AN INSTITUTIONAL THEORY OF COMMUNIST REGIMES

A publication of the
Center for Self-Governance

AN INSTITUTIONAL THEORY OF COMMUNIST REGIMES

DESIGN, FUNCTION, AND BREAKDOWN

ANTONI Z. KAMINSKI

San Francisco, California

© 1992 Antoni Z. Kaminski

Printed in the United States of America on acid-free paper. All rights reserved. No part of this book may be used or reproduced in any manner without written permission except in the case of brief quotations in critical articles and reviews.

This book is a publication of the Center for Self-Governance, which is dedicated to the study of self-governing institutions. The Center is affiliated with the Institute for Contemporary Studies, a nonpartisan, nonprofit public policy research organization. The analyses, conclusions, and opinions expressed in ICS Press publications are those of the authors and not necessarily those of the Institute, or of its officers, directors, or others associated with, or funding, its work.

Inquiries, book orders, and catalog requests should be addressed to ICS Press, 243 Kearny Street, San Francisco, CA 94108. (415) 981-5353. Fax (415) 986-4878. To order call toll free in the contiguous United States: **(800) 326-0263**. Distributed to the trade by National Book Network, Lanham, Maryland.

Cover designer: Ben Santora.
Copy editor: Frances Bowles.
Production editor: Tracy Clagett.
Indexer: Shirley Kessel.

0 9 8 7 6 5 4 3 2 1

Library of Congress Cataloging-in-Publication Data

Kaminski, Antoni Z.
    An institutional theory of communist regimes : design, function, and breakdown / Antoni Z. Kaminski.
    p.   cm.
    "A publication of the Center for Self-Governance."
    Includes bibliographical references and index.
    ISBN 1-55815-110-9.—ISBN 1-55815-174-5 (pbk.)
    1. Communist state. 2. Communist countries—Politics and government. I. Title.
JC474.K26   1991
321.9'2—dc20   91-27897
                                                                                 CIP

Contents

Foreword   *Robert B. Hawkins, Jr.*   ix
Acknowledgments   xi

I
Introduction

ONE   Explaining Communist Regimes   3

EXPLAINING AN INSTITUTIONAL ORDER • ACCIDENTAL AND ENVIRONMENTAL DETERMINANTS • COMMUNISM AS MODERNIZATION • ISSUES TO BE EXPLORED • AN INSTITUTIONAL ANALYSIS OF COMMUNIST REGIMES • THE STRUCTURE OF THIS STUDY

II
The Soviet Institutional Design

TWO   Historical Continuities and Discontinuities   29

KEENAN'S ACCOUNT • PIPES'S ACCOUNT • ORDER, CYCLICITY, AND CHANGE

THREE   Lenin as Theorist   45

STATE AND REVOLUTION • LENIN ON THE ORGANIZATION OF THE PARTY • CONCLUSIONS

FOUR	Lenin as Practitioner	67
	LENIN'S ROAD TO POWER • THE THREE DECISIONS THAT DETERMINED INSTITUTIONAL STRUCTURE • STALIN AND THE COMMUNIST INSTITUTIONAL ORDER • PROLETARIAN INTERNATIONALISM • CONCLUSIONS	
FIVE	The Communist Institutional Order: Historical Continuity or New Creation?	101
	THE OLD AND THE NEW • PATRIMONIAL AND LIBERAL ORDERS • CONCLUSION	

III
The Evolution of Key Institutional Structures: Privatization of the Communist State

SIX	Legitimacy and Corruption	121
	THE MEANING OF CORRUPTION • PUBLIC INTEREST AND THE ORGANIZATION OF SOCIETY • THE PRIVATIZATION OF THE SOVIET TYPE OF REGIME	
SEVEN	The Party in the Communist Political System	141
	CHARISMA AND CORRUPTION • PURGING • THE EMERGENCE OF INFORMALITY	
EIGHT	The Partisan State	157
	THE REVOLUTIONARY AND THE RATIONAL-LEGAL LEGITIMATION OF THE COMMUNIST REGIME • THE PARTY'S CONTROL OVER THE STATE • POLITICAL CONTROL AND PRIVATIZATION	
NINE	Factions, Interest Groups, and the Political Process	177

FACTIONS AND INTEREST GROUPS •
PARTY APPARATUS, SECURITY ORGANS,
AND THE ARMY • SOCIETY AS A
NONESSENTIAL BURDEN: THE
REPRESENTATION OF SECONDARY
INTEREST

TEN The Political Process and Economic Policies 203

THE ECONOMIC CONCERNS OF THE
STRATEGIC INTEREST GROUPS •
STATE ADMINISTRATION AND
MARKET-ORIENTED REFORM • ELITE
RECRUITMENT AND MARKET-ORIENTED
REFORM • CONCLUSIONS

ELEVEN Succession as an Error-correcting Mechanism 227

BASIC STRUCTURAL FEATURES •
SUCCESSION AND POLITICAL AND
ECONOMIC CYCLES IN POLAND •
SUCCESSION AND ECONOMIC POLICY

TWELVE The Partisan State and Civil Society 243

THE SYNDROME OF ASYMMETRY •
CONFLICT AND COOPERATION •
COERCION, CORRUPTION, AND REFORM
• THE LIMITS OF REFORM IN
COMMUNIST STATES

IV
THE SOVIET BLOC:
A SUPRANATIONAL REGIME

THIRTEEN East-Central Europe 269

FOURTEEN Patterns of Dependency in the Soviet Bloc 283

BUILDING THE SOVIET BLOC •
DEPENDENCY AND THE SOCIAL
STRUCTURE • THE PERVERSITIES OF

ECONOMIC DEPENDENCY • CONTROL FROM THE TOP

V
Transitions

FIFTEEN	The Reformability of Soviet-Type Regimes	313
	THE NOTION OF REFORMABILITY • THE SOVIET TYPE OF CONSTITUTIONAL DESIGN • REFORM AND GROUP INTERESTS	
SIXTEEN	East-Central Europe in Transition	333
	CAN THE TRANSITION SUCCEED? • GLOBAL INTERDEPENDENCE • EAST-CENTRAL EUROPE AND THE SOVIET TRANSITION	

Notes	355
Bibliography	381
Name Index	397
Subject Index	402
About the Author	415

Foreword

The foremost lesson of the Communist experience is that ideas matter in the conduct of human affairs.

The excesses and abuses of Communist regimes cannot be explained simply as three generations of aberrant political behavior. Rather, certain ideas about society, and the institutions built upon those ideas, formed the Communist social order and gave it its essential character. In this powerful book, Antoni Z. Kaminski analyzes the rise of Communism in Russia, its evolution, and the mechanics of its demise. He shows that the failure of the Communist state arises from the same source as its former dominance—the institutional structure created by Lenin in the aftermath of the October Revolution.

Kaminski convincingly demonstrates that Lenin, contrary to his own claims and to claims of many apologists in the West, had only a negative concept of democracy. For Lenin, any state was a dictatorship. His definition of democracy was the concentration of power in the hands of the Communist party, which would then exercise coercive control in the name of the proletariat. This vision of the state came together with his idea of the organization of the party—centralized, secretive, and tightly disciplined—in Lenin's institutional design.

Stalinism, according to Kaminski's analysis, was inevitable in the Communist system. It was imprinted in the genetic code of the institutional organism Lenin had created. By the time Stalin succeeded to power, society was unable to defend itself against the state, the state could not oppose the party, the party was subject to its ruling group, and the group had lost its autonomy to the general secretary of the party.

For seventy years Communist state power in the Soviet Union was able to terrorize a society into passive compliance. But the organization of the party-state was unable to deal with the problems of the modern world, and the Soviet regime was eventually forced to look for solutions inconsistent with the very logic of its institutional design. This contradiction, together with the corruption and inertia inherent in the system, undermined its internal equilibrium and brought it down. Kaminski does not discount the role of change from the top undertaken by Mikhail Gorbachev, but he observes that Gorbachev himself has not been able to control the revolutionary forces he helped to release.

Can the Soviet transition to a fully democratic system succeed? The repressive regime Lenin created has ended, but it would be wrong to believe that we have nothing to learn from this enormous failed experiment. Certainly, the best intentions of the West to help build self-governing institutions in the Soviet Union will be valueless if we do not understand the institutional order under which that society labored during much of this century. Clarifying why the Soviet experiment failed is crucial to understanding how to cope with problems of governance. The challenge of building new, healthy institutions in the countries of the former Soviet bloc requires that we not lose sight of the way in which ideas, through the institutions that embody them, can shape political and social reality.

Robert B. Hawkins, Jr., President
Institute for Contemporary Studies

Acknowledgments

I wrote this book during the three semesters of my affiliation with the Workshop in Political Theory and Policy Analysis at Indiana University, Bloomington, in 1988 and 1989. The Workshop offered an atmosphere of quiet seclusion, rare in a world of rapid change with important events occurring every day, of stimulating intellectual debate, and of friendly support. I am grateful to Professors Vincent and Elinor Ostrom, codirectors of the Workshop, for making this stay possible.

Professor Vincent Ostrom has patiently read, corrected, and commented on various versions of individual chapters and on the completed manuscript. There is hardly a sentence whose style or content is not affected by his intervention, and there is hardly an idea in the book that we did not discuss. Professors Robert Byrnes, Robert W. Campbell, and Wojciech Maciejewski have read the whole manuscript and kindly provided detailed written comments and suggestions. I have discussed the manuscript with a number of other people and have profited from their corrections and advice. They are Professors Lech Garlicki, Antoni Mrozek, Mark Sproule-Jones, Michaly Szegedy-Maszak, Alexandr Obolonsky, and Anna Garlicka, and Mr. Wlodzimierz Daab. Special thanks go to Mrs. Patty Dalecki for her efforts to make the manuscript more readable. I am deeply grateful, too, for the help and encouragement given by many others during the course of this project. They are too numerous to mention individually, but I recognize and appreciate their contributions.

I

INTRODUCTION

ONE

EXPLAINING COMMUNIST REGIMES

The October Revolution of 1917 in Russia was no doubt one of the turning points in modern history. It marked the end of the empire of the tsars and the beginning of a new institutional order that claimed its legitimacy and built its institutional structure on Marxist social doctrine. In creating this new order, the Revolution was a challenge to the liberal, democratic world. The rise of the first Marxist regime in the world also posed a grave dilemma for the socialist parties of Europe, which had to decide whether to remain autonomous or to become followers of the Russian party. This conflict in socialism eventually led to its disintegration into Communist and social-democratic movements. For decades afterward, in the deadly battle against capitalism and other associated institutions of liberal democracies, Communist parties considered the interests of Soviet Russia to be their primary obligation.

The turning point in the history of the Soviet Union came with the end of World War II, when the USSR successfully imposed its rule upon East-Central Europe and became a superpower.[1] By subduing East-Central Europe, the USSR controlled the strategic areas of the continent and made a rapid invasion of the whole of Europe possible. It possessed a military might that could not be matched by any of the European powers. The inability of Europe to secure its independence forced the United States to become directly involved on the continent. The two countries, the Soviet Union and the United States, found themselves in a conflict that could not be reconciled within the framework of their respective interests and ways of life because the United States could not accept a situation in which an expansionist empire gained dominance over the whole of Europe and imposed by force its institutional system upon nations that until World War II had enjoyed political independence. The ability of both countries to inflict mutual destruction in case of war has been an effective deterrent against war. In these circumstances, the arms race would be won by the side able to outlast the adversary, that is, by the side with adequate resources, an innovative organizational system, and political stamina.

The Soviet Union and the East-Central European Communist bloc were joined by Yugoslavia, where Tito's Communist partisans were strong enough to take over power without direct Soviet help. Soon afterward, in 1949, a Communist regime was established in China by the victorious Communists led by Mao Zedong. After the invasion of Hungary in October 1956 and of Czechoslovakia in August 1968 the popularity of the Communist ideology in Europe has gradually disappeared. But its popularity has continued to grow in the postcolonial third world. Some liberation movements among former colonies have been supported by the Soviet Union and many found in Marxism-Leninism a handy rationale for autocratic rule. Hence, the rapid increase in the number of Communist or Communist-sympathizing regimes from the 1950s until late in the 1970s.

In the face of the economic crisis in Poland, and growing difficulties in other countries of the Soviet bloc, including the Soviet Union itself, Communist regimes are demonstrating their inadequacy to address contemporary social and economic problems. Moreover, the purely economic cost of keeping the third world Communist elites in power has become prohibitive. The demand upon the resources of the USSR and of its allies has been sufficiently exhausting to call for a dramatic shift of policy.

The Soviet world system is highly complex. Yugoslavia and China are outside the system but are not immune to changes that are occurring within it. First, adherence to Marxist-Leninist ideas makes Communist countries highly sensitive to the way any other such country organizes its way of life, irrespective of the relationship each has with the Soviet Union. Second, the political interests of the Soviet Union and of Communist China were diverging long before the two countries became openly hostile at the beginning of the 1960s. The Soviet military threat brought China closer to the West and greatly contributed to its decision to reform the economy. In turn, the Chinese reforms encouraged the Soviet leadership to reform its own system. Third, both countries face similar economic and social problems, although their diverging cultural traditions, geopolitical situations, and levels of development affect their responses.

Although much of what will be said here about the functioning of the Soviet system is also applicable to China, Yugoslavia, and other Communist states, this inquiry is confined to the Soviet Union and its East-Central European dependencies. The subjugation of East-Central Europe to direct Soviet control was what made the USSR a superpower. The Soviet bloc, together with the Soviet Union, has until recently constituted the core of the Soviet world system. What happened within the bloc and to the relations among its member states affected the whole Soviet world system and was a critical issue in world politics.

The changes we have witnessed in recent years have accelerated particularly since the spring of 1989, in a way that has surprised even the most daring observers. We are witnessing a unique historical development: an attempt to achieve a peaceful revolution in a system that itself has been the product of a violent revolution. The attempt began as a revolution from above, but in its progress the support of numerous social groups has been mobilized in spontaneous or sometimes organized ways. These groups exert, in turn, pressures upon the direction and progress of change in ways that do not necessarily accord with the intentions of its main initiators. The revolution from above has triggered a wide social movement from below. It is a revolution in the Marxist sense of the term as well, because it directly affects proprietary relations and is accompanied by the shrinking influence and even the downfall of what has been the Communist ruling class. It is a liberal, democratic revolution because it proposes to make the market the main regulator of economic activities, to give a more prominent place to representative institutions, to curtail, with judiciary controls, the arbitrariness of official decisions, and to pay greater attention to the rights of individuals. We have an opportunity to witness an event rare in history: a massive process of social change compressed into a relatively short time. We do not know its final outcome, nor can we precisely predict how effective the obstacles along its way will be. But we can say in general what those obstacles are, what the general trend is, and what will happen if this trend is hindered.

With these revolutionary changes something else has been invalidated: a certain political philosophy that has guided the Marxist Left for over a hundred years.[2] Those stubborn individuals who still do not want to acknowledge this fact pretend that the Soviet type of political regime failed because it was applied in backward countries with unsuitable political cultures. This argument can be reversed: Perhaps the Soviet political system could have been applied only in such societies and only in specific historical circumstances.

But this is not a study in the history of the Soviet world. The objects of this inquiry are the institutions, the ideas on which they were founded, and the structural changes that the Communist system has undergone in its history. It is an analysis of an institutional design that was developed by Lenin and put into practice in the aftermath of the October Revolution in Russia.

Explaining an Institutional Order

To explain the origins of an institutional order is always challenging. Such a task involves both historical and functional perspectives. We try to understand the origins of such an order, that is, the factors that contributed to its emergence and that helped to determine its particular shape. We try to grasp the mechanisms of change and development working within the system and influencing its modes of reacting to environmental stimuli. These in turn reshape its environment.

The old debate on the origins of capitalism provides a relevant example of how difficult it can be to explain an institutional order. Literature on the subject abounds. Its emergence and development in Western Europe are attributed to various factors ranging from the demographic, climatic, and geographic, to the cultural, political, and ethnic. Despite the methodological honesty of many studies and the heuristic excellence of some, the problem is not resolved. None of us is able to place the developments of Western civilization into a proper evolutionary perspective and to discriminate unambiguously between what has been indispensable for their emergence and what has not.

We can find the same problems with theories explaining the origin and evolution of Soviet-type regimes. There are many excellent historical studies of Russia and the Soviet Union, and many highly informed efforts to make sense of facts and trends taking place in the Soviet type of institutional systems. Nonetheless, the problem has remained controversial because it does not consist solely in defining the concrete historical conditions that accompanied the emergence and development of the two orders, or in finding correct theoretical categories, as such, but in providing them with a historical meaning. Elements in a theory of institutional order are always worked out in the context of historical conditions.

The difficulty in finding agreement on the historical interpretation of the emergence of the Communist phenomenon and on the meaning of the relationship between the Communist order and the Western liberal, democratic order may stem from a profound inability of observers to agree upon the historical meaning of Western civilization, of which in my view the Communist order is a logical antithesis. Marxist doctrine grew out of particular conditions of nineteenth-century capitalist society, and the Bolshevik revolution in Russia was conditioned by changes in the Russian environment caused by the dynamics of capitalism. Thus, together with the usual difficulties we encounter when trying to make sense of foreign cultures and civilizations, we find ideological conflicts over capitalism projected onto an interpretation of Communism, conflicts that further magnify differences of opinion.

How can one find meaning in the Soviet phenomenon? The answer is simple if one accepts the traditional Marxist-Leninist ideology of the Soviet state. According to this ideology, the Soviet phenomenon is a socioeconomic formation superior to capitalism, a transitory phase soon to be replaced by communism. Marxism-Leninism views Communist regimes in the evolutionary perspective of its theory of social development. Treated as a general methodological orientation that emphasizes the role of material factors in generating social changes, the Marxist analysis may have some merits. However, the traditional Marxist view of the succession of socioeconomic formations does not stand critical scrutiny in light of modern historical knowledge. Moreover, one has to assume a highly peculiar position to claim the evolutionary superiority of the Soviet regime over its liberal, democratic counterparts, and an even more peculiar position to believe that this regime has an evolutionary potential that will lead to a communist order as described by Marx.

It is legitimate to talk of social development in terms of the growing complexity of institutional arrangements and the corresponding changes in technologies that result in the growing productivity of labor. In this perspective, however, the Soviet regime has not showed an impressive developmental potential. It is evidently haunted by massive institutional inertia, which makes it difficult to compete with more dynamic liberal, democratic societies.

It seems more reasonable to accept an alternative view that, for one reason or another, between the sixteenth and the eighteenth centuries, conditions emerged in Western Europe that made it possible for the market and related institutions to develop, with parallel changes in the political organization of societies and in the culture as a whole. The institutionalization of the market, together with the system of property rights that is indispensible to it, created a social mechanism that overcame the forces of inertia in institutions dependent upon political considerations. The secret of the evolutionary potential of liberal democracies lies in the pluralistic, democratic character of political arrangements on the local, regional, and national level, the international character of market institutions, and the international patterns of association among nation-states (Wallerstein 1974).

The expansion of Western Europe as a result of these epochal institutional inventions established the character of the political and economic environment of the rest of the world. Other peoples had to adjust. Sometimes they succeeded and sometimes they did not. If we view Russian history from the perspective of this expansion, we can see in it, at least since Peter the Great, a constant struggle with problems ensuing from developments in the West. I adopt this perspective in the first part of this book. I shall also use it in examining the Marxist-Leninist institutional project, in its relationships to the Russian political past and to the liberal, democratic approach.

We can view the Communist regime as an experiment consisting in an effort to use a modified autocratic regime to achieve socio-economic development. The concept of experiment as it appears here would not be acceptable to natural scientists but, in the social sciences that deal with macrophenomena, it is difficult to think of a better example of an experiment. Even when we take this general perspective, we find several conflicting standpoints that have gained prominence in studies of the Soviet phenomenon because they show the extent to which ideology interferes with apparently detached analysis. They rarely occur in particular studies in their pure form; usually writers combine two or three perspectives at the same time. Theoretical perspectives are sometimes determined by the merits of the problem at hand, but more often than not they are also influenced by ideological choices. This influence is apparent in the work of scholars from both East and West. For the sake of illustration, I shall briefly discuss two approaches that, despite appearances of scholarly detachment, seem to have been influenced by ideological bias: explanations expressed in terms of accidental and environmental determinants and explanations expressed in terms of modernization. The modernization perspective is quite legitimate but is sometimes used on grounds that are not acceptable methodologically. The same considerations apply to the use of environmental determinants in explaining social phenomena. The discussion will help to elucidate the nature of the Soviet experiment.

Accidental and Environmental Determinants

In principle, accidental factors and environmental determinants belong to two different analytical realms. We generally consider those factors as accidental that are not part of our theoretical model; we classify them as accidental for our own convenience. We establish environmental determinants by defining the boundaries of the system we intend to examine: the factors that are external to the system thus conceived and that are relevant for its functioning belong to the environment.

The course of history is often influenced by factors that must be considered accidental. It is sometimes said that only the timely death of Ogatai, the successor to Genghis Khan, in 1241, saved central and western Europe from the destruction and suffering of a Mongol occupation. But, because of their unpredictability, such factors cannot be included in theoretical formulations and we cannot make them part of scientific predictions. All we can do is to consider them, *post-factum,* as elements in the explanation of particular events.

Depending on the problems being addressed, predictions must include reference to environmental factors. Environmental considerations start with the problems of geopolitics.

> Anyone who has looked reasonably closely at political history will have had many occasions to observe that the very experience of holding and exercising supreme power in a country saddles any ruler, whatever his original ideological motives, with most of the traditional concerns of government in that country, and subjects him to the customary compulsions of statesmanship within that framework, makes him the protagonist of the traditional interests and the guardian against the traditional dangers. He cannot free himself entirely from his predecessors or his successors. (Kennan 1962, 366)

Thus, processes occurring in particular polities are conditioned by the immediate natural environment of the society under examination. But even here the point is debatable. Different societies found different ways of adapting to similar circumstances, while similar institutional solutions developed under circumstances that evidently diverged.[3]

At this point, I am interested more in the abuses than in the uses of this kind of reasoning. The abuses usually appear under a heading such as Accidental/Environmental Determinants. The approach can also be called a structural opportunism approach for it suggests that social systems passively adjust to their respective environments and/or are unilaterally conditioned by some random events. As a theoretical proposition, this approach has never been stated in a consistent way.

Advocates of this approach have attempted to point to some of the elements of the institutional design of the Soviet system and/or some of the most loathsome policies the Soviet government has pursued and explain them by referring to accidental historical conditions that accompanied the emergence of the Communist regime in Russia: the destruction occasioned by World War I, social and economic backwardness, civil war and foreign intervention, the peasants' antipathy toward communism, lack of international recognition and support, and so on. According to this interpretation, the Bolsheviks, while trying to overcome these obstacles, resorted to policies and institutions that had not been part of their initial design. These institutions have then become rigidified and have survived beyond the conditions that made them necessary. Such an interpretation is often part of a belief that Marxist-Leninist doctrine is essentially correct but, unfortunately, its practical application has been distorted by adverse circumstances. In fact, the interpretation may be treated as an effort to defend the basic correctness of the Marxist-Leninist position or, at least, as a way to justify some of the most shocking excesses of Bolshevik rule by invoking external reasons that compelled the Bolsheviks to take actions they would not have taken had circumstances been different. Let me illustrate this with a couple of more sophisticated examples.

In an interesting work on Lenin's conception of the party, the late Helena Zand expressed the following opinion:

> It may be assumed that many of the difficulties that the first dictatorship of the proletariat encountered, at least during the initial phase, followed . . . from the establishment of the monoparty system. It should be remembered, however, that this solution had not been originally considered. . . . Lenin's uncompromising posture toward the socialist opposition was caused by its antisoviet [that is, anti-councils] attitude. (1977, 197–98)

Here, Zand uses a simple propaganda trick. She associates the idea of workers' and soldiers' *soviet*s (councils) with Bolshevik rule. Thus, whoever opposed Bolsheviks, and for whatever reason, must have, by definition, opposed the councils too.[4] The truth is, however, that most of the Russian socialists supported the councils although they eventually opposed the Bolsheviks', or we should say Lenin's, methods of governing. Thus, Lenin was not forced by the stand that the socialists took (an environmental determinant) to establish the monoparty system; Lenin's actions resulted from his own uncompromising attitude toward the socialists.[5]

George F. Kennan, in his famous early article signed X, provides another illustration of this reasoning.

> The circumstances of the immediate post-revolutionary period—the existence in Russia of civil war and foreign intervention, together with the obvious fact that the Communists represented only a tiny minority of the Russian people—made the establishment of dictatorial power a necessity. (1947, 568)

If we treat the circumstances enumerated by Kennan as environmental determinants, in the sense adopted here, we find that the quotation contains the following propositions: (1) that the drama of the civil war and its character were entirely independent from the behavior of the Bolsheviks; (2) that foreign intervention was caused by the Communist takeover itself and not by any action taken by the Communist government (Kennan himself demonstrated, in *Russia and the West under Lenin and Stalin* [1962], that foreign intervention was initially provoked by Lenin's government, when it decided to get hold of Allied stores in Murmansk and Archangelsk); (3) that the Communists were a tiny minority was an accidental feature with no bearing on the character of the party or its political behavior; (4) that the implementation of a dictatorship was a necessity imposed by environmental conditions and not by Lenin's designs and strategies. The propositions are, at best, only partly true, and the explanatory power of such reasoning is null.[6]

Hard times surely influenced what the Bolsheviks did. But would the Bolsheviks have been able to make their mark in history in different circumstances? The Bolshevik party was a revolutionary organization built around Lenin's conceptions of the revolutionary class struggle. Revolutionary parties seize power either in revolutionary circumstances or not at all. It is pointless to speculate how they would have behaved had they come to power in more peaceful times: they had not been built for this purpose. To blame revolutionary conditions for the behavior of a revolutionary party is like blaming the air for the fact that it contains oxygen.

The treatment of an institutional structure exclusively as a product of a series of forced adaptations to external circumstances carries with it a strong assumption of the complete dependence of the structure of the system upon the system's environment and of a complete independence of the nature of the environment from human behavior. This assumption, as a general proposition, is obviously false. The character of an environment is to a significant extent shaped by the structural features of a social system. It is evident that, in most circumstances, system and environment are interdependent. The basic characteristics of a system's institutional structure play a role similar to that of a genotype in living organisms: They influence the way environmental stimuli are perceived and acted upon and they affect the range of adaptive changes and developmental directions the system can pursue. Environmental factors do eliminate certain types of structures and stimulate the growth of others. Explanations based upon environmental impact or accidental events must always be made with care and serious consideration.

Communism as Modernization

The notion that Communism is a modernization strategy makes it somehow familiar to Western audiences. It suggests that, while the means may be different, West and East have been moving toward essentially the same goal: the building of a modern, as opposed to a traditional, and possibly a better world and trying to find solutions to similar challenges. This notion is partly correct: Communism is an experiment with a strategy of modernization different from the one tried by the West. Communist regimes have seriously weakened or even destroyed some traditional social institutions, effectively erased illiteracy, and given broad masses of the population access to the educational system. They also achieved substantial levels of industrialization and urbanization. Some of the problems they face are universal.

These achievements may suffice for us to consider Communism a strategy for modernization. But it is a highly peculiar form of modernization. The destruction or weakening of some traditional institutions led in the West to the liberation of the individual, to greater personal freedom. The same process under the Communists produced exactly the opposite effect: the dismantling of traditional protections, however ineffective they may have been, left lonely individuals facing an anonymous, all-powerful state. If two well-known American social scientists can open their major work with the statement that theirs is a book about the political organization "of a society of free men" (Buchanan and Tullock 1965, iii), a similar work on a Communist society should start with the statement that it is a book about the political organization of a society of *bound* men. Under Communism, free individual choice is a problem that arises in situations that are, from the standpoint of the system's organization, pathological. A collectivist system must abolish autonomy of the individual by eliminating all the protective shelters that tradition and liberal, democratic institutions built around individuals. Even the interpretation of law, which until recently has been based on the principle that "what is not authorized by law is forbidden," is a testimony to the effort to eliminate individual choice. The degree to which the society achieves that goal is the best measure of its success. The question arises, How far, for how long, and with what consequences for itself can an organized system go on denying the individual?

Some authors taking the modernization perspective mention the separation of the state and religion as an aspect of the modernizing impact of the Soviet regime.[7] However, what happened in reality was not a separation of the church and the state, but an effort by the Bolshevik state to suppress and annihilate the Orthodox church and all other organized religions. Marxist-Leninist ideology superseded Russian Christian Orthodoxy as a new state religion, while the "leading role of the party" made the state Orthodox religion politically superfluous. The new panideology may have been modernistic, but it was not a religion in any acceptable sense of the term, even though it clearly reflected the aspirations of the new state that claimed full control over individual and social consciousness. Unlike Christianity, Marxism-Leninism has no genuine ethical system of its own. Its spiritual content is poor, if not entirely lacking, it has no private rituals, and treats family life and informal groups with distrust. The effective rituals that the Soviet state has developed are mass songs, solemn mass rallies, and marches. Thus, the modernization perspective is partly correct, but superficial analogies are not very inspiring and may often mislead.

For a different instance of the modernization approach and one that possesses an undoubted heuristic value, we can consider the seminal work of Barrington Moore, Jr. (1974) on the origins of contemporary political orders. According to Moore, there are regular patterns in the way in which societies embarked upon the path of modernization. The pioneering countries underwent liberal, bourgeois revolutions; those such as Japan and Prussia, that took off in the late nineteenth century experienced conservative, statist revolutions from above; the latecomers sought modernization through Communist revolutions. The important variable was, in Moore's view, the way in which the peasant problem was solved. The factors that determined the choice of modernization strategy were the country's level of economic backwardness and the moment in history at which the country started to modernize. Communism is the strategy of backward latecomers.

We should remember, however, that in Russia modernization efforts had started before the October Revolution, the most recent being Peter A. Stolypin's reform undertaken after the Russian-Japanese war and the revolutionary wave of 1905. From an economic perspective, this was a liberal reform and fairly successful. Starting as it did the process of modernization at the turn of the nineteenth century, Russia could have embarked upon a liberal strategy of economic development, taken steps in the direction of parliamentary democracy, and, most notably, implemented some elements of the rule of law to a degree unparalleled in its past. Failure may be attributed to two events that are not accounted for by any theory of modernization: Stolypin's assassination disrupted these processes, and World War I brought them to an end. In different circumstances, the historical possibility of an evolution in Russia toward a constitutional monarchy was not inconceivable.[8]

Moreover, one could mention many countries, as backward as or even more backward than Russia, that took different roads to modernization, none less effective and certainly all less costly than the Communist one. Theda Skocpol's study (1979) of revolutions shows that the Communist road to modernization is typical of agro-bureaucratic empires that moved toward reforms (weakening thereby their power base and their grip upon the rural populations) and then, experiencing a major defeat, usually in a war, and with a weakened state apparatus and the peasant problem on their hands, were not able to control the situation. Thus, the victory of the Bolshevik revolution has been the product of a conjuncture of events. This means that, though Communism may be considered a strategy of modernization, the theory of modernization does not explain the choice and the specific nature of this strategy.

Issues to Be Explored

The Communist form of social order poses a number of puzzling questions. We are familiar with social orders that have developed over centuries, sometimes through dramatic changes and disruptions, transforming their structures in complex interactions between spontaneous processes and reflective human adjustment to new problems created by these spontaneous developments. This is, in fact, the essence of learning.

Capitalism, for instance, whether we place its beginnings in the fourteenth, sixteenth, or eighteenth century, has lasted a fairly long time. By contrast, we are witnessing, after a little more than seventy years of its existence, the dismantling of the Communist regime, which professed to be the future of humanity.

Some may not like the term *capitalism*, arguing that aspects of this social order other than the phenomenon of capital are also important and that capital is an instrument and not the essence of market organization. Yet no one claims that capital is unimportant. There is a correspondence between the language commonly used to describe liberal, democratic institutions and their functioning in the real world. Followers of different scholarly disciplines and proponents of different theories may quarrel about the interpretation of some phenomena taking place in liberal democracies, but these differences of opinion can be at least partly verified empirically, and on a number of topics there is a general consensus.

Can we say the same about Soviet types of social orders? They emerged as an effort by a group of revolutionaries to implement institutional projects that Lenin had formulated in his writing. The basic constitutional design of the system had been thought out even before an opportunity for its implementation arose. It is true that, in society, a human being is both "the Matter thereof, and the Artificer" of commonwealths (Hobbes [1651] 1962, 9). Some are, however, more the matter, while others are more the artificer. Yet, one has the impression that perhaps something in the Russian political culture made it more likely that these artificers would win. Perhaps the matter have something to say about the kinds of artificers who are to work on the matter, even if the choice is simply to remain passive.

Ideas organize the thinking of individuals and the way in which human beings perceive their environments. Systems of ideas, containing conceptions of the nature of the world and value systems, affect the ways in which individuals treat one another, inform their behavior, and influence the shape of institutional structures. The emergence of the liberal, democratic order from feudal society was a gradual, evolutionary process. Individuals, trying to understand the world around them, formulated new concepts and discovered new relationships. Some of these efforts were published and gained prominence, others have been forgotten. The process was one of experimenting with the new, of committing errors, and of correcting them with every advance of knowledge.

The emergence of the Communist regime proceeded differently. The blueprint for the regime's institutional design had been ready long before the October Revolution, which opened the way to its implementation. Then it was put into effect by force. Marxist-Leninist doctrine has been subsequently sanctified and no major critical discussion about the doctrine and its practical product, the Communist regime, has been allowed to occur within the system. The doctrine provided the regime with a claim to legitimacy and, therefore, had to be protected.

Such a posture must always lead to anomalies on a wide scale.[9] Let us consider, for instance, the terms used to describe the Communist regime. One of them is *soviet,* a word that occupies the second place in the official name of the country that initiated the history of this social order: the Union of Soviet Socialist Republics. (I shall not dispute about the suggestion of a voluntary association, conveyed by the term *union.*) *Soviet* means a council in Russian. The Communist claim to the democratic character of the regime hangs upon the notion of councils that were supposed to play a real role in the working of the regime. As it transpired, active, powerful, independent councils of any kind are not and never have been the most characteristic feature of the Communist regime.

Is *communism* a better term? According to Marxist-Leninists, communism is supposed to be the end state, when the complete liberation of mankind is attained. I know of no theory that could demonstrate that any such developmental tendency is at work. The system of rule is rigid and oppressive. If any tendency is noticeable, it is in a movement toward some liberal, democratic solutions that, from the standpoint of Marxism-Leninism, must be viewed as retrogressive. Thus, the promise of communism may be considered another false claim.

Should we use, then, the term *socialism,* which is a part of the official names of some of the countries under examination? This may seem to be an appropriate term because Communist regimes evidently possess some of the key institutional features postulated by the main currents of socialist thought. This is why Marxist intellectuals in the West are sometimes so painfully ambivalent in their attitudes to the abuses committed by Soviet regimes. In the official doctrine, socialism is a transitory stage between capitalism and communism. If no transition of this kind may be seen, what is the place of such a term? Moreover, socialism grew out of a legitimate concern with the appalling situation of the working class in nineteenth-century Western Europe, most notably England. Can we discover any such concern for the situation of the working class in the policies of Communist regimes? None has been empirically substantiated. Finally, one should not forget that socialist parties were often among the bitterest opponents of Communism. The main difference between socialists and Communists resides in their attitudes toward political democracy. Thus, for the sake of intellectual honesty, one should not yoke socialists to something they consistently oppose.

People's democracies? Again, how can we use such a term to describe a system of rule in which people have no influence over public matters, but individuals whom they have not elected, and whose opinions and decisions cannot be contested, decide what is in their best interests?

Whatever name one chooses from among those officially used will be misleading because they are all based on false claims. It is not merely a question of terminology but, at the very level of basic terminology, we encounter the most fundamental feature of the social order under study: it is unable to confront its own nature. Because of that, it has had, from its very inception, to use terminology that camouflaged its essential character. This is indeed a fascinating problem for social scientists.

In view of these terminological difficulties, I shall use two terms interchangeably: the Soviet system, and the Communist system. As a Russian word, *soviet* has no automatic association with the word *council* in other languages. The term *communism* suggests a utopia in action and marks itself as a social order created by an extremist group among socialist movements.

An Institutional Analysis of Communist Regimes

An important part of our knowledge about the world comes from the mass media. They direct our attention from one area to another, wherever the more dramatic events are actually taking place. These dramatic events are, however, preceded, influenced, and underlaid by other, superficially less dramatic, but in fact more important, trends and developments. Even in the case of a revolutionary break with the past, certain continuities and stable behavioral patterns are visible under the surface to an attentive observer. To understand the present, we have to examine the past and look for those fundamental factors.

When we study complex systems of organization pertaining to a whole society, we have to concentrate on the institutional foundations of a social regime: We must take into account the institutional design, that is, the principal structural solutions that regulate the behavior of individuals and groups, govern cooperation in society, establish a way of life, and determine the main conflicts of interest. We cannot understand the behavior of people in an organized setting without a knowledge of the way in which the game of life is conceptualized and the rules of the game established. We cannot understand the problems faced by societies without knowing how the rules are being selected and altered, that is, we need to be familiar with the decision-making rules for constitutional choices. The way in which these problems of constituting order are solved affects every area of life. Whether the rules established will satisfy the social sense of fairness with the consequences this has for the stability of the system and the pervasive need for coercion in maintaining its stability will depend on the method of constitutional choice.

Aristotle, with whose work a systematic comparative reflection on the foundations of political orders began and whose idea of constitutional rule is one of the rule of law, proposed that

". . . constitutional rule is a government of free men and equals . . ." (1943, 62). Similarly, Buchanan and Tullock note that "it seems futile to talk seriously of a 'theory' of constitutions in a society other than that which is composed of free individuals— at least free in the sense that deliberate political exploitation is absent" (1965, 13). No Communist regime even remotely satisfies these conditions. The Bolsheviks established a Communist regime with the purpose of assuring themselves maximum power and maximum freedom of maneuver, and guaranteeing arbitrary power for the individual(s) at the top of the ruling hierarchy, who would be bound by no formal rules and be accountable to no one. Those who are ruled have, by implication, no rights. Yet, even a far from perfect approximation of this situation could exist only during short periods in the history of Communist regimes.

The problem with Aristotle's position, adopted by Buchanan and Tullock, is that it assumes a direct relationship between a despot and his subjects, with no institutions or structures to restrict the despot's discretion in making decisions. Were this assumption correct, the despot would know no constraints other than natural factors. But it is not so. An autocratic system of rule, if it is to last, must be organized. This generates constraints. Stalin could have purged hundreds of thousands of individuals in the party, the army, and the State Security Committee (KGB), but his system of rule could not function without those institutions. Behind the Soviet structure of government is a conscious institutional design consisting of major elements such as the party, the army, and the KGB and their relationships that constitute the system. People at all levels of the hierarchy have striven to achieve some stability and predictability in their immediate social environment by imposing upon their superiors rules of the game that would constrain their discretion. This natural tendency was one of the major sources of dynamics within Communist regimes after Stalin's death. Similarly, the expansion of the Communist system into other countries besides the USSR, and the emergence of the Soviet world system stimulated an effort to design an institutional framework that could regulate the operation of the system at the world level.

The Structure of This Study

No society can function without rules. This assumption finds its reflection in the structure of this book. The first part, the present chapter, has discussed problems of explaining Communist regimes. The second part deals with the design of Communist regimes and its implementation; the third, with the evolution of the key institutional structures in these regimes. The fourth part considers the organization of the Soviet world system, with an emphasis on the relationship between the USSR and East-Central European countries and on the obstacles this relationship poses to institutional changes. Finally, in conclusion, the fifth part explores transitions in the Soviet system. This book is, then, an analysis of the constitution of the Communist system of order, of the problems it faces, its evolution in time, and of the patterns of its disintegration and transformation. In one of the finest ironies of history, the Communist state is withering away—because it is an institutional structure that is unable to deal with problems produced by contemporary industrial, technological, and social developments. It is being eliminated by an environment to which it is unable to adapt.

Institutional design is at the root of the difficulties experienced by the Communist regime over the last decade and, in fact, since its very beginning. At the most superficial level, this regime was challenged in the 1980s by Solidarity, the grass-roots movement in Poland, and by a broad democratic coalition in Hungary. Its basic tenets have also been the target of changes occurring in the USSR that are known by the name of *perestroika*. Aspirations of nationalities enslaved by the expansionism of the Soviet regime are now threatening its very existence.

We can ask why certain societies have a higher propensity to choose a given type of institutional solution than others have. The more we ponder such questions, the closer we come to the imponderables, to questions that are difficult to verbalize and even more difficult to test empirically. Cultural patterns and institutional traditions are, to use the analogy once more, like genotypes in living organisms that are transmitted from generation to generation, affecting the choice of reactions to environmental challenges and outcomes of strategic social processes. These various patterns may, and do, affect the way in which different nationalities and nations will move away from Communism.

The intent of this work is to examine the institutional elements that have constituted the Communist social order, giving it its essential character. I will consider these elements in a dynamic perspective, tracing their theoretical and doctrinal origins and analyzing their practical consequences as they evolved over time. But mine is not a historical enterprise. I will address only those historical events that seem to mark critical turning points in the construction of the regime.

In acknowledging the relative novelty and specificity of the Communist regime, I also try to see it in a broader perspective, hoping to find in it some universal tendencies, as well as those peculiar to a broad class of systems organized from the top. This is one of the reasons for my extensive use of classical political theories and historical studies in constructing the heuristic apparatus for this study. Perhaps it is also time to draw theoretical lessons from the experience of Communist systems.

In Part 2 of this study, I examine the constitutional design of the Soviet social order from two perspectives that appear prominently in many works on the subject and that seem to be the most pertinent to our problem of the institutional design. The first is a comparison between the effect of continuities in Russian history on the design and working of the Soviet system and the effects of the practicalities of Marxist-Leninist doctrine and of Lenin himself as a public figure upon the institutional core of the Communist social order. The second is the ultimate influence of these factors upon the course of history. I assume that human action is always informed by the ideas that individuals and groups hold about the world around them. The question is, then, which ideas: those of the Russian cultural tradition, those of the new Marxist-Leninist doctrine, or perhaps both? It seems that whatever is valuable in modernization theory and in the environmental approach can be easily integrated within an analytical approach that takes both theories into account.

In Part 3 of the book, I have tried to place the Communist regime within a broader theoretical perspective. To develop this perspective, I used the tradition that has its roots in Aristotle, was further developed by Montesquieu and by Tocqueville, and still strongly influences our thinking about politics: that institutions purposefully created by human beings are problematic. This is the case even in traditional societies. They exist only so long as members of the society respect and enforce the rules that the institutions impose. When the rules cease to be observed, the institutions die. Institutions that demonstrably serve broader social interests, whatever their virtues, can be defended only when groups and individuals act jointly in supporting their existence. This support can be obtained only when the institutions are considered fair, fairness being the prime condition for their legitimacy. When institutions merely serve the interests of a particular social group, or a narrow set of such groups, popular realization of this fact makes them vulnerable and short lived.[10]

The thrust of the argument is that, as long as the Communist party was a social movement permeated by a sense of mission, its crimes and abuses served the mission, helping to maintain the depersonalized image of the party and to keep society in a state of strict submission. Only when state terrorism subsided did the party-state complex become the preserve of informal groups oriented toward the realization of their private interests. This proliferation of special interests has gradually made the system ungovernable and contributed to its present demise.

The revival of a strong society is incompatible with a system that has denied it all autonomy. This sort of revival has been in progress in some of the East-Central European countries for decades now and has been reflected in resistance to the regime. This revival was stimulated in the USSR by the changes associated with the name of Gorbachev. Broad social participation, however, is possible only when institutions that assure individual and group automony are in place. That means that market-oriented economic reform must be accompanied and even preceded by political change.

In Part 4 of the study another perspective is introduced. My key assumption in this analysis is that the Soviet bloc in East-Central Europe was the building ground for the whole Soviet world system. If this assumption is correct, an understanding of the way in which the countries of the region have been subjected politically, militarily, and economically to Soviet strategic interests is crucial to an understanding of the problems that changes occurring within the Communist world present to Soviet decision makers. An attempt is made, therefore, to look at the history of this area up to the present day and at its strategic importance for the power relations in Europe and the world. Finally, Part 5 offers an assessment of the prospects and conditions necessary for a successful transformation in the Soviet Union and, with it, a successful end to the division of Europe.

To finish this introduction, one explanation is necessary. The thrust of the argument may seem sometimes overly "polonocentric." The reasons are, first, that I am most familiar with the situation in Poland (it may well be that some of the propositions formulated in this study are overgeneralized); second, that Poland is certainly one of the key elements in the ex-Communist bloc and an important country in East-Central Europe; and, third, that certain phenomena that seem to have been peculiar to Poland have exposed features of the Soviet types of regimes that are less visible elsewhere.

II

THE SOVIET INSTITUTIONAL DESIGN

TWO

HISTORICAL CONTINUITIES AND DISCONTINUITIES

Since the beginning of Communism in Russia, writers have emphasized similarities between the Soviet and the old autocratic regimes. Readers of the Marquis de Custine ([1839] 1989), of Baron von Haxthausen (1856), and of other well-known observers of Imperial Russia are often struck by similarities between the past and the present, notwithstanding differences in historical development and other institutional arrangements. This should not surprise us. As Tocqueville wrote, nations "all bear some marks of their origin; and the circumstances which accompanied their birth and contributed to their rise affect the whole term of their being" ([1835] 1851, 1:26). To understand the present, one should study history, which is just a process of cultural evolution. The problem of continuities in Russian history is worth pondering, for it has a direct relevance to our understanding of both the constitution and the reformability of Soviet-type regimes. Problems that successive Soviet leaderships have faced were not, in many ways, very different from those faced by their imperial predecessors.

One can postulate that societies resemble individuals in that, when faced with new and uncertain situations, they tend to pick solutions that are familiar. When undergoing traumatic revolutionary changes, societies select ways of rebuilding the social order in line with important parts of their historical and cultural heritage. When we examine historical discontinuities closely, we discover interesting aspects of continuity. No society is free of its past. If this view is correct, it is legitimate to enquire about those characteristics of Russian autocracy that have survived the Revolution, as well as about the impact that cultural traditions of middle-European countries have had upon variations in the way they received and lived with an externally imposed regime.[1]

Most authors who take this perspective satisfy themselves with a rather general statement that the Communist regime emerged in Russia as a continuation of traditional Russian political culture. This tradition developed under some influence of a Byzantine culture (although one can argue that the receiving of Christianity from Byzantium was more important than anything else because it means that crucial turning points in the history of West European civilization, such as the separation of the state and church and the Reformation and the resulting intellectual revivals, have not been part of the Russian cultural heritage[2]), under the impact of Mongol domination, and through the institutional reforms and territorial expansion of Ivan IV, Peter the Great, and Catherine the Great. The only political philosophy Russia genuinely created in its history was that of *samoderzhavie*, a doctrine that gave full powers over society to the monarch, who owed responsibility for his actions to no one.[3]

Such reconstructions are essentially correct and may serve the analytical purposes of their authors.[4] Still, the question remains, what of the Russian past? Why, how, and under what form did it survive? Can we discern any historical patterns that could help us to understand the Soviet system, its present problems, and possible reactions to these problems? To answer these questions, I shall briefly discuss two theories about Russian historical tradition, those of Richard Pipes (1974) and Edward Keenan (1986). Many other works dealing with this subject come to mind, that by Tibor Szamuely (1974) in particular. I focus on Pipes and Keenan because problems of institutions figure prominently in their work. Moreover, Keenan's work grew out of an effort to develop an alternative to the approach represented by Pipes, but a discussion of Keenan's work first will offer a better opportunity for assessing the correctness of his assertions.

Keenan's Account

Keenan's subject is what he calls Russian "vernacular political culture." In his view, because of the deep-seated secrecy that traditionally characterized Russian politics, Russia lacks legislative or descriptive codifications of rules of behavior. Most attempts to construct "continuity theories" failed, he says, because their authors took some misleading self-descriptions, symbols, and ideologically communicative "noises" too seriously. Thus, the vernacular political culture has to be indirectly reconstructed by studying economic and physical exigencies of the environment and examining the external articulation of several variants of the Russian political culture: the village, the bureaucratic, and the court cultures. In order to make his analysis more substantial, he also considers deviant or "countercultural" expressions of political culture and their relationship to the official culture. While acknowledging the existence of other continuity approaches, Keenan claims that his interpretation "shares with such treatments only an appreciation of the fundamental continuities of Russian political culture; it derives from a radically different understanding of the origins and essential features of the culture" (1986, 117–18).

The difference between Keenan's approach and propositions and other works on the subject, is that he attaches less importance to such external influences as the Byzantine connection, the Kievan tradition, and Mongol domination. He is more interested in behavior and cultural norms, as he infers them from behavior, than in the institutional study of the political and economic organization of society. This leads him to question the interpretation of the Russian political system as an autocracy; it appeared as such only in view of highly deceptive political symbols. In fact, Keenan argues, it was an oligarchy. In reconstructing Russian political culture, he underlines more the routine aspect than instances of change.

Consequently, he almost ignores the reign of Ivan IV and pays only lip service to Peter the Great. Finally, he opposes the practice often used by students of Russia of comparing Russian historical developments with those that have occurred in Western Europe, for this does not explain the culture as it emerged in Muscovy and does not consider the effectiveness of the traditional Russian arrangement from the point of view of Muscovy's needs. Because of these differences, his interpretation of Russian history differs from those of other writers.

According to Keenan, the organization of the village centers on the need for collective survival. It is conservative and risk-averse. It is based upon distrust of man and is fearful of his potential weaknesses and destructiveness and of the danger he may present to the collective interests of the community. Under such conditions, a society relies less upon the internalization of norms and values than on external forms of subordination of individual to the group. Decisions tend to be made collegially; all participants are allowed to express their views, but they strive to achieve unanimity. Thus, the village life is characterized by

> a strong tendency to maintain stability and a kind of closed equilibrium; risk-avoidance; suppression of individual initiatives; informality of political power; the considerable freedom of action and expression "within the group"; the striving for unanimous final resolution of potentially divisive issues. (P. 128)

The political life of the court displayed extreme forms of ceremonial camouflage, a hermetic silence, and the denial to outsiders of even trivial information. Everything of importance took place behind a facade of complex protocol and rituals elaborated with great effectiveness and false pretensions. The court was completely isolated from the society. The main function of the Muscovite state was to preserve military and political order, that is, to avoid chaos. "This goal was accomplished primarily by curbing, harnessing, and avoiding strife among its own elites" (Keenan, 130). In managing the affairs of the state, Muscovy relied upon extreme centralization and direct sanctions. In the working of the court Keenan discovers the same tendencies that he noticed at the level of the village: the avoidance of risk and innovation. He explains these patterns of courtly life by presenting it as an oligarchy of powerful aristocratic clans that found it useful to pretend that it functioned in an autocracy, and not as an autocratic form of rule. Political conservatism of the Muscovy state resulted from the clans' preoccupation with survival, the continuation of lineages, and the cultural tradition of the warrior class.

The bureaucracy received the least attention among the three. Bureaucracy was important, for it can be argued

> that the growth of the Muscovite bureaucracy was not only the key to the growth and effectiveness of the Muscovite state, but that the vigor and effectiveness of that bureaucracy determined, through its inhibition of other institutional growth, several other crucial features of Muscovite political culture. (Ibid., 136)

At the same time, Keenan maintains that the bureaucracy was a "socially distinct, indispensable but *politically powerless,* bureaucratic subclass" (p. 137; emphasis added). The hypothesis about the powerlessness of bureaucracy is repeated on several other occasions (see pp. 145, 156–57). After the administrative reforms of Peter I, and the introduction of the Table of Ranks, the bureaucracy and the court were integrated into a single political elite. The Table of Ranks also "strengthened the hierarchical and client-patron dynamic at the expense of the principles of kinship and 'royal marriage'" (p. 160).

The four main features of the Russian political culture in all its dimensions were its informality and traditionality, the confidentiality of membership, stability and risk avoidance rather than change and progress, and the veil of secrecy over political decision making. That the system functioned quite well is proved by the incredible expansion of the Muscovite state. The aspect that seems to puzzle Keenan the most is that no one ever found it necessary to codify the rules or to develop a doctrine that would rationalize its functioning. His explanation is that, "as in other traditional systems, those who needed to know such rules knew them, and those who had no need to know were kept in ignorance" (p. 145).

The Western influences on the dominant culture could have been effectively contained throughout most of the period. In fact, according to Keenan, Russian imperial society and its political culture were vigorous and stable until the 1880s. "The structures and philosophy of the state still reflected their Muscovite origins in only slightly altered forms of extreme centralization, bureaucratization, and authoritarianism" (p. 163). With all its inefficiency and corruption, the system worked and its territorial expansion continued.

This well-integrated whole was, in Keenan's view, destabilized by the industrialization that Russia was experiencing in the fifty years between the 1890s and the late 1930s. This was a period of cultural turbulence or, in his own terminology, of an "aberrant political culture" that was followed by a period of restabilization and reintegration of the traditional Muscovite political culture. The fact that the USSR survived World War II is a good indicator that the society was stable and its political culture effectively re-knit in the early 1940s.

Keenan mentions three factors responsible for the survival of Russian traditional culture: the specific ethos of the Bolshevik party, the elimination of social groups that had been most committed to a nontraditional political culture, and the patterns of recruitment that favored persons of peasant stock who grew up in the village political culture. One can discern in contemporary Soviet political culture (Keenan's paper was published in 1986) all the major features of the traditional one: distrust of man, informality, collegiality of decision making, unconstitutionality, and the conspiratorial character of political life.

Keenan also examines the prospects for a more substantial change within the culture. His conclusions are not very optimistic in view of the nature of the "counterculture," which being stronger on the moral side than in intellectual creativity, rejects all political order on moral grounds and generates no constructive proposals for institutional reform. As a result, the social sciences do not offer interesting and adequate insights into the working of the Soviet system. An ideological camouflage fills their place and performs the traditional function of communication noise earlier performed by ecclesiastical trappings. Political dissenters do not carry a potential for more substantial change; rather they are part of the traditional vicious circle.

Keenan's position, however valuable some of his ideas and his general synthesis of the traditional Russian political culture might be, is inconsistent and sometimes plainly wrong. One cannot treat, for instance, his reservations about the usefulness of comparative studies for explaining Russian political culture with the seriousness that his study otherwise fully deserves.[5] The reason for the deficiencies may be that he wrote a polemical article without identifying the theories he criticized. The essay might have been written to a large extent in response to Richard Pipes's book, *Russia under the Old Regime* (1974)—for Pipes made most of the points and used most of the analytical instruments that Keenan rejects.

Pipes's Account

Like Keenan, Pipes started his book with a discussion of the climatic and geographical conditions of Russia and tried to assess their impact upon social organization. Unlike Keenan, however, he carefully pondered conditions under which the long process of the birth of the Russian state proceeded. Thus, the Norman elite, which organized the Kievan state, treated its domain in a semicolonial fashion satisfying itself with extracting tribute. "We have here," Pipes said, "a type of political formation characterized by an unusually sharp gulf between ruled and rulers" (1974, 34). Contrary to Keenan, who neglected the impact of Mongolian domination, Pipes emphasizes its importance:

> There can be scarcely any doubt, however, that domination by a foreign power, which in its worst form lasted for a century and a half, had a very debilitating effect on the political climate of Russia. It tended to isolate the princes from the population further than they were already inclined to be by the working of the

appanage system, to make them less conscious of political responsibilities. . . . It also accustomed them to regard authority as by its very nature arbitrary. (P. 57)

It is not difficult to agree that such a long period of particularly brutal foreign domination could have had a long-lasting and detrimental influence upon political culture and a demoralizing effect upon political elites and the population at large.

Pipes also pays keen attention to the peculiarities of the Muscovite colonization of the eastern and northern regions that proceeded on the initiative and under the auspices of the prince. People that moved to those areas had no claim to land and no inherent, personal "rights." Their status was not much different from that of slaves. "A kind of proprietary attitude thus surfaced on the northern-eastern frontier. Penetrating all the institutions of political authority it gave them a character fundamentally different from that found in any other part of Russia or, for that matter, Europe at large" (p. 40).

The last important element in the initial development of the Russian state, according to Pipes, was the way *dvor,* that is, a prince's private domain, was extended. Within his domain the prince was the sovereign and the sole proprietor. The domain consisted of slaves and other bonded persons. People living outside the domain proper had to pay tribute but were otherwise free. The state expanded by integrating the outside areas with their population into the private domain. As a result, Russia was transformed into "a giant royal estate." Pipes argues that sheer size prevented princes from making their property claims effective. They had to resort to farming large chunks of the country through the agency of landed gentry, clergy, and bureaucracy in return for taxes and services. However, ". . . the principle that Russia belonged to its sovereign, that he was its *dominus* was firmly established; all that was lacking to enforce it were the financial and technical means, and these were bound to become available in due course" (p. 22).

On these grounds, Pipes classifies the Russian empire as a patrimonial state, by which he means a regime "where the rights of sovereignty and those of ownership blend to the point of becoming indistinguishable" (pp. 22–23). Under such a system there can be no clear distinction between the state and society, for this presupposes "the right of persons other than the sovereign to exercise control over things and (where there is slavery) over persons. In a patrimonial state there exist no formal limitations on political authority, no rule of law, no individual liberties" (p. 23). Thus, the central contention of Pipes's book is that ". . . the essential quality of Russian politics derives from the identification of sovereignty and ownership, that is, of a 'proprietary' way of looking at political authority on the part of those who happen to be in power" (p. 24). At no point does this thesis deny the economic and the military effectiveness of such a regime. This is a powerful piece of political reasoning indeed. It follows a long and respectable tradition of comparative institutional studies that goes back to Aristotle and has been represented by such eminent founders of modern political theory as Montesquieu, Tocqueville, and Max Weber.

Let us examine, in this perspective, Keenan's thesis that the Russian political system can be considered an oligarchy rather than an autocracy as most historians of Russia have maintained. First, he misinterprets, in my opinion, the place and the function that bureaucracy had in the power structure of the Russian state. On its own, the bureaucracy, in a traditional society, might have been politically powerless, but it drew its importance and its power from the fact that the sovereign was its supreme head—it had to be his reliable instrument. With this instrument in hand, the sovereign could quite effectively oppose claims put forward by the aristocracy; the bureaucracy worked for and through the position of the sovereign.[6] The aristocracy was a part of the traditional structure upon which the legitimacy of the sovereign's position depended.[7] This, in principle, made its position safe. True, Peter's reforms abolished the cleavage between bureaucracy and traditional aristocracy, but the traditional aristocracy was already seriously weakened during the reign of Ivan IV, and in the Russian social structure it never approached that measure of autonomy that the nobility enjoyed under European feudalism.

Having failed to make the connection between the bureaucracy and the position of the autocrat, Keenan can pretend that the autocrat is in fact a primus inter pares. What is puzzling to him, then, is the lack of any codification of rules, of information on the operating principles of the system. He attributes their absence to the secrecy of the Russian political mores. But he fails again to consider that such a lack of codified rules must be a part of any definition of autocracy. Every true autocracy, or dictatorship worthy of its name, must do without officially accepted rules. Uncertainty about the rules of the game is a powerful instrument of domination. A dominant proprietorship over land and persons leaves no room for true contractual relations, the rule of law included. The word of the ruler is the law of the land. Keenan tries to find the solution by maintaining that there were in fact effective rules that were known only to the players and not revealed to outsiders. Here he is correct for there are always such rules, but this does not prove much, unless we misconstrue the problem of autocratic rule. (Agreements that are explicitly stated or based upon known tradition can be adjudicated. Those that are not cannot provide grounds for effective claims.)

The court of an autocrat always provides fertile ground for political struggle for influence and control. One of the natural objects of such struggles is the effort to limit the uncertainty caused by the unrestricted powers of the autocrat. Sometimes, these efforts may be successful, that is, autocratic rulers can behave predictably and, probably, usually do behave predictably. It is also true that to avoid predictability and to exploit the full potential of the autocratic system of rule, requires great effort and dedication, as can be illustrated by some of the excesses of Ivan IV. As long as there are no binding rules, the ruler's power remains unrestrained in principle. There are no grounds in Russian political tradition that could effectively legitimate a subject's opposition to the will of the autocrat. Even Karamzin, who objected when Alexander I advocated constitutional reform, may be regarded as a defender of autocracy. The lack of formal, institutionalized constraints is one of the most significant characteristics of an autocracy. The tsar was certainly not the first among equals at the court.

Order, Cyclicity, and Change

The main difference between Keenan and Pipes concerns the whole interpretation of the historical process in Russia, including the period after the October Revolution. I shall try to discuss this issue in the perspective of what Karl Wittfogel (1981, 331–86) aptly called the "developmental trap" of despotic regimes: Such regimes offer some expansionist potential, but cannot go beyond a certain level of development. Autocratic rulers strive most of all to retain power and then to maintain effective control over the population. They are willing to promote a certain amount of easy access to resources, provided that the groups directly in control of such resources do not acquire too much power. The conflict between the ruler's effort to maintain control and attempts made by strategic groups to gain autonomy is built into the structure of despotism and has important economic consequences.

It is well known that the domination of ". . . political-collective goals, by their very nature, required implementation by extensive economic and manpower resources" (Eisenstadt 1963, 318). In their efforts to expand the powers of the state, rulers often tended to go too far, overexploiting the economy of the country.

> The ruler's excessive demands and their growing expenditure, the consequent taxation and inflation, the ruler's attempts at overcentralization and overplanning, sometimes, if not checked, struck hardest at those groups whose economic positions were based on more flexible resources—thereby draining these resources. These groups became depleted by such taxation and by the inflation resulting from growing governmental expenditure. (Ibid., 318)

Thus, we have two problems that have the same root in that the "state is stronger than society" (Wittfogel 1981, 49). First, the ruler's need to maintain some form of traditional legitimation and to make his political control effective puts a practical brake upon the developmental process for, by its very nature, that process requires the provision of greater autonomy for groups that are strategic to its continuation. Second, the domination of traditional political goals gives priority in governmental spending to military expansion and the splendor of the court. The domination of political concerns deprived the groups strategic for economic expansion of necessary resources for further development. This is a repetition of the old argument about patrimonial regimes.[8] Within limits, such a political order makes it possible to develop and mobilize resources on a great scale, but these limits are fairly narrow.

Richard Pipes's definition of the problem is similar.

> The system we have described was so immune from pressures from below that, in theory at least, it should have perpetuated itself *ad infinitum*. The crown's monopoly on political authority, its ownership of nearly all the landed, commercial and industrial wealth, its tight grip on the social classes, and its ability to isolate the country from unwanted foreign influences all seemingly combined to assure perpetual stasis. (1974, 112)

Yet the Russian patrimonial state did experience important changes—though, as Pipes noted, rulers themselves induced them from above. The ability to institute such changes he attributed to Russia's proximity to Western Europe. "Furthermore, as both a Christian and a Slav country, she was culturally the most sensitive [in comparison with other patrimonial regimes] to western influences" (Pipes, 112). The most important influence was the inability of the technologically and organizationally backward Russian army to best other European armies. Still, these changes were made at a great cost and had long-term consequences that could not have been foreseen at the time.

In implementing his reforms, Peter the Great relied on groups strategic for the reforms' success and gave them de facto autonomy. These groups then started to press for de jure concessions from the autocracy. In effect, in 1762, the nobility was relieved of the burden of obligatory state service. Other reforms followed, as "the 'ranks' were set free and, transformed into estates (*sosloviya*), allowed to pursue their own interests" (ibid., 113); full property rights were given to private land-holding *dvoriane;* monopolies on trade and industry were abolished; and, finally, in 1861, the serfs were freed. Besides, Russia became open to western cultural influences. Here is the key to understanding the deep social tensions, brought about by Peter's reforms, that kept growing for almost the next two hundred years: While conceding its population increasing autonomy in the form of "considerable economic opportunities, civil rights and intellectual liberties, the monarchy insisted on retaining its monopoly on political authority" (ibid.). Even ". . . when finally compelled in 1905 by revolutionary events to grant a constitution it yielded more in form than in substance" (ibid., 114). The whole of Russian history since Peter the Great can be viewed as a saga of inconsistency in state policies. Efforts to implement a Western legal system clashed with efforts to create a police state based upon extralegal grounds (the sovereign prerogative), the abolition of serfdom with measures that further impoverished the peasantry. How to achieve efficiency and economic growth and have autocracy too?

Russia exemplifies the inherent conservatism of the patrimonial state, which, when faced with a dynamic environment (as Russia was in its proximity to Western Europe), can adapt by trying to copy new technological developments, fashions, and ideas, but will, inevitably, introduce into its culture and institutions elements that are incompatible with their underlying logic and pose growing threats to the institutional and political structure of the system. The state tries to counteract such threats by reverting to the old patterns, but only manages to diminish efficiency and exacerbate political tensions. This strategy does not allow a country to overtake its competitors; it is a strategy of the eternal follower (see Besançon 1980, 60–62). It is quite conceivable, in the light of developments that took place at the turn of the nineteenth century, that in different circumstances the autocratic vicious circle could have been broken and a liberal-democratic reform could have prevailed, a point strongly made by White (1977, 27–29).

Pipes's view of the historical "cycle" is very different from that of Keenan, who saw the Russian traditional political culture as fully mature by the year 1600 and persisting, hardly changed, until an "aberrant political culture" intruded between 1890 and

1940. At the end of the 1930s, the traditional culture restabilized and regained its grip over the political life in Russia. In Pipes's view, the inconsistencies were brought to the Russian institutional model by Peter the Great, to counteract its conservatism. The continued assimilation of western institutional patterns by rulers that succeeded Peter and the cultural westernization of the ruling elite contributed to the further destabilization of the original autocratic regime. At the end of 1917, Russia, torn between its tradition and liberal tendencies, chose a third way that led it to reject both the monarchy and other traditional institutions and the liberal-democratic solution. Paradoxically, however, this radical rejection was a reaffirmation of some of the old patterns and traditions: The Bolsheviks replaced the traditional proprietary paternalism by a socialist proprietary state. Thus, Pipes's cycle, as I see it, contains the following view of Russian history: institutional stability between the fifteenth century and the beginning of the seventeenth, the emergence of a destabilizing course of events at that time that culminated three centuries later in the October Revolution, and a return then to some of the old collectivistic proprietary patterns.

Keenan offers some highly interesting insights into the phenomenon of historical continuity.[9] Despite the intervening revolutionary changes, the Russian traditional political culture has proved surprisingly immune to powerful historical turbulences. There are, however, continuous patterns that Keenan's approach, with its preference for the stable and the routine, is unable to account for but that fit well with Pipes's cyclicity. Among these continuous patterns are analogies that Alexander Gerschenkron described.

In examining the reorganization of the Soviet economy and agriculture at the turn of the 1930s, Gerschenkron half-jokingly remarked that a resurrected Peter the Great would have no problems in understanding the changes.

> He would have quickly recognized the functional resemblance between collectivization and the serfdom of his days, and he would have praised collectivization as the much more efficient and effective system to achieve the same goals—to feed gratis the nonagricultural segments of the economy and at the same time

provide a flow of labor for the public works of the government. . . . He would no doubt have acquiesced in the tremendous human cost of the collectivization struggles, once it had been explained to him that the quantitative difference between the Soviet period and his own time in this respect was largely the result of the colossal growth in population in the two intervening centuries. . . . Neither the formidable stress on technology in the earlier portions of the period of industrialization, nor the resolute concentration upon heavy industries would have evoked the visitor's astonishment. (1960, 66)

He would not have been surprised, for the familiar techniques were used in response to the same goal: the mobilization of the economy for the sake of achieving military superiority (see Pipes 1980). Like Peter, the Bolsheviks in the 1930s and 1940s widely used forced labor. Their economic priorities were similar, and they displayed the same attitudes toward their fellow countrymen.

Gerschenkron describes (1970, 94) the characteristic feature of Peter the Great's economic strategies: economic growth was a function of the military needs of the state and entirely subjected to them. This resulted in an unsystematic pattern of spasmodic development that placed a terrible burden upon the population and required the wide use of coercion to prevent rebellion. The economic spurts continued as long as military pressure persisted or until the population was exhausted. Stagnation or a decline in the rates of economic growth followed.

In Gerschenkron's view, this pattern was equally characteristic of the industrialization spurt of the 1930s. He recognized that once more in the history of Russia an attempt to modernize it, to bring it technologically closer to the Western level of production, was accompanied by a movement away from the West toward the old patterns of oriental despotism (ibid., 117). That this happened under the banner of a Western Marxist doctrine had its precedence in the transplantation of Byzantine Orthodoxy to Russia.

One can object by saying that this so-called pattern has only twice appeared in the history of Russia. Similarly, the purges of the 1930s can be compared to the period of *oprichnina* under Ivan IV but might, like the latter, be considered aberrations. Nonetheless, for such a conservative social arrangement, any profound change in its institutions is an aberration: The system has no institutional instruments to deal with change and to routinize the processes of change. It has a built-in autocratic bias. It can function for long periods of time as a quasi oligarchy, but under destabilizing circumstances can veer toward either anarchy or full-blown despotism, or both—anarchy first and despotism second. This vicious pattern can be brought to an end only by the persistent effort of a large, well-educated and well-informed citizenry able to promote its interests effectively.

As I have tried to show, using examples from works of some of the most competent modern students of Russia, the thesis that the perspective of cultural continuity offers powerful insights into the functioning of the Soviet state has considerable merit. Most of all, this approach makes it possible to show how historical tradition affects the political behavior of groups and individuals, how it persists in the organization of the state despite deep structural changes, how it influences the way problems are solved and policies generated, and the way the population is mobilized for traumatic changes. Still, the problem remains, How exactly did this continuation of old ways through revolutions and wars occur? To try to answer this question, we have to look into the theory and practice of Leninism.

THREE

LENIN AS THEORIST

Lenin's importance for the emergence and initial development of the Soviet political order raises no doubt. Differences of opinion emerge only when it comes to the concrete interpretation of his role. Some see Lenin as a tragic visionary whose vision could not have materialized under Russian conditions.[1] Others believe in the essential correctness of his ideas, blaming unfavorable conditions for his failure. The position adopted here is that he succeeded and failed for the very same reason. He succeeded in subjecting Russia to Bolshevik rule because his institutional conceptions and the tactics he pursued were suitable for that purpose. He failed to achieve the values traditionally connected with socialism and Marxism because his doctrine was incompatible with such values. (I do not intend to outline Lenin's social and political ideas; I am interested only in the main doctrine behind the Communist institutional design.[2])

Lenin presented himself as an orthodox Marxist, but he did not hesitate to modify Marxism and reverse his ideological position whenever it suited him. Nearly all his written work consisted of polemics against political opponents in the Russian and European social democracy movements. In those polemics he always presented himself as a defender of "pure" Marxism against the "revisionists." This was related to his effort to turn the loose, freely debating association of socialists that Russian social democracy had been into a disciplined and centralized organization with a revolutionary mission. Theories of Marx and Engels provided the mission; Lenin provided the leadership. To achieve this, he had to become its only true interpreter. Thus, even in his role as a theorist, Lenin was a determined pragmatic politician rather than a student of social life. As a practitioner, he proved himself a flexible, single-minded, and ruthless leader with a good sense of timing. As a writer, he was preoccupied by tactical considerations of the power game within Russian social democracy, always ready to conceal his true opinions or to contradict himself. His arguments had mainly a tactical character; we can infer his principles only indirectly by seeing how stubbornly he clung to certain positions while changing his arguments. When we use this indirect method of examination, we find in his work a fairly consistent body of ideas, or perhaps just of predilections, that can be formulated as a coherent political and economic doctrine.

STATE AND REVOLUTION

I shall start with ideas developed in *State and Revolution* ([1917] 1971a). The choice is not accidental. The booklet was written shortly before the October coup of 1917 and has been read closely by his interpreters.[3] A. J. Polan, in a provocative work devoted to the examination of this highly relevant text, characterizes its role in the following way:

> Openly or implicitly, *The State and Revolution* has had a long career as Lenin's credentials as a revolutionary humanist, allying him with those who reject the pragmatism and brutality of subsequent Soviet history.... A political ideology based only upon a theory of vulgar *Realpolitik* (the rest of Lenin's writings) and a reality of disappointed hopes and bloody confusions (the history of the Soviet state) would be a weak one indeed. *The State and Revolution*

inserts into this unconvincing ensemble all the humanist elements that are missing: the deeply felt aspirations for a truly free society based upon tolerance, equality and fraternity. An effective and practical politics which can guarantee the birth of Utopia is surely difficult to resist. (1984, 11)[4]

Polan is correct in saying that *State and Revolution* contained a program Lenin tried to implement in practice. Some of its elements, such as the *uravnilovka* (the term was applied to the policy of equalization of incomes), have proven unrealizable and were consequently abandoned; others still hang over the institutional system of the communist regime. Thus, *State and Revolution* deserves close consideration. Whether it gives credence to claims of Lenin's humanism is a different matter.

As far as the general interpretation of the state is concerned, Lenin was mostly inspired by Engels's book, *The Origin of the Family, Private Property, and the State;* he also used Marx's appraisals of the short history of the Paris Commune. The theory of the state offered by Engels can be summarized in the following way. Primitive communist societies consisted of a community of equals who lived in tightly integrated groups and cooperated to satisfy their needs. This type of social organization was destroyed by the social division of labor that was closely related to the spread of commodity markets. Under such historical conditions the institution of private property emerged and led to the division of society into antagonistic classes opposed to one another in an irreconcilable conflict of interests. Efforts by exploiting classes to assure their dominance over the exploited resulted in the emergence of the state, that is, of an organized system of coercion serving the interests of economically dominant classes. Empirical manifestations of the state are the army, the police, jails, and the bureaucracy. A proletarian revolution, the taking over of political power by the exploited, must bring about the complete liberation of mankind, for it is in the objective interest of the exploited to put an end to exploitation— only then can the workers liberate themselves. The process of liberation goes through a series of stages: the abolition of private property and commodity exchange puts an end to the social division of labor. Only then will class divisions disappear. At that point, the state loses its historical raison d'être: the proletarian revolution triggers the process of the "withering away" of the state. The "workers' state," not being a state in the true sense of the term, is a transitory phenomenon, a political mechanism with a self-annihilating device built into it.

Analyzing *State and Revolution* is a highly confusing experience. In it Lenin embraced values that are universally cherished, but denied those values whenever he touched on problems of institutional design. Let us take, for instance, the subject of democracy, which was not high on Lenin's practical or theoretical agenda. His treatment of democracy is crucial to any understanding and assessment of his design for the Communist institutional order. One suspects that the only reason he addressed the issue was that his opponents within the social-democratic movement often accused him of autocratic ambitions and of disregard for the democratic character of the working class movement. During debates about the organization of the party, Lenin justified the antidemocratic thrust of his proposals by pointing to conditions with which the social democrats had to deal in Russia. But he also used another kind of argument that makes his thinking more dogmatic than circumstantial: A revolutionary workers' party is democratic simply because it fights a bourgeois state that, by its very nature, is undemocratic. Destruction of the bourgeois social order by the revolutionary working class will automatically result in democracy.

This idea appears in *State and Revolution*, where Lenin asserts that true democracy could emerge only under the dictatorship of the proletariat: "Democracy is a *state* which recognizes the subordination of the minority to the majority, i.e., an organization for the systematic use of *force* by one class against another, by one section of the population against another" ([1917] 1971a, 11). He continued: "Democracy for the vast majority of the people, and suppression by force, i.e., exclusion from democracy, of the exploiters and oppressors of the people—this is the change democracy undergoes during the transition from capitalism to communism" (ibid., 327). Only when capitalist resistance is completely crushed, does true democracy become possible. Then, as a form of the organization of the state, it must immediately wither away.[5] It is interesting to note that only at that point, when the state disappeared, can the term *democracy* acquire its universalistic meaning. Otherwise, it is always accompanied, in Lenin's texts, by words such as "force," "coercion," "suppression," "exclusion," "crushing," "smashing," as if those terms were defining the *differentia specifica* of a democratic social order.

One of the topics of particular interest to Lenin both in *State and Revolution* and in his earlier writings was that of centralization. He undoubtedly was among the most convinced of its advocates. To elucidate his position, let me quote directly from his work.

> Now if the proletariat and the poor peasants take state power into their own hands, organise themselves quite freely in communes, and unite the action of all communes in striking at capital, in crushing the resistance of the capitalists, and in transferring the privately owned railways, factories, land and so on to the *entire* nation, to the whole of society, won't that be centralism? Won't that be the most consistent democratic centralism and, moreover, proletarian centralism? (Ibid., 301)

He repeated this view on many other occasions. He also dismissed the problem as devoid of practical relevance. By adding to "centralism" the adjective "proletarian," he made it palatable by any socialist standards of the time. It is possible to interpret his reasoning in the following way: If a social class is bound by a common interest, then it is not important whether the coordination of its class activities is achieved by negotiations among various groups that form it (bottom-up strategy) or by hierarchically imposed coordination by a single power center (top-down strategy). The effect in both cases would be identical. This, however, contradicts his earlier position, associated with his conception of the elite party, that by themselves workers could attain only "trade-unionist" type of class consciousness; "revolutionary" consciousness would have to be brought to them from outside. There is no doubt that here

Lenin showed bad faith, for in all discussions concerning the organization of the party he consistently defended the idea of centralization and the top-down strategy.[6]

It is possible that Lenin misunderstood the problem of democracy and centralization. Comparing, for instance, the French Republic of 1792–1798 and the Swiss Republic, he wrote: "The really democratic centralised republic gave *more* freedom than the federal republic. In other words, the *greatest* amount of local, regional and other freedom known in history was accorded by a centralised and not by a federal republic" ([1917] 1971a, 316). When we consider Lenin's views on democracy and the shallowness of his arguments, his ignorance is striking.[7] As A. J. Polan has aptly remarked, ". . . it can be said that, in a literal sense, *Lenin did not know what he was talking about*" (1984, 155). This may not have always been true, but in the case of Lenin's treatment of the problem of democracy such a critical comment is justified.

Lenin's view of democracy, contrary to all his claims, was a purely negative one. He saw democracy as a centralized, coercive power acting on behalf of the majority of the population. He was not at all concerned with the crucial question about how to achieve coordination between the interests of the majority and the actions of the centralized coercive powers of the state. In his view, provided the revolutionary power was in charge, this *had to happen*.

This brings us to his ideas on the dictatorship of the proletariat. The sources of Lenin's inspiration are obvious when one considers the examples he used to illustrate his points: German state administration and German industrial planning imposed by the necessity of economic mobilization for war. Like Karl Marx, Lenin saw in monopolies the sign of the approaching socialist era. The organization that seems to characterize his thinking is the German postal service.

> At present the postal service is a business organized on the lines of a state-*capitalist* monopoly. . . . But the mechanism of social management is here already to hand. Once we have overthrown the capitalist, crushed the resistance of these exploiters with the

> iron hand of the armed workers, and smashed the bureaucratic machine of the modern state, we shall have a splendidly equipped mechanism, freed from the "parasite," a mechanism which can very well be set going by the united workers themselves who will hire technicians, foremen and accountants, and pay them all, as indeed all "state" officials in general, workmen's wages. ([1917] 1971a, 299)

Directly beneath he added:

> To organize the whole economy on the lines of the postal service . . . this is our immediate aim. This is the state and this is the economic foundation we need. This is what will bring about the abolition of parliamentarism and the preservation of the representative institutions. (Ibid.)

These statements are confusing indeed. What could he have had in mind when, having proposed the smashing of "the bureaucratic machine of the modern state" he stated that the workers would come into the possession of a "splendidly equipped mechanism"? How can one abolish "parliamentarism" and still preserve "representative institutions"?

A solution to these questions can be found in dialectic logic. The modern state is a great organizational invention, an achievement of the utmost effectiveness and efficiency. What makes it a "bureaucratic parasite" is its relationship with private property; to smash the bureaucratic state could thus mean to cut the alliance between the state and private property. If the state is the ruling committee of the dominant class, the problem for the proletariat consists of seizing the state and using it to promote its class interests. Being a neutral tool in the hands of whoever controls it, the state under the control of the majority interests becomes a representative institution. The parliament, which Lenin never held in high repute, becomes obsolete, and the market—which, following Marx and Engels, Lenin associated with private property, division of labor, and class exploitation—must disappear too. Thus, he proposed replacing a parliament and a market by a neutral administration that was also to become a representative institution.

It is not possible to dispense at once with all administration, with all subordination, wrote Lenin. These are anarchic dreams. "The subordination, however, must be to the armed vanguard of all the exploited and working people, i.e., to the proletariat" ([1917] 1971a, 298). But subordination to the armed vanguard changes the very nature of administration; it was to be based on the principle of eligibility and instant removability, in the case of abuse, of all officials. Therefore, the officials would carry on executive functions while being elected representatives of their constituencies. The only exception to the rule were those enterprises in which technology imposed the requirement of absolute discipline. In such cases the workers were supposed to elect a quasi-parliamentary, self-governing body.

An extraordinary simplification of accounting and control functions in the administration makes it possible for all workers quickly to acquire such abilities and to run the state by themselves. Lenin formulated the idea of the state *and of the economy* that emerged from this in the following words:

> Accounting and control—that is *mainly* what is needed for the "smooth working," for the proper functioning, of the *first* phase of communist society. *All* citizens are transformed into hired employees of the state, which consists of the armed workers. All citizens become employees and workers of a *single* country-wide state "syndicate." (Ibid., 336)

It would be, added Lenin on the next page, impossible for "parasites," "the sons of the wealthy," and for other "swindlers" to escape from such popular accounting and control.

Lenin's conception of the withering away of the state comes from the simplification of the tasks of accounting and control. This process consists in the transformation "of public functions from political into simple functions of administration . . ."; and, at a certain stage of this process, ". . . the state which is withering away may be called a non-political state" (ibid., 308). Thus, the withering away of the state is the creation of an order "under which the functions of control and accounting, becoming more and more simple, will be performed by each in turn, will then become a habit and will finally die out as the *special* functions of a special section of the population" (ibid., 298). Without considering the merits of the proposed eligibility of officials, which is the key to Lenin's interpretation of the withering away of the state, it is worth noticing that this is one of the few ideas put forward in *State and Revolution* that was not tried in practice.

Lenin had no theory of political institutions.

> Lenin's state form is one-dimensional. It allows for no distances, no spaces, no appeals, no checks, no balances, no processes, no delays, no interrogations and, above all, no distribution of power. All are ruthlessly and deliberately excluded. . . . The new form of state will be transparent, monological and unilinear. . . . It . . . demands a situation devoid of all political conflicts, of all economic problems, of all social contradictions, of all inadequate, selfish or simply human emotions or motivations. . . . It demands, in short, for Lenin's political structures to work, that there be an absence of politics. (Polan 1984, 129–30)

Lenin saw his communist society as one big state that, at the same time, was not a state; a huge post office in which everybody went about his or her own business without being in any way induced to do so by material rewards or organizational sanctions. But a period of severe coercion was necessary to install such habits of behavior, and anybody who disregarded such "fundamental rules of the community" would experience "swift and severe punishment . . . for the armed workers are practical men and not sentimental intellectuals, and they will scarcely allow anyone to trifle with them" (Lenin [1917] 1971a, 337).

There is an element in *State and Revolution* that permits a different interpretation of the conception it presents. Lenin often used terms such as "organized proletariat," "armed proletarians," "armed vanguard," "exploited and working people," "united workers," to denote those that were to punish, force, coerce, smash, crush, and destroy. The question is, Who were the people who were to do this? If these men and women were to have free rein, it is not a trivial matter to ask about their identity. What happens if we replace these terms with another term—the Communist party?

Lenin on the Organization of the Party

One characteristic feature of Lenin's booklet is that he wrote little about the party. It may be that in the summer of 1917 Lenin consciously avoided this controversial issue. Times were uncertain indeed. His views on the organization of the party had proved highly divisive. They had contributed to the split of Russian social democrats into the Bolshevik and Menshevik factions. His views were also unpopular among some of the leading German social democrats, most notably Rosa Luxemburg and Karl Kautsky. Lenin had good reason to avoid new doctrinal disputes.

We can assume, then, that what he meant in *State and Revolution* by "armed proletarians," "organized workers," and so on, was the party of Bolsheviks. The alternative hypothesis would be that he suddenly, and only for a very short time, abandoned his views on the organization of the party. I can see no grounds to uphold such a position. There is some circumstantial evidence that Lenin did not trust spontaneity or workers left on their own. Besides, when he mentioned "armed workers," he usually added that they were "organized." Thus, if he had the Bolshevik party in mind, it may be useful to look to some earlier works for the essential features of the party to which he wanted to grant extensive powers of coercion over society.

Lenin's conception of the Communist party is the key element in his revision of Marxism.[8] Marx considered the fall of capitalism and the emergence of communism an objective historical necessity, an unavoidable outcome of the laws of motion of the capitalist formation and of the logic of historical development. Lenin had less confidence in historical automatism. He seemed not to believe in the unavoidable collapse of capitalism, but apparently assumed that, once this had happened and all the powers were in the hands of Bolsheviks, further development toward communism would take its automatic course.

This claim found support in Lenin's conception of class consciousness. In his view, workers by their own effort could attain only the trade-unionist level of class consciousness, that is, do no more than to start organizations with the aim of fighting for better work conditions and better wages within the capitalist mode of production; workers' class interests were, thus, narrowed down to their immediate material concerns. Lenin saw the possibility of regulating class conflict within the realm capitalism formation, but did not approve of it on the doctrinal level. He envisaged a superior type of class consciousness. A group of professional revolutionaries, using refined methods of agitation and propaganda, was to bring *revolutionary* consciousness to the working class from outside.[9] Some may call this a creative development of Marxism, others "revisionism." What is relevant here, however, is that it is an important modification of the original theory.

Lenin's attitude toward trade unions was ambivalent. He never attacked them directly and even recognized their positive functions. He thought that they should be (indirectly) subordinated to the organization of revolutionaries. He saw the organizational structure as a function of organizational goals. Having different aims, the trade unions' structure and methods of work differed from those of the revolutionary party of the proletariat. Organizations of workers for the economic struggle should have a mass character, should enroll members with different levels of class consciousness, should act in the open and possibly in accordance with existing laws. This is how Lenin himself characterized the differences:

> The political struggle of Social-Democracy is far more extensive and complex than the economic struggle of the workers against the employers and the government. Similarly (indeed for that reason), the organisation of the revolutionary Social-Democratic Party must inevitably be of *a kind different* from the organisation of the workers designed for this struggle. The workers' organisation must in the first place be a trade-union organisation; secondly, it must be as broad as possible; and thirdly, it must be as public as conditions will allow (here, and further on . . . I refer only to absolutist Russia). On the other hand, the organisation of the

> revolutionaries must consist first and foremost of people who make revolutionary activity their profession (for which reason I speak of the organisation of *revolutionaries,* meaning revolutionary Social-Democrats). . . . Such an organisation must perforce not be very extensive and must be as secret as possible. ([1902] 1961a, 452–53)

In the relationship between the party and the trade unions, the party is the senior partner. It is important to start organizing a trade union movement only when the party has been organized and is safe (ibid., 460). The party and the trade unions should be formally separate, although the party should keep the key posts in the unions for its members; it should penetrate the unions.

Lenin viewed the working class movement as a series of circles ([1904] 1961e, 266). The first circle consisted of the organization of professional revolutionaries, the second circle of the factory workers' organizations and these two circles formed the party. The third circle was made up of workers' organizations associated with the party; the fourth, of workers' organizations not associated with the party but under its control and direction; the fifth, of unorganized elements of the working class in part and at times also under the control and direction of the party. This was an organizational hierarchy of the Social-Democratic party, a hierarchy of initiation (ibid., 270).

The task of the party is to educate the masses, to shape and enhance their revolutionary consciousness, to lead. For this purpose, the members of the party should constantly work upon their own consciousness and their abilities in conducting agitation and propaganda work. The supreme rank of agitation and propaganda explains the very special place ascribed by Lenin to the party's main press organ, the newspaper, *Iskra.*

Lenin viewed the party as a group of professional revolutionaries, fully deployable agents of a centralized, disciplined, secret organization, entirely devoted to the party and materially dependent upon it. This put a terrible financial burden upon the Bolsheviks. The methods through which they tried to resolve it were a source of many comic stories and of constant indignation among other social democrats.

Professional revolutionaries were to be the elite leaders of the revolutionary struggle. Commenting upon the German experience, Lenin wrote that ". . . without the 'dozen' tried and talented leaders (and talented men are not born by the hundreds), professionally trained, schooled by long experience, and working in perfect harmony, no class in modern society can wage a determined struggle." On the next page he added that ". . . Russian Social-Democracy is passing through a crisis entirely due to the lack of sufficiently trained, developed, and experienced leaders to guide the spontaneously awakening masses. . . ." ([1902] 1961a, 461–62). It is hard not to notice Lenin's manipulative attitude toward the workers on whose behalf he wanted to act.

He gave the leaders full powers within and over the party. He considered no mechanism of control over them.

> The Central Committee itself should be allowed to determine the sphere of its competence, since any local matter may affect the interests of the Party as a whole, and the Central Committee should be in a position to intervene in local affairs, even going against local interests, should such action be in the interests of the Party as a whole. ([1903] 1961c, 492)

Giving such broad powers to the Central Committee, he deprived local party organizations of all autonomy. Let us remark that this is not a conjectural argument but more a doctrinal one.

This top-down logic of organization is to permeate the whole party structure. On the lower level, the modus is the same.

> The district groups should be permitted to act independently only on questions concerning the technical aspect of transmission and distribution. The composition of the district groups should be determined by the committee, i.e., the committee *appoints* one or two of its members (or even comrades who are not on the committee) as delegates to this or that district and instructs them to *establish a district group,* all the members of which are likewise installed in office, so to speak, by the committee. The district group is a branch of the committee, deriving its powers only from the latter. ([1902] 1961b, 241)

The Central Committee must be fully informed about all aspects of work at the lower levels of party organization and about every member. The center must have a *"complete* picture" of the whole movement, to enable it to make rational decisions about party activities and personnel policies (ibid., 247). Lenin was aware that if "an *incapable* person [were] invested with tremendous power" in the party (ibid., 242), such a centralization would pose a threat, but this did not compel him to reconsider his views. To this question I shall return.

The way Lenin perceived the problem of centralization and decentralization in the party borders on myopia. In "A Letter to a Comrade," one of his most authoritative early statements on the subject of the organization of the party, he made the following point:

> While *the greatest possible centralisation* is necessary with regard to the ideological and practical *leadership* of the movement and the revolutionary struggle of the proletariat, *the greatest possible decentralisation* is necessary with regard to keeping the Party centre (and therefore the Party as a whole) *informed* about the movement, and with regard to *responsibility* to the Party. . . . We must centralise the leadership of the movement. We must also (and *for that very reason*, since without information centralisation is impossible) as far as possible *decentralise responsibility to the Party* on the part of its individual members, of every participant in its work, and of every circle belonging to or associated with the Party. (Ibid., 248–49)

Thus, with regret, Lenin conceded to party members the right and duty to inform the center on all details of their work and that of their comrades. He also delegated to them the "right" to be responsible solely before the party. The strongest, and the only, argument he could find for decentralization, in his rather curious meaning of the term, was that without it full centralization would not be possible.

No wonder Lenin's ideas encountered stiff resistance among many Russian and non-Russian social democrats. His model of organization of the party was criticized as "organized distrust," a "system of despotic and bureaucratic rule over the Party," "bureaucratic centralism," and "bonapartism." Some participants in the discussions expressed the fear that, if such a disciplined and centralized organization were controlled by irresponsible individuals, they could use their powers for whatever purpose suited them. Such completely uncontrolled form of organization presented great dangers of abuse. Plekhanov, in 1904, formulated one of the most perceptive and farsighted forecasts on the possible effects of accepting Lenin's model of the party.

> Imagine that the Central Committee recognized by us all possessed the still-debated right of "liquidation." Then this would happen. Since a congress is in the offing, the [Central Committee] everywhere liquidates the elements with which it is dissatisfied, everywhere seats its own creatures and, filling all the committees with these creatures, without difficulty guarantees itself a fully submissive majority at the congress. The congress constituted of the creatures of the [Central Committee] amiably cries "Hurrah!," approves all its successful and unsuccessful actions, and applauds all its plans and initiatives. Then, in reality, there would be in the party neither a majority nor a minority, because we would then have realized the ideal of the Persian Shah. (Baron 1962, 50)

Later on, the term *liquidation* was to lose its soft meaning and acquire a hard one.

Lenin seems to have been unable to see the problem in terms of organizational design and its consequences. Therefore, he could only answer these criticisms in terms of individual control and ideological socialization in the party. He wrote:

> *The whole Party* must constantly, steadily and systematically *train* suitable persons for the central bodies, must see clearly, as in the palm of its hand, *all the activities* of every candidate for these high posts, must come to know even their personal characteristics, their strong and weak points, their victories and "defeats." ([1903] 1961d, 117)

Thus, the argument against centralization has been turned into an argument for centralization or rather for Lenin's mix of centralization *qua* decentralization, that is, the decentralization of the duty to keep the center informed on all the details of party work and personal information about other comrades coupled with the extreme centralization of the power of decision exercised in utmost secrecy. This meant that members of the party were to act as impersonal, objective mechanisms without personal feelings and private interests. That he was succeeded by Joseph Stalin may be the best comment about the implications of his stand.

Lenin's type of party organization leaves no room for elections to party posts. The center is the key element in the nervous system of the party, it has all the information about party work and party workers. Under such conditions, the logical strategy for choosing candidates for responsible party positions is not to elect, but rather to co-opt. In fact, Lenin advocated the principle of co-optation in recruiting members of the Central Committee. In discussions during the Second Congress of the Russian Social Democracy, held in 1903 in London, Lenin strongly defended co-optation, proposing mutual control exercised by the Central Organ (the newspaper, *Iskra*) over the co-optation of members by the Central Committee, and by the Central Committee over co-optations of members to the Central Organ. However, being at that moment part of the majority within the Central Organ, he could not resist remarking that the staff of *Iskra* "was undoubtedly best qualified to judge about the personal composition of the central bodies, having as it did the closest practical acquaintance with all affairs and with all the candidates" ([1904] 1961e, 297). If central bodies of the party consist of the best of the best, then one should leave responsibility for the selection of candidates for important party posts to those central bodies of the party themselves; any interference with their judgment could have negative consequences for the quality of leadership selection.

One can object by pointing out that Lenin often wrote about "democratic centralism" and, therefore, the idea of democracy was not altogether foreign to him. Two remarks are necessary in this context. First, the question, formulated by a certain Comrade Posadovsky, was posed during the London Congress: ". . . *should we subordinate our future policy to certain fundamental democratic principles and attribute absolute value to them,* or should all democratic principles be exclusively subordinated to the interests of our Party?" (ibid., 227). Lenin enthusiastically supported the subjection of democratic principles to the party's interests. He never expressed a similar opinion concerning centralism. Thus, we can assume that in the "democratic centralist" formula, the democratic element was disposable, and facts support this assumption. To this I shall return in a moment.

Second, Lenin's conception of "democratic centralism" is rather peculiar. It seems to me that the organization whose functioning best illustrates his idea was an American bomber unit in the Pacific theatre during World War II, as characterized by Herbert A. Shepard:

> The planning before a raid was done jointly by the entire unit—the private having as much opportunity to contribute to the planning as the colonel. During the raid, the group operated under a strict military command system. Following each raid, the unit returned to the open system used in planning for purposes of evaluating and maximizing learning from each raid. (1963, 523)

This system can function fairly well only when an organization's activities can be divided into distinct phases separated in time: preparation, execution, evaluation. This was possible both in the case of the bomber unit and the prerevolutionary Bolshevik party. We can also assume that this type of organization required a strong *unity of purpose* that surely characterized Russian revolutionaries of the time and probably bomber pilots no less. There is still another similarity: the purpose of a bombing raid is to wreak havoc upon the enemy; the purpose of the revolutionary party was the destruction of tsardom, of capitalism. Thus, we have distinct phases separated in time and a unity of destructive purpose. This similarity should surprise no reader of Lenin, whose pages abound with militaristic comparisons and military language. The inspiration for his idea of the party came from the military domain; the party is an army. The appropriation of this organizational model by the party was a highly consequential act, for one justifies the existence of an army only by the existence of an enemy.

To be more specific, we propose that Lenin's image of democratic centralism had the following form. Before and during the congresses, the Communist party was to discuss proposals, engage in consultations, and formulate a joint program of action. Once the program was adopted, the party had to change into a fully deployable group, acting in harmony for the purpose established by the congress, blindly obeying all orders coming from the center. The next congress would make it possible to assess past activities and to decide upon a new program.

Let us ask a rhetorical question: What is likely to happen when such an organization gains control over the state and starts to rule? Its tasks cease to be divisible into distinct phases, clearly separated in time; the unity of purpose starts to disintegrate in face of necessity to make choices among many equally legitimate purposes; the destructive character of party aims must be, at least to some extent, supplemented by positive purposes. The history of the Soviet Union and other countries with a Soviet-type regime shows how difficult such a transition is.

But even this interpretation hardly stands up to the facts. Can we maintain that Lenin seriously treated the matter of free and open intraparty discussions and consultations, in view of his postrevolutionary record? A positive answer to this question would require the following development of events: Between the end of 1917 and the beginning of 1921, that is, when the Bolsheviks had to struggle against foreign intervention and the counterrevolution, there was little place for democracy in the party. Only when more peaceful conditions emerged could intraparty debates reappear. This interpretation would support the position that Lenin treated democratic values seriously and that he could accept restrictions upon these values only when fundamental interests of the party were threatened.

In reality it was the other way around. Some of Lenin's closest collaborators opposed him throughout 1917 and later on. After 1919, a number of very active factions in the Bolshevik party accepted Lenin's personal authority, but strongly opposed certain trends and openly criticized specific policies. Elections of delegates to the Tenth Congress of the Russian Communist Party, held in March 1921, were relatively democratic, with a true election campaign during which different factions presented their electoral platforms. It was only *after* the end of the civil war and *after* the suppression of the Kronstadt rising that Lenin introduced his resolution, "On the Unity of the Party," which explicitly forbade factional activities to the extent that any party member expressing critical opinions about party policies could be accused of factionalism and punished. Therefore, it seems that the other hypothesis is correct: as long as the party's grip upon the population, and the leadership's grip upon the party, were weak, the leadership had to tolerate a measure of intraparty democracy. When circumstances changed, this tolerance came to an end.

Lenin justified his design of the revolutionary party or, at least, its most controversial fragments, by pointing to the specific conditions under which Russian Social Democrats had to operate, to the lack of basic civic freedoms and to police terror. This might suggest that he treated these democratic elements of his design as an unfortunate necessity that should be abandoned under more opportune circumstances. The truth is that, throughout his doctrinal and political activity, Lenin consistently defended central dominance, changing only the circumstantial arguments. To put it bluntly, circumstances were always inopportune for democratic opposition. Changing circumstances did not result in a modification in the commitment to central dominance but only in the search for different arguments to justify that design. One may suspect, therefore, that Lenin treated the principle of central direction in his design much more seriously than his tactical arguments would suggest. Whatever Lenin's personal attitude, one thing is absolutely certain: All of them are a fundamental part of the everyday repertoire of modern Communist parties. The consequences in democratic countries in which Communist parties usually function at the very margin of political life are different from those in Communist countries in which these parties form the core of political life.

Conclusions

It is my proposition that the concept of the dictatorship of the proletariat developed in *State and Revolution* becomes comprehensible only when we replace such catchwords as "united workers," "organized proletariat," "armed vanguard of the proletariat," and so forth, by the term *the Bolshevik party*. When we do this, the reasoning becomes realistic and we see its true meaning. Moreover, the image we obtain, of the state in the form of the post-office system under control of the Communist party, accurately reflects the reality of the Soviet system through its existence.

We should remember, however, that all attempts to reconstruct an institutional design must be largely arbitrary. I am not aware of any analysis, in Lenin's work, that seriously considers the relationship between the revolutionary Communist party and the state. The way he reasoned about his theoretical options, omitted crucial problems from his reflection, avoided seriously considering the principles of the socialist movement makes it preferable to talk rather of Lenin's doctrinal or practical predilections than of his theories. He was not a man dedicated to theoretical and moral reflection. His writings were more a part of his contribution to political intrigue and power struggles than they were an effort to understand the mechanisms of the world around him.

For him any state was a dictatorship. Differences among states in the use made of coercion and in the way they devised peaceful modes of conflict resolution through negotiations, elections, and the rule of law were of no concern to him. A so-called democracy under the dictatorship of the proletariat was to be no less a coercive form of government than any other, the only difference being that force was to serve the interests of the majority of the population. The only condition necessary for the achievement of a truly democratic government was the concentration of full powers in the hands of (his) Communist party, which would exercise dictatorship in the name of the proletariat.

He was unable to envisage in his writings any conflict of interests other than the class conflict. The rest logically followed: If it were so, a destruction of capitalism by the revolutionary party and the subjection of the state to the control of the Communist party would have to result in the abolition of all conflicts of interest. The only needs the dictatorship of the proletariat could serve under those conditions would be to suppress the resistance of remnants of the old dominating classes and to complete the mass education of those elements of the proletariat that had not yet acquired the correct class consciousness. Having accomplished these tasks, and not generating any new interests, the state of the dictatorship of the proletariat was to wither away.

The state is only the "executive committee" of the dominant class, and class domination develops outside the state, within the mode of production. To be more precise, property relations generate class divisions. When private property is abolished, class divisions disappear, and conflicts of interests must also vanish. The state becomes a neutral tool in the hands of the proletariat. An expansion of state functions that is required for building a communist society can have no negative side effects because it is only a temporary phenomenon.

Of all this, perhaps the most significant is the formula: democracy = coercion + centralization of power + rule by the proletarian vanguard. The proletarian vanguard is the revolutionary party of Bolsheviks, itself centralized, secretive, tightly disciplined. This is the bridge between Lenin's vision of the state as the dictatorship of the proletariat and his idea of the organization of the party. We have to look at both in order to understand the design of his institutional order.

It is obvious that this institutional design makes impossible any realization of the values cherished by Marx and many other socialists in their dreams of a communist society. No institutional structure can realize utopian dreams. When one uses terror to obtain compliance, terror becomes the axis around which the new social order is built. Lenin's importance does not consist in successful establishment of a utopia but in his being the founding father of the USSR. Considering the values that communism was expected to achieve, this whole social order can be considered an unintended effect of a social action that was supposed to attain a very different purpose. Lenin sought communism and created a new autocracy: the Soviet regime.

FOUR

LENIN AS PRACTITIONER

Lenin, it seems, was made for the Russian Revolution. He had an intuitive understanding of the situation and its requirements; he felt it with every nerve of his body. Without it, he might have been an insignificant person, known only to a handful of historians specializing in Russian revolutionary movements at the turn of the nineteenth century, as merely one among a number of leaders, a difficult character, and the author of long, murky, and often boring political treatises.

The October Revolution itself can hardly be considered an inevitable event. After it started, the Bolshevik hold on power was often highly precarious. There were alternative options for constructing institutional structures. The key to understanding the strategy, tactics, and the final success of the Bolsheviks lies to a great extent in the personality and ideas of their leader, Vladimir Ilyich Ulyanov, otherwise called Lenin.[1]

LENIN'S ROAD TO POWER

The Russian social democracy movement consisted initially of loosely structured groups of leftist intellectuals with considerable influence among the Russian intelligentsia and some influence among the workers. They were part of the great political revival that occurred in Russia at the end of the nineteenth century. They were influential but represented only one among many political orientations. Most of them, with the exception of the radical right, were in favor of profound changes in the Russian political regime. The Social Democrats, together with Social Revolutionaries, occupied the revolutionary part of the political spectrum; the liberal part of the spectrum was dominated by the Constitutional Democratic party (Kadety), formed in 1905, which had a reformist orientation. Both parties, the Social-Democratic and the Constitutional-Democratic, consisted of highly idealistic individuals, the products of a long tradition of Russian radical antiabsolutist dissent. They diverged in everything else, and despite some influence, the Constitutional Democrats were the great losers in Russian history.

The problem of democracy was of crucial importance for most of the Social Democrats, too. They shared George Plekhanov's conviction that the victory of socialism in Russia should be preceded by a period during which a liberal republic would bring the country out of its economic backwardness and spread values of democracy and civic responsibility among a population that, except for a few, had known nothing but servitude and tyranny. Conducting their activities under constant police vigilance, risking imprisonment and exile, the Social Democrats concentrated most of their political activities abroad: most of the congresses and party meetings were held in Western Europe. Some of the party journals and political programs were printed there and smuggled into Russia by special emissaries. This practice created one of the main dividing lines in the movement, that between activists living abroad and those pursuing political work in Russia itself, but was not the only source of conflict within the party.

Like every group of highly motivated individuals, the Russian Social Democrats endured constant ideological disputes and personal intrigues. Efforts, often successful, by the secret police organization, Okhrana, to penetrate its ranks, and the difficult life of political émigrés created a strange combination, so typical of this milieu, of what is the most noble and most ignoble in human hearts and minds, a situation described vividly by Joseph Conrad in his book, *Under Western Eyes* (1911).

The first deep division within Russian Social Democracy in which Lenin played an active part came into the open in 1902 after he published *What Is to Be Done?* which was intended to be the program of the party and an outline for its organizational structure and methods of action. The program became the subject of hot debate during the Third Party Congress in London in 1903. The most controversial were Lenin's principles of party membership that followed from his idea of the party as a small professional elite of militants, his emphasis upon the centralization of decision making, and the idea of organizing the party from the top down. Behind it, a matter that received much attention during the Second Congress and that might have been more important than the doctrinal differences, was Lenin's attempt to change the editorial board of *Iskra* and gain control of the newspaper by eliminating the "elders," Plekhanov, Zasulich, and Axelrod.

There was a separate debate over the proposal by the Bund, the Jewish socialist party, to introduce the principle of federalism into the organization of the Russian Social-Democratic party so that the Bund could maintain its identity as a representative of Jewish workers. Discussions about the organization of the party took place at many subsequent party meetings and congresses.

Another issue that divided the Social Democrats was Lenin's personality itself. Many of his colleagues perceived him as an authoritarian with a lust for power. Reading Lenin, one often has the impression that his unending ideological quarrels were not really ideological, that the ideological language was a veil for his ambition to be the uncontested leader of the party, and that he used ideological debates to impose his authority upon others. His comrades of the period often complained of Lenin's ruthlessness, of his lack of scruples in choosing the means to defeat his enemies, of his methods of solving the financial problems of the Bolshevik faction, and so on. Lydia Dan, a member of the *Iskra* editorial board before the Third Congress, and a sister of Martov, provided one such example of suspected double-crossing of his closest collaborators.

> Since Nadezhda Konstantinovna [Krupskaya] handled correspondence with Russia, she probably had a double set of books, so to speak. That is, she would sometimes write letters to Russia that Lenin would dictate and Martov didn't know about, and she probably received letters from Russia that she deciphered and didn't show to Vera Ivanovna [Zasulich] or anyone else. This aspect of duplicity, double bookkeeping, and the embryo of subsequent factionalism appeared before the [Third] Congress. (Haimson 1987, 128–29)

The split over the issue of party organization during the London Congress in 1903 divided the Social Democrats into Lenin's Bolsheviks ("majoritarians") and the Mensheviks ("minoritarians"). Afterward, Lenin tried to build his Bolshevik faction according to the program adopted in 1903, as a small, select, disciplined group under his own authority.[2] He was not entirely successful, but did try to organize his faction according to these precepts. The Bolsheviks were certainly different in this respect from the Mensheviks who did not have a single leader who would dominate the party as Lenin dominated the Bolsheviks.

Lenin's lust for power leaves little doubt. He had no scruples about using dishonest methods against his opponents.[3] George Denike described his shock at Lenin's duplicity.

> The incredible shamelessness, not just of changing one's position and of denying that it had been different, but of violently accusing those who had accurately reminded him of his position of lying! I wouldn't say that this finished Lenin for me then, but any deep admiration and respect for him were liquidated, essentially for moral reasons. (Ibid., 331)

Yet, nobody ever questioned his qualities of leadership, his ability to present his views effectively in public, his iron will. The other side of his lack of moral scruples was his pragmatism.

To an extent, the division between the Mensheviks and the Bolsheviks was that between orthodox Marxism and pragmatist variations, with the pragmatism bordering sometimes upon moral nihilism. Mensheviks were, according to their own views, more inclined to think of their political activities in terms of "serving" the working class rather than "using" it. They tended to trust the workers more than their opponents, who feared spontaneity and trusted no one but themselves, did. The Mensheviks, according to Denike, were undecided, hesitant, they "didn't manage to come to a fully logical conclusion from their position in any direction" (ibid., 337).

These differences were much more visible at the top of the two factions than among the rank and file who often could hardly understand what was going on.

There were other differences, possibly not even fully realized at the time. The Bolsheviks recruited their supporters mainly from ethnically Russian areas; the Mensheviks came from the west and southwest of the Russian empire. "By 1907, on a line from Astrakhan to St. Petersburg, to the west lay the Menshevik support and, with the possible exception of Siberia, to the east Bolshevik" (Lane 1969, 41). The "Menshevik" territories were settled mostly by non-Russians: Georgians, Ukrainians, Balts, Jews, Poles, and others. These differences are illustrated in the table on page 72. Lane even suggests that Russian nationalism played a part in integrating the Bolshevik faction.

> National antagonisms, the strength of local ties, the binding force of language and tradition kept together the Bolsheviks and allowed for easy assimilation of other Russians into their ranks. The Mensheviks, being more mixed nationally and socially, were subject to competition from purely nationalist and nationally based parties. (1969, 215)

The majority of the Social Democrats came from the gentry or petite bourgeoisie, although the Mensheviks tended to have more members from the middle classes. This factor may explain the different attitudes of the two groups toward the bourgeoisie and capitalism; the Bolsheviks seemed to be much more radical. The Bolsheviks also seemed to have more support among Russian

Ethnic Composition of the Fifth Social-Democratic Party Congress, 1907

Ethnic/national groups	Bolsheviks		Mensheviks	
	Members	%	Members	%
Russians	82	78.3	33	34.0
Jews	12	11.4	22	22.7
Georgians	3	2.7	28	29.9
Ukrainians	1	1.0	6	6.3
Others	7	6.8	7	7.0

Source: Lane (1969, 44); see also Agursky (1987, 92).

workers, although this support seems to have varied with the changing political and economic situation.

The two groups coexisted as factions of the same party until 1912 when Lenin proclaimed his Bolshevik faction as the true Social-Democratic party and expelled the Mensheviks from it. Yet the possibility of reunification survived until the end of 1917, the major obstacle being Lenin himself.

In February 1917, Nicholas II, tsar of Russia, in the face of military defeats in the war against Germany and of growing political opposition, resigned. A new Provisional Government constituted itself out of parties represented in the Duma. The government initially consisted of a coalition of centrist and moderately conservative parties. Later, Social Revolutionaries and Mensheviks joined it. Meanwhile, workers and soldiers in the main Russian cities organized themselves into councils (*soviet*s). Soon, *soviet*s of soldiers' and workers' delegates in Saint Petersburg and Moscow became the real centers of power, effectively curtailing the government's freedom of maneuver. In dismantling the traditional imperial system of rule, the Provisional Government significantly weakened its position vis-à-vis the *soviet*s.

The economic potential of Russia had been exhausted by the war. Markets were disorganized, difficulties in supplying urban centers with food grew. Peasants started massive expropriations of private land. The Provisional Government postponed the legalization of this spontaneous agrarian reform until the Constituent

Assembly was convened, a decision prompted not only by the legalism of its leaders but also by the fear that such legalization would encourage peasant-soldiers at the front to desert in droves to take part. (Even without it, the problem of desertions was grave.)

The army was demoralized by constant defeats wrought by the Germans. The professional officers' corps, indoctrinated in the imperial military tradition, was eradicated in earlier engagements and replaced by poorly trained officers with no sentimental ties to tradition. The final blow to the integrity of the army was delivered by the famous Order Number 1 voted by the Petrograd (as Saint Petersburg had been renamed in 1914) *soviet* immediately after it constituted itself. This order called upon all the units to elect their own *soviet*s of soldiers and gave them the prerogative to make decisions about everything except matters directly concerning field command. They were to control the weapons in possession of the individual units and to mediate in conflicts between soldiers and officers. Those *soviet*s were also to cooperate closely with the Saint Petersburg *soviet*. The chief motive behind the order was to prevent the use of the army against the workers' and soldiers' *soviet*s in Moscow and Petrograd. It succeeded in paralyzing the Russian army and completely destroying its military value.

The Provisional Government decided to stick to its alliances and did not even consider the possibility of a separate peace with Germany. France and Great Britain, ignoring the Russian predicament, urged the government to increase the war effort and step up military operations. The government was waiting for the Constituent Assembly to provide it with legitimation. All the parties that were in the coalition were committed to democratic ideals. Unfortunately, however, they wasted too much time on problems of "here and now" instead of doing what really was important, organizing elections to the Constituent Assembly as soon as possible, perhaps because the organization of elections after a revolution and during a war would not have been easy.

The Provisional Government found itself in a precarious situation: It could not abandon the war, nor could it oppose the Germans in any effective way; it had no remedies to alleviate the worsening economic conditions, for that would require no less than an immediate end to war; it was losing control over the army and could only passively watch the growth of anarchy. Moreover, it did not have any independently organized support at its disposal and its claim to legitimacy was not strong.

Nevertheless, the Provisional Government, however limited its freedom of maneuver may have been, did provide Russia with effective political leadership. Confusion and indecision among other parties of the left contributed greatly to the Bolshevik seizure of power and to the defeat of the prospect for democracy in Russia. The physical exhaustion of the population and the disorganization of social life brought about by the war reduced the country's powers of resistance to an institution that denied society any active role. Besides, the situation in 1917 was truly revolutionary; the attitudes and political behavior of the population of Petrograd and Moscow were highly volatile, changing sometimes from day to day.[4]

Whatever is said about Lenin's leadership and political qualities, one thing is certain: in 1917, and the years that followed, he had only one purpose in mind, to win power for the Bolsheviks—and he was the Bolsheviks. In his absence, in March 1917, Kamenev and Stalin started reunification talks with the Mensheviks. Lenin broke off the talks after his arrival in Petrograd on April 4. Other Bolshevik leaders seemed much more conciliatory toward their colleagues from the left than Lenin was.

Lenin immediately saw that the real power rested with the *soviets* of Petrograd and Moscow. He stubbornly rejected all proposals for a compromise with the Provisional Government and advanced his famous appeal: All power to the *soviets*. He did not hesitate to back the redistribution of large estates among the peasants, and dissociated himself from the idea of continuing the war. Only later he called for a cessation of hostilities on the German-Russian front. By doing all this he simply acknowledged *les faits accomplis.* This radical stand helped him to increase his Bolshevik following, mostly at the cost of the Mensheviks. The Bolsheviks were well organized and had a strong leader who was able to make quick decisions and has been proved right in his tactical choices most of the time. All the failures of the Provisional Government played to his advantage.

After two unsuccessful attempts to bring down the Provisional Government in June 1917, the third attempt, on October 26 (the old calendar), was a success. This attempt coincided with the meeting of the Second Congress of Soviets. In addressing the congress, Lenin read two declarations. In the first, he expressed his willingness to start peace talks with the Germans immediately. In the second, he proclaimed the abolition of all private possession of land, although peasants retained the de facto right to dispose of their land as if they owned it. Both declarations were accepted by the congress. The congress also elected an all-Bolshevik Council of People's Commissars with Lenin at its head.

Thus, Lenin started by playing the *soviet*s against the Provisional Government, while assuring a majority in the *soviet*s for the Bolsheviks. He stopped the war against Germany, something he had to do in order to stay in power: he needed a respite and the support of the soldiers. The final peace treaty signed in Brest-Litovsk was achieved in spite of the initial opposition of most of the Bolsheviks. The peace gave Lenin effective support of the army, which feared nothing more than fighting against Germans. His stand on the issue of land redistribution to the peasants assured him of their temporary neutrality. His position on self-determination gave him the conditional support, at least for the duration of the civil war, of Poles and Finns who could not expect the same from Yudenich, Denikin, Wrangel, or other White (anti-Bolshevik) generals.[5]

Pipes's opinion that "their entire approach to the national idea . . . made the Bolsheviks perhaps the least qualified of all the Russian parties (save for those of the extreme right) to solve the national problem" (1954, 285) seems to be well grounded. Chicherin's statement, made at the end of 1918, to representatives of the new Polish authorities best illustrates the real Bolshevik position on the issue of self-determination. He told them that, as the people's commissar for foreign affairs, he could not recognize the legality of the Polish state because the right to self-determination applied only if it were the sovereign decision of the Polish proletariat to develop a political order corresponding with its class interest; the Polish government represented by his visitors was foreign to such interests (Lednicki 1967, 665).[6] The invasion of Georgia, with whose Menshevik government Soviet Russia had a treaty of peace and friendship, in the spring of 1921, indicates that the Bolsheviks were not consistent about this principle.

In the Bolshevik seizure of power, their stand on three issues—the rejection of the Provisional Government in the name of the *soviet*s, support for the peasant seizure of large estates, and their willingness to start immediate peace negotiations with the Germans—proved decisive. And in each case, the Bolsheviks adopted their position on the initiative of Lenin, who often had to overcome a strong opposition from his colleagues.

THE THREE DECISIONS THAT DETERMINED INSTITUTIONAL STRUCTURE

What were Lenin's strategies in molding the Soviet institutional system? Can we discern in these strategies the same predilections that we traced in his political writings? Lenin's activities during and after the Revolution have been subject to many excellent historical studies. I shall restrict myself to a cursory presentation of the way he solved some of the most crucial issues in the formation of the Soviet state. I believe that the solutions he advocated and implemented are consistent with his theoretical ideas and his personal predilections. The most important were the complete control of the state, the abolition of party factions, and economic and agricultural collectivization.

The struggle for monopoly control. The Bolshevik war against the Russian Left was much more than a simple struggle for power. It was a struggle for a monopoly of control over the whole population. What was at stake, then, were not differences of opinion, even as expressed by the Mensheviks, the Social Revolutionaries, or the Anarchists, but the existence of opinion itself. One can explain most of Lenin's political maneuverings at the time only as an effort to win complete power for the Bolsheviks. As long as Mensheviks, Anarchists, and Social Revolutionaries existed, workers could choose between them and the Bolsheviks in electing their representatives to the *soviet*s, could find support in other political parties for their grievances. The successful destruction by the Bolsheviks of their competitors on the left, therefore, opened the road to the total subjection of the *soviet*s and of the country's population to Bolshevik control.

The problem of the coalition government was decided at the very beginning of the October Revolution, at the Second Congress of the Soviets. The Bolsheviks, together with their supporters, the Left Social Revolutionaries, had a small majority. Because of major political blunders committed by other leftist groups, Lenin and Trotsky were able to elect an all-Bolshevik Council of People's Commissars, with Lenin at its head. This maneuver was not easy, for there was in the ranks of the Bolsheviks themselves considerable support for a coalition government. At that time, only Lenin, with a small group of his closest collaborators, rejected unconditionally the prospect of sharing power with other leftist parties. "Whatever the private intentions of Lenin, Trotsky, and a few other leaders, may have been, the great majority of the party expected 'soviet government' to mean a coalition of the Bolshevik and socialist parties, without the hated bourgeoisie" (Schapiro 1984, 134).

At the time, Viktor P. Nogin, on behalf of a group of people's commissars, said, during the fifth session of the Central Executive Committee of the Soviets:

> We take the stand that it is vital to form a socialist government from all parties [represented in] the soviets. Only such a government can seal the heroic struggle of the working class and a revolutionary army in the October–November days. We consider that a purely Bolshevik government has no choice but to maintain itself by political terror. This is the course on which the [Communist party] has embarked. We cannot follow this course, which will lead to the proletarian mass organizations becoming estranged from those who direct our political affairs, to the establishment of an irresponsible government, and to the annihilation of the revolution [and] the country. We cannot bear

responsibility for such a policy and therefore, in the presence of the [Central Executive Committee], resign from our posts as people's commissars. (Keep 1979, 77-78)

The statement was signed by four commissars, and seven high-ranking members of the Bolshevik party, including, according to Leonard Schapiro (1956, 75), also Zinovyev and Kamenev. Soon after, Lenin made a small concession by forming a "coalition" government with the Left Social Revolutionaries, a relatively small splinter group in the Social Revolutionary party.

The subject of the freedom of the press appeared on the same agenda.

> Right-wing papers were suppressed in the first days [of the revolution], while [the] liberal press survived little longer, according to the ingenuity and courage of various papers in evading the attempts to close them. The leading socialist papers enjoyed no security from the start of the revolution and were repeatedly exposed to forcible and arbitrary suppressions by the Military Revolutionary Committee. (Ibid., 72)

From the very beginning of their rule, the Bolsheviks showed little respect for the freedom of the press, but during the same fifth session of the Central Executive Committee of the Soviets they prepared an act that gave them formalized instruments of press control. Lenin, as the initiator of this move, defended his decree by invoking the right of revolutionary authorities to suspend bourgeois newspapers, but most participants realized that the main purpose of the act was to curb the freedom of socialist newspapers. V. A. Avanesov, one of the main advocates of the measure, put forward the following argument:

> We defend freedom of the press, but this concept must be divorced from old petty-bourgeois or bourgeois notions of liberty . . . it would be ridiculous for Soviet power to stand up for antiquated notions about liberty of the press. First the newspapers must be freed from capitalist oppression . . . and then we can promulgate new socialist laws and norms enshrining

a liberty that will serve the whole toiling people, and not just capital. (Keep 1979, 70)

This reasoning was among the first harbingers of the times to come. Some delegates still could have opposed him. Karelin, a Left Social Revolutionary, called it a "Hottentot morality," and said, "I protest at the abuse of the term 'bourgeois.' It is not only bourgeois governments which need to give account of themselves or to maintain good order in their affairs. . . . A proletarian government must also submit to popular control" (ibid., 82).[7]

The Bolsheviks' problem was clear cut.

> After their seizure of power, the Bolsheviks confronted a difficult choice. To govern alone was to bear the stigma of a minority dictatorship and to cement the strength of the opposition. To share power with other parties and to await the judgment of a Constituent Assembly based on popular elections was to risk losing the fruits of the insurrection. The path of dictatorship led irrevocably in the direction of civil war, the suppression of the opposition, and the invocation of terror. The path of coalition and constitutionalism meant compromise, concession, and the abdication of supreme power. (Fainsod 1953, 122)

Their solution turned out to be one of the most consequential decisions they made at the beginning of the Revolution and a turning point in modern Russian history.

On January 6, 1918, the Bolsheviks forcibly dispersed the Constituent Assembly, the first body in history democratically elected by the people of Russia, the object of dreams of generations of Russian democratic opposition. Among the 707 delegates, there were 370 Social Revolutionaries, 175 Bolsheviks, 40 Left Social Revolutionaries, 17 Kadets (Constitutional Democrats), and 16 Mensheviks. One of the initiators and most influential proponents of this move, in the face of some opposition within the Bolshevik ranks, was Lenin. The decision to disperse the assembly was risky (see Pipes 1988).

What is perhaps more important than the content of particular decisions is their consequences. The minutes of discussions that took place at that time show that many leaders understood exactly what was happening and what the implications were. It was obvious to many of those who took part in the debate on a coalition government that, without support from other leftist parties, the Bolsheviks would have to resort to widespread terror. If Lenin thought otherwise, he must soon have changed his mind, for on December 20, 1917, he signed an ordinary act that established the Cheka, the Extraordinary Commission to Combat Counterrevolution, Speculation, and Sabotage. The first superior of this formidable instrument of suppression was Felix Dzerzhinsky. The Cheka was responsible directly to the party leadership and was legally accountable to no one. In March 1918, when the peace treaty with the Germans was signed in Brest-Litovsk, Lev Trotsky started his organization of the Red Army, which soon became another powerful tool of internal suppression.

An intensification of repressions against other groups of the Left accompanied these measures. Some of these groups tried, without much success, to find a compromise with counterrevolutionary armies to open a joint front against the Bolsheviks. Others, like the Mensheviks, chose the role of a loyal opposition and, later, that of a loyal critic of the Bolsheviks. This did not help much. The lot of the socialist parties in Russia was described by Vera Broido in the very first paragraph of her book.

> Between October 1917 and the death of Lenin in January 1924 all non-Bolshevik parties of the left in Russia—Mensheviks, Social Revolutionaries (both Right and Left), Maximalists, Populist Socialists, Anarchists, the Jewish *Bund,* the Zionist Labour Party *Poalei Tsion* and others—were virtually destroyed. Some lucky individuals either escaped abroad or were exiled there; the rest, if not shot, lived out their lives in prisons, camps and remote places of banishment. Only handfuls of "invincibles" lasted a few years longer in deepest "underground," while funds and personnel dwindled from year to year. (1987, vi)

Parallel to these developments, the role of the *soviet*s declined. The Bolsheviks rigged elections, pressured and terrorized voters, arrested members of elected bodies, exiled and even executed them.

Lenin's call to war, "All power to the *soviets*" meant, in reality, something very different. As soon as Lenin returned to Russia in April 1917, the Bolsheviks started taking advantage "of the irregularities in the structure of the soviets to seize control of the key positions in them in many regions of Russia and to maneuver them to suit their own purposes" (Pipes 1954, 121). Later they used the Cheka and the militia to assure themselves of control over the *soviets*. It is obvious that, for the Bolsheviks, the *soviets* were no more than mere instruments. (On the expulsion of Mensheviks from the *soviets* see Dallin [1974, 159–63].)

The abolition of factions within the party. If the war against the Mensheviks, Social Revolutionaries, and other socialist groups reflected an unwillingness to share power with any other political force, the solution to the problem of "internal opposition" within the party ultimately determined the organizational structure of the Communist party and the way it functioned. The term *internal opposition* is not quite adequate, for none of the factions thus labeled ever intended to take control over the party or even proposed personnel changes at the top party positions. They fully accepted Lenin's authority and leadership. They only criticized certain practices that took root in party life during the civil war and the period of "war communism" and called for structural changes within the party that would remedy the malaise.

Debates over the structure of the party organization intensified in 1920 and formally terminated in March 1921, with the Tenth Congress of the Russian Communist Party. In those debates, four main positions emerged. Lenin's faction, the majority, represented a compromise; Trotsky's faction, postulating the organization of the state and the economy according to military patterns represented the extreme left. The "internal opposition," which consisted of two groups—the Democratic Centralists (or Detsysts) and the Workers' Opposition—shared, in spite of some serious differences, one common element, the hope of extending intraparty democracy.

The debates came to an end when the Tenth Congress voted for two resolutions, both drafted by Lenin. The first, "On the

Syndicalist and Anarchist Deviation in Our Party," consisted of a polemic against the Workers' Opposition faction and is not relevant here. The second, "On the Unity of the Party," was of a much more general and long-lasting importance, and can be compared in its subject matter to essay 10 of *The Federalist*, by James Madison.[8]

The resolution "On the Unity of the Party" appealed for the tightening of party discipline, for a struggle against factionalism, and for restrictions on internal criticism of the party. Only criticism deemed constructive was acceptable. When formulating critical opinions, party members should always take into account the existing political situation, for such criticism should not be to the advantage of the party's enemies.

> Any appraisal of the general line of the party or a summary of its practical experience, any control over the execution of its resolutions, any examination of its methods of error correction, and so on, under no circumstances should be first discussed by groups constituting themselves on the grounds of whatever "platform," etc., but should first be discussed by all the members of the party. (Lenin 1949, 803)

Intraparty discussions were to be restricted to problems raised by the *Bulletin of Debates,* to be edited by the Central Committee. The editorial board of the *Bulletin* was to decide what criticism was "constructive" and what not, which opinions were damaging to the interests of the party and which not. The idea expressed in the resolution is interesting, for it foreclosed discussion of internal party problems without prior consent of the Central Committee, which could treat any unauthorized expression of criticism as a factional activity and expel the critic from the party.

A few delegates to the congress understood some of the consequences of such a resolution. Y. N. Ignatov, a representative of the Workers' Opposition, made a dramatic comment:

> With the proposed resolution you are foreclosing the possibility of discussing whatever problems in the party. Here everything

is put on one pile and, instead of the principles of practical workers' democracy, in reality we receive an interruption of all discussion, an end to all living ideas within the party. (Russian Communist party 1970, 721)

As already mentioned, the resolution "On the Unity of the Party" is fully consistent with concepts formulated by Lenin eighteen years earlier in *What Is to Be Done?* and in all his later writings on the organization of the party. There he argued of the need of conspiracy for the party's survival under conditions of a police state. After the civil war and the war against Poland, when no independent organized groups existed to question the position of Bolsheviks, Lenin returned to his old ideas, changing only the supporting arguments. As the French say, *"on revient toujours à ses premiers amours."*

The decision forbidding factions and terminating genuine discussions within the party was already implied by the Bolshevik persecutions of Constitutional Democrats, by the rejection of a coalition government, and by the deadly struggle they waged against their former comrades in arms from the Russian Social-Democratic Revolutionary Party and the Social Revolutionaries. "How can a party," Adam Ulam asks rhetorically, "that rules undemocratically and through repression preserve or achieve democracy within its own structure?" (1976, 46)

Decisions concerning the organization of the party that were made during the Tenth Congress had wide-ranging historical consequences. Three of them were pointed out by Leonard Schapiro (1972, 47). In his view, the decision to liquidate the internal opposition in the party had the following effects:

- It destroyed the possibility of rationally formulating programs of action because, if alternative opinions cannot be expressed for fear of weakening the unity of the party, decisions will be made by one man in an absolutely arbitrary way.

- It complicated the problem of the legitimate succession of leaders, because, if no group of leaders could freely express their views, personnel policies had to be determined on the grounds of private connections, intrigue, and manipulation.

- By spreading intolerance for differences of opinion, it produced the degeneration of the party and of the state, which lost thereby the ability to reform their structures effectively and efficiently.

We have here an interesting sequence of events that relates systems of values and doctrinal convictions to institutional strategies. We start with a political spectrum divided into three elements: the pro-imperial Right whose interests rested with the stability of tsardom, the liberal-democratic center (Constitutional Democrats, or Kadety) supporting extensive reform of the Russian state and social structure, and the Social-Democratic Left, rejecting tsardom and the liberal, democratic alternative. The last group was also divided into more and less dogmatic elements. When Nicolas II abdicated in February 1917, Kadets together with more moderate elements among the right-wing members of the Duma formed a Provisional Government; some representatives of the leftist parties, with the notable exception of the Bolsheviks, eventually joined the Provisional Government. The first victims of the October Revolution were representatives of the moderate "bourgeois" parties, that is, the Constitutional Democrats, whose sad plight many, if not most, Social Democrats and other representatives of the Left accepted with indifference (Pipes 1988, 157). Soon after, the turn came for the Social Revolutionaries, and the Mensheviks did not much object; then the Mensheviks found themselves at the head of the waiting line. At that time, the Bolshevik rank and file accepted the fate of their former allies without moving a finger; finally, the turn came for the independent-minded among the Bolsheviks themselves, and the party was silent. This sequence of events had undoubtedly paved the way for collectivization, the Great Purge, the Moscow Trials, and for all the terrible crimes associated with the name of Stalin. I do not see how one could deny Lenin's moral and political responsibility for these developments.[9]

The NEP and collectivization of agriculture. Another important change initiated by the Tenth Congress was the New Economic Policy, or NEP. Although, in the long run, changes in the functioning of the Communist party were perhaps of greater importance, the congress is remembered mostly for the initiation of the NEP. The events that forced upon the Bolsheviks, or rather upon Lenin as the main initiator, a change in economic policies included the growing disorganization of transport and industry, famine caused by the desperate situation in the countryside, and growing unrest among the population manifesting itself in peasant rebellions, riots in Petrograd, and the Kronstadt Revolt. A continuation of what later was to be named "war communism" could have resulted in the collapse of Bolshevik power.

Lenin thought that the NEP was a solution perhaps not for centuries but certainly for generations; in fact it lasted eight years. It ended with the First Five-Year Plan and with the collectivization of agriculture. Tensions between the new economic policy and the institutional structure of the Soviet state became visible from the very start of the NEP.

We may consider the peasant problem, that is, the problem of Soviet agriculture, from two perspectives. The first is that of the specifically Russian strategies of industrialization that originated in the reforms of Peter the Great and continued through the spurt of industrialization at the end of the nineteenth century that was led by Sergey Witte. Second, we may examine it from the point of view of the institutional structure of the regime the Bolsheviks were trying to construct and their specific attitude toward peasants.

Witte's strategy of industrialization consisted in the development of transportation (railways), steel, and other heavy industry with a bias toward military production. This economic spurt was financed by the government mostly from foreign credits. It paid the credits back mostly from proceeds obtained from the export of agricultural products. Without investments in agriculture, in the property rights, and the political organization of villages that would stimulate the intensive exploitation of soil and of the labor force, an increase in the export of agricultural produce could be obtained only if the peasants were squeezed fiscally to consume less. The

Russian peasants were the first victims of this strategy of economic growth. The abolition of serfdom in the 1860s did not improve their lot in any way; the property rights system in the countryside and restrictions upon their personal freedoms kept them in a role of the pariahs of Russian society. The events of 1905 showed the dangers that could result from the continuation of this state of affairs—the peasant problem was the time bomb set under the social and political structure of the Romanov empire.

Between 1908 and 1911, the government led by Peter A. Stolypin introduced a series of reforms. It abolished the outstanding redemption dues that were a true curse for village communities (*obshchyna*),[10] it gave peasants the freedom to live where they wished, and the right to buy and to sell their land, in other words, the right to individual ownership. It created conditions for the development of a freeholder agriculture of a family-farm type favoring an intensification of farming techniques. At the same time, from the political point of view, that was a blow to an egalitarian, closely integrated organization of the village communities that now experienced the disintegrating growth of material and status inequalities. In fact, by 1916, about two million peasant households left the traditional village communities to start their own, fairly efficient farms (*hutor*s). This was a key element in the strategy of solving the political danger presented by the peasant class through the "wager on the strong [the more successful]" (Nove 1969, 22). In 1917 village communities, composed of the less successful, seized these farms together with the estates of the noblemen.

Soon after they seized power, the Bolsheviks were faced with the recurring problems, Who was to pay the costs of industrialization, and how could the political problem of a huge peasantry be solved? But an answer to these questions was determined by the answer given to still another, more important one: What should the strategy of industrialization be; what were the objectives of the industrialization drive? These questions are connected not only with the choice of policy but also with the fundamental issue of institutional design. The NEP was doomed because the Tenth Congress chose an organizational structure for the Communist party, and consequently for the Soviet state, that virtually made the NEP incompatible with the country's political organization. It strengthened a political arrangement that deprived people of direct influence upon governmental decisions while offering them a measure of the producer's and consumer's sovereignty.

Spontaneous expropriation of the best agricultural enterprises, in 1917, disorganized agricultural production. At the same time, as a result of the continuing war, industrial production kept declining, and cities had less and less to offer to the countryside. Thus, the exchange that was fundamental for the functioning of the social division of labor virtually ceased, further disrupting food supplies for the urban areas and contributing to the expansion of black markets for food products. The Bolsheviks, whose political support came from the main cities, reacted by sending out groups of activists who searched the peasants' households, grabbing whatever food was available regardless of the survival of the peasants themselves. This brutal robbery helped to alleviate the immediate food requirements of the urban areas, but was certainly unproductive in stimulating the long-term growth of agricultural production or winning the peasants' sympathy for the Communist regime. The first factor was more important than the second because, as private proprietors and petit bourgeois elements, the peasants were not in high repute among the Communists anyway.

The NEP brought an end to those practices. Forced requisitions were abandoned. Regular taxes were introduced, first in kind and later, after a monetary reform that based the ruble upon gold parity, in money. The peasants could start to calculate rationally, could sell on the market, and improve their material situation. By the end of the 1920s, agricultural output reached the best prewar volume. But throughout the NEP period, Soviet government economic policies in general and their policies toward agriculture in particular were far from consistent.

However, the Bolsheviks faced another problem. The destruction and liquidation of market-oriented farms and estates resulted in a substantial equalization of land holdings. The stories generated by Stalinist propaganda about rich peasants, the *kulak*s as they were called, were fairy tales. Peasants on small, or relatively small, holdings could choose between marketing their products or keeping them for their own consumption. Besides state stores and shops, there were also private shops. When the state interfered with the market, the black market appeared. All this provided peasants with some freedom of choice, which they exercised in accordance with their interests: Nobody imposed upon the peasants decisions on what, and how they were going to cultivate, and to whom they were to sell their produce. They could freely decide whether they wanted to plant this or that, or nothing at all, whether they sold potatoes to the cities or used them to feed pigs. The very fact that the peasants could achieve a measure of material independence and had some freedom of economic choice effectively curtailed the state's control over them.

Big industry, under the direct control of the state, experienced great difficulties and constantly required capital support that it could obtain only from the government. After the Soviet government expropriated foreign-owned factories and repudiated the outstanding debts made by the tsarist state during the war, any hope of the influx of foreign capital turned out to be illusive. The Bolsheviks had to rely upon themselves. There were two ways to proceed: They could reestablish the market or abolish it entirely. They could rebuild the division of labor by reestablishing a market exchange, the capitalization of agriculture, and the acquisition of agricultural surpluses through the medium of the market exchange. Industrial production would have to correspond to the needs of the countryside or, at least, the state would have to import those products that Russian industry was unable to deliver and that were most needed. Under such conditions, the needs and aspirations of the peasants would in large measure dictate the direction of the central government's investments. Economic development along these lines would also require parallel investments in the capital goods industry, in transportation, and the economic infrastructure. This could be reconciled with an important role of the market in shaping the economic policies of the Communist state. The group that preferred this solution included moderate elements in the party and economists working for the State Planning Commission (Gosplan). (Still the most authoritative source on the subject of the Soviet economic debates in the 1920s is Alexander Erlich [1960].)

The alternative was to abolish the market, to liquidate private property, and to base the management of agricultural production on an administrative apparatus enforced by police terror, that is, to build, at the cost of the peasants, an industrial structure whose output was unrelated to the needs of the countryside or of consumers. Consumers eventually appear as a political category and not as an economic one. This second strategy is consistent with the tradition of Russian industrialization used by Peter the Great and Sergey Witte.

It is not clear whether the period of "war communism" that lasted until March 1921 followed from a conscious decision to select the second alternative or was imposed upon the Bolsheviks by circumstances. Later, the Bolsheviks tended to justify "war communism" by the historical conditions under which they had acted. It is more reasonable to assume that "there was a process of interaction between circumstances and ideas" (Nove 1969, 48), with ideas playing an important role.

The characteristic features of "war communism" followed from the basic principles of the Communist creed, such as the drive to nationalize all industry, to introduce the central rationing of all resources and products, abolish private trade, and to get rid of money in economic exchange. Money lost all value and enterprises started to barter, exchanging products and services in kind and paying their workers mostly in kind. Peter Wiles fairly assessed the responsibility of Bolsheviks for the aberrations of the war economy.

> It is a great mistake to suppose that this second model was at the time conceived as a war economy. True, the war forced universal nationalization, but nationalization can take many forms. True, there is usually inflation in wartime, but governments do not normally boast of their intention further to debauch the currency. True, there is often rationing in wartime, but rations are normally paid for, and it is a far step from ordinary rationing to the actual abolition of money and the delivery of goods in lieu of wages; nor can it be held to help the war effort if the post office and the tramways cease to charge money. True, central physical planning is common in belligerent countries, but not

to anything like the detailed extent here used. Moreover there was peace in 1919, between the civil and Polish wars, and the Party then explicitly reaffirmed this second model as its peace model, at the 9th Congress. (1962, 29)

One can postulate that the war economy was in large measure a product of the Bolsheviks' conceptions of a Communist economy, at least during the transition period. Thus, we may consider the institutional design a part of the legitimate Leninist tradition within the Communist movement. Economic changes implemented by Stalin and his group at the beginning of the 1930s were a return to the conceptions of "war communism" as a form of organization of the economy more consistent with some basic precepts of the Communist doctrine and, most of all, with the organization of the Communist state, than were the policies of the NEP.

There is another possible interpretation of the outcomes of the Tenth Congress. Lenin could have been aware that with economic liberalization, the whole system might drift in a liberal-democratic direction that could finally deprive the Bolsheviks of their power. To avoid the threat, he had to strengthen those elements within the political system that were truly Communist. In his view, the most important was the party—the centralization of power, the discipline and unity of the party line, and the effective dictatorship exercised by that party through the instrument of the state. Political reform was, according to this position, forced upon him by the circumstances: The dramatic economic situation compelled him to embark upon the New Economic Policy, which in turn made it expedient to strengthen the party-state. This interpretation is plausible, but without much relevance. What is important is Lenin's role in making the crucial institutional decisions and the congruence between his theoretical views and practical measures.

STALIN AND THE COMMUNIST INSTITUTIONAL ORDER

In examining how Stalin shaped the Soviet political order after Lenin, we are faced with two sets of considerations: the tactical considerations related to the struggle for power, and the strategic considerations related to the tensions produced by the lack of consistency between the institutional structure of the state and the NEP. The tactical considerations are much more obvious. Even before Lenin died, a ruthless struggle for succession started among his closest collaborators. The most obvious successor was Trotsky. To oppose him Zinovyev, Kamenev, and Stalin, who started as a junior partner, made up a coalition. But Stalin was given control over the party organization and personnel policies in the party. This allowed him to develop a following in the party that no other leader possessed. When Zinovyev and Kamenev sensed danger, they joined Trotsky and his leftist, anti-NEP group; Stalin obtained support from Bukharin, Tomsky, and Rykov, closely identified with the NEP. After some rather inept maneuvering, the first group lost all influence within the central institutions of the Bolshevik party, leaving their place to Stalin and his new coalition. To make himself fully independent, to be the sole person in charge, Stalin had to free himself of Bukharin, Tomsky, and Rykov. He chose to do it by taking up the anti-NEP position and justifying it on the ideological and theoretical grounds developed by Trotsky and his allies, of whom Preobrazhensky was the most notable, without, of course, mentioning them by name.[11] This allowed Stalin, who now had a comfortable majority within the central bodies of the party, to represent the position of Bukharin, Tomsky, and Rykov as a "rightist deviation" in the party and to accuse them of factionalism. Robert V. Daniels provides a convincing description of Stalin's strategy, and of some of its consequences.

> Stalin was only feeling his way toward policies that would embarrass the Right Opposition. In fact, some of the extremeness of Stalin's stand on industrialization and collectivization was due to the efforts of the Bukharinists to save themselves by compromising. Stalin had to keep jumping ahead—notably in the preparation of the Five-Year Plan—by having Kuibyshev's Supreme Economic Council prepare ever more ambitious proposals to discredit the more careful and cautious drafts of the rightist-dominated State Planning Commission (Gosplan). (1966, 29)

The final strategic decision consisting in the termination of the NEP was a product of the power struggle in the Kremlin and not, as some suggest, of substantive economic considerations.

Daniels's position seems sound, although it is by no means the only interpretation of the events. There is, however, a fundamental factor, or perhaps a set of factors—the structure of dominant group interests generated by the system—that allowed Stalin to mobilize support for his stand. Stalin made himself the representative of these interests before he finally subdued them during the Great Purge of 1936–1938.

Here we must return to the Tenth Congress, and to some decisions that had preceded it. As I tried to show, the congress accepted two mutually exclusive and contradictory sets of policies, one set for the organization of the party and the state, another set for the economy. The political package was a continuation of the traditional centralizing bias, also highly characteristic of the Bolsheviks, of the effort to extend political control over society, by further restricting political and cultural freedoms. It also strengthened the position of the Cheka, whose head, Dzerzhinsky became also responsible for economic policies. The Soviet-German agreement on military cooperation, signed in 1922 in Rapallo, gave the Soviet army a chance to acquaint itself with the modern techniques of warfare and to participate with the Germans in developing new weapons and new tactical conceptions. (On this subject see Adam Ulam [1968, 149–52].)

The economic package had a strong liberal bias, including as it did the stabilization of the individual peasant property in agriculture, introduction of a rational tax system, and the acceptance of private property in small and medium-sized industry and trade. Meanwhile, the Soviet government rented many of the already nationalized firms to private individuals and cooperatives, stabilized the currency and based it on a parity with gold, opened state credits for private enterprises, and made possible private savings. Even private banks were allowed, though they had to operate under the strict control of state banks.

The political package was in tune with the logic of a system built from the top down; the economic package was consistent with the bottom-up organization of the social order. Thus, the Tenth Congress embraced two mutually exclusive principles of organization that immediately generated a conflict. One of the two had to win and impose its logic upon the other: there was no institutional means for regulating the conflict. If there had been, we might speculate that the NEP could have survived Lenin by some four years because the pretenders to Lenin's position would have closed ranks against his heir apparent, Lev Trotsky—also the most renowned opponent of the NEP. When Zinovyev and Kamenev decided a few years later to unite with Trotsky, they had no doctrinal problems in embracing his anti-NEP views; neither had Stalin when he finally made a bid for the position of the unquestioned, sole leader of the party. The only ones at the top of the party hierarchy who supported the NEP with real conviction were Bukharin, Tomsky, and Rykov, but their influence was marginal. Stalin controlled the party bureaucracy and, when he decided to abolish the NEP, he represented the great majority of the political establishment against scattered individuals and the irrelevant 90 percent or so of the nation that had no means of defending itself.

On the practical level, the conflict between the two packages appeared to lie in the impossibility of synchronizing the economic policies of the state with the functioning of the private sector. For all practical concerns, the Soviet economic system was condemned to autarky. Foreign capital was not forthcoming, because of the Bolshevik government's unwillingness to respect the prewar property rights of Western European investors and to repay its war debts. The only articles that could be exported were agricultural products, but peasants had their own "utility function" that determined their economic decisions about what to produce, how to produce, and how much food consumption they were willing to forego in order to buy industrial products.

The peasants were the only large social group connected to the economy through the market, a link that gave them considerable political power. Besides, the NEP had some liberalizing effect on social life in Soviet Russia. One can see it in the tenor of economic debates during this period. The real problem was political: continuation of the NEP put the Communist rule in danger.

> A policy of moderate tempos which would strengthen the position of the upper strata of the villages and would make the adroit balancing between them and the unruly radicals of the cities a necessity could be adopted only as a temporary expedient. Had such a course been pursued over a long period of time, the regime would have stood to lose not only from its possible failures but also from its successes. The alternative to such retreats and maneuvers leading to the gradual erosion of the dictatorial system was clearly a massive counterattack which would have broken once and for all the peasants' veto power over the basic decisions on economic policy. A high speed industrialization with a strong emphasis on the capital-goods sector which Stalin now favored provided the logical line for such a counterattack; and here the risk constellation would have been entirely different. The success of such an alternative would have been an unqualified triumph. (Erlich 1960, 174–75)

What was needed, then, was a dramatic reversal in either the economic or the political order. Economic policies could obtain from a compromise among different positions; the political problem appeared insoluble.

Stalin selected the path of quick industrialization, oriented toward the realization of big industrial projects, the electrification of the country, and the development of a steel industry, considered then as the chief indicators of a country's level of economic development. The realization of such a large program of industrialization required a parallel program for the development of urban centers for the labor force that, until then, had been "stored" in great quantities in the countryside and to provide these urban centers and labor force with food and other consumer goods. Finally, the program required an increase in the flow of food products from the villages to the urban areas to sustain the growing urban population and to increase the export of food products to provide the financial resources to pay for the increased import of capital goods. These objectives could be quickly achieved through the intermediary of the market, which implies a minimum of consent and mutual interest. But these big projects had no relationship to the concerns of the peasants and did not produce the things that the peasants needed most. The surplus population in the countryside had little incentive to go to urban areas and seek work in industry. The history of collectivization can only be compared to a conquest of a country by a foreign invader.

The political and economic system thus created was internally consistent. One can even say that it had an unsurpassed "purity of style." It brought a huge number of people to the cities, for it was safer to be in an urban area than in the hell that took place in the countryside. At the cost of millions of human lives, the flow of food products from the countryside to towns and cities and their export dramatically increased. Forced labor permitted the realization of huge industrial projects without incurring inflation.[12] This program increased the political role of the security establishment, which became now not only the guardian of the political regime but also the main overseer of the nation's economy. By giving prominence to military production, it also strengthened the role of the army.[13] It is hard not to agree with Erlich that, ". . . if Stalin's repeated warnings about the greatly increased danger of war were to be taken literally, the policy of the First Five-Year Plan would look very much like a suicide prompted by a fear of death" (1960, 167–68)—a comment that amounts to a rebuke to those who interpret Stalin's collectivization campaign as a result of his "prescient" intuition about the coming war.

The changes of the late 1920s must appear as a logical continuation of the two other strategic decisions: the rejection of any coalition with other leftist parties and the suppression of factions. The war against other socialist parties was aimed at eliminating the possibility of a reemergence of a political pluralism. The suppression of factions made such a possibility still more distant. Collectivization and the events that followed it represented an effort to destroy whatever remnants of pluralism were left.

Stalinism was inevitable in the Soviet system. It was imprinted in the genetic code of the institutional order Lenin created. Within this order, society was made unable to defend itself against the state; the state was incapable of opposing the party; the party had no means of defending itself against the leadership; and the leadership lost its autonomy to the de facto leader, the general secretary of the party.

During the decades that have passed since Stalin's death, a reverse process has occurred: the party leadership has gained some guarantee of safety from the general secretary, the party has gained some autonomy in its dealings with the leadership, and so on. We have been witnessing a gradual withering away of the system, with interesting consequences.

Proletarian Internationalism

The socialist movement, like other antiestablishment movements in the nineteenth century, took an international form very early. The rejection of nationalism in the name of class solidarity facilitated close cooperation among the social-democratic parties of Europe. This internationalist solidarity did not prove very strong when the social democrats encountered World War I, the first real test of their internationalism. Lenin was one of few socialist leaders of the time who took a firm antiwar position. Others supported the war, and those healthy enough joined the army. The Socialist International fell apart.

Following the October Revolution, Lenin took the first steps to rebuild the international organization of socialist parties. He started the Communist International, or Comintern, in 1919 in Moscow. In contrast to the loose structures of former Socialist Internationals, the Bolsheviks built Comintern on Leninist organizational principles: it was a centralized, strongly disciplined agency under the full control of Soviet leadership. The emphasis on discipline and obedience created some resentment among the social-democratic parties outside Soviet Russia. Thus, the cleavage that surged in Russia in 1903 and resulted in the scission of Russian Social Democrats into two parties repeated itself in the aftermath of World War I: Communists and Social Democrats went separate ways. The Soviet leadership had in its hands a powerful instrument of international subversion. Stalin disbanded Comintern in 1943 in an effort to win the trust of his Western allies.

At the beginning of its existence, when hopes for the world revolution were still alive, Comintern's main purpose was to spread

Lenin as Practitioner

revolutionary ideas and to encourage revolutionary outbreaks. Especially in Germany, Soviet Communists repeatedly urged their comrades to wage a revolution. At the end of the 1920s, however, when Zinovyev lost the direction of Comintern, the position of the internationalist was weak, and the world revolution was not materializing. Stalin came up with the idea of "building socialism in one country." The functions of Comintern changed. Until then, Soviet leaders had supported and helped revolutionary movements in other countries. From that moment on, all the other revolutionary movements had to surrender unconditionally to Soviet interests even to the extent of betraying their own country, as French Communists did during the German invasion in 1940. From that moment on, it became the moral duty of each member of the Communist Left to care first of all for the interests of the Soviet Union. Comintern became an instrument for the realization of Soviet foreign interests through extra-diplomatic means. No wonder then, that other governments perceived it as a means of foreign interference in the internal matters of sovereign states and as an agency serving Soviet interests. The period after World War II saw the gradual disintegration of the international Communist movement.

In proclaiming Soviet Russia as the first proletarian state in the world, Lenin ideologically identified the interests of the Soviet Russian state as those of the world socialist movement. The consequences of this move are still visible, although they had been of an incomparably greater practical significance in the past, in assuring the support of socialist and Communist parties all over the world for the Bolshevik *raison d'état*. Not less important was the legitimation this ideology provided for rebuilding the old imperial structures. That Russian imperial tradition and socialist ideology joined to defend the Bolshevik revolution was a major tour de force in political propaganda. The marriage was, unfortunately, concluded on the ruins of the Russian cultural tradition that had developed in the nineteenth century. The Bolshevik revolution moved Russia several centuries back, in terms of civilization and culture.[14]

This subjection of the world Left to orders coming from the USSR embodied the old dream of traditional Russian millenarianism (the myth, strong in Russian culture, of the coming of the Russian millennium was connected with the idea of the third Rome). Russia finally became the leader of the "good, progressive" world in its final battle against "evil" and "the reactionary." Because the geopolitical interests of Soviet Russia determined the way this mission was defined and implemented, the Communist doctrine has proved a highly effective form for the articulation of traditional Russian national concerns and aspirations. It also provided a background against which anything that the Soviet government has attempted to do could be justified in universalistic terms.

Conclusions

Combining and exploiting the support—or simply the neutrality—of strategic social and political groups, the Bolsheviks were able to impose in most of the areas of the Russian empire a political order that would not have been accepted there democratically. The order's most characteristic features are an unprecedented centralization of political decision making, secrecy in the processes of government, and an unmatched totalitarianism in state control over society. This institutional design introduced a nearly perfect blockage to the articulation of social interests in the political system. Society lost its autonomy to the extent that even the most intimate relationships became mediated by the state—parents did not trust children, husband and wife did not trust each other.

The system that Lenin so decisively helped to construct in Russia had one quality observed by Tocqueville and others. This type of political regime opened great possibilities for the mobilization of resources for the realization of a limited number of state goals. When the state dominates society, it justifies its abuses by external or internal threats to the existence of the society. The justification does not require the existence of the threats. Economic development is subjected, then, to the interests of military expansion at the cost of the living standard, and is sometimes promoted by a terrorist victimization of the population. To this Lenin gave the legitimizing conviction that whatever the Soviet state was doing for the sake of its expansion served the interests of humanity and anyone who opposed such policies acted against these interests.

The most often quoted, and most correct, empirical proof for the rightness of Lenin's theories, besides the rate of economic growth, was the military might of the Soviet Union. This is perhaps not what Lenin wanted and probably not what he considered his historical mission. But what is important for history are not Lenin's intentions but the consequences of his ideas and his actions. The theory that has been positively verified in this case postulates that systems organized from the top down have a much higher mobilization potential.[15] With great effort democracies can be mobilized to concentrate on achieving one dominant goal, but only in very exceptional circumstances.

Lenin's thinking not only decisively influenced the institutional design of the Communist system, but also provided the only grounds for the theoretical interpretation of the system. This intellectual monopoly has had the support of the political establishment with all the powers at its disposal. The monopoly created a "communication noise" that made any open public discourse impossible, thus impoverishing human thinking and imagination.

What can we say about the relationship between Lenin's earlier views and his activities in constructing a new institutional order during the first few years of the Soviet regime? First, no systematic examination of his writings would have allowed one to work out a *minute* prognosis of the positions he took on particular issues and the policies he advocated and implemented. The word "minute" is emphasized, for a number of his comrades from Russian social democracy and later some Bolsheviks had a clear idea of the dangers contained in these policies. Second, when one examines the key decisions made under Lenin's influence, one is struck by their surprising consistency with the program he had formulated before the Revolution. The NEP is the only notable exception. One can say that Lenin the practitioner tried nearly everything that Lenin the theoretician of revolution had invented. If the American and the French revolutions had a plurality of fathers, the Russian was highly unitary.

FIVE

THE COMMUNIST INSTITUTIONAL ORDER: HISTORICAL CONTINUITY OR NEW CREATION?

Recent developments in the USSR raise a question of long standing. Is the present malaise the result of Communism, or is it a product of a much older Russian political tradition? The earlier work of the Marquis de Custine ([1839] 1989, 91), recently published in the United States, supports the second argument. Thus, old debate continues: historical continuity or a new creation? To say both is surely closest to truth, but probably the least revealing. Yet, the puzzling problem remains: To what extend is the new creation part of the historical continuity?

Alexis de Tocqueville once wrote that "history, indeed, is like a picture gallery in which there are few originals and many copies" ([1856] 1955, 65). Let us look, then, for copies and originals in the organization of the Soviet regime. We can do so by, first, looking for the similarities and differences between the organization of the Soviet system and its immediate imperial predecessor; and second, comparing the Bolshevik and the liberal solutions to the problem of the political and economic organization of a society.

The Old and the New

What the "copies" are may be obvious from the earlier discussion of the Soviet order. They deserve, however, a closer look. The most important similarity between the old Russian patrimonial polity and the new Soviet regime is the political organization of society. In both cases it was founded on the total submission of the population to the power of the state. No European society has ever come closer to a model of the ancient despotic regimes than Russia. Alain Besançon rightly remarked that "the Russian people is a conquered people" (1980, 85). What he had in mind was the way in which first the patrimonial princes, then the Mongols, then the tsars, and most recently the Communist party subdued Russian society and those who fell prey to Russian expansion.

This strategy affected property relations in a way that was similar in both cases. Until the late eighteenth century, all land in Russia belonged to the tsar. He farmed out factories and mines to private individuals, who could not appropriate them. The main purpose of the Revolution was to abolish private property in agriculture, industry, and services and to subject it to the direct control of the state. This is the ultimate measure for making the population materially dependent upon the central power, be it that of a patrimonial prince or the leadership of a political party.

The difference consists in the legitimation of the two conquests, and in the concrete institutional solutions. Yet, the principle is the same: a strict implementation of the top-down organization of society, which implies a hierarchical ordering of individuals in the monocratic hierarchy of the state, and the destruction of all autonomous forms of organization of regional, religious, professional, municipal, or any other social groups, and of private property on which such an autonomy rests. The only organized force in society is the state, which serves the function of mobilizing the population for the tasks selected by the rulers. Lenin's idea of "transmission belts" is an old human invention.

Such an organization, to be effective, requires a rationale. On a general level, the rationale is similar in both cases: the spiritual and intellectual superiority of the powerholders. In the old patrimonium, the quasi-divine tsars subjected the Orthodox church to their authority: to oppose the tsar was not only a crime, but also a sin. Under new conditions, Lenin's interpretation of the dictatorship of the proletariat as exercised by the revolutionary vanguard provided the rationale. Being the vanguard, "the dozen leaders" with a sound understanding of the logic of the historical process, dedication to the revolutionary task, and respect for highest standards of moral purity had the best title to rule. If these assumptions hold, and there is no reason to doubt that Lenin honestly believed they do, then, it is in the objective interest of the proletariat to submit itself to the vanguard. One can claim that any opposition to such an authority would be against the interests of the working class and, thus, against the progress of humanity: The idea of "class betrayal" replaced the idea of sin as a guardian against dissent. The party rules because it is better equipped intellectually and morally for the task than is any other group in the society. This superiority is not to be empirically proven: it is assumed *a priori* in Lenin's work.

The same rationale that justifies the internal organization of power serves to justify external policies too. Thus, the ideas of reunifying Orthodox Christianity, of recapturing Constantinople from the Muslims, and of unifying the Slavs traditionally served as important rationales for Russian imperial expansion. The Soviet state also parades these rationales when it finds them useful: official propaganda in the Soviet Union and the Communist countries of East-Central Europe often promotes Slav solidarity. The liberation of mankind oppressed by capitalist exploitation became the main rationale after the Revolution, and a most effective one because of its universalism: the Soviet Union as leader of progressive humanity against the forces of evil. The external rationale fed upon the internal legitimation: whoever opposed the regime opposed everything that is good and noble in the world. To break the vicious circle required an enormous emotional determination. Thus, there is little wonder that Russian dissidence is emotionally stronger in rejecting the existing order than it is intellectually in conceptualizing alternatives.

Like the traditional patrimonial state, the neopatrimonial state the Bolsheviks created is a highly conservative entity that must cope with the problem of survival in an environment dominated by dynamic, democratic, fairly decentralized, market societies, organized to a large extent upon the bottom-up principle. This creates political strains, and compels the Communist states to adopt solutions inconsistent with the logic of their institutional system. Thus, we face again the cycle of destabilization, described in Chapter 2. Seen in this perspective, the October Revolution gave a second chance to the highly modified patrimonial pattern of state organization.

All the features that Keenan found in the political life of the old Russian court are alive in the Communist political system. Let us only look, as an example, at what a regular party member in a Communist state cannot know about and will be even afraid to ask about: the party's finances, its sources of revenue, the size of the budget and how that budget is spent; the number of full-time party employees (the apparatus); the scope of the *nomenklatura,* the administrative and other positions filled according to political criteria; opinions expressed at closed meetings of party committees by the elected representatives; the responsibilities of particular secretaries of the Central Committee—who is responsible for what at the central level; and the agenda of the Political Bureau meetings. One of the remarkable cases of secrecy was the decision of the Political Bureau of the Polish United Workers' Party, to keep partly secret the party statute that was imposed upon the party on December 13, 1981, as binding during the period of martial law. In this case, the party leadership did not even inform the party members of the full content of the party statute.

Keenan (1986, 168–72) explains these tendencies by recourse to Russian political culture. The fact is that requirements of a top-down organized regime also explain these features. Formalization implies responsibility. Secrecy and informality in the exercise of authority mean that the government ceases to be responsible to anyone but to itself: government turns into a conspiracy against its own people. To share information is to concede that people have a right to know. Providing citizens with information enables them to make independent judgments about decisions made by the government. In a regime organized from the top down, people must feel powerless or the regime is in jeopardy. The rulers' conviction that they are in all respects superior to other members of their society is not exceptional. As a matter of fact, this is the most common claim made in such regimes.[1] This conviction corresponds closely to the popular image that relates good government to personalities rather than institutional structures. The alternative approach, in terms of structures and institutions, is less intuitive.

Tocqueville remarked that ". . . whenever a nation destroys its aristocracy, it almost automatically tends toward a centralization of power; a greater effort is then needed to hold it back than to encourage it to move in this direction" ([1856] 1955, 60). If we mean by aristocracy, in this context, people who cultivate the values of personal dignity and public responsibility and have independent sources of support to allow them to preserve political autonomy, this proposition becomes acceptable. These values and norms form the very core of the ethos of civil society. Their relative strength within the social order becomes a guarantee of a republican institutional system, as Montesquieu ([1750] 1886) or Mosca (1939) would have understood it, but their weakness makes the top-down forms of political organization more probable. They are the bearers of a political culture that provides a particularly fertile ground for the development of democratic polities. Russia started to develop such a public-minded political stratum with an economic and social base only in the nineteenth century. The Communist revolution almost completely annihilated it. This brings us back to political culture as an explanatory factor.

There is usually an obvious and intimate relationship between an institutional order and political culture conceived in terms of a value system and the norms of political and public behavior. We have to ask first, how do past historical experiences affect strategic institutional choices? Keenan's most powerful argument in support of his position is the mistrust of individual motives and the traditional reliance of the Russian village community on external controls rather than on the internalization of norms and values. A person who grew up in such a culture, feels, in the absence of external controls, uneasy about relating to other individuals and groups and about entering a cooperative relationship.[2] In such a solidaristic culture, individual competition is rejected in the name of collective values.

Under such cultural conditions, a serious break in social order usually leads to anarchy and, ultimately, to the reemergence of an order also built upon external controls, that is, built from the top down rather than the bottom up. As resocialization takes a long time, the easiest way is to revive the external mechanisms of control and the established, traditional, authoritarian setting. Hence, it is plausible to assume that Russian political culture makes this nation susceptible to the top-down organization whenever it is faced with the possibility of choice. The two explanations may be considered, therefore, as different aspects of the same phenomenon.

The consciousness of the country as a double entity, the Russian state and Russian society, or the "official Russia" and the "popular Russia," has in Robert C. Tucker's view, characterized Russia through a large part of its history.

> The image of dual Russia is not simply a conception of the state and people as two different Russias. It also comprises an evaluative attitude, or rather a range of such attitudes. Their common denominator is the apprehension of the autocratic state power as an *alien* power in the Russian land. The relation between the state and the society is seen as one between conqueror and conquered. . . . [The state] is an active party, the organizing and energizing force, in the drama of dual Russia, whereas the population at large is the passive and subordinate party, the tool and victim of the state's designs. An alien power is, of course, one toward which a great many different positions may be taken, ranging from active collaboration through resignation and passive resistance to outright rebelliousness. (1971, 122)

This popular attitude toward the state makes democratic reform difficult. First, such reform requires broad cooperation from the people and their involvement in the public realm. Second, the lower classes perceive the intelligentsia, which is usually the main element in any reform drive, as part of "official Russia" and tend to reject their reform efforts. Third, a liberal, democratic reform must rely on individual success and competition, which contradicts the Russian tradition of collectivism and solidarism.

The Russian intelligentsia as a social stratum emerged as a product of a long sequence of changes initiated by Peter I. The intelligentsia was the only group in Russian society that developed a keen sense of social responsibility, of appreciation for education, and of ambition to lead the country toward democracy. By destroying much of the intelligentsia, the Bolshevik revolution produced a discontinuity in the sense that it arrested and dramatically reversed the trend toward democracy. The Communist party, in its effort to monopolize power, had to eliminate all independent social groups, and the intelligentsia was among the most obvious. The party consisted mostly of former peasants reclaiming the patrimonial tradition in order to establish their own power. The fact that these people came from the peasantry did not help peasants as a class, for the task of establishing Bolshevik power required the destruction of all relatively autonomous social groups, including the peasantry. This reversal did not solve, however, the problem with which Peter the Great was faced: How to deal with the challenge of the dynamic West? The problem can be solved either by joining the West, which means the rejection of the patrimonial tradition, or by trying to adapt, imperfectly and at great cost, to the formidable economic and cultural challenges originating in the West, while striving to keep traditional political patterns intact.

Yet it is evident, the similarities notwithstanding, that the USSR is very different from imperial Russia. The Bolshevik ideology, with its roots in the French Enlightenment and as part of a westernizing trend in Russian cultural and political life, is worlds apart from the traditional legitimation of imperial power. The October Revolution brought, in fact, the traditional Russian power arrangements to their final conclusion. These are, therefore, two quite different types of social order. Let us look, then, at the Soviet system from the perspective of liberalism, another institutional project that also permitted, albeit in a different way, the destruction of traditional social patterns.

Patrimonial and Liberal Orders

The intellectual and institutional roots of European liberalism can be found in the Middle Ages and even earlier. Nowhere outside

Europe has anything similar to this intellectual trend developed. Liberalism emerged in eighteenth-century Europe as a mature political and economic doctrine opposed to absolute monarchy and its mercantilist economic policies and immediately found one of its most interesting practical applications in the American constitutional debate, an argument between two highly compatible philosophies. On the one hand was the idea of a free market, first formulated by Adam Smith and further developed by the British classical economists, who proposed that, under certain specified conditions, men left to themselves and pursuing their own interests could work for the benefit of all; this result would be achieved automatically, through the working of the self-regulating mechanism of the market, without any direct intervention from the state. On the other hand was the idea of checks and balances, a tradition of thought that originated with John Locke, David Hume, and Montesquieu and was further developed during the American constitutional debate by Madison and Hamilton, who proposed that, in the interests of human welfare, freedom, and dignity, it was necessary to limit the powers of the state and eliminate, as far as possible, their arbitrariness. The powers of the state should be partitioned among three autonomous bodies: the legislative, the executive, and the judiciary.

Consequently, the joint implementation of those two philosophies resulted in estates being replaced by other forms of social stratification and differentiation, the will of absolute monarchs by the consent of the governed, royal monopolies by free enterprises competing on the market. The roles of the central government were to be limited to those of law enforcement, management of the monetary system through autonomous central banks, and the satisfaction of other indivisible needs such as foreign policy and defense. Resources to fulfill these tasks were to be obtained through taxation legislated by parliament.

This was a rational design for a social order. Trusting human reason and the ability to learn while not fully trusting human motives, it created institutional safeguards that made it difficult for individuals or groups to acquire the power to impinge upon the freedom of others. Confidence in critical reason implied an experimental attitude toward social institutions.

> The presumption that governments can be established by "societies of men" on the basis of reflection and choice has a corollary presumption that the organization of governments can be *maintained* or *modified* on the basis of reflection and choice. If this presumption is accepted as a logical possibility, then, we can infer that the "ultimate authority" to devise, revise, and alter the terms of government resides with the "societies of men" who chose to constitute themselves as political communities. *Constitutional decision making,* in such a conception, is an essential political prerogative for modifying and altering the terms of government. (Ostrom 1987, 33)

Such a political order possesses error-detecting and error-correcting mechanisms. They may not always work properly, but such mechanisms are grounded in the very organization of the system.

The basic principle of this organization is to give power to individuals, and to spread it evenly. The organization of economic life around the market gave individual consumers control over decisions about investment and resource allocation. Because the government of the country was dependent upon electoral consent individual citizens had the power of the vote. Citizenship was to be the "crystallization of rationality in the social role" (Dahrendorf 1974, 677). Human nature, in this perspective, acquires some interesting features: Man can be fully trusted only when he is consistent in the pursuit of his interests. Thus, a social order should be designed in such a way as to take advantage of this property of human nature and to exploit human ambition for public good. Such an argument stood behind the Puritan concept of community, behind Adam Smith's concept of the free market, behind Locke's and Montesquieu's idea of the division of powers, and behind Madison's solution to the problem of factions.

The liberal idea of private property also had two sides to it. From the point of view of economic theory, private property guaranteed the rationality of economic processes: An individual in charge of his own capital would take better care of it than would a proxy and would contribute to the commonweal by acting in the market for his own interest. In the political perspective, the institution of private property made people materially independent of the state, that is, of the political elite. Only people who were materially independent of the state could retain the necessary independence of judgment and participate in the political process as free individuals.

By destroying estates and guilds, the liberal system freed individuals from traditional bonds and made them dependent upon their own efforts. The play of market forces began to regulate the destinies of individuals. Some were better equipped to play the game than others, and soon inequalities with roots in the functioning of the market replaced the privileges of estate. The crux of the matter was that the market mechanism, most notably before the rise of legal trade unions, was biased in favor of employers and against employees. The perception of this marked the beginning of the democratic and then the socialist movements that eventually brought about universal suffrage and the legalization of trade unions. Through collective bargaining workers could obtain better work conditions and higher salaries, and their situation started to improve. Moreover, increases in the proportion of the working class within the total population opened the prospects for socialist parties to win power by election, not revolution. This reformist orientation developed at the turn of the nineteenth century mostly in Germany and England.

Another revolutionary orientation clung to the traditional, radical socialist ideology in its slightly reinterpreted Marxist version. It was antimarket because it saw in the market the instrument of class exploitation. It was antiparliamentarian because revolutionaries, as a rule, do not hold freedom of speech or the existence of debating societies in great repute and because the parliament was part of a "bourgeois state"; moreover, the dictatorship of the proletariat, which is incompatible with a parliamentary democracy, was to follow the revolution they dreamed of. The revolution was not only to abolish all inequalities but to eradicate the sources of private property and the market, of the state, and ultimately of the social division of labor itself. The revolutionary vanguard was to abolish the first two immediately after the seizure of power; the others were to wither away more gradually. Nothing was specifically said about the manner in which the withering was to take place, although Lenin did put forward a not altogether plausible idea in his discussion of the eligibility of all officials. Communism implies the rejection of the market and of parliamentary democracy and the establishment of the dictatorial rule of the working class vanguard. This implied the dictatorship of the Communist party over the population, which in turn implied the rule of the party leadership over the party. This metaphysical reasoning exactly fitted the needs of political propaganda, but it was based on heuristic presumptions that can hardly stand critical scrutiny.

I shall concentrate solely upon those elements of Marxist theory that are relevant to a postrevolutionary social order. Two elements are of key importance: the first is the Marxist understanding of the nature of the social division of labor; the second, the Marxist theory of the state. Both are closely interconnected. In Engels's view, the social division of labor led to the emergence of the institution of private property and to class structure. The need to secure domination over the privileged classes gave rise to the state as organized coercion. The state, as an institutional entity, had no autonomy in relation to the mode of production: it was "the executive committee of the dominant class," and the nature of class domination was dependent on the mode of production. As such, the state could generate no particular group interests. This reveals an extreme neglect of the role of authority—rules and rule-ordered relationships—in every area of social life.

If we concede, however, that government as an allocation mechanism can indeed generate powerful interests, there is a danger that dictatorship by the vanguard can quickly turn the vanguard into a classlike group seeking the realization of its particular interests by excluding other groups from political participation. A monopoly of coercion, a top-down allocation of authority, and complete material dependence caused by the liquidation of private property would create a new ruling class.[3] Second, it is difficult to imagine a society functioning on a high level of technological development without any division of labor. If there is a division of labor, what mechanisms would regulate the exchanges and interactions among the actors? Engels suggested that this task could be accomplished for a time by a "neutral" administration. The question is: Can an administration be neutral? If we answer it by saying that, in acting within the limits of law and under effective supervision, it can approach a measure of neutrality, the next question must concern the source of law and supervisory authority. Thereby, we have returned to the problem of the system of rule and of the market. Max Weber convincingly demonstrated the relationship between administrative rationality and market mechanisms both for enterprises and collectivities (see Weber 1968, 1, pt. 1, 97–100 in particular). Moreover, under the direct supervision of the monoparty an administration can hardly be nonpartisan.

Ultimately, the idea of the communist society stood upon the Marxist conception especially that expressed in Marx's early philosophical writings, of the nature of man. Some modern Marxists look at these writings with scorn, but I cannot see much sense in the "mature" Marx's theories without the background of his earlier work. If we assume that man is inherently good, and only cruel conditions of life in a class-ridden society make him evil, a change of conditions through the abolition of private property upon which the class system is founded will bring about a change in human nature and will uncover the true nobility of the human soul. If this is so, the moral foundation of the human soul could replace all other mechanisms.

Lenin took a similar, but not identical view. Most people, corrupted by capitalism, did not live up to their inherent human potential, but the vanguard possessed all those needed qualities. When the revolution eradicates the class system, the educational process would gradually spread enlightenment through the whole population.

James Madison excellently summed up the consequences of different views on the nature of man for the design of a political system.

> If men were angels, no government would be necessary. If angels were to govern men, neither external nor internal controls on

government would be necessary. In framing a government which is administered by men over men, the great difficulty lies in this: you must first enable the government to control the governed; and in the next place oblige it to control itself. A dependence on the people is, no doubt, the primary control on the government but experience has taught mankind the necessity of auxiliary precautions. (Hamilton, Jay, and Madison [1787] n.d., 337)

With only a slight exaggeration, one can say that Marx assumed that men were potential angels: social conditions made them other than that. In conditions that liberate this true potential, men will need neither government nor other regulatory agencies. Lenin decided first that the angels should govern men, and when this happens, "neither external nor internal controls on government would be necessary." Later, with time, the rest of the population would acquire the qualities of angels. Madison himself, of course, represented the liberal (republican) position. His view of mankind was much more sober and, therefore, the design of the political system that he and the coauthors of *The Federalist* developed was much more complex.

Lenin's design for the Communist system provides a perfectly logical construction. The only conflict of interests he was able to perceive in society had its roots in the institution of the private ownership of the means of production brought about by the social division of labor and guaranteed by the coercive powers of the state. Once the state and the private property were abolished, there would be no place for social conflict—we enter the world of harmony. The dictatorship of the proletariat was necessary only to eradicate these obstacles to communism and to defend the fragile new order against the remnants of the old privileged classes or people from other classes who did not understand their own interests. Thus, opposition against communism could be born either in evil motivation or in obscurantism. The evil should be brutally eliminated, and the obscurantism enlightened.

As the monopoly for this intellectual and moral enlightenment rested in the hands of the revolutionary vanguard, it was only natural that it should have all the power. In the area of economics, this notion is reflected in the assumptions, often made by more sophisticated Soviet authors of textbooks on central planning, that the Central Planner possesses perfect information, and his utility function expresses the social welfare. If these assumptions hold, there is no need for the market because any of the tasks it can accomplish the Central Planner, which is in fact the Communist state, can fulfill much better.

Conclusion

The institutional design of the Communist state differs in many important respects from the liberal design and from the traditional patrimonial system. As in the patrimonial state, the demarcation line between the private domain of the ruler and the public concerns of his social role hardly existed and state institutions were not differentiated from other institutional areas. In this sense, the patrimonial state was never a just state (*Rechtsstaat*). The liberal conception of the state rests in the separation of the private and the public. To the extent that mechanisms, such as a free press, political parties, free elections, and free associations, exist that mediate between the state and the citizens, the state is part of the public domain. The public domain sublimates private interests by transforming private concerns into public issues through the process of analytical efforts and compromises. This is nothing else than public policy making. Thus, political parties are part of a "public realm" that is neither "private" nor "state."

The Leninist project, by definition, excludes such a public realm. If the Bolsheviks were right—as they presumed that they were—people either shared their correct opinions or only confused others by trying to express incorrect and dangerous opinions. In the Bolshevik view, this confusion should not be allowed; therefore, only the party line should find expression in social relationships. But the Communist party does not belong to any mediating domain between the state and the society; the party is not a representation of the society in any rational sense of the word. The party is an internally stratified vanguard with the goal of changing society, of molding its structure, way of life, and thinking. The Leninist project conceives the party as something that is, by its very nature, outside society and above it. The state becomes a tool by which society is coerced into obedience and fulfills its impersonal and technical historical mission. The idea of the "one best way" replaces in this imagery the idea of politics. The liberal tradition, as I understand it here, focuses on constraining the powers of the state; the Leninist tradition advocates extending those powers as far as possible in serving the party's mission.

Zbigniew K. Brzezinski's (1960) distinction between different types of restraints on political power illustrates the relationship between the state and society in the three institutional designs discussed here: (1) direct restraints, among which he mentions the English Magna Carta, the Polish *Nihil novi*, the Bill of Rights, constitutional guarantees, and the rule of law; (2) indirect restraints stemming from "the pluralistic character of all large-scale societies and which necessitate adjustment and compromise as the basis for political power . . ."; and (3) the natural restraints—geographic and climatic factors, tradition, kinship structure, and the family. In Brzezinski's view, imperial Russia never accepted the first type of restraint, sometimes came into conflict with the second, and never touched the third: "The Soviets continued this subversion of the direct restraints, but went beyond that in destroying the second kind and effectively challenging, if not entirely overcoming, the third" (pp. 101–2).[4] Brzezinski explained the difference as resulting from a difference in attitude of rulers toward society: the tsar's rule had its foundation in autocratic paternalism; Soviet power is oriented toward active intervention in shaping the social structure according to ideological canons and the needs of party leadership.

It is obvious that this wider freedom of maneuver in the Soviet state contributes to its successful weakening, and sometimes annihilation, of the traditional social institutions that provided some restraint upon the powers of imperial rulers in Russia. The rejection of traditional institutions makes the Soviet regime a modernizing strategy that superficially resembles, in terms of its goals, liberalism. In terms of the strategy of institution building, it is very close to the traditional patrimonial regimes. In fact, it is a patrimonial regime liberated of traditional constraints. The modernizing element is the Marxist-Leninist doctrine with the conception of the party it advances, and of the relationship between this party and the state within the regime of a "dictatorship of the proletariat."

This treatment brings us close to the notion of the totalitarian state. What is similar, however, is not indistinguishable. The problem under discussion is not the institutional reality of present-day Soviet Union, Poland, or Hungary: it is the institutional design of the Communist system as conceived by its inspirer. The proposal put forward is that the institutional foundations from which the system started its evolution are totalitarian in nature. In its future developments, the system sometimes closely approached its institutional logic, and sometimes it looked for salvation by integrating elements foreign to this logic, creating, thereby, serious internal tensions and turbulences.

Lenin's institutional project, with its total subjection of society to the state by completely depriving society of autonomy, is utopian. Already Aristotle, in disputing Socrates's argument "that the greater the unity of the state the better," demonstrated that by creating such a unitary, homogeneous entity one can only destroy the state.

> Is it not obvious that a state may at length attain such a degree of unity as to be no longer a state?—since the nature of a state is to be a plurality, and in tending to greater unity, from being a state, it becomes a family, and from being a family, an individual; for the family may be said to be more than the state, and the individual than the family. So that we ought not to attain this greatest unity even if we could, for it would be the destruction of the state. Again, a state is not made up only of so many men, but of different kinds of men; for similars do not constitute a state. It is not like a military alliance. (1943, 81)

This could have been, had Lenin appropriated it, quite a useful argument relating his institutional design to the conception of the withering away of the state. The greatest coherence the Communist state attained was in the second half of the 1930s in the USSR and during the Cultural Revolution in China. The more the design of a partisan state is implemented, the more it destroys its population.

By rejecting market and democratic institutions of public life, Lenin deprived the Soviet regime of sensitive mechanisms of error detection and error correction. Even if errors were noticed, making an issue of it would mean questioning the wisdom of those in power. This is always risky but the presumption of the rulers' wisdom has been one of the main doctrinal tenets of the Soviet regime. "An individual can be wrong, the Party is never wrong" was the often repeated press slogan during Stalin's period, and this attitude is definitely a part of the Leninist heritage. Only during periods of leadership succession, and the weakened hold of the leadership over the party and of the party over the population, has error correction been possible.

The choice of conceptual foundations for an institutional order is always consequential, for it contains constraints upon future developments. The constraints are built into the institutional structure. A change of conceptual foundation implies a change of regime. This can create different patterns for the generation and articulation of social interests and for the regulation of social processes, thus creating a different social order. It can also result in an effort to introduce most needed adjustments without touching the essence, a result that leads to a highly unbalanced institutional system of the kind imperial Russia experienced during the last several decennia of its history.

It is proposed here that all social orders, with the exception of some of the traditional ones that evolved through long histories of often disjointed, trial-and-error learning, are in large measure man-made. There are always individuals who have the solutions to problems being experienced by their societies and are able to convince strategic political groups of the correctness of their proposals. Especially at historical turning points, one encounters political and economic doctrines that specify the institutional shape of the social order and provide it with moral and pragmatic sense. These doctrines relating means and ends are the theories behind institutional arrangements. We call them *theories of design.*

> An appropriate theory of design is necessary both to understand how a system works and how modifications or changes in a system

will affect its performance. To use one theory of design to evaluate the characteristics of a system based upon a different theory of design can lead to profound misunderstandings. To use one theory of design to reform a system based upon a different theory of design may produce many unanticipated and costly consequences. (Ostrom 1974, 102)

Marxist-Leninist doctrine provides definitely misleading insights into the working of the Soviet type of regime. However, it also provides a theory justifying this form of an economic and political organization for it establishes causal connections between institutions and events. In view of these propositions, there is no doubt that Lenin's formulation is a false theory. It also fulfilled the role of the indispensable ideological rationale for the regime, and in this role it is enforced by the powers of a Communist state. The theory served, in part, as camouflage to conceal political realities. This has far-reaching consequences for the cultural and political life in such countries. Without understanding the Marxist-Leninist foundations of Communist regimes, we cannot understand their institutional design, their workings, and the problems they face. Acting upon an erroneous theory nonetheless has consequences. To assess those consequences we turn to the evolution of the key institutional structures of the Soviet system and observe the privatization of the Communist state.

III

THE EVOLUTION OF KEY INSTITUTIONAL STRUCTURES: PRIVATIZATION OF THE COMMUNIST STATE

SIX

LEGITIMACY AND CORRUPTION

Before we turn to a more serious examination of the Soviet type of political regime and its institutional peculiarities, it may be interesting to take a quick look at forecasts two leading European political and social thinkers, Max Weber and Gaetano Mosca, made when the Bolsheviks had just installed the new institutional order in Russia. Weber deduced his prediction from the revolutionary roots of the regime that corresponded to his idea of a charismatic type of domination, to which any movement that calls for a social revolution belongs, and that always carries with it a trap: Whatever the original motives of the leader, the results are vicious because any high moral standards of its ideology turn out to be, at least among the following, a cover-up for base motives. Even those pure souls attracted by the moral values of the ideology usually succumb to temptations while in power.[1]

Mosca's prediction is related to the despotic, dictatorial character of the Communist pattern of government and to the claim by the Communist party, and more generally by socialist parties, to represent the "only historical truth." In his opinion,

> the absolute preponderance of a single political force, the predominance of any over-simplified concept in the organization

of the state, the strictly logical application of any single principle in all public law are the essential elements in any type of despotism, whether it be a despotism based upon divine right or a despotism based ostensibly on popular sovereignty; for they enable anyone who is in power to exploit the advantages of a superior position more thoroughly for the benefit of his own interests and passions. When the leaders of the governing class are the exclusive interpreters of the will of God or of the will of the people and exercise sovereignty in the name of those abstractions . . . and when no other organized social forces exist apart from those which represent the principle on which sovereignty over the nation is based, then there can be no resistance, no effective control, to restrain a natural tendency in those who stand at the head of the social order to abuse their powers. (1939, 134–35)

Then there occurs a degeneration of the whole ruling class and ". . . the vices that absolutism generates in its leaders are communicated downward to the whole political structures" (ibid.).

The problem, as it is formulated here, lies not only in the universal tendency of all power toward corruption. Mosca evidently concurs with Montesquieu, who maintained that "the principle of despotic government is subject to a continual corruption, because it is even in its nature corrupt" ([1750] 1886, 1:134). To put it briefly, despotism is corruption.

The Meaning of Corruption

Communism must from its very beginning face the problem of corruption. Before we embark upon an analysis of this it is important to introduce some terminological distinctions. The issue of corruption is so loaded with moral and ideological content that it encourages a lack of precision and, obviously, the sense in which Montesquieu used the term is somewhat different from that of its modern uses.[2]

Montesquieu developed some ideas already present in Aristotle's writings. He took the view that any system of government must be based on certain principles. These are open to corruption, at which point the regime starts to evolve into another form. Thus, for instance, "the principle of democracy is corrupted not only when the spirit of equality is extinct, but likewise when [it] fall[s] into a spirit of extreme equality . . ." ([1750] 1886, 1:126). In the first case, democracy turns into an aristocracy, in the second, into despotism. Despotism is in fact a corrupt form of other types of government. In a way, it can also be said that aristocracy is a corrupt form of democracy, but aristocracy is based on rules and normative codes of behavior, that is, on virtue and moderation; but despotism knows no rules and lasts only as long as rule is arbitrary and subjects are kept in fear. When it finds it expedient to respect some rules ". . . its nature is forced without being changed; its ferocity remains; and is made tame and tractable only for a time" (ibid., 134). When rules are established, and people cease being fearful, despotism collapses.

Under the subtypes of the republican government, democracy and aristocracy, the principle of government possesses an unequivocally moral character: it is based upon public virtue and moral restraint. Under monarchy, it has for its base "honor," whose content is a mixture of morality and vanity (lust for glory). Monarchy is a hierarchical order of estates differentiated by privileges and governed by fundamental laws. When monarchs lack public respect for the great men of the realm, "when honor is set up in contradiction to honors," when privileges are withdrawn, the corruption of monarchy occurs and it starts to evolve toward despotism. Republican and monarchical forms of government belong to the class that Montesquieu calls "moderate governments." Despotism is something else: it knows no laws and no restraints. Corruption of the principle of government specifies, therefore, boundary conditions: as a result of corruption, the system of government disintegrates or evolves into another form. Only despotism does not offer any easy way out.

This last point is not necessarily implied by the positions that Weber or Mosca took. Weber saw in the charismatic form of domination three possible kinds of transformation: traditional, the legal-rational, and democratic (1960, v. 1:249–54). The most probable effect of an evolution in the traditional direction was a patrimonial regime, which, in Weber's terminology, corresponded with despotism. Mosca contented himself, in the context in which the quotation appeared, with establishing a relationship between the form of government consisting in the coercive imposition of a single set of beliefs upon the population and the deprivation of the ruling elite and of the population at large. In a broader perspective, however, this position can be treated as a feature in his conception of the process of elite circulation.

As traditionally used in political science, the term *corruption* usually refers to a normative conception of the public domain. There are normative expectations related to the fulfillment of public roles. One can say that these expectations render a role public, that is, subject to common understanding. In view of these expectations, people occupying public positions should forget their private concerns, interests, likes, and dislikes and fulfill their duties in an impersonal, dispassionate manner according to their best technical competence and following legal rules. Legal rules may be formulated in a way that is directly discriminating but this simply indicates that corruption has already occurred at the level at which laws are formulated. (All law discriminates. The problem is, however, whether it discriminates on the grounds of particularistic or universalistic criteria.) Corruption occurs when the demarcation line between the private and the public becomes blurred, and public actors start following private criteria in the exercise of public functions. The term *corruption,* then, makes sense only if the distinction between the private and the public is itself meaningful and widely accepted, and this is rare. "The custom of refraining from using the power of public office for private gain constitutes one of the most recent and fragile conquests of the civilization, and . . . in no country in the world are bribery and embezzlement unknown" (Andreski 1970, 347).

Most modern authors conceptualize corruption in terms of an individual role.[3] They sometimes use it to denote the behavior of large organized units within an administrative complex struggling for their particular interests without regard to the commonweal.[4] Often, especially in the case of modernizing societies, corruption becomes a way of life, as obtains, according to R. B. Jain (1987), for instance, in India. But in all cases, when the distinction between the private and the public is institutionalized, that is, when it is part of the cultural endowment of a given population, the emergence of corruption is a function of control. At the level of individual roles, the most important is the informal control exercised by the peer group. At the level of the state, the way mechanisms regulating interorganizational relations work stimulates the occurrence of a collective anomie. In this instance corruption may occur when the state administration loses its autonomy to an external political force, namely, a party machine. A deciding factor in a propensity for political corruption is the sequence in which state administration and political parties develop. If political parties develop first, the state administration has difficulties in defending its autonomy and integrity against the intrusion of external, political criteria.[5] A more favorable situation arises when the state administration has time to mature and to develop its professional ethos before political parties attain importance in political life.

It is commonly accepted that the *institutionalized* distinction between the public and the private is at the core of the notion of the modern state. By *institutionalization,* I mean not only the organizational aspect of the state but also the cultural sanction of the distinction between the private and the public: There exist binding obligations toward others, some of which may be legal, that is, enforced by a generally accepted system of norms and values and not exclusively (or even mainly) by force. The notion of *public domain* becomes meaningful only in view of norms and values that are part of what we call the civic culture, the ethos of public responsibility, of civil service. These sets of norms and values create expectations and regulate individual behavior in public roles. Corruption occurs when these cultural standards are perverted or abandoned. Corruption is not a trivial matter. When kept within limits, there is nothing unusual about it; when corruption escalates, it brings about ungovernability and may eventually become a menace to civilization.

Those institutional safeguards in weaker forms appeared in all early democracies, in ancient Athens, republican Rome, and during the fifteenth and sixteenth centuries in the Polish-Lithuanian

Commonwealth. They emerged in the presence of a fairly numerous social class that controlled a strategic political resource and was geographically dispersed but not to the extent that it was unable to communicate and to coordinate its activities. In societies in which military power was based upon a military class with independent means of subsistence, and not upon a professional army, the strategic political resource was the possession of weapons and prowess in using them and the de jure or de facto ownership of land. Under such conditions, the ruler had to seek consent from this class in order to mobilize his army. One should notice, however, that such a situation could have existed only when the state, having only a limited control over the means of coercion, could not develop the high level of autonomy toward society that is characteristic of the modern state.

With the further development of the social division of labor, which created numerous social groups and institutional actors playing fairly autonomous roles in the social system, new strategic resources appeared that gave a further stimulus to the political pluralization of societies. In a state with a limited military class the autonomy of society was possible to the extent that the state's monopoly of control over the means of coercion was not complete. In the latter no such need existed: democratic control rested on the state's dependence upon the consent of the plurality of social groups. It can be easily shown that the emergence of public life was a by-product of conflicts and struggles fought for very different purposes. In both cases, however, the major problem is how to constrain and control the coercive powers of the state. The concepts of the rule of law and representative government and the development of institutions of public life that gave a prominent place to negotiation and discourse as a way of settling social conflicts served this purpose. The establishment of such concepts and institutions required a clear legal delimitation between what belongs to the public and what belongs to the private domain.

Is there a connection between Montesquieu's idea of the corruption of the principle of government and the sense in which the term, *corruption,* is actually used? There is an obvious one. The ideas of both virtue and honor provide external, normative standards of behavior. If citizens do not respect them, corruption of the principle occurs. It can be argued that it is in the collective interest of a body of citizens or an aristocracy to preserve virtue, and that it is in the collective interest of the nobility and the monarch to defend the idea of honor. But because these are group interests, an individual, in following those precepts, must often act against his own, narrowly conceived, private interests. The situation is not, therefore, dissimilar to that with which we are faced in examining corruption in the modern sense. In both cases there is the problem of how a conflict between the two kinds of interests is conceptualized and eventually resolved, and what the implications are of the choice for the nature of the government.

Furthermore, in both cases we are faced with basically the same Aristotelian idea that the task of the state is to serve the common interest, and that the state can fulfill the task only when a moral order is compatible with the institutional order. When this normative order falters, and private motives start to dominate public concerns, the government abandons its calling by conceding to the private interests of those who control it, and ". . . governments which rule with a view to the private interest . . . are perversion" (Aristotle 1943, 138).

Public Interest and the Organization of Society

There is a substantial difference between Montesquieu's vision of politics and that advanced in modern works on corruption. The modern approach to corruption often contains a bias; conveying the notion of an inherent superiority of the public over the private, and it concentrates unduly upon the state as the (postulated) representative of the public concern. This bias is rooted in much of the nineteenth-century liberal thinking inspired by the work of Jeremy Bentham, which itself is a departure from the tradition that developed from Aristotle and Montesquieu through the Scottish philosophers, the American authors of *The Federalist,* Tocqueville, and Mosca, and which has somehow lost its appeal in modern times.[6] The state is an important part of the public realm, but the concept of this realm is broad, embracing voluntary associations and religious and other institutions (Ostrom 1991). Let us try to formulate, using this pluralistic perspective, a consistent conception of a bottom-up organization of the political order. Only within such an organization does the term *public interest* make sense.[7]

By becoming socially involved with other people, communicating with them, and cooperating in crucial tasks, an individual extends his ego, starts to think in universal terms to embrace interests in the larger community, and has concerns for those with whom he works and cooperates. This does not mean that, with every new instance of cooperation and communication, we start to negotiate meanings, principles, and so on. We accept *ex ante* some rules of the game that are the products of past compromises and respect them as long as they serve their purpose. We also accept the idea of struggle and conflict as long as it is regulated and, thereby, socially legitimate, as it is in the market, sports, or many other forms of well-structured competition. Thus, the term *public* embraces any result of the ego extension that is part of *open social relationships*. The postulate of an open social relationship excludes all cases of combinations and conspiracies started with the intention of taking advantage of a combined effort to create special privileges and profits for the members of the group at the cost of others not part of the arrangement. If such a conspiratorial group seizes control over the complex of the state, understood as a monopoly of control over the means of coercion, and with its use extends this monopoly to other domains of social life, it creates the worst kind of exploitation, for other groups cannot constrain it within the existing institutional framework. Here we find ourselves again on the grounds of Montesquieu's concept of despotism.

The public realm is a hierarchy, in the sense used by Herbert Simon (1973), that, although the first ego extensions concern the family and the peer group, others will, if they occur at all, embrace more abstract social entities such as voluntary associations, clubs, unions, religious denominations, local communities, a country, and eventually the world as a whole. Family and peer group loyalties are natural and universal because families and peer groups are found everywhere and at all times; in joining them an individual exercises little freedom of choice. In most circumstances the same applies to religious affiliations. Of crucial importance are, therefore, those institutions and social relations that an individual can start or join on his or her own initiative. Hence, public life is possible only when fundamental human freedoms are respected. But in order for public life to appear at all, the family, peer groups, voluntary associations, and religious institutions must function in a way that strengthens universal moral and intellectual orientations. These preconditions of public life are recognized as a factor in shaping American prerevolutionary political life; they might have also, in an opposite way, affected the outcome of the Bolshevik revolution.

The public realm is the domain of the *intermediate,* in which various organizations and institutions communicate, negotiate, coordinate their actions, and compete. Only when this domain is sufficiently developed and diversified can society control the state and keep its powers restrained. The state becomes, then, only an element, albeit a crucial one, in the public domain. Here we encounter a historical paradox. The idea of citizenship and of the public domain developed in societies that were still largely traditional, that were dominated by religious institutions and estates that might have been formally open but de facto were closed by cultural and material barriers. Those groups and institutions, jealous of their autonomy, made great efforts to restrict the powers of the state. But when the truly liberal democratic systems finally emerged, we could see powerful forces at work that attempted to close the public realm by imposing on it their special values and interpretations and to strengthen the role of the state in social life by extending the range of its activities and increasing its redistributory powers. The public domain is the domain of discourse, and discourse can take place only where certain preconditions are met: the formal equality of parties, a commonly understood language, rules of the game that are accepted by all sides within the relationship, and a recognized obligation to honor agreements (or contracts).

In this perspective, the public and the private are not necessarily exclusive and may be mutually reinforcing. That is, once an ethos develops in the *private domain* that is functional from the point of view of requirements of the public domain, the necessary condition for the development of the *public domain* is met. Any progress in the development of the public domain will in turn enforce the underlying values of the private. For instance, the successful negotiation of a conflict of interest will enhance the probability that, if the conflict recurs, the parties would turn to negotiation and adjudication rather than to belligerence in settling it.

It is only when the community of understanding and the consensus about values and norms falters that a crisis of the public domain will occur. Then we should expect the reverse of the process described above: Broader loyalties begin to shrink, the bounds of trust disappear, and values and norms become less universalistic and more particularistic. Eventually, individuals find protection in families and other informal groups, or in small political and cultural communities trying to impose their particular ethos on society.[8] When society is unable, for various reasons, to maintain and defend the public domain, that is, the institutional diversity that, with the underlying community of understanding, provides the basis for integration, corruption sets in. On the level of individual administrative or political roles this takes the form of using a public office for the sake of personal enrichment or aggrandizement.

To what extent is the concept of corruption relevant for a study of Communist regimes? In order to answer this question, we have to consider the institutional design of the Soviet type of social order. Being organized from the top down, the Communist order reminds us of historical bureaucratic regimes. Those regimes were, however, constrained, albeit with different degrees of success, by traditional structures and by the traditional basis for legitimizing the ruler's position. The Communist revolution destroyed the traditional structures and replaced them by a revolutionary structure, the Communist party. The revolutionary Marxist-Leninist ideology provided the new order with legitimacy, but did not solve a number of theoretical and practical problems, among them the matter of boundaries between the Communist party and the state and between the "partisan state" and society, which brings us back again to the problem of sovereignty.[9] On the doctrinal level these problems have never been satisfactorily resolved because, in order to define boundaries, it is necessary to establish the rules of the game. In

Lenin's idea of the dictatorship of the proletariat there were no generally accepted rules.

Although it overhauled the social structure dramatically, in the realm of the state the revolution enforced only those changes indispensable for one-party rule. The language and content of subsequent Soviet and other Communist constitutions is not very different from that of the constitutions of liberal, democratic states (see Unger 1981). Marxist-Leninist ideologues, when faced with problems that the use of such language eventually poses in confronting reality, claim that these same notions have very different meanings for different classes (workers and capitalists), depending upon economic and political circumstances. This claim cannot be treated seriously. The use of democratic terminology to describe situations that are undemocratic is linguistic abuse and indicates serious problems with legitimacy.

For one reason or another, the builders of the Soviet state, despite their radical rejection of liberalism, never tried to (or perhaps never could) develop their doctrine of political rule. They eventually responded to contingencies providing some ad hoc pseudoscientific explanations for opportunistic decisions. These may have sufficed to fool casual observers, but did not form any consistent theoretical formulations. Keenan's remark about the imperial Russian state applies also to the Soviet state: It is a state without a doctrine of rulership or, rather, whatever doctrine it has is expressed purely in the negative.

There is indeed a Marxist-Leninist doctrine that is quite specific, although not empirically correct, in its criticism of the capitalist mode of production, and so vague as to be irrelevant and misleading when it addresses Communist societies. The only function the doctrine serves is that of producing communication noise hindering the processes of communication in society; it does not order and facilitate mutual understanding.

The distinction between the public and the private appears in the Marxist tradition only marginally. In his *Critique of Hegel's Philosophy of Right* ([1843] 1970), Marx stated quite clearly that the distinction was an ideological sham. If the state is a guardian of dominant interests, then it serves private interests under the disguise of the common good. The distinction makes sense only when a private interest is also a public interest, that is, under communism; but then no state is necessary. If Marx's analysis of capitalism is essentially institutionalist, though not necessarily correct, his remarks on communism are devoid of any institutional content. We simply do not know what social mechanisms were, in his view, necessary to assure the orderly functioning of a communist society; if neither the market nor political institutions, then what?

Marx made at least one exception to this treatment of the public and the private: he did concede in his introduction to the *Critique* that, when a class, such as the bourgeoisie, aspiring to domination mounts a revolution against the "old oppressors," it becomes for a short time the representative of the general interest of the majority against the particular interest of a small parasitic minority.

Similarly, Lenin applied the distinction to his conception of the "transitory" stage between capitalism and communism, that is, the period of the dictatorship by the revolutionary vanguard of the "exploited classes." Then, of course, the vanguard was to represent the interests of the great majority of the population against a handful of former capitalists who stubbornly defended their lost positions, or against some misled members of other classes unable to understand correctly the historical process and their own class interests. But then, also, the function of the vanguard was to abolish eventually all forms of domination in society: It was to be given the full monopoly of power for the sake of destroying all power.

Through such reasonings, the doctrine of Marxism-Leninism has delegitimized the private domain, with interesting theoretical and practical consequences. Among the former, two are of importance here. By delegitimizing the private domain, the doctrine also delegitimized society as a distinct entity and by negating the private, the doctrine also negated the public. If it is the party elite that is correctly appraising the common interest, then it must have the right to compel individuals to behave according to the definition of that interest that the party currently provides, and it will evaluate those individuals in terms of their malleability. From this point of view, nothing is irrelevant to the party, neither political nor moral convictions nor dating choices: individuals and primary groups lose the right to privacy.[10]

If the core of the public domain consists of interactions among diverse autonomous institutions and voluntary associations, of processes of negotiation and the search for consensus, one can hardly imagine a political regime more detrimental to public life than the one built upon Leninist premises. With public life suppressed, individuals can have little impact, if any, on the process of government; they can accept the government or reject it, but their attitudes do not matter so long as they remain an atomized mass. They may turn their attention only to their own and their families' immediate survival and to the use of private connections to improve their own well-being. When a state denies a place for the private realm, it leaves no place for the public one.

Also, as mentioned earlier, the motives for the abolition of private property rights follow this line of reasoning. Private property gives autonomy to individual action. A doctrine that advocates it must assume that human beings are fallible, that society must constantly make decisions on the basis of insufficient information, that is, must cope with variety and uncertainty. From this perspective, an effective institutional design requires a solution to the problem of responsibility and accountability, and private property rights allow resolution of this problem in a decentralized way. Decentralization makes it possible to exploit fully the knowledge of the circumstances of time and place that resides at lower levels of the economic and political organization (see Hayek 1945).

A theory that proposes the abolition of private property rights places power in the hands of a group of people who are infallible. According to the theory, the abolition of private property not only ends exploitation, but also eliminates all constraints upon the freedom of maneuver of perfectly rational individuals who are, as rulers, oriented exclusively to the realization of collective goals.

The Privatization of the Soviet Type of Regime

There is no private life, there are no private groups, and there are no interests outside those of the partisan state. The tension between different private concerns and various institutionalized public expectations, ever-present at the level of an individual's public role in a mature liberal, democratic society, is institutionally suppressed. An individual has no "right" to private interests. The use of egoistic motives for the attainment of a public good is considered immoral: egoistic motives can produce only evil results. The imagery may not match the reality, but it has found its reflection in the institutional design of a system based on the demand of an unconditional submission of all private interests to the partisan state. There is no institutional mechanism by which conflicts between an individual as a private person and a state agency might be arbitrated. Until recently, anyone in a Communist country who was foolish enough to sue a state agency stood no chance of succeeding.

Yet, people fall in love, aspire to careers and to better incomes, wish to have children, and want to assure a better future for themselves. When external controls are consistent with the nature of individual moral norms, all those passions and interests can be, at least to an extent, regulated so that they do not disrupt the social order. When the political order is one of many orders in a society, disruptions occurring in other areas of life will not necessarily destabilize it. In a decentralized, pluralistic system, social conflicts are largely diffuse and amenable to compromise (see Coser 1959). Because the doctrine underlying the design of the Soviet type of social order does not recognize the validity of private interests, the institutional system built upon this doctrine is unable to deal constructively with these interests once they manifest themselves. Success in suppressing all private concerns is crucial to the system's equilibrium. The partisan state must strive to become a party in all social relationships. A member of the Communist party should be, above all, a party member; a "citizen" is, first of all, the representative of the partisan state—all other roles are secondary.[11] Otherwise the system would become progressively ungovernable. A complete depersonalization of all social relations is the boundary condition for the Soviet type of social order or, in Montesquieu's terms, it is the principle of this type of government. Any personalization of social relations under such a social order must provoke the process of "corruption of the principle of government."

It is important to note that *depersonalization* is different from *impersonality*. The latter term means that, while performing public functions, an individual makes decisions on the grounds of objective, impartial criteria; usually these are moral and legal rules. Beyond such situations, one is free to act within the limits of the law and accepted moral norms. Depersonalization, in the sense used here, is the deliberate suppression of the cultural meaning of all roles other than official, social roles: An individual, free of all traditional morals and prejudices, follows the party line and obeys the orders of his superiors; he becomes a deployable agent in the hands of the party. An official in a bureaucratic organization is a wheel or a cog in the machine only during his work time; a party member is (in principle) playing his official role at all times.

The "corruption of principle" in the Soviet type of government, when it occurs, produces an invasion of private criteria into the governmental process. Without democratic forms of control, it is very difficult to oppose such tendencies successfully. Moreover, the war against traditional morality and against traditional professional ethical standards wrought great damage to the functioning of informal mechanisms of control that were operated by peer groups and oriented toward universalistic norms and values.

The term *privatization* denotes the consequences of this situation for a Communist state. We consider a state privatized when it is difficult to point to mechanisms that can be reasonably said to ensure the articulation and implementation of the general interest; there is no shared community of understanding that establishes the basis for public order and accountability. The state is privatized, therefore, when it functions in such a way that it destroys the cultural grounds upon which the distinction between the private and the public makes sense, and renders the distinction itself inoperative.

The sense in which the term *privatization* is used here is different from that popularly used in the West, where it refers to the transfer of productive facilities and services from direct management by the state to the market; that is, privatization is a change in a property relationship. However, this term has other, and in the theoretical view adopted in this study, ungrounded implications, one being that the public interest is either losing or gaining by such a transfer. The first possibility, that the public interest loses, would *a priori* suggest that the state is the center of public life and the only authoritative exponent of the public interest, so that any transfer of property rights from the state to the private sector would occur at the cost of the public interest. The second, proposing that the public interest wins when the transfer occurs, assumes that whenever a function is transferred from the state to the private sector a more efficient delivery of services must follow. This logic applies only within a liberal state.

If a state, for whatever ideological reasons, invades parts of the economy in an attempt to manage processes for which it is ill-equipped, the consequences for the quality and efficiency of the satisfaction of social needs must be unfavorable. Those invasions yield organizational problems that overburden the state complex and contribute to ungovernability. Transferring industry to where it belongs is not privatization, in the political sense of the term, for that would be to suggest that hitherto they had served public interests and from now on they will serve private interests. To the contrary, such a transfer may result in more effective public control over the processes of satisfying social needs. One can imagine many situations in which a transfer from the state to the private sector would diminish the effectiveness with which certain needs are met. The *true requirement of public interest is its efficiency and effectiveness in satisfying public needs,* including the alleviation of scarcity. A polity should select institutional patterns that regulate the satisfaction of needs on the criteria of efficiency and effectiveness and not of ideological prejudices. In identifying values unequivocally with institutions, one takes the same path Communists have taken when they condemned the market, representative institutions, the rule of law, private property, and other cornerstones of modern civilized life. The public interest is served not solely, and perhaps not even predominantly, by the state. A transfer of the delivery of services to marketlike arrangements can serve an important public purpose by making that delivery more easily controllable by the public, less costly, and more governable.[12]

In the context in which the term is used here, *privatization* describes what happens when the Soviet type of political system finds itself unable to maintain the depersonalization of social life, and society, after a long period of suppression, reemerges in an all-embracing, basically unchanged, partisan state system. Because the system is still repressive and public life may exist only marginally, a social revival of this type is not a renaissance of civic culture and democratic participation. When privatization occurs, all relations become personal again. In the absence of transcendent ethical standards and when public control has been exhausted by the war against tradition, narrowly grounded private concerns start to predominate. The term *public* is hardly applicable to the Communist state at any stage of its development, but there were periods when it was able to preserve depersonalization and appear, rightly or wrongly, to represent some general interest. Besides the fear of terror, there were other motives that provided the Communist regime with some legitimation. A political system that is unable to give, at least temporarily, a sense of a transcendent purpose to the community cannot achieve the world position that the Soviet Union attained. The terrible crimes against humanity notwithstanding, no country has ever become a great power by relying solely on the motives of fear and greed. Without a moral and historical mission, it is not possible to mobilize social energy for such a task. Max Lerner, commenting upon Aristotle's ideas, noted that

> we have come to see that the most important element of strength in a community is the sense of greatness that it can generate, and that the most important political emotion in man is the thirst for greatness which, under pressure, stretches him beyond his everyday self so that he reaches the full outlines of his human personality. (Aristotle 1943, 26–27)

In a similar vein, Tocqueville wrote:

> On close inspection we shall find that religion, and not fear, has ever been the cause of the long-lived prosperity of absolute governments. Whatever exertions may be made, no true power can be founded among men which does not depend upon the free union of their inclinations; and patriotism and religion are the only two motives in the world which can permanently direct the whole of a body public to one end. ([1835] 1851, 1:96–97)

No doubt, terror played an important role in the political life of Communist countries. But there have been periods in Soviet history when a sense of greatness permeated the life of at least the Russian part of Soviet society and gave a measure of legitimacy to whatever actions its leadership was inclined to pursue. At the beginning, it might have been the conviction that it was the historical mission of Russia to lead the world in a proletarian revolution. Later, after the victorious war against Hitler's Germany, a sense of greatness has had its source in the superpower status of the Soviet Union. There have also been periods when even in East-Central Europe communism enjoyed some, though lesser, legitimacy. However, the destructive effects of the political order, and the prohibitive price the Russians, the other nationalities in the USSR, and the nations of East-Central Europe have had to pay for this sense of greatness became clearly visible a long time ago. The crisis of the Soviet world is also a moral crisis.

Corruption is caused not by oppression, but by the growing popular disillusionment with the system of rule, by the loss of legitimacy. This confirms Tocqueville's apt remark that "men are not corrupted by the exercise of power or debased by the habit of obedience; but by the exercise of power which they believe to be illegal, and by obedience to a rule which they consider to be usurped and oppressive ([1835] 1851, 1: 7). When a Communist regime, which relies more on corruption than on coercion, tries to liberalize, and finds itself challenged by public opinion, it is surprisingly helpless—because corruption has destroyed whatever legitimate basis it may have had.

Marxism-Leninism has rejected the normative view of the state as an instrument for the realization of the general interest. Instead, it conceived of the state solely as an instrument of oppression. The Soviet state was to be superior to all other forms of state because it was the only one admitted by its founders to assure the oppression by the majority of the minority of former exploiters. Its mission, Lenin claimed, was to represent the general interest by achieving a revolutionary transformation of society that was to result in the liberation of mankind. How the state was to discover and to realize the general interest was a problem that never occurred either to

Lenin or to his successors: the Soviet state simply represented the general interest. This conviction had no rational grounds in the working of economic and political institutions.

The foregoing discussion has been an attempt to diagnose the main source of the malaise of the Soviet type of regime. In the opinion presented here, it resides in the very conception of the state that Marxist-Leninist doctrine adopted as the foundation for the design of the Communist political order. It denied the private in the name of the public. But the public cannot exist without the private; it has its roots in the private. Thus, by destroying the private, the Communists attempted to destroy the public, ending up with a caricature of a state. What may have survived did so in the underground. Any reform of a Soviet type of regime must start from this realization.

SEVEN

THE PARTY IN THE COMMUNIST POLITICAL SYSTEM

Imagine a state administrative system with no external control whatsoever. It would either have to disintegrate into some sort of a feudal order or a functional group within the system would dominate it. Usually the army or the security establishment would take control and try to assure for itself, through control over other state agencies, a dominant position over society. The army is in fact the stronger contender, for it can always justify its claim to power by an external threat; the secret police is more readily a servant of other powerful groups, but it is the kind of servant that often succeeds in controlling the master. The first outcome, feudalization, would appear in a traditional social milieu; the second is typical of modern, third world circumstances. Other agencies within the state complex can hardly provide the political leadership that would permit them to maintain the continuity of the state's functioning in the absence of external controls. When external controls are too tight and too direct, the administration loses its professional integrity and becomes a tool for the short-term interests of outside groups; its incentive system rewards political loyalty instead of professional competence. The

Communist solution belongs or rather, had initially belonged, to an altogether different realm.

At the core of the institutional design of the Communist state there is a centralized, disciplined revolutionary party aspiring to the exercise of full, dictatorial control over society in order to restructure it in accordance with its ideological principles. But, the party, to be able to achieve this aspiration, must first restructure the state in such a way as to make political control secure and effective. It must become a very special state, one that is responsible not to the population but to the party. This deprives the population of institutional means of controlling or affecting in any direct way the functioning of the government. The party leadership, and sometimes only the first secretary, has concentrated in its hands all effective instruments of control.

To make the controls effective and secure, the party must politicize the administration. It must also maintain discipline in its own ranks by using its own hierarchical supervision to enhance ideological control by peer groups and by using the security system that is responsible to the leadership to supervise the party. In any case, the Communist party is the crucial element in the political system of the Soviet type of social order.

Charisma and Corruption

Ken Jowitt developed a conception of the party that corresponds with the theoretical perspective assumed here. His interpretation of the Communist party drew its inspiration from Max Weber's idea of the charismatic form of domination and concept of the routinization of charisma.[1] Jowitt's work provides, then, a convenient point of departure for our discussion of the evolution of the Soviet-type political system and the process of privatization of the state.

Jowitt perceives the originality of Lenin's model of the party: "The novelty of Leninism as an organization is its substitution of charismatic impersonality for procedural impersonality dominant in the West.... Lenin took the fundamentally conflicting notions of individual heroism and organizational impersonalism and recast them in the form of an organizational hero—the Bolshevik party" (1978, 34 and 36). Lenin's organizational innovation consisted of combining the full personal devotion of members to the party with effective impersonal, peer group control over this devotion by enforced and unquestioned obedience to hierarchy. By becoming a party member, a person joins an order supposed to defend everything that is morally pure against social evil. The party demands of him total submission. When this devotion and unquestioned obedience falters (on a larger scale), the intricate system of organizational control begins to crack.

Having formulated the roots of the Soviet-type or Leninist, as he calls them, regimes in terms of the charismatic form of domination, Jowitt proceeds to interpret the development of such regimes as a process of the routinization of charisma. Of the three directions in which charisma could be routinized that Weber envisaged, Jowitt concentrated upon the neotraditionalization of Leninist regimes. The process of neotraditionalization leads to an escalation of corrupt practices within the party. Jowitt employs, for the purpose of his study of the Communist party, the following definition of corruption:

> *Corruption* refers to an organization's loss of its specific competence through failure to identify a task and strategy that practically distinguish between rather than equate or confuse (particular) member with (general) organizational interest. For a Leninist party, organizational integrity means the competence to sustain a combat ethos among political office holders who act as disciplined, deployable agents. Phrased somewhat differently, a Leninist party's organizational integrity rests on its regular ability to prevent both the ritualization of its combat ethos and the transformation of (deployable) party-agents into (non-deployable) party-principals. (1983, 279)

Informal practices have always occurred in the Bolshevik party. But at the beginning, in Jowitt's view, they tended to contribute to the achievement of formal goals. As neotraditionalization progressed, these practices have increasingly posed a threat to the organization's ability to preserve its general interest, that is, to maintain its impersonal competence.

The process of neotraditionalization is not a linear one. Sometimes it is curbed or even reversed.

> The tendency toward "corrupt" routinization was pronounced during the NEP, at the time of the Seventeenth Congress, and after the Second World War. But in each of these situations (different) leadership coalitions—under Stalin—succeeded in giving the party a *social combat task* that subordinated particular interests to authoritative definitions of the party's general task and interest. (Jowitt 1983, 284)

Thus, Jowitt proposes—a position shared by Friedrich and Brzezinski (1956, 150)—that the party can regain its strength and assert its competence only under extreme conditions: when it is involved in a purge of itself and/or a mass extermination of the population. This is the price of organizational integrity.

The problem with Jowitt's analysis is that it is terminologically confusing. He defines corruption as most contemporary authors do: Corruption occurs when the private interests of individuals replace the general, formal interests of the organization and public offices then lose their public character. Thus, he applied to the party the definition coined in a liberal, democratic environment in which organizations must try to win the loyalty of individuals and their submission to general organizational purposes while recognizing in principle those individuals' right to possess private interests. In the face of that, organizations have to seek ways of relating private interests to the interests of the organization through an incentive system. The crux of the matter, in the case of the Communist party, is not the maintenance of the formal impersonality but the depersonalization of social relations which, as I tried to show in Chapter 6, is something different.

Jowitt would have been in a much better position had he defined corruption explicitly in Montesquieu's terms, relating the concept to the core principle of the Soviet type of government. Weber's concept of the charismatic form of domination assumes total devotion stemming from a belief in a leader's superhuman qualities and leaves no place for private concerns and interests. Lenin, as Jowitt rightly noted, made of the party an impersonal charismatic hero, and this became part of the party's cultural ethos.

When its adherents start to use a charismatic movement for their private purposes, routinization is in progress and gives way to neotraditionalization, bureaucratization, or democratization. To Montesquieu, this would imply that the corruption of principle triggered a process of transforming the Communist form of rule into another form, that is, that the system's identity, its core organizing principle, is changing.

There arises another problem with Jowitt's use of the term *corruption,* especially with his thesis about the cycles of "corrupt routinization" within the Soviet Communist party: it turns attention away from those instances in which corruption, in its modern conventional sense, has occurred. Minutes of discussions held during the Tenth Congress of Bolsheviks in March 1921, which had directly preceded the NEP (which, according to Jowitt, was haunted by corruption), show an already quite general awareness of the widespread practice of misusing state offices and party positions for private gain. (On this subject see also Rigby 1981.) Aleksander Weissberg-Cybulski, a highly perceptive observer of the Soviet scene in the 1930s, noticed (1951) that Stalin bribed whole professional groups, the security police, lawyers, journalists, writers, and so on, to obtain their cooperation first in collectivization and later in the Great Purges: they were offered special privileges, access to special shops, and much higher incomes. Of course, those who did not cooperate faced probable arrest and death. This is a textbook case of the corruption of entire professional milieux that in prerevolutionary Russia had often possessed, with the obvious exception of the political police, a highly developed sense of professional ethics. These milieux were purged and suffered together with the rest of the population, but the suffering was individual though the rewards were collective.

Thus, during the period characterized by Jowitt as a reversal in the routinization process and, therefore, by a decline in party corruption, from another point of view, the opposite was true: this was the period of the massive corruption of large segments of Soviet officialdom and of Soviet society as a whole by a perverse form of conformism, the demand for absolute, unquestioned obedience to party authority.

In the case of the Communist regime, the two meanings of corruption with which we started this part of the study are clearly in conflict: while defending its charismatic, revolutionary character, the party must corrupt and in other ways victimize society. Jowitt might have confused the issue by using an improper conception of corruption. But here he has put his finger on the right spot.

Purging

Lenin conceived the Communist party as a spiritual order: an organization of individuals who were ready to sacrifice everything for world revolution. When the revolution erupted, this small assault group was faced with three tasks: the first, of winning and maintaining itself in power; the second, of enforcing direct control over the state administration; and the third, of keeping under control its own quickly expanding ranks. The accomplishment of these tasks required the widespread use of coercion, which is not unusual in a revolution. The party could fulfill all these functions to the extent that its leadership had at its disposal a sufficient number of individuals who were entirely, and out of inner conviction, devoted to their duties.

However, conviction in this case could not have been defined either in terms of ideological goals or in terms of the concrete organizational tasks; it required complete devotion to the party: the party sanctified the task. The confession by Andras Hegedus, the Hungarian deputy prime minister during the Stalinist period, illustrates the kind of mentality described here.

> One characteristic [of every party functionary] was his faith in the superiority of the Party above all other things—the mystification of the Party. Orders coming from the Party were, therefore, seen to be received from higher, mystical authority which *had*

to be obeyed unconditionally. The nature of this higher authority [passed] ordinary understanding. One could only believe in its omnipotence and superiority. In other words, our faith in the Party was a deep, subconscious commitment to which everything was subordinated. We lived in a state of ideology, religion, complete dedication. (Urban 1985, 19)

These were the types of people the party needed to maintain its integrity. These were not individuals who saw in the party an instrument for the realization of humanitarian aspirations (such as communism); such people belonged to the past, and in the Bolshevik party, even before the Revolution, were probably a minority. Hegedus, and others like him, perceived the party as an end in itself, an object of veneration.

There were others in the party, and these were more and more numerous, with fairly low ideological but high personal motivations, who joined the party in growing numbers for purely instrumental reasons. Initially, they were acceptable as long as the party could discipline them, although, it must have been very difficult to distinguish in practice between those who treated the party as an end in itself and those who treated it instrumentally as a means of obtaining power and the other pleasant things that the possession of power provides.[2] Thus, the party needed an organizational ethos that would encourage the emotional mobilization of its membership. It also needed specific forms of supervision for turning new members into "deployable agents" and to maintain centralized control over the membership and over the state. The main instrument for preserving the party's integrity was the purge.

One of the chief conditions required for preserving the party's organizational cohesion is the existence of a combat environment: The organization must be in a state of constant mobilization against a real or imaginary enemy. The enemy must be visible, must be believed to be a menace, and eventually must be seen to suffer. Communist propaganda presented the purge, which was nothing more than a victimization of helpless, innocent people, as a heroic and dramatic struggle. The enemy could be anyone, one's parents, brother or sister, or friends. Popular participation in purges created the fanatical devotion that integrated the party and eventually the society around the party. Purges also helped to destroy communal ties: parents feared their children, friends denounced friends, and all found a relief from guilt in the belief that they were serving an objective, universal, and humanitarian purpose. In their faith of the rightness of the cause, they found emotional catharsis and rationalized their cowardice and betrayals. They found peace with themselves but only as long as they were able to preserve a belief in the rightness of the party. Communion in crime, so well described by Dostoyevsky in *The Possessed,* cemented the regime.

An organization such as the Communist party cannot, while in power, accept individuals who possess high moral standards, for moral norms provide external evaluative criteria. A "deployable agent" is one who obeys orders without asking questions. Only a combination of fear, expectation of high reward, and faith in the continuity of Communist rule can achieve unquestioning obedience on a wide scale. In such circumstances power becomes the most important value; all the other values lose importance. Selfless obedience in a power game creates grounds for moral nihilism in its pure form.

When the idea of purge as a control device came to Lenin's mind, he presented it as a way by which the masses could eliminate unsuitable party officials, a spontaneous, uninstitutionalized control over party officials exercised from the bottom. One may doubt whether Lenin was sincere, for he never had much trust in the spontaneity of the masses. Furthermore, the idea of purges fitted Lenin's conception of centralization *qua* decentralization in the party life, that is, the duty to keep superiors informed (see Chapter 3). A purge as an occasion for the party rank and file to inform on their colleagues and lower-level party officials was, in Lenin's view, a decentralization and strengthened, thereby, the centralization.

Purges also served different functions from those Lenin envisaged. In a system organized from the top there is no place for controls from the bottom unless we think of rebellions, and Lenin would be the last to accept rebellion as a legitimate means to control the exercise of the dictatorship of the proletariat by the party. Zbigniew Brzezinski in his classic work on the subject mentioned several functions that purges served.

> Totalitarianism needs the purge. Disloyal and potentially deviant individuals or groups must be unmasked and their followers liquidated. The tensions, the conflicts, and the struggles within the totalitarian system must somehow be released or absorbed lest they erupt into disintegrating violence. The problems of promotion and circulation of the elite must be solved within the monolithic framework of a system which eliminates freedom of choice and free competition. Corrupt and careerist elements must be weeded out periodically in order to maintain revolutionary fervor. The purposes of the purge are accordingly many and varied, and the need for it ever present. The purge thus becomes permanent. (1956, 168; see also p. 36)

This diagnosis may seem incorrect now, for purges are rare, their scope is narrow, and victims may lose their positions but usually survive. Yet, the problem is a real one. After Stalin's death, for reasons to which I shall return shortly, the Communist system could not continue purges. But this renunciation created serious functional problems. Purges preserved the depersonalization of social relations; without them, the road to privatization lay open.

I can see, therefore, one reasonable objection to Brzezinski's opinion: it seems that he overrationalized the choice of culprits in the purge. The rationality of the purge can be found in the process itself rather than in the choice of objects. A purge is an act of terror by a state over society. An act of terror strikes at random. A remark made by N. V. Krylenko, the public prosecutor and later minister of justice, proves that the terrorism was intentional: "We must execute not only the guilty. Execution of the innocent will impress the masses even more" (Corson and Crowley 1985, 74).

The tension between the private and the public, the particular and the general, that a liberal, democratic system resolves with a complex system of counteracting measures based mostly on institutionalized consensus-building processes, is supposedly nonexistent in a Soviet type of political order. The system does not recognize and rejects the private: it identifies the general welfare with the line of the party and with decisions of the party and administration officials; individuals and primary groups are expected to give priority to collective interests not private ones. Yet, people have private interests and, possible ideological objections notwithstanding, usually try to pursue them, even when the supposed general interests are formulated in vague, abstract terms malleable to different interpretations.

The purge, not as a rational strategy aimed at the elimination of a certain kind of people but as an act of blind terror striking people in great numbers in an accidental, unforeseeable way, becomes an instrument to assuring the subordination of individuals and categories of individuals to the will of the party leadership. The victims are "categories of individuals" because groups, understood in any sociopsychological sense, disappear: state terror prevents groups from forming. When terror devastates groups of professionals and employees, people distrust one another; they cannot combine to subvert the execution of orders or to misinterpret them. Purges destroy the private realm by destroying the society as a moral and cultural community. Purges become, therefore, a functional substitute for the rule of law, for the free press, and for other institutions that maintain the demarcation line between the private and the public in a liberal, democratic society. They serve, through the maintenance of depersonalization, to preserve the governability of the Communist system of rule. The only other policy that could serve the same purpose would be permanent shifts of officials from one position to another.

Thanks to purges, individuals and groups were unable to take over institutions and, profiting from the inadequacies of centralized control, manipulate them in their own interests. Individuals feared denunciation, and groups, undergoing a continuous change of membership, had no opportunity to form. Purges were directed against ordinary people, members of the party organization, officials in the state administration, officers' corps in the army, and the security hierarchy itself. Institutions and collectives were rewarded; their staffs were decimated.

When the party renounces purges, the problem of the private and the public reappears under the guise of the privatization of the partisan state. Enemies are no longer easily available, the party loses its ability to maintain "cadre-impersonalism" in its ranks and ceases to be perceived as a "collective charismatic hero." Ideology gradually weakens its grip over people's minds. The party becomes then, to borrow a phrase from Robert C. Tucker, an "extinct movement-regime" (1971, 13).

The purge is a way of assuring the ascendancy of the top leadership, and ultimately of the leader over the society, of maintaining the impersonality of the partisan state. Defending the state against the invasion of the particular, private interests of primary groups is very costly in every sense of the word. Even when the enemy is imaginary, the battle waged against him must be real and will have significant and sometimes prohibitive economic and social costs. According to Swianiewicz (1965), for instance, the use of forced labor in the Soviet Union in 1930 could have been economically rational, but there was a marked decline in its marginal utility in the aftermath of World War II. It is doubtful whether one can apply the notion of economic rationality at all to a system of production that is so wasteful of human resources. (See Rosefielde 1981 and 1983 and the classic account by Robert Conquest [1971].) Even in the purely economic sense, such an assessment raises a number of questions concerning the forgone alternatives. When the mastering of modern technologies requiring the exploitation of human brains and goodwill, rather than muscles, proved to be decisive for economic success, the unsuitability of the Stalinist economic system became evident. But the same applies to the economic system that evolved after his death and still prevails in Communist countries.

The Emergence of Informality

One of the first problems that the Soviet party leaders faced at Stalin's deathbed was how to ensure their survival during the coming months and years of acute factional power struggles.[3] Probably after they neutralized Beria's attempt to seize power, they reached agreement to spare one another's lives. This need not have been technically difficult, in view of Lenin's earlier warnings against the use of physical terror in solving conflicts among the Bolsheviks.

The death of Stalin completely changed the Soviet system of government. It took Stalin many years to win unquestioned authority, although as the true organizer of the party administration he was in a far better position than anybody else was to achieve the aim. Only after Stalin eliminated Bukharin's "rightist deviation" did all top-level party officials owe their positions to Stalin. Even then, until the purges of the late 1930s brought a definite solution to such obstacles, Stalin on some occasions had difficulties in having his proposals accepted by the Politburo and even faced a challenge to his leadership during the Seventeenth Congress.

Whoever wanted to lead the party after Stalin had to win the support of his colleagues: that meant to negotiate, to compromise, and to make promises. Those requirements created favorable conditions for the emergence of an oligarchic system of rule in which the first secretary still had a very strong position but was obliged to take into account the views of other members of the leadership who possessed ample means to stop him whenever it was necessary—even if it included deposing him, as the group led by Brezhnev and Kosygin disposed of Khrushchev in 1964.

This change increased the personal security of incumbents at all levels of the party and state hierarchy. Leaving aside the problem of an external threat, the search for enemies as a technique of control is effective as long as it is possible to accuse any official of being an enemy irrespective of what he does or thinks. When it is not possible, party careers become more stable. People are less personally threatened, have more time to combine in helping one another to carry on with their daily, sometimes official and sometimes private activities, the difference between the two being blurred. In the new circumstances, the party has no use for believers; it needs most of all efficient and discreet operators.

Competition for the leadership positions takes place in the party hierarchy and that of political youth organizations that provide a ladder to those aspiring to the leadership. This is a tough struggle. Some lose their positions, others reach higher positions. But there are rules of the game that everybody has to respect; these are mostly informal but they are known to everybody who enters the party from Communist youth organizations. These rules include loyalty to the organization; observance of the current party line; unconditional obedience to superiors; readiness to disavow losers, good contacts with peers, combined with an ability to intrigue successfully against potential competitors; and, most important, effectiveness in fulfilling tasks, even when their accomplishment requires breaking the law. These rules mean that an individual, in political conflict, has either to act against his own convictions and more probably against the convictions of his social milieu, or he must give up his political ambitions. Every party activist has had to pass a number of such tests before he can rise to high office in the organization.

These rules are typical of most organizations in which people are struggling for power. Less typical is the level of tension between the organization the individual serves and its social environment, the degree of informality of intraparty relations as well as relations with outside organizations, and the fictitious character of most assignments. This last point means that the same result can either be considered a success or a failure according to the interpretation formulated at higher levels.[4] Everything can be manipulated, the party is an artificial world in which all that counts are informal, private connections and secret deals. But even this informality is not unusual. To find the *differentia specifica* of the Communist party, we have to see it from the broader perspective of the political order it has shaped.

It is important to bear in mind that these private connections are not the well-known "old-boys networks" that often improve the efficiency of a bureaucracy in *solving* real-world problems and frequently serve practical public concerns. The intraparty informal networks are different. They are entirely devoted to the internal power game; there is no world outside that game, no external controls, no public opinion, no independent mass media. Briefly, there is no mechanism to assure the accountability of the rulers to the ruled. I shall return to these problems in the next chapters.

The relaxation of tension in the functioning of the party had an important effect upon its relations with its environment, the state administration, the society, and also the international environment, all of which I shall describe very briefly because we shall have occasion to return to them frequently during the course of this study. What is obvious for the evolution of relations between the party and the state administration is that a decline in the importance of ideology means at the same time a decline in the importance of the party relative to the state administration.

The oligarchization of the party leadership stabilized relationships between the partisan state and the society. There were no more witch-hunts, imagined enemies, or persecutions of whole categories of individuals. Some groups were still distrusted or discriminated against, such as, until recently, peasants and the private sector in Poland and in Hungary; but to become an enemy one has had to declare himself as an oppositionist and undertake actions of protest, openly express opinions considered detrimental to the interests of the Communist state, the USSR, or the Communist bloc.

These changes have even found a reflection in the constitutional domain. In the preamble to the Soviet Constitution that was adopted in October 1977 is the statement: ". . . having fulfilled the tasks of the dictatorship of the proletariat, the Soviet state has become an all-people's state" (Unger 1981, 233). There are no more *objective* enemies in the population.

Finally, these developments have changed the perception of the international environment. The fundamental ideological conviction, based on the assumption that the Communist revolution was imminent, first gave way to a more skeptical view that the revolution may be a matter of some future developments, although Communism was still believed to be demonstrably superior to liberal democracy. This change occurred after Stalin's death, in particular during Khrushchev's opening to the West, and continued throughout Brezhnev's period. Obviously, the Kremlin leadership continued to consider the Western liberal democracies a mortal enemy who could be cheated and used in every way possible, but it recognized the need for a modicum of cooperation. Thus, more and more, the ideological conception of a worldwide revolution has been replaced by a conception formulated in terms of the imperial interests of a superpower. Although in principle the entire liberal, democratic world is a foe, the real foes are those countries that oppose Soviet imperial interests, those docilely accepting Soviet claims may even become friends. But now even that revised belief in Communism has been undermined by the inability of Communist states even to keep up with technological developments in the West. The regime has obviously failed to pass Marx's test of superiority.

Like the individuals living in Soviet-type states, the governments of foreign countries are no longer classified as allies or enemies depending on their political regimes. They themselves "decide," in taking positions toward the Soviet Union or its particular foreign policy strategies, whether they are friends or foes. Communism, in dealing with its environment, has become more open to negotiation and compromise in resolving conflict. This does not mean that Marxist-Leninist ideology has lost its relevance for explaining events in the world, but surely its role has changed.

Many authors, in explaining changes in the Communist party, often mention other factors that are not directly central to the points I raise in this chapter. They concern the impact on the institutional system of changes in the population produced by increases in the levels of education, urbanization, and industrialization. This is a highly complex topic, and certainly I cannot treat it satisfactorily in a few paragraphs, but will return to it later. At this point, I shall only try to address one issue briefly: How does the improvement in the education and professional experience of recruits affect the ideological integrity of the party?[5] Within limits, it is obvious that the more educated a party official, the more his attitude toward ideology will be rational and instrumental rather than quasi-religious, the higher his tolerance of differences of opinion, and the more pragmatic his approach to policy problems. These correlations are universally present in Western civilization. However, a pragmatic individual is not necessarily guided by professional criteria; one can imagine situations in which decisions made on professional grounds would be highly impractical for one's career. It seems that a rise in the educational level of the party apparatus contributes to the corruption of the founding principles of this type of regime rather than to the rationality of government policies. Gorbachev's war against the functionaries stems from the realization of this fact and this group, which is part of the problem, tries to subvert his reforms.

Education and the professional experience of party officials have certainly played a role in speeding up processes of routinization, processes that, as Weber and Mosca point out, occur universally in this type of regime. One has to see these developments in the proper perspective. Taking a superficial view, one could claim a causal relationship between the diminishing rates of economic growth apparent at least since the 1950s and the rising level of education in society. In both cases, we are discussing structural tendencies that are not directly dependent on demographic and other changes in the population.

To conclude, the changes in the structure and ethos of the Communist party, that is, in the very core of the Soviet type of political system, have had a decisive impact upon the evolution of the regime. After the heroic period of the Revolution, and a slightly less heroic period of the collectivization and the purges, came the stage of stabilization, during which private concerns revived but without the intermediation of a public domain. Thus, individual interests appeared as family- and peer-group concerns without regard to broader national interests. This resulted in what we are witnessing at present. The system is unable to cope even with those tasks that it had been capable of managing until quite recently, such as the maintenance of a relatively high rate of economic growth, keeping the population in check, and controlling (within limits) its executives.

EIGHT

THE PARTISAN STATE

When in November 1917, the Bolsheviks seized power over the remnants of the old Russian empire, they found themselves face-to-face with the problem of fulfilling their dreams of the dictatorship of the proletariat, of creating Utopia. In the first part of this book, I explored the political philosophy behind their institutional design, the way they came to dominate Russia by initiating the practical implementation of their ideas. Here, I shall discuss the institutional system they created, its evolution over the past seven decades, and the unintended consequences that the Soviet political order produced, in terms of the causes for the specific successes and the ultimate failure of the Communist institutional project.

According to Marxism-Leninism, the seizure of power is only the beginning of the road toward communism. The final stage in social development requires a dramatic change in the social structure, property rights, cultural patterns, and individual consciousness. The doctrine reserved for the revolutionary party the active role in the process of total transformation; it conceptualized the state as an instrument in the hands of the party; it reduced society to a mere object of the vanguard's creative efforts. Given the range and depth of transformation necessary to attain a social order corresponding in any way to Marx's utopian dreams and the qualities ascribed by Lenin to the vanguard, it was necessary to construct the institutional system of the transitory period so as to give the vanguard, that is, the party leadership, maximum freedom of maneuver. The maximization of the power of the party leadership, in terms of the range and specificity of its control over the society and of its ability to exercise arbitrary rule has become, thereby, the *constitutive principle* of the new social order.

As the principal instrument for implementing the party's designs, the state has been granted a special role in the doctrine of the Soviet type of social order. "As such a [reified, hypostatized] power," wrote Herbert Marcuse, "the state, according to Soviet Marxism, becomes the Archimedean point from which the world is moved into socialism, the 'basic instrument' for the establishment of socialism and communism" (1957, 104–5). The fact that the party was to carry out the revolutionary transformation of society through the intermediary of state instrumentalities had important implications. The constitutive principle formulated above contains two postulates: first, the vanguard must obtain full monopoly of control over the administration of the state; second, the state must exercise to the maximum its direct control over all aspects of social life. This chapter will be devoted to the first part of this constitutive principle.

The key to any understanding of the Communist political order is the recognition of the fusion of the revolutionary Communist party and the state. During Stalin's rule, the party and the state were said to form one consistent whole, the state being completely subjected to the party's domination. This was the partisan state in its pure form.[1] Yet, even then the problem was complex. What was at stake was not the maximization of the party's power over the state but of the party leadership's control over the political system. This implied that the leadership needed an instrument of control over the party's functionaries. The secret police, initially called Cheka, among others, fulfilled this role. It was responsible to the party leadership and was controlled in turn through its own party organization.[2] The leadership exercised its control over the political system by exploiting the competition between different organizational hierarchies. At the roots of these apparent party/state redundancies were the imperfections of purely hierarchical controls that can paralyze any system of centralized rule.

After Stalin's death, the problem of the relationship between party and state kept reappearing in both constitutional debate and as a practical problem of responsibility during political crises. The gradual weakening of the role of Marxist-Leninist ideology over the past thirty-five years gave additional importance to this issue. The formula that "the party should guide and the government should govern" means nothing unless the relationship between the Communist party and the state is formally regulated, and the boundaries between the two are clearly drawn and linked. The separation of the party and the state is, however, impossible in a one-party state.

The Revolutionary and the Rational-Legal Legitimation of the Communist Regime

The reemergence in the post-Stalinist period of the state as an institutional complex endowed with some autonomy, and the tensions this development has produced in the working of the system, are a manifestation of a more substantial conflict about the legitimacy of the partisan state, a contradiction between two different (and logically incompatible) doctrines articulated in two different types of political language. There is, first, the revolutionary ideology of Marxism-Leninism with its idiom of class struggle and its dichotomous, Manichaean view of the world in which there is a clear-cut division between the forces of good and the forces of evil. This language justifies the special position of the party within the political system, the arbitrariness of its rule, and restrictions imposed upon human freedom. The language of class struggle in a contest of good and evil comes to the forefront during periods of intensive political struggle when either the party fights to extend its extraordinary prerogatives or when it defends them in the face of mounting opposition.

Simultaneously, and to some extent independently from the first idiom, there is another doctrine and a different idiom. The doctrine is derived from a modified liberal, democratic tradition and its language has a legal rationality.[3] A rational-legal order is one characterized by the rationality of law. Constitutions and other fundamental legal documents, many legal and political science treatises on the Communist state and its institutions, and official discourses on "law and order" use this idiom. The party invokes this doctrine to oppose the political demands of the democratic opposition. It has several variants; the one that is most often used for legitimation purposes consists of a mixture of etatist and nationalist ideologies.[4]

During the initial phases of the Soviet system, rational-legal language played an accessory role to revolutionary slogans. With time, the situation has changed. When General Jaruzelski tried to justify the imposition of martial law in Poland, he paid only lip service to Marxism-Leninism and concentrated on such issues as "the reason of state," "threats to the constitutional order," and eventually "dangers to national existence." Some of his supporters within the political establishment are even ready to go further than that. Consider, for instance, the following explanation, given by one of the prominent political writers in favor of martial law, for what was called "the present crisis in Polish political thinking."

> The crux of the matter is that the present Polish state is grounded in two different and irreconcilable traditions: in the thousand-years-old tradition of political existence, and in the tradition of the revolutionary working-class movement. Meanwhile, there can be no co-existence between national legalism and revolutionary legitimacy. There is a contradiction between legalism which is a necessary condition for state authority, and the principle of effectiveness which is the necessary condition for a victorious revolution. So, we have to choose. And we can choose, when we realize that socialism, though it is undergoing processes of change, cannot be improved by revolutionary methods. Hence, now we must above all rebuild the weakened authority of the state. (Adamski 1984, 90)

Such a statement made by a member of the Communist political establishment in Poland indicates a loss of faith in the Leninist doctrine, which alone can justify his position. Both doctrines are in fact indispensable for the preservation of the Communist system. The advocates of "national legalism" are not calling for democracy; they represent interests generated within the state hierarchy that resent the party's interference as much as they would resent popular control. They need a party to keep democratic forces at bay, but they prefer the party to be relatively weak and submissive. At the same time, both legitimating ideologies are like an ill-fitting shoe: the bureaucratized, routinized party is anything but a revolutionary force; the regime it supervises is anything but a rational-legal order.

The revolutionary doctrine was absolutely dominant during Stalin's rule. But once oligarchic change took place within the party leadership, the doctrine became incompatible with it. The stabilization of the system required the weakening of the revolutionary component and a greater emphasis on routine, everyday operations. However, as the revolutionary ideology is the sole legitimating factor for the positions of power occupied by the most powerful political groups within the system, it is hard to imagine their possible survival without the ideological rationale. Even so, the elite is strongly attracted by the prospects of stabilizing its positions in a rational-legal way. But, having seized power through a revolutionary upheaval, one that involved a cultural and physical annihilation of former elites, the leadership has to live with its original sin.

The problem of the autonomy of the state in a Soviet type of political system is both critical and insoluble. On the one hand, the relative autonomy of the state is functionally indispensable for the efficient exercise of authority. On the other, because of the nature of political controls, autonomy can be achieved only to a limited degree. To this, one important point should be added. In the absence or weakness of all forms of democratic control over the state, should the fetters of party controls be eased, the only outcome would be neither an increase in effectiveness nor an improved efficiency of state activities, but disintegration and disorder countered to some extent by a growing importance of the army or the security police, the obvious reason being that the whole institutional setup that is needed for a responsible government controlled by and accountable to the population is absent.

The Party's Control over the State

Let us take a brief look at the three principal methods of party control over the state administration and at some of their consequences: control through the legal system and legislation, control over personnel assignments (the so-called *nomenklatura*), and control through parallel organizational hierarchies.[5]

The first type of control consists in setting and enforcing legal rules that regulate administrative activities and the relationship between the state administration and the society. This type of control is known to anybody familiar with liberal, democratic political systems. The fact that the Communist system is a one-party system profoundly affects the exercise of this form of control. The logical and practical problem that one-party (revolutionary) rule poses in this context is that the party, by setting legal rules for the administration (and for the citizenry), provides it with autonomy within the bounds those rules define and restricts, by the same token, its own freedom to intervene arbitrarily. This restriction contradicts the very doctrine of the dictatorship of the proletariat on which the system is built.

Even the introduction of the principle, foreign to the liberal, democratic tradition, that only that which is explicitly stated by law is permitted, has not helped resolve the contradiction. Moreover, a reliance on this type of control implies the need to strengthen the independence of courts of justice, further curtailing the party's arbitrary powers. In the 1930s, an effort was made to solve the problem by changing the character of law.

> Soviet criminal law in the early 1930s experienced a sharp decline in the stability of its provisions. Indeed, the very idea that law should have stability was itself attacked. . . . Soviet legal theory at that time proclaimed that in a period of rapid transition to socialism, the law should have maximum mobility and should

be merged with a policy preparatory to its complete "dying out." (Berman 1966, 38)

Under such conditions, arbitrariness replaces law, which stops functioning. The opposition between the rational-legal foundations of the state and the revolutionary effectiveness of the state is one of the fundamental sources of tension within the system.

The party has an extralegal status, that is, its functioning is eventually regulated by some formal and more often informal rules, while its powers of control over the state are not specified in any legal document, even the Constitution, which mentions only its "leading role." *The revolutionary character of the Communist system* consists in the fact that the principal element in the system of power is entirely extralegal in its nature and prerogatives.[6] At the same time, there exists a highly complex, though not internally consistent, system of laws—there are courts and law enforcement organizations.

> There is a multitude of laws and codes which really do operate in the Soviet Union, on the basis of which the courts decide on disputes between citizens, try crimes, resolve labor disputes, and so forth. Nevertheless, the principle of legality does not operate in the Soviet Union; since the regime does not consider itself to be bound by the law, any organ within the system, from a district council to the Supreme Soviet, and any court, from a people's court to the USSR Supreme Court, can—indeed must—violate the law upon orders from its opposite number in the party *apparat*. (Simis 1982, 17)

This arbitrariness has had some positive consequences for the efficiency of the administrative process.

The immense bureaucratization of social life has produced insurmountable problems of coordination. Administrative coordination requires fairly unambiguous, stable, formal rules; administrative efficiency requires that officials be secure while acting within the bounds of these rules. The minuteness of administrative control produces a situation in which no legislative body is able to formulate a legal decree detailed enough to cover all situations facing officials.

Therefore, the "parliament" must delegate an important portion of its legislative powers to the administrative organs themselves. By being unable to control their legal activities, legislative organs de facto relinquish also the right of control over legal acts the administrative organs concoct. Such regulations are produced at all levels of the state hierarchy without regard to legal regulations of a higher order, parliamentary decrees included. The proliferation of these so-called duplicator's laws creates a legal jungle. Moreover, faced with contradictory legal rules and fearing political responsibility for improper actions, officials will do nothing unless they are officially ordered, by their superiors, unofficially ordered by the party, or have a personal stake in the decision. This obviously applies also to the management of industrial and commercial firms.

To this picture of administrative paralysis, one can add the well-known and widely analyzed bureaucratic dysfunctions produced by overcentralization, internal struggles for resources and simple inertia that haunt the Communist system to a greater extent than they do any other regime because it relies so heavily upon bureaucratic devices.

Under such conditions, arbitrary political intervention becomes a necessity. Party leaders suspend some laws while allowing others to be ignored; they give certain state activities an absolute priority in access to resources. The price of this method of crisis management is paid by other sectors of the administration. The combination of the dictatorial powers of the party and the lack of essentially nonpolitical controls over the state results in a crippled legal order: decrees the Communist party introduces through its "legislatures" are subsequently violated in the case-by-case interventions of the top leadership in a so-called rule by exception.

Control through personnel assignments means that all decisions about appointments, advancements to higher position, and dismissal of personnel are made on the basis of opinions formulated by party organizations. Regional or central party committees decide promotions to all positions of authority above a certain level.[7] The party initially justified its interference in personnel decisions by citing imperfections of other types of control over the administration and a fear of subversion. Because the state is a tool serving the dictatorship of the proletariat, individuals who fill important positions within the state administration should be not only professionally competent but also politically reliable. If only politically trustworthy but professionally incompetent individuals are available, mere loyalty should suffice.

This policy, which supports the *nomenklatura* system, has had a long-term, unintended effect in bringing about an erosion in the quality of personnel.[8] Instead of being guided by the imperative to find the best professionally qualified candidates, the party leaders rely upon loyalty. They award jobs to individuals with political merits or a given group (faction),[9] and, in order to enhance its powers, places party members, irrespective of their qualifications, in as many positions as possible. One may be reminded of the familiar institution of spoils in the American political system, but the extent of the practice overshadows anything experienced in the United States. There are other, more striking differences between the Communist system of *nomenklatura* and other familiar forms of control of personnel policies.

> There are three aspects . . . which make of the nomenklatura system in the USSR and other communist countries something qualitatively new and unique among modern societies: first, the concentration of important positions in all official and "voluntary" organizations in the *nomenklatury* of *party* committees; second, the inclusion of *elective* positions (and most of the more important ones are in form elective); and third, the *comprehensiveness* of the system, which omits no position of any significance in society, and thereby converts the occupants of nomenklatura positions into a distinct *social* category. (Rigby 1988, 524)

When the party's ideological integrity weakens, only one step separates this arrangement from the practice of selling administrative positions. Party leaders in Soviet-type states have taken this step on a number of occasions.[10]

Thus, positions in the hierarchy acquire a dual function: on the one hand, they retain their bureaucratic character—that is, incumbents are expected in principle to maintain some standard of administrative performance; on the other, these individuals, as part of the *nomenklatura,* have a *right* (which has no particular relationship to professional experience, educational achievement, personal integrity, or other objective criteria) to occupy their positions. One may be sure, however, that they owe special obligations to their patrons and their peers.

What is exceptional here is not the practice, for this exists everywhere, but its organization and scale: the *nomenklatura* fill virtually all key positions of power and responsibility. What happens, therefore, is the virtual appropriation of state offices and their perquisites by the Communist party, or rather by its leaders and members of the apparatus.

It is obvious that an indispensable condition for organizational efficiency, where other factors are held constant, is that an organization be allowed to conduct its personnel policies according to its own needs and functional criteria. Only then can the organization enforce those attitudes and abilities that are functionally proper for the accomplishment of its tasks and eliminate those that are not. A serious loss of control over personnel policies to an outside agency with different goals and evaluative criteria has a detrimental effect on administrative performance, for the necessary relationship between the contributions of individuals to the organization and their abilities, on the one hand, and the rewards they receive on the other, is broken. When there are no links among goals, incentives, and performance, it is difficult to expect either efficiency or effectiveness.

The third technique of control consists in the coexistence of two parallel and interconnected hierarchies. The party hierarchy exists and functions within the state's administrative hierarchy. Besides these, there is a separate, territorial party hierarchy parallel to the hierarchy of the state administration and to which corresponding levels of the state administration are accountable. The number of hierarchies can be multiplied at will: Communist trade unions, secret police, and so on. In each administrative unit, party cells with executive committees discuss the unit's problems and policies, the activities of particular employees and officials, and broader issues of the current political national and international situation. The executive committee presents opinions about employees, advises management on personnel decisions, and appraises management's performance. The executive committee, through the person of the secretary, is in constant touch with the regional, district, or county committees. Party organizations in big industrial enterprises or other important institutions may even have direct access to the Central Committee.

This arrangement implies that party activists can intervene in matters of concern and eventually impose their will upon the administrative supervisors at each level of the state's administrative hierarchy. Thus, although formal powers to make decisions and take responsibility for those decisions are vested with the administrative hierarchy, the party hierarchy has arrogated to itself the real power to make decisions. The informality of the arrangement shields the party leaders from any responsibility for the decisions they make and "nothing encourages corruption so much as the diffusion and blurring of responsibility" (Vankatappiach 1970, 276).

This effect is often recognized during political crises, and results in a call to return to Lenin's principle, that "the party should guide and the government govern." As I mentioned earlier, no one has ever found an institutional method of assuring a dictatorial position for the Communist party while providing the government autonomy. The two are in conflict—that is, the government can make gains in autonomy only at the cost of the party's control, but then it quickly finds itself under the control of other agencies, a change that affects the working of the political system. The relationship between the party-state complex and society is transformed but there is no increase in the level of public control over the state.

Political Control and Privatization

The forms of control described above have various damaging social consequences. Wherever such control techniques are "successfully" applied, they have destroyed or at least seriously weakened the relevant normative professional ethos. The bureaucratic ethos of public service, wherever it had existed, has disappeared. The same has happened, albeit to a more limited degree, in the legal, academic, and medical professions, with significant loss to civilization. The most serious effects of these control techniques may not be, therefore, a current loss in efficiency, but a long-term debasement of the habits, norms, and values that ultimately sustain a civilized society. The political establishment in all Communist countries officially recognizes and often openly discusses some of these problems. Unfortunately, like some primitive peoples who, it has been said, fail to see a relationship between sexual intercourse and the birth of a child, the party's leaders encounter great difficulties in establishing a connection between the institutional design of the regime and its practical consequences.[11]

The second and third forms of control are among the principal contributors to the virtual ascendancy of informal relations in the party-state complex. Let us examine this result from the perspective of two types of individual roles that are crucial in this context and of interests related to these roles: that of a party activist in the state administration, and that of a functionary in the party bureaucracy (a so-called *apparatchik*).

The party closely monitors administrative activities both externally and with the help of party activists employed by the agency in question. The activists may fulfill their tasks out of loyalty to the party (belief in its charismatic powers), out of fear, or out of concerns for their own well-being or careers. Since Stalin, the first two kinds of motivation have lost much of their relevance. Party activists have an obvious vested interest in defending the role of the party because its existence may be crucial for their social advancement. Too aggressive a defense, however, may damage their status among their colleagues and detract from their professional position.

For a party activist interested in a professional or a political career, the best strategy is to try to strike a balance between the requirements of the party apparatus and the expectations and needs of the professional milieu. The way he does this will, in turn, depend upon two factors: the political attitudes prevailing in the work milieu or the power of the party relative to the power and influence of his professional milieu; and on his career orientation, that is, whether he is professionally oriented, politically oriented, or connected with the security services. The former factors depend upon the general political situation. The latter, which is influenced to a degree by the former, one can formulate in the following way: an activist may treat his party work as useful for his professional career, he can use his professional activities in his party career, or he can have connections with the secret police and his behavior will depend upon the nature of the connections. These factors can sometimes be successfully accommodated in a party career.

The party activist may represent some specific interest of the party in his professional milieu and, to legitimize and/or establish his position within that milieu, he will articulate some of its interests to the party or promote through the party the interests of those individuals whose support is crucial for his position. Whether he prefers to legitimize his position in the group and articulate some of its interests or to establish his position by buying off key individuals depends upon the integrity of the group. The outcome in both cases is different: In the first, we have the articulation of some functional interests and concerns to the party hierarchy; in the second, we face a textbook case of political corruption. In both cases, however, the party activist must make a compromise with his work group on the one hand and with responsible *apparatchik*s on the other. His career prospects depend in large measure on how well he does it.

Party functionaries are as interested in arranging informal deals with party officials in the administrative units under their supervision as are the party activists themselves. The responsibilities of party functionaries are not clearly defined, but they must produce results without committing political blunders. They can obtain results only with the help of those they are supposed to supervise. Without such help they are ineffective and risk losing their positions in the apparatus or succeed in involving the party hierarchy in a costly battle against officials and party activists of the agency in question, which is usually detrimental to their own standing. Thus, an accommodation is desired by both sides. This results in bonds of mutual dependence that unite party *apparatchik*s with party activists outside the party's central or regional organization. The functionaries are able to produce results that please their superiors; the activists can gain some legitimation for their position and/or through their cronies to establish their position in the agency. These informal networks also serve to protect executives in the administration against responsibility for errors of their own or someone else's making.

In periods of stabilization, such compromises can work fairly well, helping sometimes to articulate interests that under different conditions would not have access to the decision-making centers. They do at least assure control and stabilization through the corruption of the professional milieu. During periods of political crisis, the intricate system of deals and tacit understandings often disintegrates, eventually to be rebuilt during a return to stabilization.

Two points should be made explicit about the working of these arrangements. First, they result in an informal decentralization of the system: lateral connections over which the political center has little control start to play a role in policy making. Second, they are the product, and they further contribute to, the routinization of the party: both sides to such agreements treat the party instrumentally. The party's ésprit de corps undergoes further disintegration.

The first point deserves some comment. The ability of a professional group or a sector in the administration to articulate its interests and to influence outcomes depends upon the role it plays in the social and political system and upon its ability to act as a group vis-à-vis the party. Only then will it have enough power to force the other side to take its concerns into account.

There is, however, another powerful, informal mechanism acting in the party-state complex that helps to preserve its vertical character: patronage. Contributing extensively to the development of patron-client relations under communism is the *shortage* of resources, an inherent feature of the Soviet type of economic order. By far the best-known analysis of the phenomenon is offered in Janos Kornai's book, *Economics of Shortage* (1980). When the means necessary for the performance of administrative tasks are in short supply, people responsible for the execution of the tasks turn to those who control the distribution of the needed resources. If those in control occupy positions at the same hierarchical level, they will tend to develop an informal relationship regulated by the norm of reciprocity. If they occupy superior positions in the party-state

The Partisan State

complex, the officials from inferior levels will try to enter an informal relationship of a clearly asymmetrical nature. Jacek Tarkowski described the motives of those in high administrative or party positions who assumed the role of a patron.

> The systemic principle of consensus and unity, the principle of subordination of particular interests to national interests, and a ban on factional activities make the organization and effective use of associational interest groups very difficult or simply impossible. In this situation, mobilization of influence on a personal basis seems to many leaders a safe and effective way of consolidating their power. They look for people who, although located below them in the hierarchy of the superorganization, control important resources. These may be material resources, such as jobs, hard currency, construction capabilities, and luxury goods, or they may be influence and control over particular organizations, branches or regions, especially over the party, administrative, and economic apparatus. In spite of the high degree of centralization and concentration of power at the top of the superorganization, the support of the lower levels is of crucial importance for the central leaders. (1983, 503)

Patrons may use these informal networks to promote the interests of the center(s), but it is more likely that they use them to advance their own political interests.

The picture presented above would be excessively simplified if we do not take into consideration some secular trends that have appeared in Communist systems after Stalin's death, namely, the gradual deterioration of the party's influence within the system. In some Communist countries, this tendency has gone further than it has in others. The best indicator that such a change has taken place can be found in the domain of the *nomenklatura*. At the beginning, it was the exclusive preserve of the party apparatus; secret police or army officers were spending their professional lives in their respective organizations and eventually retiring. At some point, however (in Poland this occurred at the end of the 1960s), the security establishment broke its isolation and started invading the foreign service, foreign trade administration, scientific institutions, and other potentially attractive areas. The *nomenklatura* has become a shared preserve. In the 1980s in Poland, the army officers' corps joined in.

Let us distinguish now between the pure party career, and the mixed party career. The typical pure party career would start in a high school with a boy or a girl joining and becoming an activist in a Communist youth organization. (As is generally known, the party's recruitment procedures are heavily biased against women, so I shall dispense here with she or he, for in reality, it is nearly always he.) Then it would continue through the youth movement hierarchy, as the activist undertakes university studies and joins the organization at a higher level, or directly with the local party organization. In either case the person's whole career is spent within the party and/or its auxiliary organizations. Such a person can be "delegated," even for long periods of time to positions outside the party hierarchy, but even in those positions an individual is only a party *apparatchik*.[12]

The mixed career is typically a mix of professional and political careers. A person following such a career has a mixed allegiance and a confused sense of identity. He may be basically oriented to a professional career and may use his party connections only for fast promotion, but at the same time he may be willing to perform party functions professionally. The preponderance of individuals representing the mixed career type over the pure career type in the party leadership is a good indicator of the weakening role of the party in the political system.

Poland provides an extreme example of this trend, which is less advanced in other countries. If we examine the composition of the Politburo and the Secretariat of the Central Committee elected at the Tenth Congress of the Polish United Workers' Party in 1987, only six out of the twenty-four members of these bodies had spent their entire careers in the party, but among those six only two had any political experience and influence, the other four simply added to the decorum. Three-quarters of the top party functionaries represent the mixed type of political career. Ten years earlier the situation would have been completely reversed. Since the Tenth Congress, because of personnel changes introduced by the party's Central Committee, the situation has turned even more to the disadvantage of the dedicated party careerist.

These trends are very important, but they should not be misread. In most Communist countries, with the exception of Poland and Hungary, the party administration still plays an important role. The central party organs remain the main supervisory institutions in the system. The question is, Who controls the functionaries and the central party institutions? I would suggest that the administration has less and less control over them. More and more, it is a coalition of outside interests that predominates.

Let us look at the problem of economic reform and economic policies from another angle. As I suggested earlier, in the partisan state the important groups are those that are derived from the structure of the state itself: the place occupied by a group in the party-state complex and the type of relationship between this complex and society determine a group's influence and its way of using its influence. The important groups are those involved in the central decision making and policy implementation. The ruling elite is internally stratified both in terms of the overall hierarchy of the party-state complex and in terms of the less formal hierarchy of priority among administrative units. In the latter case, one can stratify administrative sectors according to the size of their budgets, and even more accurately according to the sensitivity of their budgets to the policies of governmental savings; by the ability to obtain special privileges for their employees in terms of health care, recreation, and access to consumer goods that are in short supply, at special prices; and finally, by their access to the *nomenklatura,* that is, by their ability to place their career employees in other attractive sectors of the state complex, such as the diplomatic service. I have already tried to characterize the way a market-oriented reform could affect the interests of some of the key groups in the establishment. Now I shall try to look at the issue from a different perspective.

The structure of the partisan state generates the political establishment. Some groups within this establishment have a closed, corporate character, others are open. One of the more interesting questions is the recruitment of the members, a great majority of which, virtually all except some window-dressing "nonpartisan comrades," belong to the party, obviously the major channel of recruitment.

The weakening of the party and the disastrous failure of ideology, at least in some Communist countries, made the tasks of control and coordination urgent. Until recently, the informal networks partly took care of fulfilling these tasks. Thanks to those networks, certain things that would not have been done in their absence are indeed done; the networks are certainly part of the system. But, in the informal area between the party and the state administration, a massive process of the appropriation of state resources for private use has developed.[13] Maria Hirszowicz summed up the problem in the following understatement:

> In extending the advantages of their official positions to practices which were illegal, officials were helped by the general habit of bending rules and cutting corners. Since almost all of them did it in the course of their official activities, many of them found it easy to do for their own personal benefit. In an atmosphere of universal deception, that is falsifying statistics, patching up official reports, and entering fictitious figures in order to obtain extra funds for wages or investments, party and state officials became used to irregularities, and to some extent did not perceive that many of their activities were corrupt. (1986, 139)

All actors behave rationally, but their rational behavior only helps to further their private interests to the detriment of the public interest and induces profound irrationality in the social order. It is virtually impossible to formulate an overall rationality for the Communist system in terms that would not be particularistic. The system was designed under the assumption that it was impossible to construct a system of interactions that could combine private motives with the public interest: outcomes are good only when motives are good. Therefore, when it comes time to defend the public interest against the invasion of privately motivated actions, Communists and the party are helpless, there is no institutional arrangement to provide such protection. They can only turn to the old liberal precepts and "correct" Leninist principles, a tactic chosen until recently by the "reformist" leaderships of Hungary and Poland and used even longer in the Soviet Union.

NINE

FACTIONS, INTEREST GROUPS, AND THE POLITICAL PROCESS

In the political order dominated by a state accountable only to the Communist party leadership, the interests represented in an institutionalized way are only those generated within the realm of the party-state complex, that is, the partisan state. Other interests such as professional associations of lawyers, economists, engineers, and so on, may eventually have an indirect and less systematic access through "associations of higher social utility," which may be represented at parliamentary hearings or at the plenary sessions of the Central Committee of the Communist party. It should be added, however, that basic interests truly relevant in the Soviet system are articulated or attended to secretly, never *publicly*. This is probably one more indicator of their marginal legitimacy to the society.

A political system that is organized from the top down must have at its disposal a powerful apparatus of coercion because it does not have enough voluntary cooperation from the ruled. The state as an institutional domain that is not directly dependent on the society develops interests of its own that do not coincide with those of the population.[1] It is possible to assess the discrepancy between the priorities of the state and those of the society only when one considers the stable priorities of the state and their social relevance. An obvious and generally acknowledged priority that has no serious justification in terms of public interest has been the absolute priority accorded to heavy industry in all investment programs and the systematic neglect of consumer-goods industries. To conceal this bias and to preserve a socially unresponsive form of political domination, the rulers maintained a powerful apparatus of repression, justifying its existence by the Marxist-Leninist claim of the threat of the "capitalist conspiracy" to the existence of the new "workers' state."

Consequently, it was also necessary to build powerful armed forces to spread the revolution and/or to defend the Communist order against the external, and sometimes an internal, enemy. The mission of the army varies in time but in all Communist regimes it has never lost its special position within the system of priorities. In a social order organized around the repression of independent internal and external forces, and for a dictatorial system of this type, everything that is independent from direct political control is a source of threat. Hence, the functional sectors directly connected with the use of coercion and the suppression of autonomy must be especially privileged.

The political core of the hierarchical instruments of control consists of the *apparatus* of the party: that is, the party's administration. This, as I explained earlier, permeates the whole complex of the state, though it is accompanied sometimes by auxiliary hierarchies such as, for instance, the Main Political Administration of the army. The apparatus consists of two sets of positions: those to which one is "elected" and those to which one is nominated. "Elections" are, in this case, a ritualized form of nomination, but elected positions are leadership positions and they provide incumbents with some autonomy and good career prospects.

The focus and source of power in the Soviet type of regime is the center. The institutional meaning of the term *center* changes in time. I understand by this term a complex of institutions that provides guidance and coordination to the system of government. Traditionally, different bodies fulfill those functions in the Soviet type of political regime. They are part of the Central Committee of the Communist party, being to some extent the Central Committee itself, but most of all they consist of the Secretariat, the Politburo of the Central Committee, and the office of the first secretary, which must be considered separately. Sometimes this institutional complex is well integrated and disciplined and can be treated in its entirety as the center; when it disintegrates and succumbs to the influence of outside groups, the concept of the center must be defined more narrowly. I would relate such variations to the mechanism of the political cycle in the partisan state, a topic to which I shall return in the next chapter.

The society can have varying degrees of autonomy. Its needs and interests often find expression only when statistical data of mortality rates or of the level of productivity in the economy force the leaders to envisage the possibility that their survival depends to some extent upon the survival of the society too. Sometimes it becomes vocal by rebelling. But more often, it has been the political activities of émigrés in the West and programs on foreign radio stations that have forced the authorities to respond. A society can sometimes preserve or create independent institutions that are able, within limits, to speak out on its behalf, enhancing self-confidence and integration outside the realm of the partisan state complex.

What is striking here is that in the "normal" functioning of a Communist system, these pressures have usually had little impact upon strategic decision making. Only when pressure becomes open revolt that authorities have difficulties containing, will serious policy changes take place. The society may also be taken seriously into account in a deep economic crisis, when change requires broad social cooperation. But, as a Hungarian political scientist remarked, ". . . activities aimed at representing interests and opinions coming from under appear as disturbing factors against the detailed political control that has everything decided upon well in advance" (Bihari 1986, 304). Thus, for the moment, we can forget society and focus upon the institutional core of the Communist political order, that is, upon the crises-generating mechanisms in the social order.

The oligarchization of the system of power that occurred after Stalin's death led, on the one hand, to the growing "formalization" of relations among the main political actors and, on the other, to an escalation of informal "combinations." The formalization of political influence emerged with the growing role of the articulation and negotiation of interests within the setting of the Central Committee. The main segments of the party and the state administration and some professional groups in the society have direct access to the Central Committee; that gives them some influence. Some especially privileged segments can exercise influence at the level of the Politburo: the Economic Planning Commission, which represents the economic administration rather than the economy itself, the armed forces, the security establishment, and the foreign service. Being represented in the Politburo provides an institutional complex with a rather more symbolic than real political importance. The weight of the security and defense interests in the Communist system of power is independent of their formal presence in that body.

To the extent that the political process in a Soviet type of regime takes on institutionalized forms, mutual relations among the main actors within the partisan state are negotiated and conflicts among them resolved at the level of the central party organs. In maintaining the system's governability the fundamental task for the party leadership is to keep the control hierarchies in check. Mutual animosities and competition among some of the hierarchies, between for instance the Ministry of Defense and the Ministry of Internal Affairs and even between the regular militia and the secret services, facilitate to some extent the fulfillment of the task. These animosities allow one hierarchy to neutralize or check upon the activities of another one, a system of checks and balances in reverse. They thus help make the system more manageable.

We can conclude, therefore, that under the monolithic appearance of the partisan state there is constant political struggle among the groups created by the state that are striving to control important policy areas. We can also conclude that some policies and developments that may be regarded as accidental or caused by an error of judgment are outcomes of the structural regularities of the system. We may talk about structural regularities if we establish empirically that when a certain factor occurs, under a given set of circumstances, a specific set of consequences shall follow; that is, other factors held constant, the system responds to a set of inputs with a predictable and fairly uniform set of outputs.

FACTIONS AND INTEREST GROUPS

I shall discuss the political process in the Communist political system in terms of two distinct types of interests: those of political factions and those of interest groups. Both have their roots in the structure of the partisan state.[2]

The distinction between factions and interest groups corresponds to the classic distinction between two elements of the political process: interests that are related to the intentions of a given group of persons to seize power or to improve the probability of their seizing power, and the functional interests of groups in the social division of labor that engender efforts to increase influence upon policy decisions of the state and to strengthen the bargaining position of a particular group. There is no doubt that the connotation of these distinctions is different in the Soviet type of political system and in liberal, democratic regimes.

The turning point in the history of factions in Soviet politics came with the Tenth Congress of the party in March 1921, discussed in Chapter 4. The resolution, "On the Unity of the Party" brought about, though not immediately, an end to interparty ideological debates, to electoral platforms, and to any influence the rank and file party members could have had upon the selection of party leaders and on policy decisions within the party. These results contributed in turn to the bureaucratization of the party and the ritualization of the ideology, so that political influence was restricted to those occupying the top positions within the party-state hierarchy. The rank and file members of the party, deprived of all influence, became passive observers of political struggles they were usually unable to comprehend. Power ceased to be perceived as an instrument for the attainment of important social goals and became completely detached from other cultural values.

The resolution did not manage to erase political rivalries within the leadership, although the present-day factions are very different from those Lenin sought to abolish. By the term *faction* I understand an informal, loosely structured group of people who occupy positions that cut across the hierarchies of the party and of the state, are bound with ties of loyalty and obedience to one of the members of the top party leadership, and who intend to secure their positions and/or move up the power ladder. The basic rule governing the relationship between the leader of a faction and his supporters is the *principle of reciprocity*. His supporters offer to the leader their loyalty, obedience, and political support and in exchange receive security of position, prospects of further advancement, and other special favors. This is the classical patron-client relationship: the exchange of support and obedience for favors and protection.

The leader can use the faction in a political struggle, though open factional wars are usually avoided, because the party leadership must present an image of unity. More often he uses the faction to fulfill his political tasks within the party and to extend his influence: it provides him with the information and resources necessary to get things done. Factions are, therefore, not only instrumental in power struggles within the party but are also important tools of control exercised by members of the party leadership over the party-state complex or fragments of it and are an important part of the mechanism of distribution of goods and values in the system—on this subject see Tarkowski (1983).

Long ago, Kremlinologists noted that party activists advancing in the hierarchy draw behind them a "tail" of their subordinates whom they try to place in those positions they patronize. A numerous and well-placed clientele is an important resource for a leader in political infighting. Moreover, the power of a party leader grows as he is able to increase his influence over decisions about personnel. Factions are not channels for the articulation of group interests: the leader takes care of the interests of his clients on an individual basis. A reliable faction member is someone who forgets about most other concerns except the wishes of his patron and his own private interests.

In a sense, factions are embryonic political parties. Political parties grow from informal coteries of people brought together by common interests and who seek to win and wield power. The difference is that from the faction nothing of structural significance is likely to develop. Political parties in liberal, democratic states organize themselves around electoral processes. They strive to win the support of the electorate for their candidates and their programs. Their field of action is public opinion. In the classical Communist system, elections are a ritual supposed to provide appointments and self-appointments with the illusion of legitimacy. Factions do not formulate programs, neither do they organize public opinion; in fact, they carefully avoid public exposure. (In the last part of this study, I shall return to the problem of the recent changes that have occurred in the Communist bloc countries.)

In the absence of true elections, there is no need to formulate political programs. A program implies a commitment, something a reasonable faction leader will make only under exceptional circumstances, such as an open struggle for power. Usually, factions coalesce around a leader and not around a program. Relations are personal and private. When one faction strives to win broader popularity it most often spreads gossip, leaks, and political jokes enhancing its own image in society and belittling its competitors. In official presentations, the fiction of the "moral and political" unity of the monolithic party are maintained. Only the first secretary can make public pronouncements, on behalf of the whole party, that provide a binding interpretation of the current party line. A member of the leadership who too openly distances himself from this fiction will do himself no good because other members of the leadership will consider any action that extends social participation in political life through even limited appeals to public opinion a major betrayal. Such lack of discipline among individual members of the leadership would menace the long-term interests of the whole political establishment and is the best indicator of the weakness of the first secretary. Open conflicts in the Politburo are rarely articulated publicly. When they cannot be contained within the Politburo, they spread to the Central Committee and only then will the public become involved. Such was the situation in the conflict within the Hungarian leadership in the mid-1950s, the Polish leadership in 1956, in Dubcek's ascent to the position of first secretary in 1967, and in the highly publicized dismissal of Boris Yeltsin from the Soviet Politburo during the struggle of the reformist group against Ligachev. Generally speaking, reformers are always eager to extend their political participation because they know that it is their only chance for success. These examples concern, however, critical situations in the history of communism. As long as society is excluded from political participation, which is the key to the institutional design of the Communist order, factions will remain personal coteries, and interfactional struggles will remain interpersonal intrigues, confined to the back rooms of central party and state institutions.

Similarly, interest groups are not, in the Soviet type of state, what they are in a liberal, democratic state. As Leonard Schapiro remarked, the effective functioning of interest groups, in the sense in which it has been accepted by liberal political doctrine, requires a number of conditions: (1) the right of citizens, unrestricted by any party or state power, to associate freely and undertake voluntary collective action, (2) the existence of a lively public opinion that can be easily mobilized to put effective pressure upon the government, (3) a high standard of professional ethics among lawyers, medical doctors, scholars, and other leaders of public opinion, and (4) the availability of material resources independent from the political authority (1972, 7–8). Most of these conditions do not appear in the Communist system of rule.

The monopolization of control by the party over the state, and of the partisan state over the society, has effectively eliminated the right of citizens to associate in defense of commonly held values. It has suppressed public opinion, subjected all material resources to political control, and initiated the political and moral corruption of professional groups. Most of all, however, when all concerns other than those of the top leadership are considered private and, therefore, illegitimate, there is no place for formally legitimate interest groups. When, during the last decade, some genuine representation of interests was (quasi-) institutionalized in Poland and Hungary, the political system was destabilized but policy priorities were not significantly affected. In the case of Hungary, see the contributions of Mihaly Bihari and Bela Pokol (in Andorka and Bertalan 1986). Both authors, Bihari in particular, see no possibility for the representation of democratic interests within a one-party system. In such circumstances, the only really important interest groups are those that emerge within the structures of the party-state complex.

Yet, some sectors in the administration that are crucial to the functioning of the Soviet type of state, enjoy a broad autonomy because of their importance and are able directly or indirectly to affect policies bearing upon their well-being. Obviously, the more these sectors turn into interest groups and become directly involved in the political process, the less they are executive instruments of the party and government. This brings us back to the topic already mentioned and that will reappear later in the context of this discussion, the meaning of the notion of the center. The greater the autonomy of the executive instrumentalities, the weaker the center, the more power will be seized by executive hierarchies and informal groups.

For several reasons the economy draws the attention of all factions, irrespective of the formal responsibilities of their leaders. First, the domain of economic policies is the area of *positive* action: economic policies and decisions about changes in economic structures have far-ranging social and political consequences that might threaten the position of particular factions or even the whole leadership group. To watch this area attentively is the equivalent to an instinct for survival. Second, until recently, Communist leaders considered the accomplishment of economic tasks to be the true measure of success in the Soviet regime and a proof of its superiority over the liberal, democratic alternative and to contribute to this noble cause gave prestige. Third, an interest and some competence in economic matters has been beneficial to the image of the leader, whatever his true formal responsibilities in the party administration might be. Fourth, economic policies directly affect the distribution of material resources in the society. In this context, the importance of a faction depends upon the influence it can exert in the process of economic decision making: it can use this influence to "buy" the support of regional or functional interest groups.

It is worth remarking that none of the interest groups belonging to the core of the party-state complex has a direct connection with the economic domain, though it is of importance to all of them. Most industrial interests, though influential, are articulated to the political system indirectly through factions and interest groups in the state administration. Only the politically dominant industrial sectors have direct access through the regional state administration and the central planning hierarchy. The economic hierarchy can exert influence by using the discretion of its different levels to reinterpret orders coming from the top in accord with their interests, a strategy that, obviously, contributes to ungovernability. Thus, paradoxically, the area of economic policy is much less professionalized and specialized than are most other policy areas in the Soviet type of state. It is also much more politicized.

We are faced with an entirely different situation when we consider the domain of the state's interests in terms of security and defense for which policy making is much more autonomous and specialized. Interest groups, that is, the relevant administrative sectors are hidden under the veil of state secrets, and themselves decide what should be secret and what should not. They directly control the instruments of coercion, which are strategic resources in any political order that has been organized from the top down, and they also exercise a measure of control over the processes of communication within society by censoring the mass media and private correspondence and to a large extent controlling the information that reaches the top decision makers. Being keys to successful repression and suppression, such groups are fairly autonomous within the political system and use the license for their own purposes.

In the economy and in security factions have to cooperate directly with major interest groups seeking support and offering theirs in return. But the relationship between factions and interest groups is different in each case. A striking example of the deliberate subordination within the party-state complex of economic goals to political interests is the lack of autonomy in the economic domain that manifests itself in the sensitivity of economic policies to all changes in the political domain.

This lack of autonomy is also apparent in personnel decisions, which in the economic sector are subject to diverse political influences. The economy is virtually colonized by the party administration, security organs, and the army, that is, the sectors realizing the state's purposes, all of which have a large measure of effective control over their own personnel decisions. (That does not mean, however, that the criteria of political allegiance are not important in making personnel decisions. Those who are known for having political opinions considered inappropriate are passed over or fired. To have the right political opinions is one of the rules of the game. But, once political requirements are met, decisions on advancement are made on the basis of internal considerations.) Relationships between factions and economic interest groups are usually asymmetrical; the relationship between factions and the core interests is more like that of a true partnership.

Factions can increase their political relevance by using various strategies. They can increase the scope and importance of the positions occupied by their people by extending influence upon personnel decisions whenever possible. They can broaden their scope of control by seeking the support of functional interest groups. They can try to bring about changes in the structure of the leadership to increase the value of resources under their control. The first two strategies are in fact *opportunistic:* they do not directly result in, and are not aimed at, systemic changes. The third implies a change in the system of political priorities and can be called, therefore, a *reformist* strategy. Opportunistic strategies involve no risk and are commonplace in the history of Soviet-type politics. Reformist strategies are used by those political groups that attempt to promote market-oriented economic reforms and by other similar groups, such as the one led by Piotr Jaroszewicz that attempted to strengthen governmental positions at the cost of party positions by reforming the state administration in Poland in 1975. The adoption of a reformist strategy by a faction threatens other factions and some interest groups and eventually leads to a countercoalition that can also articulate a reformist ideology, but will at the same time subvert the practical measures of the reform. Thus, a reform movement is often stultified before an open conflict is created in the leadership of the party.

Most factional struggles are positional wars: The opponents try to defend positions under their control and, whenever possible without undertaking a risky conflict, broaden the policy areas under their control. Commonly other groups treat an excessively brutal action as breaking the rules of the game and undertake a counteroffensive. A system of authority built on the rejection of the idea of the "sovereignty of the people" cannot be accountable before the society. It has to maintain the appearance of a monolith and pretend that it always adheres to the "one best way": it is an order without reasonable alternatives. An escalation of factional struggles to the point that they become public creates the danger, as has been shown on a number of occasions, of the possible reemergence of the society as an independent actor in the political arena. No faction or functional group in the Communist political establishment desires such an outcome.

Factions in the leadership of the party run a certain risk if they cooperate too closely with core interest groups. First, these groups are too specialized and conscious of their importance to be of direct political advantage to leadership factions. Second, their importance and autonomy makes them dangerous in a power struggle. The importance of the minister of internal affairs, Mieczyslaw Moczar, in Poland during the 1960s, and the successful subordination of the party apparatus by the army in Poland in the 1980s are good examples of the risks involved. Since the instrument of the purge has been abandoned and the party's position has started to deteriorate, such gradual emancipation of core interest groups has become unavoidable and creates problems with political integration and overall policy coordination within the partisan state.

Party Apparatus, Security Organs, and the Army

Let us examine in turn each of the three core interest groups of the Communist state: the party apparatus, the security organs, and the army. I shall analyze other aspects of the party apparatus in greater detail later, while discussing the succession of leadership groups in Poland; here I shall describe briefly its place in the political structure and its functions. As mentioned earlier, the party apparatus is a powerful tool of control used by the leadership to supervise all party and state activities. It is also the most important channel for the selection of the party leadership; top party officials who attained their positions through other channels are usually outsiders without real political influence, unless they represent the security establishment or the army.

Careers in the apparatus start quite early in the political youth organizations. Future party *apparatchik*s undergo a process of effective socialization in the specific and highly homogeneous ethos of party life. Because of the social isolation of the milieu, most of their friends and colleagues are party activists and officials. This socialization and community of experience creates an ésprit de corps and respect for such norms of behavior as loyalty to superiors and to the party as a whole, discretion and discipline, and an ability to get things done regardless of the legality of the methods used. With this background, an activist who is later directed by the party to work outside of it remains, still, only a party activist delegated to accomplish an outside task.

The party apparatus is, therefore, a corporate group. It has a closed, secretive character, its hierarchy consists of levels of initiation at the bottom of which are rank and file members who know hardly anything. It is seldom an object of empirical research and, when it is, usually only the lower, if not the lowest, levels are studied. Then only the most trivial results of the research are ever published.

The political interests of the party apparatus are mainly defensive. It tries to defend its role as the main recruitment channel for the top leadership; it also strives to defend its right to supervise other functional areas within the partisan state and to control personnel policies in these areas through the system of *nomenklatura*. But most of all, it must defend Marxism-Leninism as the one official doctrine, for only this ideology provides the legitimation and a rationale for the privileged position of the party and its functionaries. This is easier to achieve in the Russian Federation of Soviet Socialist Republics (RFSSR) where the party can make a more convincing link between national interests and the Communist regime than it can in other Soviet republics. It is more difficult still to make this link in other countries of the bloc, where the regime is a tool of external political, economic, and cultural domination. There, the only available argument is "Without us you would have been subjected to direct Russian rule." But the party cannot use the argument too openly, lest that undermine the claim that ties between Communist countries are based upon "friendship and a community of interests." In the face of growing economic problems, an effective defense of apparatus' claims and interests has become more and more difficult.

The army, like the other two main pillars of the Communist state, is also isolated from the society. But this isolation is somewhat diminished by the fact that it is based on conscription, that is, all young males who reach a certain age and are reasonably healthy must serve. Therefore, the army is infused with a diversity of opinions and attitudes that are more representative of society than those to be found in the security services or the party. This diversity, however, is to be found more often among the rank and file soldiers than among noncommissioned officers and officers, and rarely in the separate caste of generals and, in the USSR, marshals, the latter being especially closed and impermeable to external influences.

The army is distinguished from the other two hierarchies in that it has an independent basis of legitimation. Every army is based on a patriotic, or nationalist if one prefers, system of values and so shares at least a fragment of its value system with society. It, therefore, enjoys more trust and sympathy in society than its partners in the system of power.[3] This creates some problems for the integration to which I shall return later, of the Soviet bloc as a whole, and to the integration of the Communist system of power in particular countries. On a number of occasions, the Soviet party leadership has perceived the army, with its independent legitimation, as a potential threat to the more specifically "Communist" hierarchies (Kolkowicz 1967). Thus, the army is subject to special political controls to prevent its excessive autonomy.

But too direct a political control would impair the efficiency and discipline of the army.[4] One political form of control of the party over the military is the Main Political Administration, with its separate hierarchy drawn mostly from officers trained also as political officers. Many officers who reach the top positions of command in the army have seen service with the Main Political Administration (Colton 1979, 90–95). This service, like membership in the Communist party, socializes the officers corps politically.

The Main Political Administration seeks to reduce the role of nationalism as a source of integration in the officers corps and substitute for it or, at least, supplement it with "Soviet patriotism," or "internationalist," Marxist-Leninist "class" ideology.[5] The intention is to diminish the probability of fraternization between the army and the masses during revolts against the authorities and to preserve the loyalty of the army during periods of heated social conflict.

In addition, the army's own counterintelligence and, externally, the security services supervise the armed forces. Control by the latter started in 1918 when the *Osobyi Otdel* (Special Department) was created in the Cheka to supervise the army (see Corson and Crowley 1985, 39–42). The external control has been especially resented by the army.

According to Roman Kolkowicz, the army has the following corporate interests. It is interested in maintaining a high level of investment in heavy industry, the sector most directly tied to the satisfaction of the military's material needs. It is interested in assuring the high level of military expenditure that is obtainable only under conditions of international tension. It strives to defend the professional and corporate autonomy necessary to fulfill its professional tasks: to formulate strategic military doctrines, to devise defense plans, and to conduct necessary preparation (1971, 140–45).

In view of recent developments, it is possible to amend this list somewhat. A change in the strategic conception of defense, with less reliance on the ability to deliver the first conventional attack, makes the army more dependent on modern technology and less on heavy industry. But it is unlikely that the initiative to change the focus of its interests would come from the army; in fact it came from Gorbachev's civilian advisers.

Political control, the purpose of which is to link the defense of the Communist system with the army, does not necessarily diminish its ability to press for its group interests. The reconciliation of the two interests is more natural in the Soviet Union, but may create latent conflicts in the Soviet bloc where the armies may compromise on the issue of their patriotic ethos, but win in terms of the chunk of the gross national product (GNP) that they get as their budget, a point made convincingly by Douglas A. MacGregor (1986, 242). The institutional design of the Soviet system is built around the mobilization of resources for the internal and external defense of the regime to the extent that defense (and sometimes offense) has become the regime's main purpose.

For a number of reasons, the security organs are closer to the core of the political system than is the army. The party bureaucracy has an alliance with the security services to limit the influence of the army upon internal and foreign policies (see Barghoorn 1971, 98). Thus, the security services contribute to the overall balance of the system of power. Their task is to keep society well in hand, to suppress dissent and resistance. They are the necessary guardians of the dominant position of party leadership in the system of government. The security services provide the party leadership with information about attitudes and opinions circulating in society and keep a close watch on the opinions and behavior of people occupying important party and state positions.[6] The Ministry of Internal Affairs has under its command special military units that it may eventually use against the army and also has units specially trained to fight street riots and demonstrations. It is involved in intelligence and counterintelligence activities, it is engaged in economic activities in managing the forced labor economy, and it keeps close watch over economic processes through specialized departments. It performs a variety of functions within the system, most of them under a close veil of secrecy.

Security services form an organizational complex with considerable autonomy, a distinct ésprit de corps, and considerable isolation from society. In the Soviet Union they are supposed to provide their members with social prestige and other privileges. In the countries of the Soviet bloc, security services may be more or less feared, but because they enjoy neither respect nor sympathy their isolation is reinforced. According to some, the proportion among new recruits of sons and daughters of employees of the security services is much higher than it is in other professional groups and marriage between employees is much more common.[7]

Outside control should be easier because the security establishment consists of a variety of services and hierarchies. Nonetheless, the control is rarely effective because of the size of the complex, the secrecy that permeates its activities, and its complete lack of respect for legal considerations. From time to time, the party conducts purges of the personnel but these cannot be done too often if the services are to be efficient. This would explain the paradoxical confession that was supposedly made by a Polish minister of internal affairs to one of the Catholic bishops: "There are some areas in this ministry over which I have practically no control."

The security organs, too, have a number of interests. They wish to maintain a high level of expenditure for the maintenance of internal security; to limit external oversight over the revenues and expenditures of the Ministry of Internal Affairs;[8] to increase the influence of the security establishment over personnel decisions, especially in attractive occupations, such as the diplomatic services and foreign trade that offer the possibilities of travel; and to minimize formal legal restriction on the methods they choose for fulfilling their duties, an interest that also affects the immunity of security officers and their dominant position in their dealings with the public prosecutor's office and the courts.[9] They advocate the continuation of a hard line in the politics and economics of internal and external affairs. They oppose any democratization or liberalization for fear that such developments would destabilize the system.

It is worth remarking at this point that the security establishment also legitimizes itself by association with nationalist motives. While the army has done this with some success, the security forces have failed miserably. Thus, the nationalist elements in the ethos of the security organs take a special form: they see themselves as possessors of secrets about international and other conspiracies aimed at the well-being of the country. Those not having access to similar intelligence, it is suggested, do not understand their tasks. The "conspiracies" take the traditional form of suspicious forces such as Freemasons, Jews, imperialists, and so on, working against the nation. They perceive the world as a gigantic conspiracy incomprehensible to people outside the security organs.

It follows that the basic set of interests in the Communist system of power consists of three groups that are in many ways alike: They all have a closed corporate character, they are highly disciplined and have a clear-cut hierarchy of authority, they are isolated from their social environment, and they maintain this isolation because of their separate organizational ethos and ésprit de corps. They act on the basis of internal regulations and informal rules of the game (this does not apply so much to the army), their accountability to external agencies is minimal, they manage their affairs in a highly secretive way, and they have a stake in maintaining a certain level of tension to legitimate their interests. Their organizational subcultures present the society as an entity devoid of reason, incapable of understanding the general welfare, the requirements of state, and the international situation, and open in its naïveté, to foreign propaganda and manipulation. Thus, the security services must, in the best interest of the society, keep it on a leash and guide it in fulfilling tasks the leadership selects for it.

In this triangle, the administration of the party is more closely related to the security establishment than it is to the army. The extralegality of status and interest in defending "power without responsibility," makes both the party and the security establishment staunch defenders of the revolutionary genealogy of the Communist state.[10] The security establishment has built its position on its claim as the chief defender of the leading role of the party and of the Communist regime. Consequently, the probability that the security establishment will assume control over the party and win a dominant position within the power structure of the partisan state is slim. Its legitimation depends upon the position of the party; it can exercise its influence only through the party. It can manipulate the party and, under favorable conditions, impose its interests upon the party establishment but its interests are irrevocably tied to those of the party. The army's external legitimation gives it more room to maneuver and a measure of autonomy within the political establishment.

Factions and functional interest groups belong to two different political realms. When a strong leader dominates a strong center, which does not happen often, factional struggles are practically nonexistent and interest groups are reduced to the role of executive instruments for central decisions. Any weakening of the position of the first secretary in the face of a strong political center encourages the development of active factional strife because members of the leadership have more freedom to use resources under their control to improve their own chances of succession. A relatively strong party leadership may effectively keep interest groups away from conflicts in the center and thus exercise effective control over these groups. A weak center has to broaden "participation" in decision making by giving voice and autonomy to interest groups, a concession that makes it difficult to develop a consistent political strategy. A weak first secretary and a weak center imply a critical increase in ungovernability exemplified recently during Jaruzelski's term as first secretary of the Polish Communist party.

The privatization of the Communist state emerges when the Central Committee's governing bodies start to weaken and when the party loses its autonomy and its sense of identity. Then factions turn into cliques, interest groups play their own particular games, and the entire political establishment loses a unity of purpose. The most important political resource in the system, the control over personnel decisions that in turn provides control over the functioning of the party-state complex, becomes an object of dispute between groups in the leadership and by major interest groups. The logic of this mechanism of political struggle imposes upon the administrators the necessity to use particularistic criteria of decision making instead of the criteria of professional competence and legal rules. If someone is nominated to a position of responsibility not because of his professional abilities but because of personal connections and association with a clique, he will first of all try to satisfy those on whom his tenure and further promotion depend. Thus, state and economic administrators perceive their posts as feudal endowments, not as positions of public responsibility.

Society as a Nonessential Burden: The Representation of Secondary Interest

As I have indicated on a number of occasions, the seizure of power by the Communist party brought with it the need to break all effective constraints on the expansion of state power. It liberated the state from social control at the cost of its complete subjection to the revolutionary party and with the result of a change in the structure of the state. The Bolsheviks reduced the state to those elements that, according to Engels and to Lenin, were the true essence of the state, that is, to the administration of coercion in all its forms. The state became isolated from the society. Marxist-Leninist doctrine provided a rationale for these developments. The partisan state was said to be devoid of special interests: it was to serve exclusively the interests of the toiling masses who constituted the great majority of the population. The doctrine also posited the cognitive superiority of the vanguard over the masses and its unique ability to grasp its historical mission to realize communism, the essence of the general social interest.

One can presume that Stalin's purges were partly a reaction to problems created by deficiencies in the design of the Soviet institutional system. The use of the purge indicated that the political system had no effective institutional instruments with which to defend its integrity in the face of the particular interests it generated. Purges were the costs society had to pay for maintaining the integrity of the state. Beside being excluded from any form of participation, society had to pay a prohibitive price for the maintenance of this order. The partisan state does indeed generate particular interests, but the task of preserving its integrity has nothing to do with any reasonably conceived notion of the general welfare. Such a state is simply incapable of serving society: it serves the interests of the groups that control it.

This explains an apparent paradox: The state treats even those services for which the population pays in full as a cost. In a system that gives priority to state-generated interests, any allocation of resources for other purposes occurs at the cost of the state's interests. *Society can only satisfy its needs at the cost of the needs of the state and of those groups that control the state.* The state cannot live without the society, but regards it as a nuisance that must, unfortunately, be tolerated.

The economic system poses the most effective constraint upon the domination of state priorities. Hence, it becomes the most painfully sensitive element in the organizational system of Communist political order. The economy owes its crucial role to three factors. First, the rate of economic growth has tremendous ideological and propaganda value, for it is the only indicator acceptable, on traditional Marxist grounds, for the superiority of the Communist system; it is, thus, the only true ground for the legitimization of the system. Second, the amount of resources that the government can divert for the realization of state priorities depends upon the general level of economic development. Thus, ultimately it depends on economic growth. Third, the economic situation and standards of living influence the attitudes and behavior of the population. As economic growth depends upon the productivity of the labor force, and this partly depends upon motivation and material rewards, the government must take into account the consumption needs of the population. A persistent neglect of such needs can have highly dangerous political consequences.

State priorities decisively affect the strategy of economic growth, both in its organizational and in its developmental aspects. The orientation of economic growth to those areas that serve the external and internal expansion of the state has two consequences. First, the expansion of the state in the economic domain increases the powers of the central planning apparatus and contributes to the bureaucratization of management, so that the economic system becomes one huge bureaucratic complex. Second, state priorities imply the need to build a powerful energy- and raw materials-intensive heavy industry that requires parallel development of the sources of energy and of raw materials. Besides, the chronic shortage of resources that haunts every Communist economy appears under the disguise of a labor deficit. In order to find workers, enterprises must provide those who do work in the state-oriented industries with greater material and other advantages than are offered to workers in consumer goods industries, a necessity that has built inflation into the structure of the Soviet type of economy.[11] Inflation is also part of the liberal economy, but is produced by a different mechanism. Inflation in the Communist countries is a typical war inflation caused by the inflationary financing of military expenditure.

What happens, then, to interests and needs that are not directly related to the core interests of the Communist state? Among these one can mention health, education, science, recreation, ecology, and law and order. How are these needs articulated and satisfied within the Soviet type of political order?

In a liberal, democratic system, the private market economy and state services satisfy these needs. For some, such as recreation, the direct involvement of the state is fairly limited. In health care, the role of the state varies from country to country, but in most instances is important. Law and order are typical public goods and belong, therefore, to the traditional concerns of the state.

Particularly after World War II, we witnessed in liberal, democratic regimes the growing role of the state and the shrinking role of the private sector in the satisfaction of social needs, a result of the Great Depression, the war, and a burgeoning egalitarian philosophy. Some efforts are being made at present to reverse this growth and to make more use of the non-state public sector and the private sector in meeting public needs. Yet, the limits of the tax state, as they were described by Joseph Schumpeter, have never been definitively established. The Communist state, which, especially since collectivization, has passed these limits, destroyed the distinction between the public and the private, replaced free choice by rationing, and penetrated deep into the social structure. From the very beginning, the state found itself facing the consequences that, according to Schumpeter's diagnosis, must follow such decisions.

> What we call the modern state would itself change its nature; the economy would have to be driven by new motors along new paths; the social structure could not remain what it is; the approach to life and its cultural contents, the spiritual outlook of individuals—everything would have to change. ([1918] 1954, 6)

If the tax state, Schumpeter proposed, is abolished, together with competitive markets, and economic growth is to continue, new cultural and institutional arrangements would be required. Communist leaders, who constantly spoke about a new type of motivation connected with the collective ownership of the means of production, about the new socialist human being, and a new socialist culture, understood this from the beginning. They spoke about it, but it did not materialize. Human nature has proved less malleable than has the world of institutional structures.

Thus, the Communist state is a form of state built around certain core interests that it has itself been generating, and it is forced to attend to other interests that are external to it. At the same time, it cannot allow those external interests to be served by private groups in the society. To do so would be to countenance the freedom of initiative that is considered a direct threat to Communist rule. The Achilles' heel of Communist regimes is that they require reference to society.

We concluded earlier that interest groups belonging to the core of the Communist power system enjoy an important, though varying, degree of autonomy in their dealings with the party/state leadership. The same cannot be said about functional interests related to the secondary goals discussed in this chapter. For instance, personnel decisions in those secondary areas are entirely subjected to political supervision and it is these subsystems that have to bear the cost of any adjustments necessary to remedy critical situations that might emerge in the more strategic domains. Budgetary savings begin when the state experiences economic difficulties; a hardening of the party line directly affects the standard of living, the universities and schools, the safety of individuals, the rendering of justice, and so on.

Whenever the core interests might be in jeopardy, the party and the government sacrifice secondary interests, with far-reaching consequences for social life. Interests that have a direct or indirect influence upon the processes of biological and cultural reproduction in society are in a state of permanent disequilibrium and crisis. Health care, education, science, recreation, and ecology are neglected, but the neglect does not produce political turmoil and mass social protests, or even strong resentment in society. Those who suffer most belong mainly to minorities of one form or another, such as the sick in hospitals, and the old. From time to time, a group of doctors may sign a petition informing authorities about the state of health care, but censorship insures that the text does not reach the public. The same has been true about ecology. The result of this neglect shows up in the rise of mortality rates, which for males of all age categories, in some Communist countries, began in the mid-1960s and is particularly marked among those between the ages of thirty-six and fifty-five.[12] "As wealth declines, emigration and higher death rates thin out the poorer classes, and finally the exhaustion of the entire body occurs. These phenomena are observable whenever a bureaucratic regime declines" (Mosca 1939, 86).

From time to time, the party and the government undertake a highly publicized, and usually make-believe, project to prove that they care. Instead of building dozens of hospitals that would be expensive and would not excite the public imagination, they build one, highly publicized, huge hospital-monument. Or they start an impressive campaign that does not go beyond the level of propaganda but will be following the Communist regime's old tradition of waves of mobilization campaigns. Under the system of overcentralized decision making, consistent systematic attention to any policy area outside the core ones, upon which the regime's survival depends, is impossible. Decentralization, by giving peripheral policy areas a necessary level of autonomy, by building into their organizational structure self-regulatory devices and by enabling them to generate fairly stable revenues from sources other than the state budget would be beneficial. But decentralization would require a reexamination of the property rights system and, consequently, a restructuring of the entire political order.

Thus, the Communist regime subjects such policy areas to strict bureaucratic supervision, while decisions concerning insignificant policy details are often made at the center. The center attends to problems by focusing attention sequentially on one at a time, usually by organizing the occasional plenary meeting of the Central Committee in charge of whichever department—education, health, youth, ecology, the intelligentsia, or the rule of law—is under scrutiny. At these meetings, the Central Committee formulates directives for the affected ministries and other administrative organs. The directives are usually put in very general terms open to a wide range of different interpretations. No adequate provision of resources follows; there is no independent control over implementation. Each policy area is discussed separately from others, as if there were no interdependence, and even problems encountered in the same policy area are considered to be independent from one another. The center makes all its policy decisions separately and handles operational problems case by case. Considerations that might concern the overall system never appear on the agenda. What can result from it are moral appeals to responsible officials to take better care of this or that matter. But a ruling group that wishes to keep direct control, at any price, over all the domains of organized action has no other option than to proceed in this way; any more rational solution implies the sharing of power.

There is another interesting aspect of this method. Officials responsible for the area under consideration themselves prepare materials for the plenary meeting of the Central Committee and other decision-making bodies; they serve as experts and suggest solutions. Given such an important role in preparing policies for their own administrative sectors, they can eliminate any information and policy alternatives that they find detrimental to their own interests.

As mentioned earlier, the secondary interest sectors are most vulnerable to political criteria in decisions about personnel. Most individuals who occupy positions of responsibility are political appointees for whom the prevailing concern will be with maintaining effective political and administrative control rather than satisfying social needs.

Sessions of specialized parliamentary commissions provide another occasion on which we may observe opportunities for the articulation of professional standards, those of lawyers in particular. Those sessions give experts an opportunity to voice their opinions. Sometimes this makes a difference. But this channel of representation of interest is effective only if the matter under examination does not affect the dominant interests. When it does, the Communist legislature disregards all public and professional considerations.

In summary, the dominant interests are guaranteed continuous priority; the secondary interests are neglected. The cleavage between the state and society has an institutional character: interests that are illegitimate in the public view dominate the policy area.[13] Changes in priorities, or rather fluctuations in priorities, do occur, but they are part of the political cycles that are caused by the changing power of society in the bargain between the partisan state and society to which I shall return later. This bargain has neither a formal nor an institutional character.

The main symptom of the weakening of the center that is treated here as a secular trend developing in all Communist states is the emergence of groups that are able to exert an influence far beyond that required to meet the needs that enable them to fulfill their functions. At the same time, important social needs are systematically neglected so that the demands of the primary interest groups may be met. The growing ungovernability of the partisan state is accompanied, therefore, by the growing frustration of the population. The problem has a structural character; it cannot be solved by a simple change of policy.

TEN

THE POLITICAL PROCESS AND ECONOMIC POLICIES

It is commonly assumed that Marxism emphasized the technological and economic aspects of social organization and neglected the political aspects. There is no question that it reserved the active role in stimulating social change for the economic forces, or at least those forces generated by particular economic relations. The state passively registers and adapts to changes in the economy. It is also evident that this theory is useless in explaining the emergence of the Soviet institutional order. The Soviet political order grew from the realities produced, to use traditional Marxist terminology, by the political "superstructure" rather than from the economic "substratum."

Douglass C. North formulated an alternative to the Marxist view and one that seems a better fit for the problems we are dealing with.

> The forms of cooperation and competition that human beings develop and the system of enforcement of these rules of organizing human activity are at the very heart of economic history. Not only do these rules spell out the system of incentives and disincentives that guide and shape economic activity, but they also determine the underlying distribution of wealth and income of

a society. The two essential building blocks to understanding the structure are a theory of the state and a theory of property rights. A theory of the state is essential because it is the state that specifies the property rights structure. Ultimately it is the state that is responsible for the efficiency of property rights structure, which causes growth or stagnation or economic decline. A theory of the state, therefore, must provide an explanation both for the inherent tendencies of political-economic units to produce inefficient property rights and for the instability of the state in history. (1981, 17)

But even here, in a general sense, one can reasonably argue that what is needed is a political theory that is more than a theory of the state, that is, a theory that would take account of factors and political processes other than those occurring exclusively within the narrow realm of the state (Ostrom 1991). Yet, in the case of the Soviet type of regime, society has been given the role of passive object of the state's creative endeavors. The Communist economic system can be considered, though with some exaggeration, as a simple projection of the partisan state's administration.

The *etatization* of the economy—to coin a word meaning the way by which the economic domain is made an integral part of state activities—has some very important implications for the functioning of the Communist system, both on the global level and at the microlevel. Although its consequences for the microlevel of analysis in the form of minimal labor productivity, inefficiency and waste of resources, and lack of innovation are important for our discussion, not every feature of the institutional order of Soviet-type regimes can be examined in a single volume.

One can claim that economic development in a market economy is a relatively autonomous feature built into the institutional structure of a liberal social order. The essential characteristic of this order is that the institutional complex of the world market, which is not under the control of any one state, provides one of the most important links among particular states. Policies of particular states affect the functioning of the world market, but no single government can in the long run manipulate it; the game has to be played according to market rules.[1] Of course, any government strives to influence world markets in a way that is advantageous for its own economy, and world markets influence the internal situation of every country. However, the smooth functioning of world markets requires that the political factor, which by its very nature represents national interests, be kept within limits. The Bretton Woods agreements in 1944 made the world market a common good and created specialized institutions to safeguard and regulate it.

As I have tried to show, the goals of the Communist system are also conditioned by its institutional structure. The economy has no autonomy within the political order: it is part of the partisan state complex. Its function is to provide the means for achieving those goals that are the priorities of the partisan state. The interests that dominate the political system, the bureaucracies of the party, the security services, and the army, and patterns of factional politics ultimately determine the goals. These interest groups are functionally indispensable for the survival of the regime. When their interests become seriously threatened a transition to a qualitatively different political system has begun.

The sovereignty of the state over the economy, if not constrained by traditional or other relatively autonomous structures, must result in decisions that from the standpoint of economic criteria are arbitrary, that is, are not dictated by or run according to the dictates of economic rationality. The effective imposition of state priorities on the economy requires its complete submission to the administration. The isomorphism between the economic organization of society and its political organization becomes perfect: only when decisions are made centrally will, according to Marxist-Leninist political economy, the "maximalization" of the public interest be assured. Rationing completely eliminates the consumers' freedom of choice, and administratively regulated prices prevent consumers from exercising any influence over production and investment decisions. The assumption that there is "one best way" suggests that the center has a legitimate monopoly for defining the general interest.[2]

It is important now to establish analytically the relationship between the interests of the dominant groups in the system, the institutional structure of the economy, and the economic policies of the government.

The Economic Concerns of the Strategic Interest Groups

The strategic interest of the party bureaucracy consists in defending its monopoly position and privileges. The emergence of a multiparty system implies the loss not only of the party's privileges but also of its raison d'être. All other concerns have, beside this one, only tactical relevance. The next important goal is the preservation of the role of the administration as the main recruitment channel for political leadership in its broadest sense, that is, for the recruitment of the political class in the Communist regime. From this point of view, control over the personnel decisions, the *nomenklatura,* is of crucial importance, making it possible to place party activists outside the party hierarchy proper, extending, thereby, their career opportunities and giving the party control over other sectors of the partisan state. The preservation of the *nomenklatura* system is of paramount importance for the party bureaucracy. But this type of control functions effectively only within the realm of the state administration: the *nomenklatura* cannot formally influence private agriculture or industry, although it is well known that good political connections are important in these areas too.[3] Market-oriented economic reform is not, therefore, in the interest of the party apparatus, whether we consider the apparatus as a corporate group or as a set of corrupt activists. To the contrary, effective market reform with its indispensable changes in the position of the legal system and the judiciary poses a direct threat to the position of this group.

Let us turn now to the security establishment, for which society pays a high price. In any country in which rule is based upon coercion, the expenditures of the security organs are an important, although concealed, item in the state budget. The incomes of people employed in the security organs must be sufficiently high to make that employment attractive. Besides high salaries, security officials have other expensive privileges: They have separate health care and recreational facilities and schools of different levels. They do not pay for medicine. They obtain housing easily and cheaply. They were granted virtual immunity from prosecution. Security services need modern devices for the surveillance of the opposition, of foreign diplomats, and of trade representatives and equipment to suppress street riots. They drain the labor market of young healthy men and women who could be employed in more socially useful ways elsewhere in the economy. Finally, the priority given to political security shortchanges the criminal, the narcotics, and other socially relevant divisions of the police.

The priority of state security is apparent not only in the internal politics of the Ministry of Internal Affairs and the KGB, but also in the functioning of the system of justice (penal law is repressive and excessively punitive) and in many areas of state administration (in the virtual explosion of "state secrets," the divulgence of which may be punished severely). Such repression hinders the exchange of information and limits innovation, its dissemination in the economy, and opportunities for cooperation.

All over the world, security services investigate candidates for top governmental positions, but this is an accessory function. In the Soviet type of regime, the security organs actively shape personnel policies in the state administration. Clearance from the security services is required even for managers of civilian plants. Foreign service and foreign trade are virtually monopolized by people from the security establishment, who consider such positions as rewards for past services. Strong support from their institutions puts those people virtually outside the reach of the law and weakens the jurisdiction of the ministries that employ them.

One of the main tasks of the security services is to survey the contacts between the citizens of their country and those of the West, including representatives of business firms conducting business negotiations with local enterprises. This supervision, and pressures of a type that have nothing to do with business, hinder international economic contacts and badly affect the economic position of the country. Hedrick Smith provides a good illustration of the obsession with security concerns and its consequences.

> Détente itself was a policy launched by the leadership for its own purposes and it has been carefully controlled by the leadership ever since. What little change it has brought has been kept in check within parameters that precluded fundamental reforms.

What has been at work is a process of grafting on, of adapting techniques from the West, of making exceptions and piecemeal adjustments but not of radical transformation. Western technicians may now be allowed to look at some gas and oil fields in Siberia and to encourage Western investment, but they are kept away from scores of other industrial sites to which their businesses would logically take them. IBM may be asked to install a computerized type-setting for *Pravda* and *Izvestiya* and a computerized control system for the Kama River Truck Plant, but it is required to house most of its specialists in Western Europe and fly them periodically into the Soviet Union to do their jobs because Moscow will not grant visas for more than two IBM men to live in the country at one time. Security and control of contract take precedence over convenience and efficiency. (1976, 675)

It should be noted that security services use some surveillance for corrupt purposes. Some activities, such as protection in exchange for a share in profits, are clearly illegal. Some are quasi-official. For instance, many of the foreign-owned firms in Poland have in recent years been forced to employ a security officer who comes once a month to collect his salary. This may be interpreted as tribute extracted by the Ministry of Internal Affairs or some of its units from organizations not sufficiently protected by the law to withstand such pressures.[4]

There is no reason for the security establishment to oppose economic reform as such. But they have every reason to oppose democratization, that is, effective public control over the functioning of the state and the development of a rule of law, and so on. The security establishment is all-powerful only when coercion is the main instrument of rule. When the political support of the population becomes an important consideration and when individual freedoms are institutionally enforced, the role of the security establishment becomes less central, its powers are more effectively restrained, and its opportunities for illegal dealings and outright corruption are limited. But economic reform without accompanying deep political change is impossible. In opposing democratization, the security establishment willy-nilly opposes economic reform.

I have already discussed some of the main concerns of the armed forces. Let us focus now on their economic interests. Defense is costly, and the military establishment strives everywhere to gain the biggest possible chunk of the state budget for its needs. Military expenditures are a burden for every economy, though in some very rich countries an increase in military expenditures can have a short-run, positive economic impact. It has no such impact in Communist countries, in which the normal situation is one of excessive demand and chronic shortage. A Communist government can only maintain high military expenditures at the cost of an underdeveloped consumer-goods industry, resulting in a low standard of living. It is possible to keep society in a state of economic deprivation only if it does not know that a better life is possible,[5] and is unable to voice its discontent with the way of life imposed upon it. Limits upon democracy that will hinder the articulation of aspirations and economic demands by the society are, albeit indirectly, in the interests of the army. No democratically governed society, except under conditions of war, would accept the level of military expenditure imposed upon the population of the USSR and other Soviet-type countries. According to some students of the Soviet armed forces, the Red Army opposed the NEP, supported the program of industrialization that required the collectivization of agriculture, and opposed Malenkov in his attempts to change economic priorities to raise the standard of living of the population and Khrushchev in his efforts to decentralize the economy (Kolkowicz 1967, 43, 50–55, 245–47; Holloway 1984, 9, 159).

Among the priorities of economic policy that the army has consistently supported is the development of heavy industry, the basis of the military industry. It is a highly capital-intensive industry that requires the parallel growth of other capital-intensive industries and has highly detrimental results for the ecological environment. The crucial political role of the military has led to the emergence of a pattern of industrialization that, from the point of view of the needs of a society at peace, is useless. The argument that this pattern helps to preserve peace comes from the traditional militarist's arsenal.

The satisfaction of military requirements in an inefficient economy means items produced under a Communist regime are incomparably more expensive than their equivalents are in liberal economies. But, economic inefficiency is not something external to the militarization of industry, it is an outcome of the centralized planning and bureaucratic management implemented to mobilize the productive resources of the country for military purposes.

In a market economy, the military economy must compete at least in some markets with the civilian economy, and military investments need public support. Only during a war will public opinion accept serious limits upon the market, as occurred with wartime planning in Great Britain. A system based upon rationing will do more to maintain high military expenditures than will a market system. Rationing and secrecy help to conceal the level of military spending although it will eventually manifest itself in patient lines in front of shops and in the biological exhaustion of the people.

An economic strategy dominated by defense concerns creates other serious disadvantages. The army, in developing its own industries and research facilities to diminish its dependency upon the civilian economy and research, creates a great military-industrial complex that drains the civilian sector in at least two more ways. First, it is the only customer in the Communist economy who does not face a "producer's market": its needs have priority. Second, the diffusion of new technologies from the military into the civilian sector is less likely than it is in liberal economies.

> The high priority of the defence sector has helped to make it different from the rest of the Soviet industry. It has tended to receive the best machinery and instruments. Pay is higher than in civilian production, and the defence industry can offer its workers more benefits. . . . High priority is reflected also in the arrangements for day-to-day management. Defence plants have the power to commandeer what they need from civilian industry, and this must be an important advantage in an economy where supply problems are chronic. Economic planning agencies will deal more quickly with requests and orders from the defence industry, and this too must be an advantage in a system where bureaucratic delays can be considerable. (Holloway 1984, 119)

Taking into account the level of military spending, and the insatiable needs of the armed forces, the Communist system provides a much more favorable environment for the satisfaction of military aspirations than does a liberal, democratic system. The side effects of such political priorities are a low level of innovation in the economy, technological backwardness, and an obsolete industrial structure.

The research and development facilities of the Communist military-industrial complex can only be relatively better than those in the civilian economy. The advantage is not enough to compete effectively with Western efforts to develop new military technology, so the armed forces must use secret ways of acquiring modern military technology from the West. This is not easy, however, and the general backwardness of the Soviet industry makes it increasingly difficult to keep pace in the armaments race.

Some Western observers have speculated about the possible role of the military in supporting Gorbachev's economic reforms. The declining growth rates in the economy make the choice between spending on armaments or permitting civilian consumption increasingly difficult. Technological requirements may cause the military establishment to give more active support to the reform strategy.

> In the face of continuing economic difficulties, and given [the] military attitude toward the other options . . . the military as an institution may find that the protection of its institutional interests and the fulfillment of its role as a guardian of Soviet national security are becoming increasingly problematic and that reform measures are required. Given the coalition of interests likely to oppose reform under almost any circumstances, the support or, at least, the tolerance of the Soviet military establishment for a reform-minded leadership will be crucial. (Bova 1988, 397)

There is no clear indication that such a support for reform is actually developing in the army. But it would not be inconceivable. Condoleezza Rice described an action undertaken by Czechoslovak officers during the Prague Spring (1968). They proposed profound changes in the military doctrine that contradicted the doctrine of the Warsaw Treaty Organization and determined the Czechoslovak army's support for the economic and political reforms initiated by

Dubcek (1984, 133–44, 154–56). It is worth remembering that a change in military doctrine directly affects the relative position of various services in the armed forces. Thus, there is a potential problem of conflicting loyalties within the armed forces.

Many of the problems caused by the present stagnation of the Communist economies have an indirect impact upon the army: as the rate of economic growth declines, it is difficult to maintain the usual rate of growth of military expenditures, the biological exhaustion of the society manifests itself in the worsening health of draftees, the ecological crisis (e.g., the toxicity of the water) affects the defense potential of the country. The military establishment is aware of these difficulties, but its relative isolation and functional specialization within the power structure make it difficult to turn the awareness into a determination to exert effective political pressure for reform.

STATE ADMINISTRATION AND MARKET-ORIENTED REFORM

Let us consider now the impact of the central economic administration and the territorial state administration upon the reform of economic policies. For many reasons the central planning administration is one of the main sources of support for heavy industry. First, state administration is no less prone than most other social institutions to bureaucratic inertia; traditional investment priorities are built into its structure with highly conservative results. Second, it promotes large, highly visible enterprises with a direct access to top political institutions over smaller ones, and the large enterprises are all in the heavy-industry complex. Third, the economic philosophy that has accompanied communism from the time of its victory in Russia in 1917 has treated the production of steel and energy as the only adequate indicators of the level of economic development. Finally, the center has to take into account the interests of the most powerful regions of the country, and most powerful regions represent the interests of the heavy industry. Consumer goods and service industries have no allies in the central economic planning and management institutions.

One cannot expect innovative ideas from central planning institutions because market reform would create a revolutionary change in their powers, structure, and operations. From a huge bureaucratic complex with extensive powers of direct intervention in the operation of individual industrial branches or into particular plants, economic planning under reform conditions would have to provide a highly professionalized service whose main tasks would consist in gathering information, formulating forecasts, and eventually suggesting solutions. Most of the officials and employees of the central planning agencies would become obsolete, because they do not possess the qualifications and experience needed in the new circumstances.

The subversion of economic reform by the central planning and management bodies under the leadership of the deputy prime minister Zbigniew Szalajda in Poland during the mid-1980s offers a revealing picture. Of the three guiding principles of the reform—autonomy, self-government, and self-financing—the central economic administration attacked the third one. An elaborate tax system was created that brought every enterprise to a state of near bankruptcy. At the same time, although the income tax paid by subsidized industries (such as metallurgy or electrical machinery) increased by nearly a third, sales in these industries did not grow sufficiently to support the increase, and the subsidies they received were raised by *more* than one-third. Thus, the rate of subsidy growth was higher than the rate of growth of the income tax. This phenonemon may have been to the short-term advantage of the subsidized enterprises, but it was hardly economically sane.

An enterprise maintained through subsidies was as dependent on the central administration as it had been before the reform took place, with one difference. The system had become still more arbitrary. Examples of the central economic administration's resisting, and effectively subverting, attempts at reform abound.

As far as the territorial state administration is concerned, we have first to consider its financial situation. In a centralized administrative system, all resources come from the top down. Local administrators are not interested in local needs; they are interested in the items for which the center allocates funds. An enterprising local administrator is the one able to choose the correct item and to persuade the center that his region is best suited to receive funds from the relevant program. His success will depend on whether his region specializes in agriculture or industry. Agricultural regions will eventually get money, but only when they can persuade the center that they should be industrialized. Money usually flows to already industrialized regions that are politically powerful and is spent mostly on developing heavy industry. Regional pressure will act, therefore, mostly in the direction of maintaining the priority of heavy industry. But the regional administration is probably not the main opponent of reform. A change in the fiscal organization of the state would effectively and definitely change the priorities of a regional administration without generating much opposition within its ranks.

It is easy to demonstrate the damage factional politics has upon investment priorities and economic reform. The essence of factional politics consists in the extension of control and the acquisition of support. The economic domain has little autonomy in its dealings with the political domain and is under the strong influence of political factions. As it is in the interests of factions to win powerful allies, the main beneficiaries of such a mechanism of policy making will be those economic branches and regions that are already strong, that is—under the Soviet type of condition—heavy industry and auxiliary structures and regional authorities are all closely linked to heavy industry.

Elite Recruitment and Market-oriented Reform

I have distinguished earlier between pure and mixed party careers. I shall now distinguish between two groups within the ruling class of a Communist state: the internal and the external elite.[6] The external elite consist of people who have had a mixed party career outside the army and the security services; the internal elite consists roughly of those who have had the pure party careers and the officer corps of the armed forces and the security services. The two groups fulfill different indispensable functions within the system. The internal elite assures the maintenance of order and stability; the external elite initiates adaptive change. They constitute a crucial part of a mechanism that assures some flexibility of response while upholding the system's identity. Their interests in the survival of the regime also vary. The internal elite risks losing everything; representatives of the external elite have more universal professional competencies.

I would propose two general hypotheses. First, each group in the elite recruits its members in a different way. Second, in the Soviet type of political regime, the internal elite tends to be recruited from socially marginal groups. The level of marginality, however, varies in time and among countries: it is lower, and perhaps nonexistent, in countries in which the partisan state is considered legitimate and higher in those in which its legitimacy is questioned. Moreover, this type of career further marginalizes the recruit by isolating him from his original milieu. The thesis is qualitative rather than quantitative. The mere fact that Russians dominate the Soviet political class does not prove that the Soviet Union represents extreme marginality. The question is rather, What is the social background of those Russians? It is quite possible and even highly probable that the level of marginality of the Hungarian political elite is more extreme than that of the Polish elite.

The notion of marginality lacks precision. It would be difficult to find for it unambiguous quantitative measures or even qualitative indicators. To give just one example, it can be said that, in a country in which over 90 percent of members of the population professes to be Catholic, a political elite open exclusively to atheists must have evidently been socially marginal. In the Soviet Union, where nonbelievers constitute the majority, it would be difficult to defend the thesis of marginality if it is expressed only in terms of religious preference, though this is not sufficient to reject it.

The term *marginality* is not related here to the idea of statistical representation. A rural community of which 10 percent consists of relatively wealthy peasants and 40 percent of poor ones does not imply that the representatives of the 10 percent are socially marginal. Nor is it that rich people dominate the community and occupy privileged positions in its institutions. These people are central to the community because they take better care of their farms and are more industrious: they are the core of the community. Thus, if in positions of authority in such a community we find exclusively or mostly people belonging to the 40 percent group, this indicates, in most situations, that an outside agency fills those positions for the purpose of destabilizing the community and controlling it better from outside. This is exactly what Lenin did by pitting the poor peasants against the more prosperous ones.

This point may seem trivial, but it is a key to understanding one of the properties of the Communist system: it has not developed an intergenerationally stable political class. There is much nepotism during the lifetime of a leader, but after his death new people come. His family may still enjoy some privileges, but it has no position of power. There is much self-recruitment, as children of party bureaucrats take jobs in the administration, but only at lower levels. They eventually can reach higher levels in the external group of the ruling class. I would suggest that the recruitment mechanism within the party, the security services, and the armed forces makes the internal elite function like a suction pump: it reaches out to marginal elements in the mostly less successful groups of the population and opens before them the possibility of careers in the power hierarchy of the system. Thus, among higher party officials the sons of peasants predominate; if they come from the intelligentsia, they are mostly children of teachers from provincial centers. When they come from the working class, they are usually from small, weakly industrialized towns. Among army officers, careers are often connected with an extensive technical training and continuing education. For careers in the party or secret police, technical competence is not so important.

One can consider this type of recruitment proof of the regime's egalitarian character, if it were not so reminiscent of all other top-down organizations. By drawing administrators from lower and marginal classes and giving them special privileges that could be taken away at any time, rulers have made their officials utterly dependent upon their will, and therefore more faithful and reliable than potential recruits from traditionally privileged groups would be. I would even suggest that this pattern of recruitment is necessary for the existence of a social order organized from the top down. The interesting difference between a Communist regime and its predecessors is that the latter were ruled by dynasties, the former are not.

The thesis about the marginality bias in the elite selection is of major importance for the theory developed in this work and requires some empirical support. That this empirical support comes from research carried on in Poland is hardly surprising in view of the traditionally greater freedom of investigation enjoyed by social scientists there. For these reasons and because of the clearly minimal level of legitimacy for its Soviet type of regime, Poland is an extreme case. Similar tendencies probably appear in other East-Central European countries and in the Soviet Union.

Jacek Wasilewski, in an interesting and methodologically rigorous study (1981), examined the recruitment of managerial elites in Poland at the end of the 1970s. Wasilewski studied the biographies of most of the top directors of large industrial associations. He distinguished a number of career profiles and found two that were distinctly political. He described as having political careers people with comparatively little education, who started at low levels of the hierarchy, switched back and forth between the party and administrative positions in industry while obtaining some formal education in the meantime, and made it to the top. The development of these careers usually took a long time and the individual occupied a number of positions before reaching the top. Political affiliations were crucial throughout. People who made political-technocratic careers, which are typical of the external elite, started their careers with a college diploma and, as students, became ranking, salaried activists in student political organizations. From there, they moved to high party or administrative positions and quickly reached the top directorial posts in industrial associations.

What is interesting about both types of political careers is that most individuals studied came from the countryside and small towns in the economically backward areas of eastern and southeastern Poland. Those who had political careers came from peasant families; those who had political-technocratic careers came from the small-town intelligentsia. People from urban centers and more industrialized regions usually had slow, apolitical, professional careers. A study by Aleksandra Jasinska-Kania (1987) supports these findings.

The political careers of members of the internal elite, especially of the party activists, start early, often in high school. The decision to embark upon such a path in most cases isolates the person from his peer group and limits his social contacts to like-minded people. The greater the unpopularity of the Soviet type of regime in a given milieu, the more isolated are members of the elite and the more closed is the group they form. One study conducted in the 1970s by Gawda, Kowalczyk, and Rychard (1981) of values and opinions among members and activists in political youth organizations in Poland showed no statistically significant difference between those of the rank and file members and of the youth population at large. However, the higher in the hierarchy a respondent was, the greater was the disparity between his views and opinions and those of the rank and file and of the youth population at large. If membership alone does not distinguish individuals from the rest of the population, a career in the organization does.

The interesting question, to which the study did not provide an answer, is about the extent to which the organization selects its activists from among people who already have attitudes and opinions that differ from those of their peer group and the extent to which attitudes are the result of an effective socialization process in the hierarchy. Whatever the answer, the differences between those individuals advancing in the political hierarchy and those who choose other careers create a cleavage between the two groups. Not finding understanding in the society, such an elite rationalizes its position by perceiving its social environment with an air of superiority and paternalism that makes understanding still more difficult—a cleavage clearly illustrated by reactions of the Communist leaders in Poland to their electoral defeat. They took the position that the results did not reflect the true will of the people; that the electorate was motivated by emotions and not by reason.

Thus, the internal elite consists of closed, isolated people whose opportunities in life depend, to an extent greater than is the case for any other group, on the survival of the institutional order.

The military, or at least its nonpolitical part, is an exception insofar as hardly any society can live without an army. Otherwise, the future of party *apparatchiki* depends on the preservation of a one-party system; the political police, when it is of the size and professional orientation of those that flourish under Communism, has a vested interest in preservation of a police regime. A truly democratic reform would wipe out both groups, depriving them of their power and special privileges.

The external elite is a more diversified category of people who attained their positions of power by combining elements of a political career with those of a professional one. These are individuals of various social backgrounds, careers, and psychological motivations. They are sometimes acknowledged specialists in their respective professions and have broad social contacts. Frequently they speak foreign languages. They are often well traveled and enjoy a measure of social acceptance. Their attitude toward Communism is skeptical; they use the Marxist-Leninist language cynically and for purely instrumental ends. They are more oriented to the West than to the East, which scares them, but which they treat with tacit disdain. Hence, they are more receptive to Western criticism of policies pursued by Communist governments than are their colleagues from the internal elite. Their elitist aspirations make them feel superior to their colleagues from the internal elite, for whom they feel, however, a deference that naked power always provokes in socially aspiring intellectuals.

Members of the external elite hold most of the staff positions at the Central Committee of the party and many ministerial posts with the government. Often they are personal advisers to men in top leadership positions of the party-state complex, to secretaries of the Central Committee, and to members of the Politburo, though sometimes they occupy administrative posts in the departments of the Central Committee. Their broad social contacts and key positions in the power structure provide them with fairly realistic information. Occupying staff and advisory positions, they exert influence mostly through persuasion and personal contacts with incumbents in the top positions. They set agendas and influence decision makers, but they usually do not make decisions, nor do they implement them. In a change of regime, they could lose their social visibility and importance, but the loss would be small relative to that of the people in the administration. Their acceptance by the professional milieu is due in large measure to their support of reform. Thus, they are its staunch supporters. When reforms go too far, and the social pressure goes up, they either leave the party and continue a purely professional career or hide under the mantle of the internal elite.

The main function of the internal elite is to preserve the identity of the system and to protect the status quo; the external elite initiates liberal policies and institutional changes and is the major political force behind reforms. The two parts of the elite are often in conflict, tacitly obstructing each other's plans and, at times, engaging in open battles. One should not, however, exaggerate this. First, the two groups are in large measure interdependent and are in constant contact with each other over policy issues. Second, the boundary between them is not as clear as the above description would suggest. Both groups are internally diversified and often internally divided by bitter conflicts of interest. Furthermore, the external elite is only relatively less marginal.

When the internal elite strengthens its grip over the center, the party and state policies take on a hard line. A growth in the external elite's influence brings about liberalization and general relaxation. Too much influence in the hands of either may dangerously destabilize the system. A Communist regime is constantly vacillating between reform and entrenchment. This shift has been going on for twenty years in Hungary and for nearly as long in Poland. In other countries of the Communist bloc, the equilibrium might have been skewed more to the advantage of the internal elite. But even there, one can discern such vacillations. This indicates that Soviet-type regimes may talk reform but are not necessarily reformable.

CONCLUSIONS

In summary, the dominant constellation of interests strongly favors the traditional form of economic organization and industrial development. The army and major economic interests tend to support the priority of heavy industry and the preservation of existing quasi-rationing. Because rationing implies a bureaucratic management of the economy, it suits the interests of the central economic bureaucracy, the party, and the security establishment. Political frustrations that result from the discrepancy between what the consumers need and the priorities determined for the centrally planned economy make the security establishment a key partner of party leadership in assuring the survival of the regime. One can legitimately ask, How is it possible for a change of priorities to occur? Why is it that party leadership constantly ponders the idea of reforming the economy without achieving any basic change?

If our analysis is correct, the Communist institutional system has no mechanism that would limit the tendency toward bureaucratization, the centralization of decision, the explosive growth of a perverse economic structure devoid of any connection with consumer needs, and economic autarky. Yet, some errors and discrepancies are corrected, and priorities do change. There must be some, though varying, limits. These limits are largely informal and external to the Soviet type of institutional structure. The internal environment of the system, the society itself, does somehow matter, even though it is denied basic political rights. There is an external environment consisting of international political, economic, scientific, and cultural developments over which the Communist world system has little control. In spite of its self-imposed isolation, the Communist world has been faced with economic and political competition from liberal, democratic countries.

Let us assume a situation in which the inner tendencies of the system develop in accordance with the logic of its institutional inertia. The proportion of resources spent on investments rises at the cost of consumption; investments in heavy and energy industries become larger at the cost of consumer-goods industries, centralization in decision making grows along with an extension of administrative supervision at the cost of individual initiative and the market. The private sector, if it still exists, is subjected to persecution and its share in the supply of goods and services becomes negligible. Political criteria take a predominant role in all decision making. In every area of social life the system becomes more and more isolated from the external world so that an economic autarky is reinforced.[7]

This is a fairly accurate description of the situation at the apex of Stalin's rule. But similar tendencies have appeared time and again, though they were never as marked. Externally, such developments must lead to international tensions, militarization, and the political polarization of the world. Internally, they have to lead to the pauperization of society, a growing sense of frustration, and an intensification of terror. This pattern of economic and political development cannot be maintained for long. Having reached a certain critical level, investment in heavy industry creates a demand for further investment in heavy industry: the development of heavy industry becomes its own goal. To maintain such a vicious circle is more and more costly for the economy and can be done only at the cost of shrinking consumption. Under such conditions, a Communist economy acts like a parasite; instead of serving society, it lives off it. An economic policy fitting the logic of this institutional system would, without political intervention, end in catastrophe.

There is possibly one element in the political system that could undertake such an intervention and reverse the course of events: the top political leadership. The ability of the leadership to perform such a reversal depends on several factors. It can do it when it is strong and well in control of events. A strong leadership is usually the one that has successfully passed the initial period after succession; that is, it has already sufficiently strengthened its position but has not been in charge long enough to be burdened by the responsibility for existing difficulties. It can still blame its predecessors and can propose corrections for the most visible mistakes. A seasoned leadership might eventually try to introduce some corrections and adjustments without admitting responsibility for wrongdoing, but this hardly ever happens. Transitions are, therefore, the only times when error-correcting strategies can be found in the Communist institutional order. Transitions are usually provoked by natural causes, sometimes they are a product of struggles at the top of the party, and sometimes the leader may be removed under the pressure of a social revolt. The third variant occurred in Poland with the fall of Gomulka in 1970 and of Gierek in 1980.

Of direct relevance to these considerations is a discussion that was published in the periodical *Soviet Studies* at the end of the 1970s, and initiated in an article by Bogdan Mieczkowski, who proposed that "in the Polish postwar experience growth of consumption has been inversely proportional to the power of the Communist Party (CP). It may be that the Polish experience can be generalized to other countries of Eastern Europe" (1978, 262). Mieczkowski's view of Polish political and economic cycles takes the following form: the strengthening of the party, which leads to social protests, and eventually to a change of leadership. The new leadership, to appease public opinion, reduces investments and allows consumption to increase.[8] When public passions cool off, the leadership reverses its policies and, in the logic of the system, the hard-line situation leads to new social protests. Mieczkowski supported his model with statistical data about the distribution of the national income between capital investments and consumption and on changes in the personal consumption per capita. He did not present any convincing evidence or even theoretical hints that would suggest that patterns found in the Polish case could be generalized to other countries of the Soviet bloc.

This weakness was immediately picked up by Philip Hanson, who argued (1978) that Mieczkowski's model was not applicable to other Soviet-type states. He questioned the relationship that Mieczkowski postulated between changes in economic policies and social unrest. In particular, he could not understand why party leaders would neglect consumers' needs if this neglect would invariably lead to their demotion from office.

The third participant in this controversy was Valerie Bunce, who argued

> that there is a consumption cycle in Soviet bloc polities (particularly Poland, Czechoslovakia, the GDR, and the Soviet Union), but that it is governed not by protest, as Mieczkowski argued, but more generally by *succession*. While protest does, obviously, play a role in Poland, it is in fact unnecessary for the operation of a politically-based consumption cycle. Communist leaders do not need riots to find out that the mass public would

like a higher standard of living—they know this automatically and answer these demands *when* they feel it is imperative to do so. The imperatives can come from riots or from the perception of the leaders that unrest could be imminent—that is, in the uncertain aftermath of a succession crisis. Thus, overt pressures *or* the anticipation that such pressure might develop would seem to encourage a short-term policy of raising consumption levels as quickly as possible. (1980, 281)

Bunce's cycle starts with a succession crisis that weakens the regime and causes fear of mass dissatisfaction. The new leadership tries to appease the public to win some legitimacy for the regime and rearranges its priorities to meet public expectations. The more it succeeds in attaining these goals, the more it will be tempted to return to traditional priorities.[9]

Bunce supported her hypotheses with data on the growth of consumption in the German Democratic Republic, Poland, Czechoslovakia, and the Soviet Union, on the growth of the consumer-goods industries in Poland and the Soviet Union; on the shares of light industry and housing in capital investment; and on the share of welfare in public expenditures in all four countries during succession periods and non-succession periods. She found that, invariably, consumption and consumer-goods production as well as investments in light industry grew faster during succession periods than at other times, and that the shares of light industry and housing in capital investments and of welfare in public expenditures also tended to be higher during succession periods.

A more recent contribution to the study of the political and economic cycle was provided by Piotr Strzalkowski (1987), who found that each succession crisis in Poland had been preceded by increased expenditure on the military and the justice and security administration and followed by an increase in budgetary outlays for education, health care, and culture.[10] This would suggest that the cause is more complicated. In taking a closer look at the mechanism of succession, I shall use Poland as an example because the changes accompanying successions were pronounced.

The data referred to above seem to support the model of the political process in Communist regimes that I have tried to develop in the previous two chapters. They also confirm the existence of tendencies in the Communist political order that push society to the brink of catastrophe. The special role of the leadership would consist, then, of taking corrective action in alliance with the liberal elements in the political class that conflict with the tactical interests at the core of the establishment, but at the same time help to assure its survival. They also support the contention that the structural conflict in the institutional system designed according to the precepts of Marxist-Leninist doctrine is one between the political ruling elite and society.

None of these authors considered that the crises in Poland might have been a warning for the Soviet Union and other Communist countries. If the violent successions in Poland induced the correction of errors on a wider scale, they might be considered part of a global adjustment mechanism.

ELEVEN

SUCCESSION AS AN ERROR-CORRECTING MECHANISM

The inability of Communist regimes to implement purposeful changes in their policies and in the institutional structure of the economic and political order has been remarked upon frequently. There is also a rich body of work dealing with the problem of succession. The perspective that prevails in this research is empirical and historical, the authors—among them, Rush (1974, 1980), Beck, Zarzabek, and Ernandez (1976), A. Korbonski (1976), Flerou (1971), and A. Brown (1982)—usually examining concrete cases of successions that have occurred in various Soviet-type regimes and the disturbances in the power structure that followed. Succession, when it is not subject to institutional routines, is always dramatic. Only Janos Kadar's resignation in 1988 seems to have occurred normally and relatively quietly. But, the succession itself took place during the most dramatic, and perhaps final, crisis in the history of world Communism.

I am assuming that the existing institutional system constrains the choice of reform and the breadth of the policy change open to the first secretary and the new leadership and am excluding the possibility that a leader will dismantle the regime, creating, in the name of some nationalist ideology, a new institutional basis for his rule. Such a possibility may exist but manifests revolution, not reform.

I shall try to develop here a synthetic model of a forced succession developed from five historical cases: three in Poland, one in Hungary, and one in Czechoslovakia. I am not taking into account the successions that took place in 1989, because they are part of a process of transition that revolutionizes the institutional structures in the region. Similarly, I shall not consider Khrushchev's fall in 1964, because it was a typical coup, and the political crisis was contained at the top of the party leadership.

The successions are those of Wladyslaw Gomulka in 1956, Gierek in 1970, Kania in 1980, Imre Nagy in 1956, and Dubcek in 1968. The fourth, and the last, one under the "old regime" was Jaruzelski's ascent to the position of first secretary and prime minister as part of the succession crisis started by the events in Gdansk in the summer of 1980 and in the resulting fall of Gierek. The Polish successions were in a sense more successful because they did not provoke direct Soviet invasion, as did the Hungarian and Czechoslovak successions. The ability of Polish society to get rid of Communist party leaders when they lose all credibility indicates that the influence of the Soviet regime has been the weakest there.

Each of these succession crises had a different character, occurred in different circumstances, and produced different results. Each has become part of a strange learning mechanism in the mutual relationship between society and the political ruling classes in Communist countries. I shall present here no specific account of any particular succession, but shall attempt to construct a general model of a succession crisis to show some of the structural features of the Soviet type of political order that have not yet been discussed.

It seems that forced successions are costly and unsuccessful mechanisms for correcting political errors, but, once a political system embarks upon this path, there is no way out. The decline in legitimacy of the Communist regime caused by each succession weakens the system to the extent that a fragile equilibrium develops between the ruling class and society, an equilibrium susceptible to disintegration.

Basic Structural Features

For the sake of simplicity, I shall limit the discussion to processes that occur within the hierarchy of the Communist party and shall initially treat society as an undifferentiated mass of individuals and groups having no direct impact upon the processes occurring in the Communist hierarchy. I view the hierarchy as consisting of four separate elements: the rank and file members organized in basic party cells; the middle level, the party bureaucracy, or the apparatus proper; the central party institutions; and the position of the first secretary.

Basic party cells exist in all units of the state administration, in cooperatives, factories, state farms, in trade and service firms owned by the state, and so on. They provide the main contact between the cadres of the partisan state and society. Party activists at this level mediate the relationship between the rank and file party members and the hierarchy, and also between the party and the non-party world. To mediate effectively, they must have a certain autonomy, they have to be on good terms with everybody. They are well informed about the work conditions and problems in the lives of their colleagues and often know their opinions and attitudes. The level of conflict, which stems from split loyalty, experienced by individuals in these roles is a function of the general political situation. If the party is relatively strong and enjoys some passive acceptance, the level of conflict is fairly low. When tensions rise, and people start to criticize the party publicly in their work places, when family members openly express their disapproval of the party and its activists, the level of conflict may become unbearable, forcing party activists to make dramatic choices. (The loss of over one-third of its membership by the Polish United Workers' party during the years 1980–1982 shows how unbearable those pressures can become.) The functioning of this level is critical for the party's ability to control its social environment; weakness here results in weakness in the party as a whole.

The next key element in the vertical organization of the party is the apparatus that links the center and the basic party cells. Activists at this level are close enough to reality to have an idea about what happens in the areas under their jurisdiction. At the same time, their isolation makes them much less sensitive to outside pressures than are activists at lower levels. They work in the party administration. Their prospects depend upon the fate of the party. They do not make important decisions and usually are not responsible for the content. But the apparatus has a broad, albeit unintended, autonomy in its dealings with the center because of the inability of the center to supervise the main function of the apparatus, the transmission of orders coming from the center to the basic party cells and to the heads of state organizations and the execution of the party line in areas under its jurisdiction. At this level, we find individuals who treat their party work as a professional career and look for further advancement. They go to work outside the party administration only when the party assigns them such positions.

The strategic interest of the apparatus consists in preserving autonomy in its relations with the basic party level, and organizations external to the party, and in developing effective defenses against encroachments from the center. It may seem a paradox that the party bureaucracy is most interested in the centralization of political decisions. The reason is that the higher the level at which decisions are centralized, the greater the discretion of the bureaucracy.

This can easily be demonstrated. In any organized social whole, there is a tendency of elements to gain their autonomy. In a relatively closed social system, an increase in the autonomy of some elements can occur only when other elements lose a comparable portion of their autonomy. Variations occur within the system. First, the apparatus strives to increase its autonomy in relation to groups whose situation it controls and who will, for this reason, attempt to win some influence over the decision-making process at this level. From this point of view, centralization provides the apparatus with important advantages. Activists at this level can informally put the blame for any controversial decision on the center, with a very low probability that the interlocutor would be able or willing to check. (Any information in the party is strictly informal, though this informality has its shades.) Central decisions must be formulated in a general way as directives; the center intervenes in concrete matters very rarely, and its freedom of interpretation gives the party bureaucracy considerable discretion in its rule over its jurisdiction. Central directives are usually based upon information provided by the bureacracy, so there is ample opportunity for manipulation from the bottom. Moreover, the greater the centralization of decisions, the smaller the ability of the center to supervise in detail activities at the middle level. The result is a vicious circle: increases in the centralization of decision making broaden the autonomy of the apparatus, contributing to an increase of ungovernability in the system to which the center can react only by further centralization. In this way, the system of rule over the party moves toward increasing rigidity and disorder.

Thanks to centralization, the functionaries of the apparatus have a large measure of arbitrary power without being accountable for their decisions. It is worth noting, however, that this is a purely negative power consisting mostly in obstructing the initiatives of the center. Activists have no motivation to undertake creative measures to solve social problems. Creativity is outside their duties and carries with it some risk. These circumstances create opportunities for corruption: the power of the apparatus is used to paralyze the center and promote the private interests of activists and their allies. To break the power of the apparatus would require the abolition of secrecy that envelopes the party operations and would make the party accountable to the public—a flagrant contradiction to the principle of the leading role of the party within the Communist political system.

Thus, within the institutional boundaries of the Communist system, no remedy is available for the problem of control over the party bureaucracy, with the exception of multiplying independent hierarchies of control; for instance, pitting the security system against the party apparatus. This might have been possible in the early (Stalinist) days, but the reverse situation is more frequent now. By close cooperation, party bosses, heads of internal affairs departments, and other regional dignitaries protect one another and jointly exploit the opportunities for corruption that are offered in the exercise of power without responsibility.

From the perspective of the center, the de facto autonomy of the party bureaucracy implies that the center has limited control over the implementation of its decisions. Central decisions are interpreted and selectively implemented depending on the corporate interest of the apparatus. This explains to some extent the phenomenon one can often observe in Soviet-type polities: a lack of fit between centrally adopted measures and processes taking place in reality. When information about the discrepancy reaches the center, it has no other means to remedy it than further centralizing decision making, thereby further restricting its own freedom of maneuver.

The party leadership often falls prey to a temptation to see reality as being more advantageous than it really is. This happens most often to first secretaries after a prolonged period in the position. Also, a proclivity to excessive trust in the reports of the special services can cause a profound discrepancy between the beliefs and ideas that members of the leadership hold about reality and reality itself. Nonetheless, the belief that individual members of the party leadership are misinformed most of the time is exaggerated. What really happens is that because, as a group, they do not allow certain topics to be discussed even in their restricted circle, information held privately by each individual has no effect; it is repressed from the collective consciousness. The initiators of critical debates would be promptly accused of factionalism and dismissed. Members of the leadership want to maintain their positions. To do this they have to respect rules of the game.

Succession and Political and Economic Cycles in Poland

Let us start with the moment in the political and economic cycle when the center is paralyzed as it was in Hungary and Poland after Stalin's death, from 1953 until 1956, in Czechoslovakia in 1967, and again in Poland between 1968 and 1970 and in the second half of the 1970s.[1] A growing centralization of decision making was accompanied by growing economic and political problems. Society was more and more frustrated. Political jokes about the regime, the leadership of the party, and the first secretary escalated. This situation caused some anxiety among the party leaders, and some started to prepare for an eventual succession struggle; open factional intrigues became commonplace. Declining rates of economic growth posed a dilemma for the leadership: Should they maintain the rate of investments in heavy industry, or reduce the rate of growth in investment in general and restructure them by giving priority to the consumer-goods industries? To maintain the existing rate of growth of investment required a reduction in the standard of living. The second option was not even considered. Each time the decision was made to maintain the traditional priorities, at the cost of consumption. The leadership also decided to strengthen the loyalty of the security services and the army by raising their salaries. Price increases for consumer goods, especially food, triggered strikes and open demonstrations. The leadership reacted with the use of force. When this did not stop protests, an internal opposition within the party leadership developed and, to appease society and open for itself new opportunities for advancement, forced out the first secretary and his closest collaborators and blamed him for the party's shortcomings and difficulties. The explanation offered to the public is that the system is sound and good; errors of judgment of the leadership, notably of the first secretary, caused problems.

The key figure in the political game at this stage is the new first secretary, who has to appease the masses by winning public confidence. He must present himself as a decent human being who understands the average working people and shares their concerns. But he must also introduce himself as a competent organizer, able to get things done. During the first two years his public pronouncements are full of democratic symbols and of promises of market-oriented economic reforms. He also maintains that to introduce such economic and political reforms does not require deep institutional changes; the system is sane. One needs only to return to the fundamental Leninist principles that the former first secretary and his cronies had violated. At the same time, party leaders make more or less open suggestions that if social demands go too far, people should expect the intervention of the Warsaw Pact armies.[2]

The new secretary, therefore, presumes to guarantee the implementation of economic and political changes and the safety of the country from foreign threat. Some improvements in the economic situation accompanies his promises. He uses existing reserves and/or foreign credits to raise the standard of living and alleviate shortages. He stops some investments and directs more resources to consumer-goods industries and to social services. There is a relaxation of censorship, some of the most scandalous cases of corruption in which members of the former leadership participated are made public, and some of those guilty are punished. This process is called "the renewal." The new leader tries to put into leadership posts as many friends and coworkers as possible in order to strengthen his own position.

The most important task at this moment is to win a measure of social support and to recover some of the lost legitimacy for the regime. The second necessity is to resist and diffuse pressure for institutional reform. The new leadership is aware that a reform that would satisfy public opinion would create not only external but also internal threats to its survival. The margin for "reform" is narrow, being a matter of generating some improvement while keeping institutional change to a minimum.

In some cases, public pressure recedes. Sometimes—in Hungary in 1956 and in Poland in 1980–1981—it did not and it was impossible to diffuse it within the existing institutional order. Then, the Soviet leadership had to apply more drastic measures to save the system.[3]

In periods of mounting social pressure, the basic party cells become externally invisible. They may hold meetings, vote resolutions and join in criticizing the deposed leadership, and ask for sweeping personnel changes, but do not make more dramatic demands for institutional reforms. The apparatus, too, reduces its activities and becomes hardly noticeable. During that period, the center obtains effective control over the apparatus because hierarchical controls are enhanced by a more open press that makes public some of the activities of local party cliques. This provides the center with greater freedom of maneuver. But, any weakening of the apparatus, one of the key conservative elements in the political system, also weakens the leadership's ability to resist public pressure for institutional reform. At this moment, the leadership makes an effort to change the direction of central policies. More and more frequently members of the leadership start to use phrases such as, "the party has renewed itself," "public confidence in the party has been effectively restored," "the party has regained its ability to lead," and so on. What these phrases mean is that the party leadership has decided that the time for reversal has come, a decision justified by the claim that any effective implementation of economic reform requires political stability. Whatever the true motives for this maneuver, it has one unavoidable implication: by enhancing the powers of the apparatus, it stultifies reform.

Thus, theoretically, the new political leadership is faced with the following dilemma: It must either limit the powers of the apparatus and implement economic reform or rebuild the position of the apparatus and abandon the idea of reform. (Later, in discussing the limits to reformability, I shall return to the problem of the meaning of the term *reform*.) Practically, the first option is improbable. The leadership would not willingly weaken its own position with society and with the security establishment, the military, and parts of the state administration. Nor would it be likely to provoke the unfriendly reactions from neighboring states that might lead to armed intervention.

Within the party leadership reformists are prohibited by the rules of the game from trying to win support for their views outside the party establishment, unless they are led by the first secretary in an intraparty struggle.[4] The reason is that such recourse to public support is considered by the Communist political elite a betrayal, because it is a strategy that questions the basic principle of its political order: the submission of society to the dictatorship of the revolutionary vanguard. Society can be manipulated, but under no circumstances can it be called upon to serve as an arbiter in intraparty disputes. Hence, at that point, even if the leadership clings to the phraseology of reform, words are not followed by acts.

The period that directly follows a change in leadership, even if no decisive institutional reforms take place, is rich in important events. First of all, the government corrects some policies and revokes its most unreasonable decisions. The new leadership initiates changes in the legal system. Some of the most unpopular politicians lose their positions. Freedom of the press grows and, in this revival of public life, the administration starts to pay attention to private individuals and groups. This transitory period between a succession crisis and the stabilization period may last a couple of years or even more, depending upon the strength of revolt and the breadth of change forced upon the establishment.

In all these chains of events, the first secretary plays a key role. He is not only the leader of the party, he is also the most powerful man in the country. His main task is to integrate the party and society under the umbrella of the accepted political line, to build a measure of consensus, and to inspire. But the role is laden with conflict. The more the first secretary tries to win the support of the party bureaucracy and its political allies, who are by their very nature highly conservative, the more he loses popularity in society. The more he strives to win social popularity, the more dangerous this becomes for the political establishment. If the secretary persists in his popular aspirations, he will circumvent the conservative opposition by strengthening public control over the functioning of the partisan state. This, with some simplification, is what happened in Czechoslovakia in 1968 and has been happening in the Soviet Union since 1987. Thus, if he wants to survive, he must skillfully balance his popularity (and unpopularity) within the establishment and in society.

The most rational strategy of the party bureaucracy when presented with the first secretary's policies is distrust concealed behind the veil of warm support. Close and loyal cooperation is in the long run unprofitable. Lack of attention to the activities of the leader can be dangerous. The apparatus must watch closely the policy decisions made at the center and try to subvert those that create the danger of drastic political and economic change.

The first secretary can break the resistance of the apparatus by changing the personnel, by putting his loyal followers in strategic positions in the party hierarchy and removing his adversaries. But the subversion of the center's initiatives by the apparatus does not consist in active opposition. To the contrary, the party bureaucracy manifests overt support for the new leader. What happens is a spontaneous, uncoordinated subversion in executing some of the center's key decisions. It is difficult to control this sabotage, for the controllers themselves are the political allies of the apparatus. Personnel changes, although helpful in averting an open political conspiracy against the first secretary, are not an effective tool for breaking the resistance of the apparatus toward any liberalization.

Lack of respect for basic human rights denies a public life, destroys the traditional civic culture with its sense of responsibility for the affairs of the country, and makes of society a disintegrated collection of individual families and informal groups devoid of any sense of control over the affairs of their village, town, region, or the country as a whole. The intensity of these disintegrating tendencies changes in time and from country to country. One might say, in a travesty of Marx's description of classes, that a society without public life is a society "in itself," and cannot become a society "for itself." Some elements of public life, a limited crystallization of political opinion, and an articulation of demands and interests, appear only during a relatively short postsuccession period. The necessary condition for *an institutional stabilization of the Communist regime is a demobilization of the society as an autonomous social agent;* it is social apathy. Peoples become masses. The problem is that social apathy hurts the system in other ways, such as low productivity, alcoholism, indifference to the outside world, and so on.

During the period following the succession, the attitude toward the first secretary that predominates in society is (to a varying degree) favorable. He has made an official pledge to implement changes and taken upon himself the obligation to meet social demands. He has become, therefore, a party to a sort of a social contract. Even if he does not act upon his promises, he is preferable to someone who has made no pledges. This initial support for the first secretary, although it is rather grudging—lack of an alternative, the choice of a lesser evil, and so on—obviously contributes to political stabilization and is, therefore, important in the political and economic cycle of succession.

Another stabilizing factor is related to the specificity of the rules of the game at the top level of party leadership. Those closest to the first secretary are other members of the Politburo and the Secretariat of the Central Committee, which is the main center of factional intrigue. The principle of such intrigue, as was explained earlier, is to create and maintain informal networks through the party and the state hierarchy and to limit the first secretary's freedom of maneuver. While the first secretary is involved in a broader political context as a de facto head of state, his closest collaborators are all involved in intraparty work or in the management of sectors of the state administration. In both cases, their work milieu has a conservative character. The only likely representatives of liberalism among the top leaders are, in general, political outsiders devoid of significant political support either in the party bureaucracy or in other essential interest groups.[5]

The dominant position of the first secretary derives from the uniqueness of his role: being primus inter pares, he alone can alleviate intraparty conflicts and mediate among opposing tendencies. Thus, he will tend to assume a moderate posture, trying to maintain an equilibrium among the different groups and orientations represented within the leadership. The critical moment comes when the party leader is no longer able to control factional strife. Then, the danger of the disintegration of the party leadership and of the spread of the conflict outside the narrowly conceived limits of the top political establishment emerges. At that moment, some party leaders will try to form a consolidated opposition to the first secretary to dislodge him and replace him with another leader. This is never easy. The first secretary has his own following and is usually able to wage an effective defense, although at that point in the cycle he is no longer able to unseat his rivals; the best he can expect is a compromise.

One can imagine two situations in which an attempt to dislodge the first secretary may take place. One may occur when he involves himself too deeply in the process of reform. If he is a popular person, indirect means will be used to paralyze his policies. Internally it is very difficult to move him out; under such conditions only external intervention can bring back stabilization. But if the peak of his popularity has passed, he can be removed by a coup in the leadership, like the one staged by Brezhnev, Kosygin, and Suslov in deposing Khrushchev, or through a political crisis that cannot be contained within the top leadership and spreads outside to the party and society, as happened to Nagy, Gomulka, and Dubcek. The other may occur when the first secretary has made the full cycle, has started from some flirtation with reform and then returned to traditional practices and priorities, and the country finds itself in the grip of an economic crisis, in the face of rising political tensions to which the ruling groups cannot find a reasonable remedy. Then succession becomes the only solution that fits the survival instinct of the political establishment and will appease society.

Between 1956 and the early 1970s, the first secretaries in Poland began their duties as fairly popular men (this may even be true, to a lesser extent of Kania and Jaruzelski), gradually lost popularity, and finally also lost their positions. There is an element of perversity in this: When a leader of the party yields to the pressures of the apparatus and other dominant interests, economic difficulties and political tensions follow within a relatively short time. This deterioration in the political situation results in an erosion of support by the conservative political class. By implementing the dominant political interests, the first secretary finds himself in trouble and becomes a liability. His role is not, therefore, an easy one. He can survive only when he is strong enough to defend his superior and sovereign position in the face of organized interests. If he can do that, factions remain only as informal channels for the more efficient execution of orders from the center; interest groups remain what they are intended to be, the executive hierarchy, and the meaning of the term *center* becomes an inclusive one.

The succession crisis is the period when the power structure is at its weakest and society is at its strongest. This manifests itself in the decision to risk an attempt at reform or to make vague promises and some tacit policy changes without risking a serious reshuffle in the institutional structure. Until recently, the choice of the first option by an East-Central European partisan state would have provoked the intervention by external Soviet forces. Now, with changes initiated in the USSR itself, the situation has, to an extent, reversed. In 1989, the Soviet leadership consistently undermined conservative leadership in East-Central Europe, fearing the consequences of their support for opponents of Gorbachev's team.

Succession and Economic Policy

Let us reconsider the specific connections between this political and economic cycle and the economic policies of the Communist state, starting with the moment of the leadership succession. At that point no attempt at reform is yet made; reforms are promised and discussed, and a general relaxation of constraints makes social pressures more effective. This results in some rationalization of economic policies, at least within the limits that the existing economic organization allows, which is reflected in cuts in the general level of investment, change in economic priorities, and the devotion of more attention to such previously neglected policy areas as health care, housing, education, and science. Change in economic policies is manifest in the revocation of strikingly unreasonable legal limits upon the autonomy of decision making at the plant level,[6] in the reduction of the number of plan-fulfillment indicators for enterprises from a couple of dozens to a few, and in some minor organizational adjustments. There is also a change in the official attitude toward private agriculture. Where agriculture is fully collectivized, farm workers are encouraged to use more intensively the individual plots awarded to them by state farms or by the cooperatives.

This is also the period of intense public deliberation about reform. Everybody supports reform, but views of what reform should be differ considerably. Each group wants to see its interests safeguarded against the costs of reform. Practically, the interests that must be protected are those of the party bureaucracy, the army, the security establishment, and those in control of the economic administration and of some regions and, if they are, there can be no reform. Leaders in Poland have often demonstrated the propensity, which has been reflected in the Western press, to accuse Polish workers of unwillingness to accept the costs of the reform. The principal problem, however, is not whether the workers are willing or not to accept such costs, but that the regime itself resisted the reform. The workers' resistance to reform is only now becoming important, with the present political and economic changes. The practical viability of economic reform without a profound change in power relations is null.

The stabilization of the economic situation, as a result of policy adjustments and the liberation of some hidden reserves within the system, makes it possible to slow down the reform and return to the old patterns: the tendency toward overinvestment, the maintenance of traditional industrial priorities at the cost of consumer-goods industries and services, and an increased control over the private sector in agriculture. There is a marked growth in the centralization of decision making and the bureaucratization of management. In the domain of politics, the repressiveness of censorship and the level of police harassment increase. In the face of rising shortages and inflation, which under a system of regulated prices manifests itself in the length of waiting lines, society becomes more frustrated, workers (mostly women) spend more and more time shopping during work hours, and productivity declines. Soon heavy industry starts to experience shortages of equipment, energy, and raw materials, and presses (at this point still effectively) for more investment. In the hope that the accumulated investment will soon be producing goods that will alleviate shortages of both capital and consumer goods, the leadership accepts these demands. The investment further contributes to the general disorder and to the disorganization of economic processes. At that point, the only maneuver still available to the leadership is the further centralization of decision making to counter spontaneity. But, as I tried to demonstrate earlier, this contributes to disorder. A visible decline in the self-confidence of the party bureaucracy occurs, the leadership disintegrates, and information about economic absurdities spreads to undercut morale. All social groups start to think of alternatives. For the political establishment, the question becomes, Who will replace the current first secretary? In this way, political succession has been the only response available to the political establishment in the face of catastrophe.

The above picture does not correspond exactly to any particular succession crisis. Moreover, no other Communist country besides Poland has moved through the full succession crisis. I have tried to present an analytical model descriptive of the political cycle. The nature of the cycle changes, however, with the process of learning. I shall return to this in a moment.

There is another question: Why are the variations between specific moments in the cycle so much more pronounced in Poland? Valerie Bunce demonstrated (1980) that the succession crises produced similar results in all the countries she investigated. What makes Poland different is that successions forced from the bottom were not followed by a full-blown invasion of troops from the Warsaw Pact.[7] Each successful "dethronement" strengthened the self-confidence of Polish society. Also it may be that the crises of forced succession in Poland act as an error-correcting mechanism for the whole bloc, causing changes elsewhere in policies and in political priorities. This last point remains to be empirically demonstrated.

Thus, the forced successions could have detected and corrected some errors while they left less and less opportunity for the menaced ruling elites to detect and correct errors by themselves. At each succession, society became more integrated and had fewer illusions about the nature of the system it dealt with. The Communist elites were more hesitant and insecure and less able to resist popular demands. Succession struggles have worn the Polish Communist regime out to such an extent that, when strikes started in the spring of 1988, it was clear that its end was near.

TWELVE

THE PARTISAN STATE AND CIVIL SOCIETY

The previous chapters focused attention on the institutional structures of the Communist political system and on the social arrangements these structures generated. The society, and its characteristics, was mentioned only when it was directly relevant to the topic under discussion. Yet, the society with its centuries-long historical tradition and more recent experience of World War II and of the imposition of Communist rule, is an important actor, although most of the time it is important only indirectly through its behavior in everyday life. There are long-standing cultural differences among the peoples of Romania, Hungary, Bulgaria, East Germany, Russia. The object of this chapter is not to examine these differences but to show the ways in which society is relevant to the Soviet type of institutional order and to explore different effects of the interplay between the society and the partisan state.

THE SYNDROME OF ASYMMETRY

In the doctrinal blueprint for the Soviet type of system, the party was to be the all-powerful initiator, the state was to serve as an instrument, and society was to be the object molded. The Bolsheviks translated this image into an institutional pattern built around the idea of the unlimited power of the partisan state. The more effectively the conception is implemented, the more society is reduced to an aggregation of individuals.

Thus, the relationship between the partisan state and society, as postulated in the doctrinal blueprint for the Soviet type of order, is highly asymmetrical. This asymmetry characterizes every area in which members of society come into contact with the state. In the domain of politics it manifests itself in the "politician's arena," that is, in the lack of connection between the priorities of the state and the needs and aspirations of the population. From this basic asymmetry, others follow: in economic life, it is reflected in a "producer's market," that is, in the lack of fit between the consumers' needs and preferences and the supply of goods and services. This results in a situation of permanent shortage, both in the capital- and consumer-goods markets, and in a low quality of product. In the domain of social communication, this phenomenon takes the form of the "broadcaster's scene,"[1] that is, a lack of correspondence between the content and the language of messages disseminated by the mass media and the opinions, attitudes, interests, and linguistic conceptualizations of most of the population. In the area of justice, it takes the form of what one may call the "prosecution's court," where the prosecutor has more weight in the court than the defense, while at the stage of investigation, the position of the prosecutor is in turn weaker than that of the investigating officer. In the Soviet Union until very recently, an accused before the court stood little chance of being found innocent.

These asymmetries appear when a society faces a monopoly of power in the hands of a small, organized minority that controls the state and is not responsible to the society. Under such a regime it is in the vital interests of the ruling class to show members of society that they are helpless against the partisan state. The effective intimidation of society is a necessary condition for the "smooth" functioning of such an institutional order.

Some authors believe that the true *differentia specifica* of the Communist system in the history of political regimes is to be found in the effort to impose upon society an artificial language, a "newspeak," to use Orwell's famous concept. Marxist-Leninist language replaces the traditional, everyday language of ordinary discourse. Aleksander Wat (1985, 28–30), a poet and a perceptive analyst of the phenomenon, enumerates its characteristic features:

- The rigorous regimentation, systematization, and codification of language. For practical purposes, the language becomes a political instrument of the party leadership.
- The imposition of the language upon society by terror as a binding one in all situations.
- The creation of a totalistic, semantic caricature embracing the whole of the language, all significant words, and relationships between words and objects.
- The isolation of Communist semantics from natural socially and historically formed semantics. This language replaced true reality by a postulated "reality"; for instance, people were sent to concentration camps, with long sentences, simply for having revealed in a private conversation that they had not eaten butter for many years, the remark being construed as anti-Soviet propaganda.

But the situation is changing. Nearly everywhere natural social semantics is gaining ground on Marxist-Leninist semantics.

The reason for such treatment of society by the partisan state is obvious. No institutional constraints in Communist regimes compel leaders to take into account interests that are not those of the narrowly conceived ruling class, or aspirations that cannot be expressed in the peculiar semantics of the Communist party. Interests taken into account are first of all those that matter: the party bureaucracy, the security establishment, the armed forces, and traditional heavy industry.[2] Other interests and concerns merit attention only sporadically, when the situation becomes critical. When critical situations are produced by powerful interests and when effective solutions would threaten those interests, no effective solution is possible. The problem is then not only one of error detection but also one of error correction: the system is opaque, and behind the veil of secrecy are hiding powerful groups whose survival depends on their being able to maintain their lack of accountability to the public. Not only is the Communist regime's ability to correct errors limited but also, within limits, it is an error-amplifying arrangement.

The relationships among the party, the state, and society are those of the relationships among the actor, the tool, and the object, and the constitutive principle consists in the maximization of control by the party over the state and of the partisan state over society as the object to be transformed. This situation implies an inherent conflict between the partisan state and society. Paradoxically, party leaders can disregard society entirely only when they strip it of its existence, that is, only when members of society are unable to organize themselves for action. Society approximates this state only under intense terror. A totalitarian state attains as much power as it can when it approaches the physical annihilation of society.[3] This may sound absurd, but we are discussing utopias in the process of realization. The Soviet Union somehow approximated this point at the end of the 1930s, the People's Republic of China during the Cultural Revolution at the end of the 1960s. Only an external territorial expansion can replace, within limits, terror directed against the population of a country. Marxist-Leninist theory becomes enshrined in patriotic symbolism. There is no doubt that this can only be done at a very high material and physical cost to the population, at the cost of the destruction of society as a cultural community.

A totalitarian regime that is, for whatever reason, not involved in constant external expansion, that is, in war, must mobilize energies for the sake of expanding its internal control, a venture that is no less costly to its population than is external aggression. When it ceases to invade its own country or those of outsiders, the regime loses the ability in which it really excels: its mobilization drive.

Thus, the Soviet type of political order is structurally based upon conflict between the party-state complex and the society. A strong partisan state implies a weak society, that is, a society denied the opportunity and, eventually, the ability to articulate itself, to organize, a collection of families at best, an aggregate of individuals at worst.[4] The partisan state can achieve such atomization of society only when it embarks upon a course of intense terror. Because the costs of such a system quickly become prohibitive in every sense

The Partisan State and Civil Society

of the term, a trend toward stabilization and routinization emerges once the chief ruler (Stalin, Mao, or any other) dies. The initially dominant motives, the compound of faith, fear, greed, and ambition, with faith and fear dominating, are gradually replaced in the political establishment by more so-called civilized motives: the self-interested combination of lust for power and material acquisitiveness. As I have tried to show earlier, this shift brought conflicts between the institutional interests of the party and the state bureaucracy into the open, and consequently affected relations between the partisan state and society.

The impact of these changes on the relationship between state and society depended very much upon the condition of society. Societies that have been effectively atomized have difficulty in regenerating their cultural patterns; in such societies, anomie reigns supreme.[5] At the opposite pole, a society able to defend some of its institutions regenerates itself more rapidly and can eventually pose a threat to the survival of the Soviet type of regime. (It is obvious, for instance, that the ability of the members of society to defend the role of the church in Poland during the Stalinist period and after, and the survival of the large private sector in agriculture, paved the way for other, more differentiated forms of institutional autonomy.) These defensive efforts take the form of individual or collective efforts to overcome the state monopoly of power in social life and range from such innocent, individual activities as listening to foreign radio stations to organized efforts to contest the monopoly of power by the Communist party.

However, a passive, atomized society has certain disadvantages for the partisan state because passivity and indifference do not foster purposive activity and voluntary cooperation. With the decline of competitive ability in economic, cultural, and possibly military areas, Communist elites are forced to realize the strategic importance of self-motivated activity and cooperation for their survival. Unfortunately, this realization has led them to a dead end. The suppression of society resulted from the basic design of the Soviet regime and not from errors in policy, so the position of the Communist elite is based upon the continuation of this socially alienating arrangement. When the institutional structure changes, they have to go

(Djilas 1957, 45–47). They have no other justification for their privileged position besides Marxist-Leninist doctrine and, possibly, the survival of the Soviet empire.

Conflict and Cooperation

Before we consider the strategies of conflict and cooperation used by the partisan state and a society (by which I mean a collection of individual members and groups and their mutual relationships), we must take into account the general conditions in which these strategies are pursued. Most of all, we have to consider the social mechanisms that regulate and determine access to resources. For individual households, this means the availability of durable and nondurable consumer goods; for formal organizations, access to capital investments, the possibility to increase employment by obtaining a bigger budget, and so on.

The reason behind the denial of autonomy to society, although this particular reason was initially unintended, is simple, and is neither ideological nor traditional: The political class uses the system for its own interests, a purpose that society is unlikely to find acceptable; so the political class has to organize the political system in such a way as to enable itself to disregard society. Operations on the language and the liquidation of the most important elements of the market mechanism by the imposition of the administrative, centralized management of social life that is part of the consistent top-down pattern in the organization of the Communist social order, show just this. Let us return once again to the consideration of one unintended result of the system's design: the phenomenon of *shortage*.

The Communist economy has been described by Janos Kornai (1980) as an "economy of shortage." In Kornai's view, shortage in the Communist economy is not an indicator of crisis. To the contrary: a chronic shortage of resources is the normal state of any economy limited not by demand determined by market price, but by the physical magnitude of the resources. Kornai traces the factors contributing to shortages, starting at the plant level where no incentives exist to use resources efficiently, but there are plenty of reasons to build inventories without limits in expectation of future shortages. At the middle levels, incentives exist to exert constant pressure upon the center to improve access to resources. At the center, those pressures cannot be ignored, and the center reacts by offering "soft" financing—transferring funds without adequate links to performance—which creates a potentially inflationary situation, but because the state controls prices, it can suppress the effects of its actions by not raising prices. Economic systems constrained by demand do possess economic means to balance supply and demand, but economic systems constrained by the size of available resources are regulated only by shortages. Access to political influence, or political pressure by any given industrial concern or organization to alleviate its shortages, does not resolve the problem. The soft financing that is at the root of the problem results, of course, from the politicization of the economy. But here, at the threshold of the political and institutional problems, Kornai's analysis stops.

The situation in the consumer market is similar. So long as the Stalinist system lasted in the Soviet Union and East-Central European Communist countries, the standard of living could be kept very depressed. Family budgets, under the traditional Communist economy, experience hard constraints: one cannot spend more than one earns, and the workers and employees have a weak bargaining position. Soft budgeting in the state sector and hard budgeting in the private households led to the situation in which investment quotas in Five-Year Plans have always been exceeded, but consumption quotas never attained. According to some estimates, the standard of living prevailing in 1928 was not reached again in the Soviet Union until thirty years later. The low standard of living was rationalized by an argument according to which economic development was created by the growth of the capital-goods sector of the economy, and consumer-goods industries would follow suit, a growth strategy based upon deferred gratification. After seventy years of this system, the question emerged, How long would gratification have to be deferred? It became obvious to some economists (and perhaps even more to satirical writers) by the middle of the 1950s that Communist economies had acquired an interesting feature: the capital-goods sector was producing mostly for the sake of satisfying its own needs. Its functioning served no useful social purpose other than to sustain further increases in capital goods. Under such conditions, the gratification of consumer demands would be deferred forever.

This realization, and the decline in the use of force, made it very difficult to oppose pressures for wage increases and still more difficult to raise prices to offset the demand generated by increasing wages and salaries. At that point, the Communist elite had to take the society into account, to give consideration to the growing shortages of consumer goods, access to which was regulated by the black market, rationing, the privileges of the *nomenklatura,* and lines of shoppers. This circumstance meant that the Communist elite, though unaware of it, had to determine the structural conflict between its own interests and those of society.

The problem of shortages can be seen as a general feature of Communist society, going well beyond the domain of economics. As a producers' market leads to shortages, the politician's arena is accompanied by shortages in the rights of citizens, the broadcasters' scene in the shortage of relevant and correct information and the shortage of a language to communicate intelligibly. We can discuss shortages in connection with all the basic social needs and values. Conflict between the partisan state and society becomes a zero-sum game: in every area of life, whatever is won by society in terms of autonomy implies a correlative loss to the partisan state in dominance. Thus, from the point of view of reformability, which I discuss later, there is no apparent basis for a compromise.

The strategies available to the society in the post-Stalinist phase, can be classified according to two sets of criteria, passive or active and individual or collective (see the figure on page 251). There are four possible combinations of the variables: individual and passive, collective and passive, individual and active, and collective and active. The first combination takes the form of indifference or resignation and is indicated by, for instance, high levels of alcohol consumption (the only good that is rarely in short supply); the second excludes the self-organizing activity of social groups. The active combinations can take two distinct forms: activity within the system—an acceptance of the regime and concentration upon efforts

Strategies Available to Society

	Individual	Collective
Passive	Resignation	None
Active Within the system	Corrupt behavior	Acceptance of corruption Participation in spoils
Against the system	Individual moral protest	Different forms of action in defense of certain values Mass protests

to obtain as much as possible within the limits set by the monopolized distribution of goods and resources—and activity against the system—different forms of individual and group resistance based on the moral rejection of the regime.

Passive strategies are a product of the feeling of hopelessness: "Whatever one does cannot succeed; we have to accept what we get. The world is as it is; we cannot change it." It is a fatalistic view often taken by the victimized. When such individuals meet, they drink and share their gloomy views of the world. They know no sense of responsibility and their sense of worth is irreparably broken.

People who are active as individuals within the system will use informal and often illegal ways to satisfy their needs and aspirations irrespective of what others do; their activities are mostly economic, pursued in the party-state domain, in the gray area between the state economy and the private sector, or in the black market. Informal networks develop that supply their members with the goods and services to meet their needs. They govern themselves by the norm of reciprocity. Everybody, irrespective of his or her moral and ideological convictions, will, when faced with problems of everyday life, participate in this way (Wedel 1986).

Individual activities against the system take the form of moral protest and are often purely symbolic acts. The two forms of active behavior by individuals are not mutually exclusive; the same individual will engage at times in one or the other. Often one's political convictions will provide a rationale for undertaking something that may be damaging to the interests of the state but useful from a selfish point of view.

The collective active strategy, within the system, may take the form of moral support for corrupt behavior. Reasons for this may lie "in the conviction that, in a state of permanent scarcity, people were entitled to cope with their problems as best they can, extorting from the state sector what was due to them anyway" (Hirszowicz 1986, 141). A state alienated from society cannot evoke any moral sentiments or sense of loyalty among its subjects. The collective action strategy may also take the form of pressure exerted by regions or industrial branches to increase their share in the distribution of resources, irrespective of the needs of the country.

There is a point at which some versions of the collective active strategy meet, as in the defense of the family as a social institution. If family ties are defended, other forms of solidarity can develop within society but outside the realm of the state. A lot of research on this subject has been done in Poland. It has been discovered in a number of studies on social consciousness that individuals tended to turn their attention away from public issues, restricted their participation in secondary groups, and focused instead on the values of private life and the enhancement of their activities in primary groups made up of families and friends. The late Stefan Nowak called the ethos that has developed on such grounds a sociological vacuum (1980) because there is a void between a sense of national identity and the primary group identity.[6] Antoni Sulek, in discussing results of surveys of the younger generation in Poland, remarked that

> the orientation [toward the family and peer groups] . . . could have been a reaction of a defensive nature against a world of formalized social relations, unfriendly institutions and incomprehensible large groups. The family, the circle of friends, oneself—these became sanctuaries, where one can hide and be "oneself." (1985, 39)

Individuals try to nurse their public wounds in their private nests, if they possess them. There were times and societies where Communist institutions succeeded in penetrating family life by making heroes of those who betrayed their kin.

The family may be the last line of defense, but from that trench offensive actions can be mounted. The concrete form that action would take depends upon the values socialized in the family, which probably differ across social strata, and upon the existence of a public institution independent from the state. The only institutional domain that was, in certain cases, able to defend its relative autonomy was that of organized religion. The effectiveness of religious communities in defending their autonomy has varied from denomination to denomination (Sharlet 1989). Protestant denominations, which are fairly decentralized and highly institutionalized, probably had more problems in preserving their autonomy than did others, with the exception of the Orthodox church in Russia, Bulgaria, and Romania because it has had a tradition of complete subjection to the state.[7] Under conditions of severe persecution, Baptist sects, which are decentralized but not so institutionalized and have a strong evangelical bond, were much better adapted to survive in the underground, winning converts from the Orthodox church and causing, especially in the Russian Republic, serious problems for the KGB. The Catholic church, with its international connections and highly developed hierarchy, was perhaps the most vulnerable to terrorist activities by the state. Once those became more restrained, however, it was best able to resist pressure and to defend its autonomy against encroachments by the party and government because of the popular and international support it enjoyed.

Whatever its other significance, a religious mass or service is a public meeting, and a sermon is an occasion to share values and attitudes without direct intervention by the state. Participation in organized religious life, even if limited to common prayer, creates bonds of trust and community on the basis of which other forms of participation can develop.

Thus, the successful defense of the family, although accompanied by an absence of intermediate loyalties that would fill the space between the realm of the family and that of the nation, can lead to a strong identification with family members and groups of friends and only a symbolic identification with the society or the nation.

In these circumstances, moral regulators and informal controls work only at the level of primary groups; what is outside of those is "up for grabs." When individuals and groups decide to exploit existing opportunities, they may become politically active, overtly accepting an ideology that is not theirs, but using their political positions to promote the interests of the family and of allied primary groups. Then, when the political leadership abandons the use of terror, which is the only instrument available to preserve the depersonalization of the Communist state, informal relations and clique networks start to permeate political institutions, and the phenomenon of the *privatization* of the state begins to escalate.

A successful defense of the family, when accompanied by effective socialization in a democratic tradition of public life or in a universal morality stemming from religious or other socialization principles, can also lead to the active and individual or active and collective behavior against the system that is aimed at broader, rather than particularistic, values and interests. The second case results, for rather obvious reasons, directly or indirectly, in various forms of political opposition.

In view of the considerations formulated above, I would qualify Alain Besançon's proposition that corruption is a sign that the "civil society" has survived. In his words, " . . . in the opposition between *them* and *us*, between the Party and the civil society, corruption is a sign of sanity. It is a sign of life, of a pathological life, but that is better than death" (1980, 302). (I also think that he too easily sees in corruption the rebirth of the market. Corruption is no market, and it existed for millennia in ancient empires without resulting in anything even approaching a competitive market economy.) Besançon is surely correct when he says that under such conditions individuals start to matter and to reject the language of an artificial ideology and false values. But the culture of the society in which the sociological vacuum is an omnipresent reality is devoid of the values that make public life possible. It is not a civil society in terms of a *community* built upon universal values. When loyalty centers on the family and friends, national allegiance is either purely symbolic or takes on highly particularistic, tribal forms.

Neither can we postulate that the rejection of Communism as such creates conditions sufficient for the emergence of a civil society. Opposition is based first of all on negation. The bonds that unite individuals and groups in opposition have a strongly moralistic, negative character. But a civil society requires a positive vision, an ability to cooperate in a constructive—not only destructive—way, a respect for other persons that precludes the development of a zero-sum game. A *civil* society reflects principles of socialization implied by the acts of being civil and partaking in a civilization. From the fact that Communism is effectively opposed in a given country, one should not deduce the existence of a civil society there.

A factor that can contribute to the emergence of the civil society is the enormous progress that has been made in education. But, to assess the weight of this factor properly, one has to bear in mind that educational advancement has been used to mold the thinking of the Soviet population in a way that was functional for the regime, education having been part of the propaganda effort. Its content directly contradicts the idea of the civil society. It promotes political passivity, obedience, and a view of the world in which the only measures of correctness and legitimacy are the interests of the Soviet state. People educated thus are good material for corruption; they are not good material for democratic revolution.

Although cultural traditions, historical circumstances, and other characteristics of Communist-ruled societies can affect the strategies pursued by individuals and groups, they represent only part of the picture. It is an important part if we consider that, despite a great effort made in the 1940s and 1950s to homogenize Soviet-dominated East-Central European societies institutionally, these societies are as diverse as ever. But it is quite obvious that the structural characteristics of particular Communist states and the policies they pursue are universally relevant to the kinds of strategies adopted by individuals and groups in satisfying their needs. Let us consider the strategies of the partisan state and their impact upon the strategies selected by and in particular societies.

Coercion, Corruption, and Reform

Elsewhere (1989) I consider policies of the partisan state toward society in terms of three strategies: coercion, corruption, and reform. What we encounter in reality are usually different mixes of the three. Besides, a Communist government can use different strategies in dealing with different groups; for instance, it can try to bribe workers in big enterprises with wage increases and "special shops" while it persecutes the dissident intelligentsia, or vice versa. It can coerce society while providing individuals with rewards for cooperation. Before we consider the factors behind the predominance of this or that strategy, it may be useful to examine the impact of *pure strategies* upon the behavior of individuals and groups.

Widespread and persistent coercion, if successfully applied, results ultimately in passive submission. An individual's social environment changes fairly quickly as his friends and colleagues are arrested and liquidated; attachments become weak and superficial, no personal loyalties develop. This is the picture of a perfectly atomized and atomic society, clearly exemplified by the Stalinist period in the Soviet Union.

The process of de-Stalinization has pushed to the forefront the problem of individual and group interests. A regime that either rejected or at least mutilated all impersonal, objective control mechanisms is badly equipped to deal with individual and group autonomy. When terror is relaxed and life stabilizes, the reappearance of particular interests is tantamount to an escalation of corruption in all its forms. These impersonal regulatory devices were created to mediate between the domain of the private and the domain of public interests through public discourse and negotiations, through rules of the game that are specific for market mechanisms, or, through the coercive elimination of certain forms of behavior judged detrimental to social life. When those mechanisms are absent or deficient, a system is unable to produce anything that can be reasonably conceived as the public interest.

The problem is not that some officials are dishonest and take bribes or use their positions in other profitable ways. Most of all, when the party is organizationally integrated, all other control mechanisms disintegrate. The declining effectiveness of social controls coupled with changes in social consciousness and systems of values has left a lacuna that is gradually filled by informal relations and clique networks. The domain of the state becomes a playground for narrow private interests: the most attractive game in town is exploitation of the state.

> In the state sector . . . the most important [advantage] is the possibility of re-privatising, the appropriation of control over state property by individuals and groups. In consequence, the second economy loses its parallel character, becoming just one of the forms of behavior of the official system. Individual opportunities for participation in the second economy become dependent upon the position occupied in the state sector. (Wisniewski 1985, 556)

The state and the private intertwine, becoming scarcely distinguishable. Official positions acquire a new character: they become a patrimonial "endowment," whose incumbents appropriate them in their own name and that of those who support and protect them. Official organizational goals are often reduced to fiction and replaced with informal, privatized criteria of evaluation and promotion.

This change in attitude toward position and formal duty is not an exclusive feature of those who occupy upper- and middle-level positions in the hierarchy. Workers who fulfill private orders on factory machines from stolen materials and during work hours, salespersons who exchange scarce goods among themselves ("internal trade within the commercial sector") or pass them to black-marketeers, the son of a prime minister whose house is built free of charge by convicts and soldiers from materials for which he pays a fraction of the official price and which are normally unobtainable anyway, all these people manifest the same basic attitude toward their positions: they treat them as their private preserves.

These are individual undertakings, but in engaging in them one is safe only as long as he is part of an informal network and willing to share his proceeds with others. This is also a sort of entrepreneurial game, but without constraints imposed by law and without the discipline of the market. The picture that emerges is the invasion of the partisan state by private interests. Besançon (1978, 8) once compared the Soviet type of state to a parasite preying upon civil society. Here we have the parasite preyed upon by other parasites of its own making: a parasitic state in a symbiosis with a parasitic society.

We can treat this type of corruption as an unintended consequence of the institutional structure of the Communist system and its evolution. Yet, it fulfills important functions in contributing to the survival of the system by enforcing conformist behavior. If one has no rights, or those he formally has can be freely abused by the authorities, which is nearly the same, then the cost of a decision not to comply is very high indeed. The stronger the partisan state is, the higher this cost.

The same applies to collective corruption. The concept of "right" under this type of political organization is dubious.[8] Let us take, for instance, a "hypothetical" situation described by the Hungarian sociologist, Elemer Hankiss (1986). Assume that a group of people takes over power and deprives society of basic human rights. Then, the same group, under conditions of duress, proposes a barter: society can regain some rights in exchange for conformity and obedience. In Hankiss's view, and in the view adopted here, this constitutes an act of corruption. The only objection that can be legitimately raised against this reasoning is that we are not talking here about rights; these are rather *privileges* that are revocable.

This type of collective corruption, aimed usually at some important groups in the society, consists in providing the group with privileges that the rest of the society does not possess, such as access to special shops or the special provision of certain services. Once those privileges are accepted by the group, the group starts to put informal pressure upon its members to conform. Furthermore, in cases of collective revolt, the group makes itself vulnerable to all sorts of propaganda attacks exposing the privileges it alone enjoys. This creates a favorable atmosphere for a little purge. Thus, *to the extent that coercion loses its paramount importance in keeping society in check, it is replaced by corruption.* Some is unintended and undermines the *governability* of the Communist state, while some is partly intended to destroy the ethical integrity of professional and other functional groups. A partisan state needs an atomic society, otherwise it is under threat.

Corruption, as a technique of rule over the society, is a negative strategy aimed at demoralizing and disarming a potential internal enemy, or at winning over an ally by compromising his moral integrity. Used widely, it demoralizes society and corrupts the apparatus of the state itself: a corruptor cannot escape corrupting himself. A positive strategy, aimed at providing the state with some political support and legitimacy, is *reform*. This strategy carries with it some serious risks.

For the last thirty years, advocates of reform have tried to sell reform measures to the ruling elite as being *exclusively* "economic." Reform was only considered and to some extent implemented because the traditional Communist system of bureaucratic planning and management of the economy has not worked. But, as soon as the process of implementation starts, it becomes obvious that other reforms and institutional changes are needed for the reformed economic system to work. Thus, we rediscover the obvious: economic processes are part of the broader system of social structures and processes.

Let us consider Janos Kornai's formula that an economic reform is a change in the organization of the Soviet type of economy that "diminishes the role of bureaucratic coordination and increases the role of the market" (1986, 1691). When one assumes, as we did, that the fundamental characteristic of the Soviet type of regime is that it is organized from the top down, then it follows that an economic reform that gives power to consumers to influence allocation decisions made by producers breaks the logic of the system and is, thereby, a traumatic event. A superficial look at attempts to implement market-oriented reforms during the past thirty years in Poland, at the shy flirtations with the idea in the Soviet Union, and even at the supposedly most successful Hungarian case, where they already have twenty years of experience with economic reform without achieving much success, suffices to demonstrate the correctness of this diagnosis.

The political problem with reform is that not only do people's preferences and tastes start to influence production and investment decisions—this in itself would be an important restriction upon the arbitrariness of the state—but also that economic reform requires far-reaching changes in the role of law in the organization of social action, in the organization of the judiciary, in the secrecy that covers budget decisions, in the process and criteria of making personnel decisions, and in relationships among firms and other economic institutions, such as banks. It would require a profound intervention in the domain of property relations whose significance cannot be underestimated, even if access to the capital market remains restricted to private persons, which seems rather a temporary restraint. It implies the emergence of a pluralistic political order in place of a monistic partisan state.

To be brief, the implementation of a fairly consistent and efficient economic system based upon market principles would require the broad and fundamental restructuring of the Communist state—an inference drawn from commonly adopted blueprints for reform—to make a Communist system workable and efficient is to transform it into a liberal, democratic regime. How to do so while guaranteeing a privileged position to the Communist elite is the basic puzzle. As long as this question remains unsolved, any market-oriented economic reform will be a deadly threat to the ruling class of a Soviet type of regime. The Chinese attempt to confine reform to the narrow arena of economics ended in the massacre of students in Beijing. Yet, with the economic failure of the regime, the issue of reform is inescapable. This is the nature of the present crisis facing the Communist world. As Vincent Ostrom aptly remarked, "when the *possible* becomes *impossible,* we have reason to believe that problems of institutional failure have reached massive proportions" (1974, 121). To the extent that the partisan state has become privatized and society has accepted corruption as a solution to its individual and group problems, no effective reform is possible.

In theory, the difference between ruling through corruption and ruling through reform is more profound than it is in practice. In the first instance, the ruling class attempts to pit one social group against another, demoralizing and atomizing society, and directing social frustration against scapegoats. It uses power against the interests of the society, and can find acceptance only when it deprives society of the ability to evaluate its own situation objectively. Reform, by contrast, implies the integration of social groups around tasks that are in their interests. Even when participation in reform is restricted, and the reform does not produce the expected economic advantages, it may be favorable to the emergence of an ethos of public responsibility that is crucial for any democratic society.

In practice in Communist states, reform, corruption, and coercion coexist in various mixes, with one or another usually playing a dominant role. Reform may be used, for instance, to appease intellectuals; corruption, to neutralize the apparatus and the workers; coercion, to deal with those who demand more respect for human freedom. We can also expect different strategies to predominate in different social groups depending, to some extent, on how they are related within the structure of the state.

The Limits of Reform in Communist States

I shall now use a highly simplified model of the Communist social order as consisting of two elements: the partisan state and society. The partisan state, in turn, consists of the center and the bureaucracy. The center is the top leadership of the party; the bureaucracy is made up of party and state hierarchies crucial for the existence of the order. Society is an external amalgam of various individuals and groups. The partisan state, like the society, can be strong or weak. But the same characteristics may apply to the two elements within the partisan state. However, when we consider the two elements of the partisan state separately, the question arises: strong or weak in relation to whom? A bureaucracy that is perceived by society as being very strong because it is under the effective control of the center, will, from the point of view of the center, look weak.

Let us assume, first of all, that the center cannot be strong without having at its disposal effective and strong bureaucracies. Otherwise, it will lack the instruments necessary to implement its will. If the bureaucracy can be strong when the center is weak, the outcome is ungovernability: finally, both can be weak. Although the number of all combinations is eight, in fact, we have three realistic possibilities. The others can be eliminated on logical grounds. Considering society, for instance, it is obvious that under a strong center, society must be weak, as it will be when the bureaucracies are strong under a weak center; although this last situation, because of anarchy, and a lack of coordination, opens the possibility for enhancing social integration. Society can be strong only when both the center and bureaucracy (the partisan state) are weak, but unless its strength is translated into an institution-building activity that leads to a new political order, the result will be still greater disorder and anarchy. These three realistic theoretical cases are not only probable but also approximate real situations in the post-Stalinist Communist world.[9]

The first case offers a number of possibilities. If the economy develops satisfactorily, we would expect conservative policies, with reliance on coercion and strong discipline. This was exemplified by Bulgaria and the German Democratic Republic. About the latter, we must remember that it was heavily subsidized by West Germany and, considering its political situation, had little incentive to risk a reform. It is only when the economy starts to falter, and there is no reasonable alternative, as occurred in Hungary at the end of the 1960s, that the Communist leadership seriously considers reform.

But even then there may be variations. In Romania, for instance, economic difficulties resulted only in more emphasis being placed upon terror and coercion; there was an outright rejection of reform. The outcome may depend upon the personality of the man in charge (the first secretary) and some aspects of his environment including the political traditions of his country. When a decision to embark upon the path of reform is made, as it was in Hungary, the first important consequence of the decision is political co-optation of professionals who are offered the prospect of participating in something legitimate and of using their knowledge and competence to implement a program of rational social change. In return, they have to conform and, at least overtly, identify with the system. They have to pay a price for the right to participate. In time, the system can evolve in the direction of extending the scope for participation, reducing its reliance on coercion, developing in the elites a sense of responsibility, and the ability of perceiving at least some professionals, if not the whole society, in cooperative terms, until the point is reached that whatever participation is possible under the system is not enough to satisfy social demand, and the party control becomes questioned, as occurred in Hungary.

The second situation is that of a relatively weak center, strong bureaucracy, and a weak society. The center follows conservative policies that correspond to the interests of the control hierarchies. The predominant instruments of government are coercion and corruption. Elites use coercion against any independent movement that emerges from society and prefer to corrupt individuals from crucial professional groups and whole groups, such as, highly qualified workers in heavy industry, the police, and so on. There are no grounds on which to integrate society around any positive political values. The system is able to persist only as long as it successfully coerces, disintegrates, and demoralizes its social environment, as happened until recently in Czechoslovakia or happened in Brezhnev's USSR.

The third possibility is that of a weak partisan state facing a fairly strong society. It is too weak systematically to apply the strategy of coercion, especially as this would require a strong center and, however weak, the bureaucracy is not interested in effectively strengthening central control. Its corruptive efforts are useless because corruption becomes too costly and ineffective when strategic groups are well integrated and have deprived the government of the last remnants of moral authority. Reform is difficult because it further strengthens society and the bureaucracy can effectively oppose it. Thus, the partisan state tries to coerce, corrupt, and reform all at the same time. Eventually, corruption starts to prevail as it works best in an already privatized political order. The only hope that remains is that, finally, the society will be worn out to such an extent that it will surrender all resistance to Communist rule. It is a process that can be compared to a war of attrition and occurred in Poland with the tacit support of some of the Polish party leaders.

To summarize this discussion, we can say that it is possible, when a group possesses adequate means of coercion, to terrorize a society into passive compliance. However, when the cooperation of society is needed, coercion will not serve the purpose. Corruption, in various doses, may work for some time, but it demoralizes both the rulers and the ruled. The limits of reform that are consistent with the power interests of the ruling elite are narrow.

The probability that a civil society will emerge is only partly dependent upon the strategies pursued by the state, and directly dependent upon the degree of control the Communist state is able to exercise. The probability is close to zero during a period of state terror. It is much higher when the strategy of corruption predominates, but then the intervening variable is the ability of the society to defend itself against demoralization by the state. A reform strategy presents better possibilities for participation, but these concern mostly the intelligentsia; workers become entirely involved in the struggle for material survival.

A society that has preserved some institutions independent of the state will present the greatest challenge to Communist elites. Under such a challenge, an effective reform is unlikely because political elites would find it too risky to relinquish control. Thus, corruption is the most probable outcome. But a corrupt state decentralizes corruption, weakening even further its ability to control society. When an acute conflict comes, it is hardly able to defend itself. But this does not mean that by toppling the Communist state a society can emerge as a "civil society," ready to implement democracy.

Putting aside other unfavorable circumstances related to the economic situation, the problem remains with society itself. Its sense of reality is weakened; its leaders are sometimes adventurers without a sense of responsibility for their actions. Years of political alienation leave an imprint difficult to erase in a short time.

The fundamental problem at the roots of the crisis in the Soviet world is the separation of the state from the society on which its political order was built. If the state is an institutional device serving the general interest of the polity, the seizure of control over the state by a revolutionary vanguard could have led only to a permanent oppression of those subjected to the power of the state. This was effective as long as the Communist state remained an integrated whole. When it started to disintegrate into a collection of power centers oriented toward the satisfaction of their own interests, the separation may have become less dramatic, and life more bearable. But this has clearly visible costs to civilization, though they are not so easy to identify. They relate to moral order and its relationship to autonomous standing of individuals and their capacity to associate with others in self-organizing and self-governing endeavors.

The civilizational consequences of Communist regimes are most directly visible in the degeneration of ethical norms and behavioral patterns upon which all social order must be founded. These are not only the norms and patterns connected with such values as reliability, honesty, and trust, but also the automatic reflexes that determine, without any conscious intellectual effort on the part of the actor, what is appropriate in given circumstances and what is not. Such automatic reflexes are needed everywhere and at all times as they are when, in driving a car, an individual executes dozens of actions every minute without even thinking about them. The intrusion of the state into all areas of social life, the effort to control and manage all social choices and activities directly, have eventually produced the gradual eradication of automatic social reflexes.

The key point in the process of change is the reclamation of the mechanisms of collective decision making and action by the society; "the expropriation of the expropriators." This can happen only when the diverse mechanisms of collective action emerge again to serve the common good of the society. In order to achieve this, it is first necessary to reevaluate the private; in order to re-create the public, it is simultaneously necessary to re-create the private. Individuals, groups, and communities of people functioning in a society need autonomy if they are to develop the critical self-consciousness to address themselves to situations confronting societies as something more than grains of sand.

IV

THE SOVIET BLOC: A SUPRANATIONAL REGIME

THIRTEEN

EAST-CENTRAL EUROPE

The history of East-Central Europe has been long, rich in events, and tumultuous. It is not possible to render justice to it in one chapter (or in one book). This general background information is important to an understanding of the situation in the region as it developed before, during, and after World War II. It is also important to understand the history of this region in view of the disintegration of the Soviet bloc and the potential it offers for the development of new political and economic relationships in this part of Europe. What happens during the coming years in this region will be of crucial importance for the future of the continent and, considering the importance of Europe in world affairs, may have a much wider resonance.

East-Central Europe encompasses a portion of the areas referred to in the English-speaking world as Eastern Europe and is central for many reasons. First, it is geographically located in the very center of Europe.[1] Second, it is central in the sense of political and military strategy: Whoever controls it is in an excellent position to dominate the continent.[2] Third, it is central in a cultural sense, for it has been closely integrated with Western Europe since the early Middle Ages, directly participating in, and sometimes contributing to major

European cultural and political initiatives while it had direct contacts with the Ottoman Empire and the Crimean khanate in the east. Russia, by contrast, accepted Christianity from the Byzantine Empire, found itself under Mongol rule, and later developed a regime that had no counterpart in European history. Russian contacts with Western Europe intensified late, in fact, on a wide scale only in the nineteenth century. Hence, one is left with the choice of either excluding Russia from Europe, which is not justified, or treating the areas between Russia proper and Western Europe as Central, or if one prefers, East-Central, Europe.

Geopolitically, East-Central Europe is an area that has been, at different times in history, militarily and politically contested by Bohemia, Poland, Hungary, Germany, Turkey, Sweden, Russia, and Austria. Some of those attempts to dominate, such as the one made by Sweden in the seventeenth century, were short-lived and involved only parts of East-Central European territory. The Ottoman Empire, whose expansion started in the early fifteenth century, lasted longer. German political influences were initially represented by the emperors of the Holy Roman Empire of the German Nation, later, by the Teutonic Knights, and, since the late seventeenth century, the Kingdom of Prussia, culminating in Bismarck's second German Empire and Hitler's Third Reich.[3] The Germans were also represented by the rise of Austria. The Habsburgs' expansion in this region started in the sixteenth century and intensified with the decline of their fortunes in Western Europe. Russia's expansion into this region started in the second half of the seventeenth century and ended after World War II with its effective domination over the whole area.

This highly diverse region can be roughly divided into two parts: that contested by Poland, Lithuania, Sweden, Russia, and later Prussia in the north and east, and that contested by the Ottoman Empire, the Habsburg Empire, and later Russia in the south and southeast. The eastern border of the northern part follows the Dnieper River, overlapping with the prepartition frontiers of Poland and Lithuania. To the south, the northern part embraces Czechoslovakia, and Hungary is between the two parts. What divides these parts is not only climate and geography but also cultural and historical experience. Within each there are great ethnic, religious, and cultural diversities.

The Polish-Lithuanian Commonwealth, or republic, may be viewed as the only genuine and successful effort to create a federal political structure with the purpose of defending the region against external invasion. At the peak of its power, the commonwealth included the area of the present Baltic Republics, the Smolensk region, the whole of Belorussia and the Ukraine, and Moldavia with its access to the Black Sea.[4]

At the end of the eighteenth century, on the Prussian initiative, the Polish-Lithuanian Commonwealth was partitioned among Prussia, Russia, and Austria. This opened a new period in European history, giving rise to two great imperial powers, Russia and Germany. According to Lord Acton:

> Till then no nation had been deprived of its political existence by the Christian Powers, and whatever disregard had been shown for national interests and sympathies, some care had been taken to conceal the wrong by a hypocritical perversion of law. But the partition of Poland was an act of wanton violence, committed in open defiance not only of popular feeling but of public law. For the first time in modern history a great State was suppressed, and a whole nation divided among its enemies. (Fears 1985, 413)

The partition of the commonwealth created a dangerous precedent. Since then we have been accustomed to even worse crimes, often committed by the same perpetrators.

Partition opened the way for the quick political ascent of Prussia and Russia. Until the 1790s, Prussia lacked the territorial basis to become a first-rate European power. By expanding into Polish territory, Prussia overcame this handicap. For Russia, partition moved its frontiers several hundred miles to the west, giving it the highly fertile Ukrainian black soil, great natural resources, and comfortable access to the Baltic Sea.

The next political reorganization of East-Central Europe took place after World War I ended with the defeat of Germany, the demise of the Austro-Hungarian Empire, and the Communist revolution in Russia. At the Conference of Versailles, in the aftermath of the war, a new European order was established. The puzzle that the politicians gathered in Versailles had to solve was how to redesign the territorial and political map of Europe to avoid a major conflict in the future. Roman Dmowski, a highly perceptive, conservative Polish statesman, in a brochure published in English in July 1917, remarked that "the solution of the great problems of this war lies neither in the Balkans, nor in Asia Minor, but in Central Europe itself" (p. 14). The key to East-Central European problems was, as usual, Germany and Russia, their policies and relations between the countries.

Among changes that appeared on the map of Europe after World War I, the dismemberment of the Austro-Hungarian Empire was of major importance. The Habsburgs lost their empire and Austria became a minor secondary state. Hungary suffered territorial losses that left large numbers of ethnic Hungarians outside Hungarian frontiers. Comparing Poland and Hungary between the world wars, Vojtech Mastny remarked:

> The reverse minority problem plagued Hungary, whose postwar territorial amputations—the worst in the region—consigned too many Magyars unwillingly to the neighboring states. . . . Punished more than it deserved, it became the most bitter of the revisionist nations dedicated to undoing the postwar settlement. This overwhelming preoccupation diverted its attention from the long overdue reform of its political and social structures. (1989, 22)

This revisionist bitterness, and fear of Germany and Russia, dragged Hungary into joining Germany, Italy, and Japan in the Anti-Comintern Pact in February 1939.

Slovenia and Croatia, the southern Slav territories of the Habsburg Empire, together with Serbia as a dominant power, and Macedonia, formed the Kingdom of Yugoslavia. The Yugoslav problem from the beginning has been its diversity of cultural heritage and history, although the peoples of the kingdom were mostly Slav. Croatia, Dalmatia, and Slovenia, all with Roman Catholic populations, had been under strong Italian and Austrian influence; in

Serbia, Macedonia, and Montenegro the population is mostly Greek Orthodox and there are significant Muslim minorities. Serbia and Macedonia had for centuries been under Turkish domination and later, in the nineteenth century, they developed close ties with the Russian Empire.

Of all the states created in the territories of the former Austro-Hungarian monarchy, Czechoslovakia was perhaps the most successful. Bohemia and Moravia were industrially the most developed parts of that empire. Slovakia was agricultural and much less industrialized. The country was able to create and preserve a democratic regime throughout the period between the world wars. Yet, even then Slovaks bitterly complained of having little say in running their own country. Once in control of Czechoslovakia, Hitler skillfully exploited the Slovaks' dissatisfaction.

The frontiers of Poland, both east and west, were subject to controversy throughout the interwar period. The Polish-German frontier was established by a referendum and two Silesian uprisings; the Polish-Soviet frontier was defined in the Treaty of Riga, which ended the Polish-Bolshevik war in 1920; and the Polish-Czechoslovak frontier was also a subject of controversy. Internally, Poland had serious problems with its minorities: Ukrainians, Jews, Germans, and other smaller ethnic minorities comprised nearly one-third of the population.

Soviet Russia had never fully accepted the territorial losses caused by the secession of Finland, Poland, the Baltic states, and by the loss of Bessarabia to Romania. But there was another reason for the Soviet revisionist posture that may have been even more important: Soviet Russia had a vested interest in international destabilization, an interest that was grounded in its ideological support for revolutionary movements in the West and in its aspirations to be a superpower.[5] The Bolsheviks accepted in principle the idea of self-determination of peoples, but they saw it as a provisional concession forced upon them by unfavorable circumstances (see D'Encausse 1983, 48). Had they consistently applied the principle of self-determination for nations throughout the former empire, Soviet Russia would have been reduced to inhospitable areas of northeastern Europe. Thus, self-determination was a solution that the Soviets had to avoid at all cost, unless it was to be applied as Stalin did in 1939 and 1940, to the Soviet-occupied territories of Poland, Lithuania, Latvia, and Estonia, where either 100 percent of the respective populations, or 100 percent of the members of parliaments, "voted" for the incorporation of their countries into the Soviet Union.

Both Germany and Soviet Russia considered the existence of a Polish state as a temporary arrangement: a "seasonal state," to use the term of the period.[6] In such circumstances, a Polish government could only try to prevent an alliance between Russia and Germany because, such an alliance had to be directed against Poland.

> Poland had to rely chiefly on herself. To do this successfully, she had to maintain good neighborly relations with both Germany and Russia, based on reciprocity and bilateral nonaggression pacts. She had to maintain a balance between Moscow and Berlin, avoiding collective security schemes, particularly if they were directed against either of her neighbors. Finally, she had to preserve her freedom from foreign influences or pressures. (Karski 1985, 172)

Relations between Germany and Soviet Russia were changeable. Close military cooperation between 1922 and the early 1930s started with the Treaty of Rapallo, but did not prevent the Soviet government from continually subverting the Weimar Republic by supporting Communist rebellions, describing German Social Democrats as "social fascists," and forcing the German Communist party to support the Nazis in their struggle for power. There is no doubt that Stalin and Soviet Russia bear full responsibility for the rejection by German Communists of the Social-Democratic initiatives to form a common front against Hitler, a rejection that significantly, if not decisively, contributed to Hitler's ascent to power. Later, in the early 1930s, Soviet leadership, realizing the gravity of the Nazi threat, signed a series of nonaggression treaties with its neighbors. Having come at the end of the 1930s to the realization that war was unavoidable, the Soviet government sought to direct German aggression to the west and, eventually, to take part in the spoils of German aggression in Poland, the Baltic region, and in the Balkans.[7] At the same time, from the German point of view, an invasion of Poland, and confrontation in the west, in which Hitler did not believe but had to account for as a possibility, made any understanding with the Soviet Union a valuable asset. These incentives and calculations led directly to the Ribbentrop-Molotov Pact (the German-Soviet Treaty of Nonaggression).

Thus, the major political problems the area faced were the problem of revisionism in the relationship among states and the problem of ethnic and national minorities within particular states. Revisionism had a different weight in different countries. The most consequential for the policies that other countries of the region pursued was the fear of German and Soviet revisionism, a fear that led to a system of defensive alliances, with France to counter German aggression and among Poland, Romania, and Hungary to counter a Soviet invasion. There was no provision for joint German-Soviet aggression.

The main strategic political flaw originating in East-Central Europe was the relationship between Czechoslovakia and Poland, two countries that should have been natural allies. They were divided by natural frontiers, and their long-term interests coincided. The Polish government blamed their bad relations on Czechoslovakia which, according to the Poles profited from the Polish-Soviet conflict in 1919 and 1920 by forcibly incorporating Teschen Silesia, an area with a predominantly Polish population.[8] The Czechoslovak government was also criticized for supporting German territorial claims on Poland, for giving refuge and financial support to Ukrainian extremists in Poland, and for its supposedly pro-Communist sympathies and close cooperation with the USSR. The Czechoslovaks were not interested in close cooperation with Poland, whose difficult position with regard to Germany and the Soviet Union made it, in their view, an unattractive partner. Behind those policies and those recriminations were prejudices and an unwillingness to understand each other's perspectives that prevented the neighborly cooperation that could have enhanced the viability of the arrangement reached at Versailles.

If the Czechoslovak government could be blamed for the bad start in its relations with Poland, the finale belonged to the Polish side. Polish participation, with Hitler's Germany, in the partition of Czechoslovakia confirms Talleyrand's opinion that in politics errors of judgment are worse than crimes. One of the questions that, to my knowledge, has not been satisfactorily answered is, Was there a possibility in the 1930s for closer cooperation in military and economic affairs between Poland and Czechoslovakia? It seems that these two countries acting together would have provided a substantial defense and could have made an important contribution to the security of the region and to the durability of the Versailles settlement. Another question is, What did France do to improve relations between them? France, itself weak and divided, was, apparently, more interested in a radial network centered on Paris than in developing a viable security system. The role of Czechoslovakia in East-Central Europe, because of its economic importance and geographic position, could have been much more constructive. Unfortunately, its relations with Hungary and Romania were as neglected as were those with Poland.

During World War II, the Polish and the Czechoslovak governments-in-exile engaged in serious talks about forming a federation. They were interrupted in 1943, when Benes opted for closer ties with the USSR. After the war, both governments again made an effort to establish a close economic and political collaboration (see Brzezinski 1967, 57–58), but such plans conflicted with the Soviet interest in creating a radial structure of bilateral relations centered on Moscow. Whatever institutionalized forms it takes, close cooperation between Poland and Czechoslovakia and extending to other countries, such as Hungary, Yugoslavia, and Romania may be of crucial importance for the future political and economic reorganization of this region of Europe.

Some authors claim that the Central European order, as designed at Versailles, was not workable and, therefore, could not have survived for long anyway.[9] The problem lay, however, not in the Central European region but in the political situation in all of Europe. Economically, the interwar period, the 1930s in particular, was difficult for everybody: East-Central Europe was no exception. A more critical factor was the lack of a clear political conception among Western European political leaders of how to manage European political affairs. There was a lack of the will, courage, and understanding necessary to avoid catastrophe.

The British government after World War I decided to return to its old policies of maintaining the European balance of power. Having perceived France as the main power on the continent, it distanced itself from French initiatives. Even when it supported France, it did so with caution. This attitude badly affected British relations with Poland and those other countries of the region, in particular Czechoslovakia and Romania, that Britain saw as allies of France. Moreover, after World War I, Great Britain found itself under the spell of an intense pacifism that moved to France in the 1930s when France faced economic decline and mounting domestic conflict. The United States withdrew entirely from European politics.

> The status created by the Versailles Treaty was artificial insofar as it did not express the true relations of forces once Great Britain and the United States declared their hostility to it or showed their indifference to it. If the Soviet Union and a rearmed Germany united to destroy it, France with only her continental allies, did not have the force to save it. (Aron 1966, 42)

The problem was not with the order itself. It may not have been perfect, but perfection is not of this world. The essence of the problem was the lack of understanding among western political elites of the political situation in Europe in general and of developments taking place in Germany in particular, and their lack of determination to maintain order. The maintenance of a balance of power requires the determination to resolve problems of interdependencies by active political measures rather than by pacifism and isolationism.

The German-Soviet Nonaggression Pact of August 1939 brought about a new division of East-Central Europe and the final destruction of the Versailles order. Europe was to be divided between the Third Reich and the Soviet Union. But the same reasons that produced collaboration now led to a military conflict: Hitler found Soviet territorial appetites in Europe incompatible with German expansionist designs. In large measure, World War II was fought over domination in East-Central Europe.

The main issue for the countries of the region, in the face of German threats, was a choice of strategy. Some of them, such as Czechoslovakia, were destroyed without being given a choice. For Poland, the choice was spurious. To accept German conditions, which were lenient in view of the circumstances (the main demands were the return to Germany of Gdansk, which at that time was a free city under the supervision of the League of Nations, and an extraterritorial road through the "Polish corridor"), probably would have led to Polish participation in a German war against the Soviet Union, with the promised territorial reward of the Ukraine, which would be a liability rather than an advantage.[10] The position taken by the Polish government determined the direction of the German attack: acceptance of the German conditions would have resulted in an immediate invasion of the USSR. Such an option was unacceptable for many reasons, the most cogent that it would eventually have made the country entirely dependent upon Hitler's Germany. Thus, the Polish choice was one between two evils. In Hungary, Bulgaria, and Romania, some form of cooperation with Germany was chosen. No country chose to cooperate with the USSR.

Poland and Czechoslovakia had their governments in London, and their armed forces were part of the anti-Nazi coalition. In the Polish case, these consisted of air, navy, and ground forces, and numbered in 1944 about a quarter of a million troops. Moreover, there was a large and well-organized underground army in Poland itself, and another army that fought the Nazis along with the Red Army.

The problem of Polish-Soviet relations emerged immediately after the German onslaught upon the USSR and was to haunt the Allies until the end of the war. It confronted Churchill and Roosevelt with difficulties in mediating between the Polish government and Stalin's government. With the progress of the war, the problem of Polish-Soviet frontiers gained in importance. The Polish government had no choice but to stand by the prewar frontiers. The Soviets clung to the Ribbentrop-Molotov frontiers which they, incorrectly, called the "Curzon line."[11] General Sikorski's argument that Russia, being a multinational state itself, had no right to impose ethnographical frontiers on Poland was valid but did not have the necessary political weight behind it to make any difference.

For the Americans and the British, who were most of all concerned with maintaining the harmonious cooperation of the Soviets, the Poles, no doubt, were a nuisance. Even so, Roosevelt's decision to delay all discussions about territorial questions in Europe and about political solutions for the postwar period was naive to say the least, because, as Clausewitz noted, "War is not merely a political act, but also a real political instrument, a continuation of political commerce, a carrying out of the same by other means" (quoted in Aron 1966, 23). To have pretended that the purpose of the war was exclusively to defeat Germany was short-sighted. Besides, as far as East-Central Europe was concerned, all important decisions were secretly made in Teheran. For Stalin, the purpose of the war was to obtain political advantage for the Soviet state; he subjected the conduct of the war after 1943 entirely to political goals, goals that had not changed since 1939. Stalin presented Churchill and Roosevelt with the same demands that he had earlier submitted to Hitler: the incorporation of the Baltic states, a major part of Polish territory, and Romanian Bessarabia. In Teheran, Yalta, and Potsdam, his demands were specified and sometimes extended. The Western allies, constrained by their democratic regimes and by contingencies of war, had no effective way to oppose Stalin. Roosevelt and Churchill simply accepted all the Soviet desiderata without even considering their merit.

Poland was compensated for its losses in the east with German territories in the west. The British, American, and Soviet leaders reached this decision without consulting the Polish government. At an earlier stage, such a consultation would have been pointless, for the Polish government could not accept the territorial revisions proposed. When finally some of the representatives of the Polish government were ready to negotiate a territorial compromise, the matter had become inconsequential: in Stalin's postwar plans for Poland there was no place for either the government-in-exile in London or for any other democratically elected government.

World War II gave the Soviet Union important territorial gains: nearly half of prewar Poland, the Baltic Republics, Bessarabia taken from Romania, and Karelia from Finland. But most of all, the USSR was able to impose its political regime on Poland, East Germany,

Czechoslovakia, Hungary, Romania, and Bulgaria. In Yugoslavia and Albania, the Communists won power by their own efforts and remained more independent. With control over Poland, Eastern Germany, and Czechoslovakia, the Soviet Union found itself militarily and politically in the center of Europe. In this situation, Western Europe lost the ability to survive politically and militarily on its own. The United States of America had to become a party to the European balance-of-power system.

The argument behind the American and British acceptance of this "sphere of influence," an expression still used, was that the USSR needed a *cordon sanitaire* to protect its frontiers against foreign aggression.[12] One must remember, however, that the three great invasions of Russia in modern times, by Napoleon, during World War I, and by Hitler, had either been preceded by the partition of Poland in which Russia joyfully participated with Germany or were conducted after Poland had already been partitioned. The argument about the need for a buffer zone is so misleading that one wonders how it can be accepted at face value. One could venture the argument that Russia would have been much safer with an independent Poland between herself and Germany.

The motive behind the direct subjection of East-Central European states to Soviet control has little to do with security concerns.

> For purposes of security alone, the Soviets did not need to Leninize six East European nations in what has become a process of perpetual intervention necessary to enforce the Leninist model. The fact is that the Soviets have two main goals at their periphery: one is political-ideological, the other military-security. (Walenta 1986, 276)

From the point of view of Soviet safety, the prewar situation would have been quite sufficient provided the Soviet government abandoned its efforts to destabilize the region and advance its political and ideological cause.

The postwar notion of "military-security" concerns, as formulated by the Soviet government, had obvious aggressive undertones.

> The Stalin-Hitler pact of August 1939 made history by implementing the new Soviet concept of security by imperial expansion —which was more threatening, because more viable, than the previous concepts of security by world revolution or partial collaboration with the West. (Mastny 1989, 24)

Such security can be attained only when the whole world is subjected to direct control by the power that wants to achieve it. Hence, the Soviet conception of security that required the unconditional submission of East-Central Europe to Moscow's interests was the real cause of the Cold War. The Cold War can end only when the Soviet Union decides to change both its concept of security, and the way it defines its interests in East-Central Europe. Changes in both of these concepts now seem to be taking place. To this I shall return in the last chapter.

FOURTEEN

PATTERNS OF DEPENDENCY IN THE SOVIET BLOC

The implementation of the Communist system of rule in East-Central Europe differed initially in each particular country. The first period, between 1945 and 1947, was marked by some tolerance for internal diversity. Local Communist parties only gradually asserted their control over society. This moderation was dictated by internal and external considerations. Haste could provoke active resistance against the Soviet Union and its clients. Stalin thought it wise not to challenge openly his former Western allies too early. Two years later the movement from diversity toward institutional unity was in full swing (see Brzezinski 1967).

The geopolitical changes that occurred in Europe at the end of the war made the USSR the dominant European power. The dramatic change in the frontier of Poland and Soviet Russia pushed the Soviet boundaries 120 miles to the west. Control over East Germany and the subjection of Poland provided a strategic advantage that could be neutralized, in case of war, only by a direct American involvement. Moreover, as a result of Soviet military operations and the American and British concessions made to Stalin in Teheran and Yalta, the USSR initially had full control over the

Balkans, although this control was weakened with the defection of Yugoslavia and later of Albania. Geopolitical changes in postwar Europe created the foundations for a Soviet world system. The use of the term *world system* in connection with the Soviet bloc is not free of ambiguities. Immanuel Wallerstein (1974) defines a world system as a closed system of relations, that is, one in which the component processes can be completely explained without recourse to external variables. One can doubt if the Soviet bloc is, in this sense, a world system because it is impossible to explain some of the key events that have taken place within it without referring to influences exerted by its liberal, democratic environment. One can even claim that, in the absence of competitive market mechanisms, governmental policies oriented toward generating enonomic growth were externally induced. But also, it is difficult to explain many changes in liberal political and economic regimes without taking into account the presence of the Soviet bloc. The conceptual roots of the welfare state are part of the liberal, democratic tradition, but the Communist ideological thrust no doubt helped in its implementation. There is also little doubt that the postwar militarization of the world was to a large extent induced by the Soviet expansionism that was rooted in the Soviet institutional structure. Thus, I shall use the term *world system* in a weaker sense than Wallerstein does to allow for external influences.

I shall not dwell here on the shortcomings of the world-system theory or of the ideologically and conceptually related dependency theory. I borrow, however, some of the concepts developed in those theoretical orientations, including those of the world system, the distinction between the core (metropolis) and peripheries, and the term *dependency*.

Dependency in this context implies an acute asymmetry in the relationship between two countries, or between one country and the others in a set of countries. Dependency may take different forms, according to its causes. The essential problem is, What are the goals and expectations of the dominant country and what strategies are available to dependent countries to diminish their levels of dependency? Dependency theorists reduce the issue to the relationship between the Latin-American and possibly African states and the highly industrialized nations, most notably the United States. They usually exclude from their consideration Southeast Asia, because relationships there are more complex than their simple theoretical (and ideological) assumptions could accommodate. For the same reason, they tend to exclude from their field of inquiry relations between the USSR and its East-Central European dependencies. When some writers on dependency theories feel obliged to address the problem, they usually try to demonstrate a lack of substantial difference between American and Soviet dependencies, holding that, in both cases, mechanisms and effects are similar.[1]

Among many differences in behavior between the two superpowers, one is worth mentioning. It is in American interests, and it has been American policy during at least the past two decades, to support agrarian reform and the establishment of democratic regimes in Latin America. Then, when they meet with no success, and a choice has to be made between a rightist and a leftist dictatorship, Americans prefer the former. Until 1989, the Soviet Union did not accept among its dependencies any other regime than those ruled by the Communist party. Finland has been the notable exception. Moreover, the whole situation is changing now, but that is because we are witnessing in the USSR an institutional revolution that spells the end of the Communist system.

Thus, I am using the term *Soviet world system,* of which East-Central Europe is the most important part, because it forms a distinct political and economic entity, different in its goals and the ways it functions from the liberal, democratic world and, to a large extent, coordinated in accordance with Soviet strategic interests.[2] It has had a supernational institutional order that was until 1989 an extension of the Soviet internal organization. I use the term *dependency* because the Soviet world system was constructed in a way that assured political, economic, and military domination of the USSR over its satellites.

With progress in communications, the world has become interdependent to an extent that the idea of national sovereignty must be treated with caution. In the game of interdependence, some countries are more and some are less dependent. The position of a country in an interdependent system is determined by the kinds of resources it controls. A country with a well-qualified labor force, sound and numerous academic and research institutions, and an adequately developed infrastructure will be in a far better position than will one that has no such assets, even if it is rich in oil and raw materials. Thus, market-generated dependencies stem mostly from differences in the place occupied by two or more countries in the world division of labor.

Because of its origins and organization, the Soviet world system tended to establish interdependence by direct political domination rather than by the social division of labor mediated by competitive markets. Under competitive markets, interdependency is regulated mostly by lateral mechanisms. Under a Communist system, a formal hierarchy of command and control systems coordinated the interdependence, and the peripheral participants were made dependent by force. The dominating relations were those between a particular country of the region and the USSR. "There is surprisingly little economic or political integration among the Eastern European countries," Paul Marer noted in 1989 (p. 37). There are good reasons for this. First, a system organized from the top is designed in a way that makes any form of cooperation not mediated by the center (the top) difficult, if not impossible. The radial structure so characteristic of the economic system in the Communist bloc stems directly from the basic Marxist-Leninist design upon which it was built (B. Kaminski 1989; Maciejewski and Nutti 1985). Second, the limits this pattern of organization placed on interactions among East-Central European states with one another prevented the creation of a politically and economically stronger and, therefore, more autonomous East-Central Europe (see Marer 1984). Dependency here has resulted entirely from a situation in which political and military domination is the primary ordering principle.

Countries that are administered on a day-to-day basis by external agencies and whose dependency is enforced by a threat of military invasion have much less freedom of maneuver and chance to find rational solutions to their problems than have those that depend upon market exchanges. The way the Soviet bloc was organized deprived its members of the possibility of choice among rational alternative solutions to the problems confronting them.

Building the Soviet Bloc

The organization of the Soviet bloc started long before the war ended. Communists from East-Central European countries were brought to Moscow, often directly from forced labor camps. There, they established "patriotic" organizations, as a first step toward forming Communist provisional governments, with splinter groups from other parties of the Left. These governments were then taken to the countries they were to rule by the Red Army.[3] Once installed, they became part of the organizational pattern set in motion to promote Soviet interests in the region.

What were these interests? Some I have already mentioned. Control over a large territory in the very center of the European continent with over a hundred million people is a considerable political and military asset. The creation of a Communist bloc enhanced the legitimacy of the Communist system in the Soviet Union itself because the Communist system was no longer confined to the Soviet Union; other countries had "chosen" it, a development that was an important ideological argument for the dynamism of the new social order. Some writers also suggest that there were economic motives behind the establishment of the bloc: the free use of resources from other countries for the economic reconstruction of the Soviet Union. (Important as they were, economic motives played at best a secondary role.) Soviet domination over East-Central Europe posed a direct threat to Western Europe. This strategic position, combined with the weakness of Germany in the postwar years and the strength of the Communist parties in Italy and France, stimulated Soviet plans to dominate all of Europe.

The initial strategic objective in the organization of the Soviet bloc seems to have been the incorporation of the East-Central European countries into the Soviet Union (see D'Encausse 1983, 276–80). This was not a secret plan. Soviet leaders believed in the superiority of the Communist system and that, as other Communist parties established the system at home, full unification would occur in a matter of time. The institutional and cultural homogenization of the bloc had to precede the final unification in which the East-Central European countries, having adopted Soviet patterns of organization, cultural values, and behavioral norms, would merge with the parent country.

Teresa Rakowska-Harmstone (1976, 38–39) points to three major assumptions underlying the Soviet theory of relations among Communist states. First, relations among these states are "identical to that of relations between nations and nationalities within the Soviet Union . . .," that is, based on "proletarian internationalism." Second, these states "are proceeding on an 'irreversible historical course' of gradual *rapprochement* which eventually leads to their 'merger.'" Third, the rapprochement process is already in progress and is accelerating. It "occurs at three basic levels: economic integration within the framework of CMEA [Council for Mutual Economic Assistance], the political integration on an interstate basis within the Warsaw Treaty Organization [WTO] and on an interparty basis, and the cultural integration through all-embracing multilateral and bilateral contacts." This suggests that successive Soviet leaderships perceived the Soviet bloc as a transitory phenomenon.

Unification was a natural objective of the basic design of the Communist institutional system: in particular countries the organization from the top had to be matched with the same organizational principle in the world. The firmer the grip of the Communist party on a given country, the greater the progress toward "building Communism." Similarly, progress on the world level depended on the degree of unification in the organizational structure of the bloc. To illustrate this point, let me quote a prominent liberal Soviet economist, the academician, Oleg T. Bogomolov.

> It is clear . . . that Lenin's conception of the world economy of the socialist type was linked with the attainment of a definite international unity of the economic activity of various countries, and in close cooperation, regulated according to an overall plan in satisfying their needs and interests. . . . The form of the world socialist economic system as described by Lenin, with a single overall plan and without any national partitions, can at present be regarded only as a thing of the future. (1986, 12)

This is not mere theory. Joint economic planning, however imperfect it has been, practiced within the Council for Mutual Economic Assistance, was surely a step in this direction.

The policy of unification was also apparent in military cooperation. Contrary to NATO practice, the Warsaw Pact "does not even have an operational command in the usual sense of the term, for the functions of the joint command have been limited to matters of administration, training and organization" (Hutchings 1983, 234). (Hutchings considers this an indicator of the weak integration of the Warsaw Treaty Organization forces. But it is just the opposite. It shows that the WTO has no autonomy, being under the complete control of the Soviet military command.) They did not have a joint operational command because in any war they would function under unified Soviet command.[4] The Polish leadership had apparently agreed not to have a Polish military representative or even a liaison officer with the Soviet command. Altogether about 90 percent of the Polish army would have found itself under direct Soviet command, which would have the right to deploy Polish units without needing to consult with the Polish authorities. Thus, the Soviets had complete jurisdiction over Polish soldiers and political education work was coordinated by the Soviet political department at the supreme command of the Western Theater of Military Activities (Kuklinski 1987, 52–54).

Thus, at the level of the Soviet world system we encounter some of the same tendencies we have seen at the national level: an effort to centralize decisions and to place control over resources at the very top of the world-system hierarchy and to attain full administrative unity and integrity.

As the last colonial power, the Soviet Union has peculiarities of its own. Its expansion to the west extended its direct control over areas that were not backward in the way that areas subject to traditional colonial expansion were: "We do not know any one example in the history of modern empires where the superiority of the metropolitan power in fact, and especially in the perception of its subjects, depended so uniquely and overwhelmingly on military power, seldom applied but always present" (Bialer 1989, 403).

(Lenin expressed a similar opinion during World War I; he was referring to the Russian Empire.) Despite some similarities, the East-Central European countries were not colonies in the traditional sense of the word. Nor were they a "sphere of influence," a term often used by some specialists in international politics, and one that, as I understand it, implies control over the military and foreign policies of a given country, but not any forced imposition of institutional structures by the dominant power. A forced imposition of institutional structures is something new, at least in the annals of European history.

Dependency and the Social Structure

In the East-Central European countries, with three exceptions, a victorious Red Army forcibly imposed, in the aftermath of World War II, the Soviet regime. The exceptions were Yugoslavia and Albania, where the Communists won power by their own efforts, and to some extent Czechoslovakia, where, even without the aid of a Soviet military presence, the Communist party emerged after the elections in 1946 as the most powerful single party with nearly 40 percent of the vote.

The imposition of the revolutionary regime by a foreign army in cooperation with small, local Communist minorities without political support in the population had some important, often overlooked, consequences. In traditional colonial conquest, the invaders either coerced the elites among the conquered into submission or tried to win their cooperation. Only occasionally were elites, or even whole populations, entirely exterminated. The conquest of Nizhny Novgorod by Ivan IV, called the Terrible, ended in the extermination of part of the population and the deportation of the rest. In recent Soviet conquests, the local Communist parties, with the help of the Soviet army and the KGB, immediately started a revolution by destroying the old political, intellectual, and economic elites and implementing a new social order.

The technique used by Communists in bringing about the revolution is widely known. First, popular proposals, such as for agrarian reform, the nationalization of industry, and free medical services, all accompanied by assurances of democratic intentions, are put forward to win broader support and to extend the power base. In carrying out these reforms, Communists have political purposes, not welfare objectives, in view. All these countries needed agrarian reform. Aiming to win the support of the poorer peasants, the Communists implemented changes that resulted in an overfragmentation of the land and multiplied the number of small, inefficient farms at the expense of larger, economically sounder ones. They also intended to pit different social groups and classes against one another: poor peasants against the richer ones, workers against intelligentsia, later non-Jews against Jews, and so on. The success of these measures varied from country to country. In Hungary and Poland, the Communists, viewed as agents of a foreign power and traditionally distrusted, had problems in winning broad political support.

Second, by presenting themselves as a patriotic group with a broad democratic program of economic and political reform, the Communists initially succeeded in tempting into coalition at least some factions of the leftist parties. Then they started gradually to radicalize their policies and to harass those who opposed them. This was the essence of the so-called salami technique—cutting off a bit at a time. Eventually, they used indiscriminate terror against all those who dared to demonstrate any independence of judgment. It is estimated that, during the first three years after the war, up to one hundred thousand people were deported from Poland to the Soviet Union. Another one hundred fifty thousand were killed in what virtually amounted to a civil war. The massive expropriation of private homes and apartments, and a change in incomes policy favoring physical work at the expense of intellectual and managerial occupations achieved the rest: the social status of the old propertied classes and intellgentsia was decisively changed.

Poland, which had experienced five years of German occupation before being "liberated" by Stalin's armies, suffered particularly tragically. Beside Jews whom the Nazis subjected to total extermination, the other group that paid the highest price was the urban intelligentsia. Until July 1941, the Germans cooperated closely with the Soviets in a deliberate policy of destroying the intelligentsia.

The murder in April 1940 of thousands of Polish officers, most of whom were highly skilled civilian specialists, is a striking example of this cooperation; another is the deportation of about 1.5 million people from what was formerly eastern Poland to Kazakhstan and other areas in the USSR. One-third of them died before June 1941. In accordance with the same policy, tens of thousands of Hungarians were deported to the Soviet Union after the Red Army crushed the Hungarian insurrection in October 1956.

Social elites in particular fell prey to the destructive vigor of revolutionary passions. The task of subjecting the East-Central European countries to Soviet domination was accompanied by another, that of implementing revolutionary changes in the society. The two purposes were not contradictory. The destruction of traditional elites exactly suited the purpose of national subjugation.

> When a class has taken the lead in public affairs for centuries, it develops as a result of this long, unchallenged habit of preeminence a certain proper pride and confidence in its strength, leading it to be the point of maximum resistance in the social organism. And it not only has itself the manly virtues; by dint of its example it quickens them in other classes. When such an element of the body politic is forcibly excised, even those most hostile to it suffer a diminution of strength. Nothing can ever replace it completely, it can never come to life again....
> (Tocqueville [1856] 1955, 111)

Nothing could serve better the purpose of breaking the resistance of indigenous populations to Soviet domination than an externally induced social revolution. In Poland, the elites that, with great physical sacrifice and moral stamina, guided the country through the Nazi occupation received the final blow from the Soviet secret police and its Communist allies inside Polish society. At all levels, the old political and cultural elites were replaced by a new one. The war against the so-called *kulak*s, for instance, was waged to destroy the traditional village community.

As already mentioned, the selection mechanism to establish a new elite favored socially marginal groups. At the beginning,

Communists of Jewish background played a prominent role. Soon they were replaced by a new political elite whose core came mostly from the countryside. Gradually, the level of education of these people improved. The important factor was that they knew that they owed their positions to political considerations.

The difference between the original ruling elite, consisting of people who had joined the Communist party when it was no more than a small band of revolutionaries, and those who enrolled when it was in power, was that the former were motivated by conviction and romantic aspirations and the latter were opportunists. Leaders such as Imre Nagy or Alexander Dubcek were among the earlier generation of Communist leaders. Those who came later had no illusions about the nature of the system they served or about the internal vulnerability of their positions. It was to support their own positions that they promoted domination by the Soviets.[5] The result was an appalling mediocrity. "The national Communist elites ruling in Eastern Europe, installed and protected by the USSR, have been embarrassing economically, retrogressive socially and reactionary politically" (Triska 1986, 3). The following important elements characterize the structure of this situation:

- An externally imposed political regime, whose legitimacy in the eyes of the population is doubtful. (John Van Oudenaren's opinion, that "the imposition of complete Communist party hegemony deprived the East European governments of any real political legitimacy in the eyes of their own populations. Henceforth, to be an Eastern European leader was to be, in effect, the agent of a foreign power" [1989, 103–4], is hard to quarrel with.)

- Political leadership recruited from socially marginal groups and, what seems to be even more important, the feeling of insecurity that may result from marginality but may also be caused by other factors. One observer has noted the propensity of Walter Ulbricht, the long-time first secretary of the East German Communist party, to place former Nazis in key party and government posts and gave the following explanation:

> In [Ulbricht's] opinion it was preferable to fill important posts with former Nazis rather than with convinced Communists who had survived Hitler's concentration camps. For he possessed complete dossiers on the Nazis. They were well aware of this fact and so made obedient followers. (Weit 1973, 185)

- A socialization process that places a premium upon strict obedience and disrespect for traditional moral values.

These elements powerfully enhance the feature inherent in all regimes organized from above: that the political order thus imposed and maintained is seen by the population as illegitimate. The problems that this creates have been solved in different ways by various Communist elites under different historical circumstances. I have already discussed the strategies used in addressing these problems, coercion, corruption, and reform.

The dominant strategy during the Stalinist period in East-Central Europe was the use of force justified by Leninist ideology. The political elites of those countries displayed unquestioned loyalty and blind obedience to decisions coming from Moscow. Native Russians or former Comintern and NKVD (People's Commissariat of Internal Affairs) agents of local provenience occupied strategic positions in the party, the government, the security services, and in the armed forces. Rulers forced their populations to obedience by terror and they in turn were kept in check by Stalin through purges.

When Stalin died, the renunciation of purges affected not only the internal situation in the USSR and in other Communist countries but also relations between the Soviet Union and its satellites. A new way of relating the partisan state and society in those countries had to be found. Coercion was still necessary, but it had to be supplemented by other kinds of motivation and by forms of ideology other than Marxist-Leninist "internationalism," namely, by nationalist forms. But what nationalist rationale could be found for an elite imposed and maintained by a foreign power? At first, the elites tried to convince the population that they were the continuation of the most valuable national traditions, that they grew from the nations' historical past. This was easier in countries, such as Czechoslovakia and Bulgaria, that had traditionally been friendly toward Russia. It was also easier if the Communist political system were congruent with elements in the political culture of a society.

> It appears . . . that the intensity of political demands is directly related to the type of political culture: the more authoritarian it is, the fewer demands there are for basic political changes and the easier it is to accommodate the pressure under the party's umbrella. But if democratic or antiauthoritarian elements exist in a political culture, they reinforce the impetus toward democratization fostered by modernization to form an explosive political mix. (Rakowska-Harmstone 1979, 319)

Teresa Rakowska-Harmstone perceived authoritarian elements in the political culture of the German Democratic Republic, Romania, and Bulgaria and a strong antiauthoritarian, individualist tradition in the political culture of Czechoslovakia, Hungary, and Poland.

To be successful in "nationalizing" a Communist regime, the ruling group had to demonstrate convincingly some independence from its Soviet mentors. Gomulka did so during the first years after his ascendence to power in October 1956, and Ceausescu repeatedly demonstrated his autonomy. Manifestations of independence worked, but naturally were not popular with the Soviet leadership, and satellite leaders could not indulge in them too frequently.[6] The elite would also have to convince the population that the Communist system served national interests efficiently and effectively and that an alliance with the USSR was the best arrangement for the welfare of the nation.[7] An elite used this rationale when it had achieved some success and tried to reinforce its position with a propaganda campaign. If that did not work, the elite might have tried to suggest to the population that it did its best within the realm allowed by external circumstances and that it served the national interest as best it could. It was understood that no other regime would be acceptable to the USSR and any attempt to change would, thus, be suppressed by a Soviet invasion. For obvious reasons the political leaders of dependent countries did not usually express such views in plain words but when necessary they reminded the society of the risks involved.[8] Two arguments were used to win legitimacy for Communist elites in East-Central European countries. The negative argument was the lack of any alternative; the positive that the elite defended important national interests.[9] Whatever the measure of nationalist ideology in political propaganda, no Communist elite, without critically undermining its internal position and existence, could entirely renounce Marxism-Leninism.

The role of a peripheral first secretary was loaded with conflict. He often had to choose between his loyalty to the Soviet leadership and to the society he ruled. The dilemma confronted him not only at the symbolic level but also at the level of strategic economic and political choices. If not kept within limits, the conflict could threaten the integrity of the Soviet bloc but was alleviated by the awareness of most Communist leaders that they owed their position to factors other than popular support and that they could rely on such support only under exceptional circumstances. A leader sensitive to the feelings and needs of the population, as were Nagy and Dubcek, was dangerous to the integrity of the bloc.

The precarious position of the peripheral ruling groups is important for the bloc's integration. Communist parties that seized power on their own, as they did in Albania, Yugoslavia, and China, without decisive external support, will not offer direct and unconditional submission. Romania demonstrated that a Communist leader who had nationalist ambitions and was able to subdue the power apparata to his will and to subject society to his control could win a large measure of independence. To change such a situation could be very costly. Thus, the best situation, from the point of view of the Soviet world system's integration, was to be found between the point at which the peripheral elite's position was directly threatened by the population and the country became ungovernable and the point at which the elite was so certain of its control over the population that it felt free to challenge Soviet leadership.

Besides coercion, the elite could use, and at a later stage had to use, corruption to divide and weaken social resistance to its rule. It is obvious that an elite that lost faith in the historical mission and belief in its ideology had to find instruments of power appropriate to, in Vilfredo Pareto's metaphor, an elite of foxes rather than of lions. Corruption by demoralizing the society, contributed to the growing inefficiency of the system and, resorting to corruption, the ruling class demoralized itself. Corruption helped to maintain, at least in appearance, the principle of the top-down organization. But it created parasitic elites, socially irresponsible, contemptuous of their own society, without strategic conceptions of the future. Opportunism reigned supreme. Indirectly, internal corruption exacerbated the difficulties of Communist regimes. It disorganized economic processes and contributed to their inefficiency. Whatever political elites gained through corruption, the economic losses became in time prohibitive.

A market-oriented reform was an effort by the elite to relate positively to society and to the problems it faced. In reforming the regime the ruling group would have been true leaders. This was a difficult task. Although ruling elites have often considered reforms, they rarely tried to implement them seriously. Reform, not only in its final outcome but also at the stage of preparation and implementation, forced the political elite to permit the direct participation of various professional groups in the government. It also forced the elite to accept constraints upon the use of coercion. Thus, a coalition emerged reaching outside the traditional Communist circle of power; managers, intellectuals, and other experts became involved in shaping policies and structural changes. Serious reform helped to maintain some sort of understanding between the Communist elite and society and to preserve a sense of social responsibility in some significant circles of the ruling class and of the opposition.

From the point of view of the integrity of Soviet world order, any move toward wider participation from below was a direct threat to survival. Whenever leaders turned to their fellow citizens for guidance and approval, instead of gratefully receiving it from Moscow, the very essence of the Soviet world system was in danger. Thus, each time such a tendency has developed in the past, the

Soviets resisted it with force. Now that tendency has developed in the metropolis itself.

The Perversities of Economic Dependency

Robert W. Campbell characterized the Communist economy as

> an economy perpetually in crisis, wasteful and inefficient in the use of resources, bureaucratically musclebound in efforts to innovate technologically and institutionally, and scandalously callous and inept at meeting the Soviet population's consumption wants. Despite all this, its growth performance has been impressive. Lurching though its progress seems, it overcomes crises rather than allowing them to accumulate to the point of collapse, and year after year significant output increments become available, expanding the leadership's ability to achieve its goals. (1983, 68)

The first part of this description is still correct, the second, in the USSR, at least since the end of the 1970s, is not.

In the aftermath of World War II, the USSR forcefully imposed its economic system upon East-Central Europe. Some East-Central European countries, seeing all the shortcomings of the Communist economic system that Campbell described, began, by the mid-1960s, if not earlier, to find that they could not overcome the crises. There were some failed efforts to implement economic reforms in the mid-1950s in Poland. The conceptually better prepared Hungarian reform started in the second half of the 1960s. The Czechoslovak attempt in the spring of 1968 ended with an invasion by Warsaw Pact troops.

As shown earlier, the economic organization and, to a large extent, economic policies of Communist governments can be directly derived from the concept of the partisan state and the structure of interests it has generated. Its basic features were: the centralization of decision making, at first real, and later formal and illusory; the extensive use of rationing in the distribution of consumer and capital goods; the collectivization of agriculture; and the favoring of heavy industry and neglect of consumer needs. This form of economic order wastes human effort, energy, and materials. Arbitrariness in economic decision making, low productivity, lack of innovation, and constant problems with agriculture are its basic characteristics.

The uniformly imposed structure of economic organization and the strategy of economic growth designed to maximize the mobilization of resources for military purposes has contributed, albeit in a highly perverse way, to the integration of the bloc. The dominance of heavy industry, together with its technological backwardness and the lack of motivation in the labor force that are caused by the centralized and bureaucratized organization of the economy has led to an unusually high waste of raw materials and energy. (This waste is measured by the use of raw materials and of energy per unit of output, or in terms of the energy cost of growth in the GNP—the percentage rise of energy consumption needed to obtain 1 percent in GNP growth.) Technological backwardness, the bureaucratization of control and of techniques of work organization, and the structure of industrial output in Communist economies result in goods that are not competitive in the world market. Communist economies do not even realize the potential of products that could be competitive because of the bureaucratic organization of foreign trade. Profits realized from the export of goods that do happen to be competitive are invested in noncompetitive branches of industry that are considered essential for political or military reasons. Long-range economic interest is sacrificed for short-term political expediency.

East-Central Europe is not rich in raw materials and sources of energy. Even Poland, which was relatively better endowed, is quickly depleting its resources. Therefore, the region has to import energy and raw materials to satisfy the requirements of an energy- and materials-intensive industrial structure. The lack of competitiveness of their products on world markets, posed and still poses problems with the balance of trade with the West, forcing the East-Central European states to turn to the only country in their political environment that is well-endowed in resources, possesses a fairly undemanding internal market, and with whom they already have a special relationship through the Council for Mutual Economic

Assistance: the USSR. Thus, paradoxically, the economic weakness of the Soviet-bloc countries and the subjection of their economic policies to the political and military needs of the USSR increased their dependence upon the metropolis and contributed to the system's integration. In the long run this mechanism of integration has had a devastating effect on the Soviet Union and its dependencies, for it further corroded their economies and contributed to their structural and technological backwardness.[10] In addition, a continuation of this situation made market-oriented reforms impossible.

This impossibility was clearly apparent in the 1970s. The decision to stop market-oriented reforms in all Soviet-bloc countries and to use Western credits to assuage popular pressure in support of reform and higher living standards placed in a particularly awkward position those national elites already facing mounting social resistance. The pressure was augmented by the existence of joint investment projects situated in the USSR that required vast expenditures of hard currency by the dependent countries. Under the traditional Communist economic organization, and with increasing bureaucratic integration within the CMEA, large borrowings in the West resulted in the insolvency of countries ruled by elites who tended to look abroad for solutions to their internal problems. Brezhnev's policies, which were designed to stabilize and integrate the Soviet bloc, in the long run only contributed to its destabilization.

In 1973 the rise in energy prices combined with unchanged priorities in industrial development meant that the Soviet-bloc countries continued to build energy- and raw-materials-intensive industries in complete disregard of changes in world prices. The result was a dramatic increase in dependency on the main supplier of energy and raw materials, the Soviet Union, and a change in the terms of trade between the peripheries and the metropolis (see Csaba 1988; Maciejewski 1989). Growing indebtedness to the West has become paralleled by growing indebtedness to the Soviet Union. Poland was the most important victim of this situation.

The tendencies described above are not accidental aberrations of policy and they do not result from any plan to make the East-Central European satellites dependent. They are regularities produced by the structure of the Soviet world system. Yet, by opposing market reform and the conversion of the East-Central European economies and by defending the cohesion of its world system, the Soviet Union has contributed to its own backwardness and economic decline. Take, for instance, the much publicized and widely debated issue of so-called subsidies paid by the USSR to East-Central European countries in the 1970s and early 1980s (see Marrese and Vanous 1983). These payments resulted from the way prices are set in the CMEA and the conditions created by the price increases instigated by the Organization of Petroleum Exporting Countries (OPEC) in the 1970s. Everybody agrees that the resulting situation was more advantageous to the satellites' economies, although the size of the transfer is a topic of controversy.[11] One of the central differences is about whether the transfer resulted from a deliberate policy by the Soviet government or whether it was a temporary phenomenon created by procedures to establish prices. According to the second view, transfers are cyclical, sometimes favoring the USSR and at others, favoring its partners. Prices set within the CMEA are based on five-year moving averages, that is, the average world prices for the same or similar goods becomes a basis for internal CMEA transactions. Until 1975, the prices were calculated and adjusted every five years. After the price increases demanded by OPEC, the Soviet Union proposed an annual recalculation of prices to make them more sensitive to variations in world prices. Thus, we have a procedure according to which, if a country supplies other countries belonging to the club with a certain product, and there is a steep increase in the price of that product on the world markets, the supplier "subsidizes" the other countries until the CMEA price is adjusted. If the price falls steeply, the supplier is subsidized by the buyers. The rules of the game sometimes favor one participant and, at other times, others. Such fluctuations in comparative advantage cannot be regarded as subsidies, which would suggest a policy of economic aid.

(There is another aspect of this problem. By opposing economic reform and the restructuring of industry in East-Central European countries, the Soviet government made it very difficult, if not impossible, for those countries to reduce their requirements for energy and raw materials. The continued demand put an additional economic burden on both the Soviet Union and its satellites.)

There is indeed a cost involved, but it is related not to subsidies but rather to the economic burden imposed by the specific structure of political power. At the bottom of this structure are the requirements of political control over consumers, producers, scientists, and engineers; at the top are the requirements imposed by a system that controls and coordinates a number of states from a central point.

CONTROL FROM THE TOP

The Soviet world system consisted of a number of formal hierarchies and of networks of less formal relations that converged in Moscow. This did not mean that everything was decided there or that whatever was decided there met with immediate acceptance and execution in the dependent countries. This arrangement might have prevailed under Stalin, but not afterward. The Soviet Union indisputably formed the core of the system, but it did have to take into account the interests of its satellites. The change that occurred in the system of government after Stalin's death had to be reflected in the way the Soviet world system operated.

Stalin did not have to waste time on formalities; his rule was personal. He also did not have to take world opinion into account. His word was an irrevocable order that subordinate leaders had to obey. Khrushchev encountered an entirely different situation, to which he had to adjust the whole system of rule. He found the solution in the formulation of intrabloc relations. Krushchev resurrected the inoperative Council for Mutual Economic Assistance and made of it an instrument for the coordination and control of the Soviet-bloc economies. In 1955, he created the Warsaw Treaty Organization, which was to coordinate and control the military forces of the bloc. Bilateral and multilateral party conferences under Khrushchev became more frequent and more significant.[12] Soviet embassies in the capitals of East-Central Europe continued their active surveillance of the local cultural and political life, and ambassadors often expanded the traditional bounds of their role (a striking example of which might be found in the activities of Stanislaw Pilatowicz, the Soviet ambassador who virtually ran Warsaw when Gierek was first secretary).

Sometimes coordination and control were exercised through secret and often informal channels. There were people in ministries and in key party organs of satellite states whose power and influence could not be explained either by their official position or their professional competence.[13] Direct intervention in personnel decisions were common. Some nominations were vetoed, others suggested.[14] The Soviet influence on personnel decisions in the peripheries has been considerable, but not without certain constraints. For instance, the Soviets always found it difficult to upset a hard-line first secretary who had strong support among the internal party elite.

Let us start with economic integration. The national economies of individual Communist countries are integrated in the network of the Moscow-based Council for Mutual Economic Assistance, which was formed in January 1949 as a reaction to the Marshall Plan. Before 1956, however, the Soviet leadership had preferred other, more direct forms of integration. At that time the CMEA was a dead letter. Nikita Khrushchev's revelations at the Twentieth Congress of the Communist Party of the Soviet Union and the unrest in Hungary and in Poland in 1956 changed the situation. The Soviet government acknowledged some of the harm it had done to the satellites' economies, Poland received compensation for its underpriced coal, and other countries obtained Soviet credits (see Brzezinski 1967, 86–89, 125–29).

The dramatic change in the system of rule, brought about by Stalin's death, made the old instruments of overall bloc coordination through direct commands obsolete. What was needed were more institutionalized, that is, more formal and stable, patterns of coordination and integration of the bloc economies. This brought about a more active role for the CMEA: the international bureaucracy destined to manage the Soviet world system and its economic processes started to grow. The organizational logic of the CMEA conformed to the logic of the fundamental institutional design of the Soviet type of system: It was centralized and had a visible radial structure stemming from the economic and political dominance of the Soviet Union.

> CMEA members have had neither incentives nor opportunities to develop mulitlateral ties with other than the Soviet Union. The striking feature of [the] CMEA has been the growth of integration along the lines of the radial pattern centered around the USSR and, in contrast, the dependence of smaller East European CMEA members on the West. (B. Kaminski 1989, 414)

The organizational structure excluded the market mechanism and currency exchange. (What are called transfer rubles are not properly speaking the currency of the CMEA—they serve only for accounting purposes.) The members had to think in terms of foreign trade balances with other members of the group, a form of organization that would guarantee the dependency of the weaker member on the Soviet Union, but would not contribute to the integration of the CMEA as an economic entity.

Efforts were made to coordinate national plans on the CMEA level, but considering the imperfections of this tool for guiding the economy even at the national level, this was hardly practicable. Thus, planning was restricted to specifying the size of trade and product exchanges among the CMEA countries, without direct interference with other aspects of the economic processes in the member countries.

For other reasons joint planning was not a workable solution. It would mean the integration of the bloc along Soviet lines, a development that would further limit the autonomy of the member-governments and make their internal economic and political situations yet more difficult.[15] One of the significant sources of tension apparent below the superficial harmony is the conflict between those governments supporting integration through the market mechanism and those supporting traditional adminstrative methods. In the first group one may find Poland and Hungary, which in differing ways tried to implement some market-oriented changes in their economies. The Romanians opposed integration too, although for different reasons. The bureaucratic organization of the CMEA was an obvious external constraint on market reform in any Soviet bloc country, including the USSR (see Hutchings 1983, chap. 6).

Another factor that contributed to the disintegration of the CMEA was the importance for the member states of Western currency, which enabled them to purchase the modern technology necessary to make their products more competitive on world markets and more interesting to the Soviet Union. To the extent that they succeeded, their position of power in the Soviet bloc was enhanced. It was soon apparent that, with their economic regimes entangled in the organization of CMEA, the satellite countries could not compete on the world market, yet, it was only on the world market that they could find what they badly needed.

The political integration of the post-Stalin Soviet bloc has taken more diversified institutional forms. The Warsaw Treaty Organization played a crucial role because defense strategy is a key to the foreign politics of any state; however, but the way in which Soviet-bloc countries were militarily integrated seriously limited their autonomy. Officially, the WTO was an answer to the creation of NATO.[16] In fact, it was a response to the internal problems of the Soviet bloc.[17] At the beginning, the satellite armies were under the direct control of the Soviet Union. In Poland, the minister of defense was a Soviet marshal, and most top officers were Russians, as were the head and ranking officers of the feared Information, that is, the army security services. As the behavior of the Polish army during the 1956 crisis showed, this control was not as effective as one might suppose. The situation was less drastic in other countries, but not that dissimilar.

Among the changes that occurred after Stalin's death was a "nationalization" of the armies in the satellite countries, which meant that gradually the Soviet government replaced direct control by other forms. Soviet leadership had to create a more formal organizational framework to provide grounds for military integration and the control of national defense policies. That was the function of the WTO. But it became fully operative only in the 1970s, as part of Brezhnev's effort to proceed with an effective integration of the Soviet bloc.

The question often posed after the invasion of Czechoslovakia in 1968 was, What purpose does the WTO serve? Is it there to defend East-Central Europe and the USSR against a Western military attack, or is it there to keep the satellites in order? Most share the opinion that the second function was the more important. This view has been explicitly stated by D'Encausse (1983, 325, 331). See also Kolkowicz (1969, 86, 101) and Zimmerman (1986, 95). "Successive Soviet leaderships have evidently never been entirely clear in their own mind whether Eastern Europe represents a socialist commonwealth to defend or a Russian empire to garrison" (E. Merton 1981, 178). In all probability, successive Soviet leaderships have not been aware that there was a problem; they were never forced to clarify their thinking.

The Soviets have imposed on their allies their own military conceptions, as some say, "to prohibit the Eastern Europeans from developing anything resembling an independent military doctrine" (Herspring 1989, 147). Nearly all the ranking officers in the satellite armies have graduated from one or more of the Soviet military academies, where they spent a number of years. They often have Russian wives. They take part in military maneuvers of the WTO, during which they work closely with Soviet officers.[18] Their careers depend on Soviet judgments, military competence being only one of the criteria. Some commentators believe that this arrangement eroded feelings of national identity and helped to create a value system that was useful for the Soviet empire but detrimental to the security of the satellites (see D'Encausse 1983, 337). The army, instead of being an institution supporting the national identity and serving the defense of the citizenry, became an instrument of foreign domination.

Other aspects of the integration by means of the WTO also served the corporate needs of the military. First, it helped to preserve a regime that assured the military a privileged position. Second, the regime itself has been built upon principles borrowed from army organization.

> Militant political systems on the Soviet and Warsaw Pact model are characterised by a normative theory of government which assigns a premium to strict control and heirarchically authoritarian chains of command. The underlying unconditional conflict with

> an intransigent, Western enemy rationalises the pact's centralization and mobilization of diverse economic, political, and social entities under communist party leadership also benefits the region's military elites. Without the existing system's ties to the Soviet military establishment, Eastern Europe's military elites would probably be relegated to a position of relative insignificance in a region of rising consumption demands. (MacGregor 1986, 242)

This statement probably goes too far. But it identifies real interests that affect the perception of reality and the behavior of ranking army officers, especially those in the political hierarchy of the army. At some critical moments in the history of Communism in East-Central Europe, the Warsaw Pact has been a reliable instrument of Soviet domination over the area.[19]

The degree of political integration of the bloc was manifest in the constitutional changes that occurred in the 1970s.[20] Bulgaria in 1971 and Hungary in 1972 adopted new fundamental laws; Poland in 1976, the German Democratic Republic in 1974, and Romania in 1975 revised theirs. The changes consisted in formal recognition of the constitutional role of the party in the political system, in emphasizing respect for internationalist principles in the conduct of foreign policy, and in a pledge of loyalty to the USSR. The simultaneity of these changes and a uniformity of direction indicate the direct involvement of the USSR in their orchestration.

The differences in the specific constitutional provisions adopted in various countries are revealing. The most outspoken on the role of the party, friendship with the USSR, and the principles of international socialism were the constitutions of the German Democratic Republic and Bulgaria, followed closely by that of Czechoslovakia. The constitutions of Poland, Hungary, and Romania were more reticent about acknowledging some of these principles. These differences show not only the will of political classes of some of these countries to assert themselves or the resistance of the population to the legislative changes (as occurred in Poland in 1975), but also the attitude and expectations of the Soviet leadership toward the various countries (D'Encausse 1983, 293).

Perhaps the best illustrations of the underlying divergences among the countries of the bloc are the dramatic events. There is hardly more dramatic an event than a challenge to the leadership position of the Soviet Union. The Titoist challenge of the late 1940s, the Chinese and Albanian challenges of the early 1960s, and the Romanian stand since the mid-1960s are similar in that the reaction was always anger and annoyance, but no more than that. The Polish challenge of 1956, the Czechoslovak challenge in 1968, and events in Hungary in 1956 and in Poland in 1980 and 1981 provoked the use of force to crush the reform movement.[21]

At least two not mutually exclusive theories explain the differences in reaction. One takes the geopolitical perspective, the other, that of the threat to the institutional order. According to the former, Soviet strategic interests lay in the "iron triangle," consisting of Poland, the German Democratic Republic, and Czechoslovakia. Well-entrenched in this region, the Soviet Union took hostage all of Europe (see D'Encausse 1983, 323–25). Whatever happened in the iron triangle was of vital importance to Soviet interests. China is an altogether different problem; besides, intervention in China would require an all-out war, which the Soviets sought to avoid. The Balkans had a secondary strategic importance. The traditional Russian strongman in the region was Bulgaria. Romania was strategically insignificant: "Bordered on all sides by Communist states, it was not crucial to Soviet defense or offense and has remained the least important of all the Eastern European states in terms of Soviet strategic considerations" (Brown 1989, 291). Yugoslavia and Albania do not have common borders with the USSR. The proposition that follows is that the USSR intervened only when its vital military interests were threatened, and they were threatened most in the iron triangle that was the key to their strategic position in Europe. Intervention in Hungary could be explained, then, by its proclaimed intention to leave the Warsaw Pact, and the destabilizing influence that could have had on Poland and other countries of the region.

According to the second approach, the relevant difference is that in Yugoslavia, China, Albania, and Romania, the challenge was waged by conservative hard-liners who questioned the position of the USSR among the Communist nations or criticized Soviet policies, but otherwise were close adherents to Marxist-Leninist orthodoxy. In Poland, Czechoslovakia, and Hungary there was no criticism or verbal attack on the Soviet Union: so-called revisionist political leaders were trying to use their sovereign rights to introduce internal political changes. Even Imre Nagy's decision to leave the Warsaw Pact belonged to this type of decision. The leaders enjoyed broad popular support and felt responsible for their countries.[22] On the grounds of Marxist-Leninist orthodoxy, a concern for one's country is a major sin. The proposition that follows from this theory is: The USSR had a genuine propensity to defend a Communist regime whenever it was threatened. Nicolae Ceausescu did not constitute a threat to the Communist regime in his country, nor did Mao Zedong, but Nagy and Dubcek did, albeit without being fully aware of it.

We can conclude that the decision to invade a country never came easily to any Soviet leadership. They examined each case on its own merit. Soviet leaders took into account all sorts of factors, including geopolitical ones. While preparing the invasion of Czechoslovakia, they also observed the tacit acquiescence by the Western powers. They must have reflected upon the low probability of encountering resistance. They also had to be aware of aggressive lobbying by the German Democratic Republic and Bulgaria, as well as of Gomulka's smug willingness to participate.

In a way, both theories are correct. The geopolitical theory holds because control over East-Central Europe is indeed essential to the Soviet military and political position on the continent and in the world. The theory that attributes Soviet intervention to perceived threats to the institutional order has implications not covered by geopolitical considerations: it accentuates aspects of control over satellite states that reflect the ability of the Communist regime to survive. First, there is the aggressive posture: The Soviet political and military establishment was convinced that it had somehow earned the right to dominate the East-Central European countries. Any challenge of this right by the inhabitants of a satellite country amounted to a lack of gratitude.[23] These convictions, also widely spread among the Soviet population, were often used by Soviet authorities to manipulate popular attitudes toward events in other countries. There is some evidence, for instance, that in 1981 Soviet agents themselves conducted the widely publicized desecration of the graves of Soviet soldiers who perished in Poland during World War II to temper Russian support for the Solidarity movement.[24] Many Russians have deeply identified themselves with Communism: Russian nationalism and Marxist-Leninist ideology became for them intimately connected. When Poles or Hungarians questioned Communism and dependency, many Soviet people reacted as if this were an insult to their deepest sense of decency.[25]

Finally, a crucial factor in analyzing the Soviet attitude toward East-Central Europe is the relationship between events taking place in the satellite countries and behavior and aspirations of ethnic and national groups within the Soviet Union.

> Relations between the Russians and other Soviet nations are not those among equals. The Russians ultimately rule the Soviet Union. The multinational character of the Soviet Union and the ethnically unequal distribution of power therein are of major importance for Eastern Europe. Irredentism from any source in the East European empire feeds irredentism in the Soviet Union, and vice versa. This limits the room for maneuver of the Soviet leadership in dealing with Eastern Europe. In sum, more is at stake here than "only" the fate of Moscow's outer empire. (Bialer 1989, 403)

The sensitivity of the Soviet leadership to Ukrainian reactions to events in Czechoslovakia during the Prague Spring and the reaction in the Baltic republics to events in Poland in the 1970s and 1980s show that the dependent status of East-Central Europe was the *conditio sine qua non* to the existence of the Soviet empire and a factor in the Soviet Union's ability to survive.

All these considerations make the East-Central European problem a key to the existence of the Soviet Union. Far-reaching political and economic changes in the USSR imply basic transformations in the relationship between the Soviet Union and its former satellites. The desatellization of East-Central Europe has become a reality. To these issues I shall return in the last chapter of this book.

V

Transitions

FIFTEEN

THE REFORMABILITY OF SOVIET-TYPE REGIMES

Our country is in the middle of a crisis of an immense gravity. Russia, in its millenarian history, has experienced difficult moments, but rarely ever has it found itself in the presence of a situation so complex, so confused, in the presence of a future so rich in dangers.
—Petr Dolgorukov, 1862

With the words of the epigraph a Russian aristocrat, a prominent representative of the party of reform during the reign of Tsar Alexander II, started his book, published in Paris 128 years ago. In similar terms, we can describe the situation we are witnessing now. Much of what Petr Dolgorukov had to say then is still relevant. Now as then, the major problem is the liberalization of the state, making it accountable to its citizens, more predictable, and efficient. The similarity suggests that the task facing the Soviet leadership is more serious than is often assumed. More is at stake than merely a reform of the Communist state. The question is, Can Russia break out of its centuries-old tradition of autocratic rule? Can it change from a xenophobic, militaristic bully into an economically dynamic, democratic society?

The Notion of Reformability

The practical issue of reforming the Communist economy has existed for the last thirty years. It is as old as the theoretical debates about whether Communism is reformable or not. (Among publications on the subject see Daniels 1988 and Pipes 1984.) Those who think it reformable and those who do not usually discuss very different issues. The former mention, as an empirical proof of reformability, that Communist regimes have undergone important changes during their history. This argument misses the point, for no one, at least since Heraclitus, ever questioned the fact that the world around us is in a state of flux.

Another argument used in support of reformability consists in pointing to intentional institutional change introduced by successive Soviet, and not only Soviet, leaderships. Let us consider, for the sake of illustration, a list of such reforms, provided by one of the leading intellectual inspirers of *perestroika*, Fyodor Burlatsky (1987). Burlastsky mentions the nationalization of industry, the tax in kind, the establishment of cooperatives in agriculture, school reform, and other changes made in recent years in the Soviet bloc as examples of successful reforms. Each of Burlatsky's cases, however, represents a decision that belongs to a different order of things. The nationalization of industry and the collectivization of agriculture laid down the constitutional foundations of the regime that made nearly total control by party leadership possible. As key elements in the institutional design of the Communist economic and political order, they neither prove nor refute the reformability thesis.

The tax in kind was part of the NEP package required to save the Bolsheviks from a disaster. The NEP was introduced at an early period of Soviet history as a temporary device that did not survive beyond the 1920s. Even Lenin thought that the NEP was based on an institutional logic foreign to Communism and treated it as an expediency. All the examples mentioned concern the period when the regime was being formed. They may indicate that Communist governments were able to respond flexibly to external stimuli and that they could temporarily introduce structural changes foreign to the basic institutional design when their survival was under threat. These examples do not provide, however, sufficient support for the reformability thesis.

The school reform and similar changes in particular areas of social policy present a special problem. Here Burlatsky is correct, though misleading. A plentitude of such changes has occurred in the Soviet Union and other Communist countries. Communist leaders for a long time have been aware of serious problems with health care, education, agriculture, and ecology, and they have been trying to find solutions to these difficulties within the social order.[1] Each time they have perceived a difficulty, they immediately assumed that it was produced by arrangements peculiar to the area in which it emerged, or by human error. If university education is ailing, they seek the solution in improving work at the university level, and it usually consists in strengthening administrative controls. They rarely, if ever, consider the possibility that the real difficulty may lie with the system of administrative controls, the centralization of decisions, and the dominant position of the party, the *nomenklatura*, that is, with the constitutional foundations of the Communist regime. This is what the proponents of the thesis of unreformability have in mind.

Thus, the reformability issue is not reducible to examples of reform within a specific domain of state activity, such as education or health care. Such reforms have abounded in the history of Communism. One can view them as a proof of changeability, which is pointing to the obvious. One cannot see in them an argument for structural reformability: they belong to a different order of intentional change. The imperial, prerevolutionary regime was also able to initiate such changes, but Prince Dolgorukov surely had something else in mind when he spoke of reforms. It is no different now. When reformist politicians, professional practitioners, and dissidents in Communist countries discuss reform, what they have in mind, perhaps not being fully conscious of the logical implications of their stand and often not acknowledging it in public, is a change in the institutional foundations of the regime.

They are aware that reforms generated by existing institutional structures represent, to use Karl Deutsch's (1967) terminology, a case of pathological learning.

To change the existing institutional structure requires more than the invention and implementation of intentional change, that is, reformability in the sense suggested by the example of educational reform. It requires, in fact, a basic change in the regime, the ability to carry on systematically with a peaceful revolutionary change in the social order. It is important, then, to consider what is meant by reformability, and especially the difference between reformability and revolution, before one starts to assess the prospects for, and possible consequences of reform, or revolution, in the Soviet Union and East-Central Europe.

The reformability of a system is the ability of strategically placed actors to prepare and implement reforms, that is, intended, purposeful change in the institutional structure meant to alleviate difficulties or to overcome critical states produced by a system's interactions with its environment. Reform is a rational activity; means are applied to attain a desired state of affairs. It follows that a theory establishing causal relationships among events lies behind every reform. Such a theory need not be explicitly formulated; it need not be consistent nor correct. More often than not, in its public expressions, it is a loose set of ideological clichés. But, if intended and implementable institutional changes are not to be merely chaotic and accidental acts of despair, one should always be able to reconstruct a theoretical explanation lying behind any blueprint for change.

Reform affects human behavior by changing the rules of the game by which the system of action is regulated. Any major intervention in the basic rules of the game in society produces deep changes in all walks of social life: in fundamental goals and values, property relations and social power, individual motivations and life-styles. Thus, before we answer questions about changes that a given reform brings about, we have first to possess a clear idea of the essential characteristics of a system, that is, we must be able to determine its basic identity.[2] Only when we have properly defined the identity of the system under examination can we decide whether the implemented changes transform it into an entity with completely different properties or whether it is the same social order modified in important ways but with its original constitutive principle still clearly distinguishable. Japan after the Meiji reforms is an instance of the first situation. Changes in the world market economy after the Bretton Woods agreements that created a new international monetary system illustrate the second case. This is the distinction between a reform and a revolution, something that is much easier to determine in the abstract than to decide in practice.

In social theory, we define the identity of a system of action by the conceptualization that best reflects in the view of a particular social scientist the properties of the real social order. Such a conception becomes the "theory of design" of an institutional order, a tool necessary to its intellectual understanding. Thus, to paraphrase Vincent Ostrom's argument quoted in Chapter 5, serious sources of misunderstanding and confusion will arise when "one theory of design [is used] to reform a system based upon a different theory of design" (1974, 102).

The essence of a theoretical endeavor is then to abstract from what can be reasonably seen as accidental and unimportant and to focus on significant relations and uniformities. All important theories of the liberal order contain a definition of its identity and, by the same token, a definition of its structural characteristics and limits. These characteristics of an organized social system are those conditions that must be met to preserve its identity. Karl Marx's theory of capitalist formation and of its dynamics can be interpreted as a statement of the boundary characteristics of this type of socioeconomic regime: when these no longer hold, a new socioeconomic formation is to emerge. Similarly, a precise definition of the essential features of the liberal (tax) state was proposed by Joseph Schumpeter in his now famous essay, *The Crisis of the Tax State* ([1918] 1954). Besides the purely theoretical question of conceptualizing a social reality to grasp its essential properties, there is a practical one: the identity of the system, and its elemental features, is constitutive of significant constellations of interests as social realities.

On the level of theory, the conception of the constitutive principles determines the identity of a social system, that is, of the basic organizational relationships that affect all other forms of organization that emerge in the social order. The constitutive principle determines, in large measure, the functional logic and developmental tendencies in the system. To the extent that the model correctly represents social reality, these tendencies should be observable on an empirical level.

The problem of reform appears when a simple policy change is insufficient to meet social expectations and a more dramatic change in the rules of the game that govern socially significant relationships is deemed necessary. The essence of a reform consists in an effort to readapt the structure of a system to its environment, that is, all those factors that are not under the control of the system in question that affect its ability to attain goals, survival and expansion being the most prominent among them. Thus, those changes that are designed to preserve or improve the ability of the political system to achieve its tasks are reforms.

The concrete meaning of the term *environment* is a function of how we define our system of action. In the partisan state, we can distinguish between the internal environment, that is, the social and physical processes that occur within its domain, and the external environment, consisting of processes occurring in the world outside. Of key importance for the theoretical approach developed in this work is the notion that both the basic goals of the system and the way it applies resources to achieve them are largely shaped by its constitutive principle. Thus, a reform consists in redesigning the rules of interaction between the system and its environment in a way that would not decisively affect its constitutional foundations.

Limits to reformability are determined, then, by the constitutive principles of the system. The principles allow us to identify the system, although perhaps it is not wholly unchangeable. For instance, in Schumpeter's view, the tax state can expand the sphere of its activities as long as this expansion is not incompatible with the profit motive in the private sector. When a state fiscally infringes upon the private sector so heavily that human efforts do not bring sufficient payoff to stimulate activity, the private sector begins to shrink. If economic expansion is to continue, or the existing level of economic development is to be maintained, said Schumpeter, a new organization of activities and a new motivation system must be invented and put into practice.

When a grass-roots social movement disrupts the existing order, then, either there are opportunities within the system for the movement to carry on with its tasks or an effort is made to suppress the movement by force. The first solution is typical of liberal, democratic regimes because it is consistent with their bottom-up logic of organization: a new power center can be added to a polycentric political order, a new organizational principle can be introduced into the working of the system, and new conflict-regulating arrangements can be introduced to reduce disruptions caused by changes in the power structure. In systems built from the top down, the emergence of a new power center, if it had not been prevented, usually leads to a highly unstable political situation, as did Solidarity in Poland. The decision to suppress ends either in an effective repression, or in failure that leads to a stalemate, civil strife, and possibly revolutionary change. Thus, systems organized from the top down, based on the monopoly of power and control from the very top, have a limited possibility of significant structural change. We should rather expect popular rebellions to occur in such social orders, or a revolution "from above" initiated by a group within the ruling class (see Trimberger [1978], an important study). Revolutions from above often result in authoritarian regimes, although, as Prussian history demonstrated, this does not necessarily preclude an important role for a parliment, and a strict adherence to the rule of law in many aspects of the social order. Modern mass revolutions "from below," led by revolutionary parties, have tended to result in totalitarian regimes. By destroying the self-governing institutions that as part of the ancient regime protected the society, they open the road to the centralization of power and total control. The combination of changes that results in a democratic system is not easily obtained.

As already indicated, in the Soviet bloc a tendency prevailed to reserve the notion of reform to market-oriented changes in the organization of the economy, which also implied a measure of political liberalization. It was assumed that a process of reform would result in greater economic rationality, productivity, and ability to generate and use innovations, as well as in an increase of internal diversity and organizational complexity of the system. This meant broadening the range of goals that the society could realize and enriching the range of possible reactions to environmental challenges. Although, out of habit, people used the term reform in this sense, it should be remembered that changes in the opposite direction were no less rational from the viewpoint of their proponents. There is no valid reason, therefore, to reserve the term for only one direction in the process of political change. There were reforms that detracted from the expansion of market mechanisms. They were implemented much more easily and smoothly than were market reforms that whenever they were tried, dragged on for years without clear success.

Limits to reformability are those institutional structures or organizational principles that cannot be fundamentally altered without a complete overhaul in the pattern of institutional design, that is, without a change in the system's identity. It follows that without a fairly elaborate theory of the Soviet type of regime, one would not be able to assess the internal modifications this system can sustain. By the same token, we cannot specify its limits. Most of the important elements of this theory were formulated in earlier chapters. Let us consider them from the point of view of the reform potentials of Communist regimes.

THE SOVIET TYPE OF CONSTITUTIONAL DESIGN

What are the essential features of a Soviet type of political order? We can start by remembering that in its basic institutional conception the Communist state is a logical negation of liberal democracy. Instead of the market as the fundamental regulator of economic processes, it proposed the concept of central planning and management by a supposedly neutral and scientific state administration; instead of what it called "bourgeois democracy" with its elected parliament and legal guarantees of individual liberties, it proposed the "true democracy" of the dictatorship of the revolutionary vanguard; instead of the plurality of political parties, it proposed the rule of one party; instead of the pluralism of ideas, it proposed the idea of the "moral and political unity of the nation"; instead of the institution of private property, it proposed collective, state-managed property, and so forth. Above all, it proposed, instead of the bottom-up strategy of building the sociopolitical order, its own, top-down strategy.

This design has been consistently put to practice. The Communist regime attained its highest measure of internal cohesion in the USSR between the early 1930s and Stalin's death, when opposition to liberal, democratic regimes reached extreme proportions and produced a state that freed itself from all constraints. As the Marquis de Custine aptly noted in 1839, "Under an absolute despotism it is the government which is revolutionary, for the word revolution signifies arbitrary system and violent power" ([1839] 1989, 534).

The change in the property rights system produced by the massive expropriation of the property of all who owned the means of production and of trade and services facilities assured the decisive dominance of the state over society. All sources of income independent from direct state control disappeared. This destroyed any grounds for individual rationality of economic processes, as Ludwig von Mises, Max Weber, Friedrich von Hayek, and others correctly explained and predicted. The abolition of the private ownership of economic resources was necessary to guarantee the monopoly of power at the center. The state's ownership of the means of production was the precondition for the dictatorship of the revolutionary vanguard.

The design of a liberal order is founded upon a complex set of political and economic doctrines. These doctrines, and the corresponding institutional orders, were developed in the context of intensive and serious debate and practical experimentation. The system design enabled society to exercise significant, although varying, measures of control over the processes of government. The liberal design allows for the coexistence and horizontal cooperation of different sectors in a system of the social division of labor and of different organizational principles in interdependent systems of interactions. This internal diversity assured the reformability and adaptability of the social order. Because of the limited role of the state, major adjustments were possible without direct intervention by the government. In particular, in political systems based upon the federative principle, effective decentralization of decision prerogatives made it possible to adapt independently at different levels of governmental organization (Ostrom 1991). Reliance on the market mechanism makes all errors in governmental economic policies easily detectable, and parliamentary democracy enhanced discussion about ideas and error-correcting potentials.

The architecture of the Communist regime demonstrates that a state without institutional constraints has limited learning potentials. The regime was introduced as the ultimate solution. Its leaders legitimized their power by claiming infallibility, that is, they could not acknowledge that they might make mistakes. Where there is no error, there is no need for correction. To make it impossible, or at least difficult, for the citizens to discover errors, all important government and party proceedings have been covered with a veil of secrecy. Until Gorbachev's *glasnost,* Communist rule has been, to use Custine's words, a "conspiracy of silence." Successions have become the only error-detection and error-correction mechanism available.

The work of Karl Marx, which inspired the design of the Soviet type of social order, is a critical theory of capitalist societies at quite an early stage of development; it contains little on the future organization of communist society, or the "intermediate stage" of the dictatorship of the proletariat. Lenin was more specific, but it is impossible to treat his work as a mature political and economic doctrine, or even as an adequate foundation for such a doctrine. Yet, his work is sanctified as the sole source of truth that the Communist leaders who succeeded him could expound and correctly interpret.

With slight exaggeration one can say that, until recently, Soviet social scientists have been allowed only to celebrate the ideas of their first secretaries. This intellectual imposition has been enforced with the coercive powers of the state. True, in some Communist countries control over intellectual endeavor was relaxed, but there was never a fully open, critical discussion of the basic assumptions of Marxist-Leninist doctrine and of its practical applications. Thus, we had a regime with a rigid ideology that was devoid of a normative theory that would establish in a rational way, subject to empirical scrutiny, the relationships between the domain of values and ideas to the domain of institutions, and to patterns of interactions in a way of life.

This lack of scrutiny impaired the quality of reform proposals and the ability to assess obstacles to their implementation and predict their side effects. Reforms are adaptive changes. The identification of factors that generate difficulties and lead to the formulation of proper remedies requires a theory establishing causal relations and helping to select possible solutions. Reform is a learning process through which societies acquire a better understanding of themselves, their situations, and their potentials.

In Soviet-type regimes, the range of public discourse has been limited by an artificiality of language with little relationship to reality. The language was derived from a theory that in its essential rhetoric is not verifiable, and in those parts that can be empirically verified, has been proved incorrect.[3] It has often been embarrassing to watch the acrobatics performed by intelligent people who wanted to be intellectually honest and, at the same time, be listened to by the top Communist officials. To give one example, let us look at the interview given by Leonid Abalkin, a leading Soviet economist and a deputy prime minister.

> Social property as an attribute of socialism cannot be the cause of negative phenomena in the economy. I want to repeat that such phenomena appear when the concrete forms of its realisation do not correspond to the nature of the property itself or to the changing conditions of economic life. (1987, 51)

When asked about specifics, he said, "The question of these forms [of the realization of social property] is a fairly new one for science and is still insufficiently elaborated" (ibid.). Hence, says Abalkin, we do not know what social property is. But, what we do know *a priori* that it is not the cause of negative phenomena in the economy.

Yet, when he came to the issue of investment decisions, he made a statement more familiar to the "secular" mind of one who is not a true-believer: "It would be a good thing here to use a system of competitive resources allocation. Resources will go to those industries which guarantee the maximum economic effect" (ibid., 53). It is obvious that such a competitive allocation requires a well-functioning market mechanism, one of these liberal devices that has been traditionally rejected by Marxist-Leninists. But, says Abalkin,

> it is wrong to say that we have borrowed these [commodity-money] relations from capitalism. They stem from the activity of our enterprises and associations, which are socialist commodity producers. The possibilities of using commodity-money relations for planned and balanced regulation of the economy and an efficient distribution policy are by no means exhausted. Thus, social property simply cannot be realised without financial instruments. (Ibid., 55–56)

What Abalkin is telling us is that the idea is good, the system is basically good; what is bad are the concrete forms of its realization.

When a critical situation emerged, top officials and their academic advisers looked to the Western, most notable American, patterns of organization, wrapped them in the language of Marxism-Leninism, and sold them as a genuinely socialist package. By doing so, they fooled the public but they achieved something else. Pretending that an incorrect theory was correct, that an unreformable system was reformable, they lulled the ruling class into a belief that it was possible to implement a market-oriented reform without endangering the survival of Communism. Had they tried to formulate and publicly present a specific program of broad economic and political reform, the influential groups within the partisan state would more accurately assess its impact upon their own interests and would more easily form a united opposition.[4] By blurring issues, pretending that black is white, proponents of reform were able to overcome, within limits, this danger, and to be politically acceptable. Alas, everything has a cost. The cost in this case is that the false pretenses made impossible a serious discussion of the program, goals, and the social doctrine behind the reform. The critical assessment of the institutional design for the future organization of society suffers.

Soviets can reintroduce private property and present it as "socialist" private property, pretending that nothing has changed, that the tenets of Marxism-Leninism still hold. But the lack of open debate results in the situation they are facing now: there is no clear conception of the program of change, and moves in one direction are followed by immediate countermeasures that neutralize advantages that the initial moves could have produced. Claiming that no dramatic change is taking place and hiding from the political establishment the truth about intended changes may be wise politically. In the long run, however, the reformers who try to fool others can fall victim to their own deception. A reform that is not well prepared and conceptually sound can backfire on its proponents.

An interesting aspect of the Soviet type of political regime is that the vestiges of a liberal, democratic order have not been entirely abandoned but have survived as decorative elements, as a part of the official ritual; they exist and play a function in legitimizing the system. The Soviet Constitution grants all the basic human freedoms, those of speech and association included. "Representative" institutions, "elections" to those institutions, and a "formally" independent judiciary all exist. Though these institutions are largely make-believe, their existence shows that the system needs a democratic legitimation of sorts. These "survivals from another formation" gain in importance with change with the progress of reform. Furthermore, the only direction for reforms considered reasonable by the politicians in their public pronunciations and by the informed public is the revival of whatever is left of these liberal, democratic institutions. This implies a parallel weakening of the elements specific to Communism. To liberal, democratic reforms belong the market with its institutionalized distinction between the state and the economy, an independent judiciary and the rule of law, a greater measure of lawful political participation, an enhanced position for a parliament and other representative bodies, and a revival of those norms and values that until recently had been considered bourgeois. This course of change has been reversed from time to time, in particular when the political elite panicked at the prospect of losing power.

To the autocratic reforms belong the unlimited power of the party over all spheres of social life, the omnipresence of the state, the special position of the secret police, and so forth. The less legitimate the system, the more constrained it is in the use of coercion, the more it will rely in its propaganda and policy rationalizations on legal rationality grounded in Western jurisprudence as opposed to revolutionary, Marxist-Leninist arguments. The weaker the Communist state, the more liberal and democratic it will appear to be. These appearances further erode the legitimacy of the system and the self-assurance of its ruling class.

It is evident that, if the institutional design of Communist regimes is in a logical opposition to liberal principles of institutional design, market-oriented reforms contradict the logic of its organization. They weaken, therefore, the constitutional foundations of Soviet-type regimes, both directly and indirectly, for the market implies a far-reaching redistribution of power and gives autonomy and self-assurance to individuals and groups outside the realm of the state. That is why the progress of reform is so painful and slow.

It may be worth noting that some political change has been made with no difficulty whatsoever. The three instances I shall mention from Poland are not particularly different from changes that have been experienced in other Communist countries. First, of the program of market-oriented reform to be carried out in 1973 (the so-called WOG-reform), the only part that was successfully implemented included measures aimed at increasing the concentration of the economy through the absorption of small and medium enterprises by big ones. As a result, profitable, market-oriented firms were incorporated into giant businesses and forced to operate within the context of the dominant, heavy industries typical of the Soviet type of economy. Overconcentration and a greater market disequilibrium were the most important effects of the reform.

Second, in May 1975, Gierek's leadership began implementing an administrative reform that replaced a four- with a three-level administrative structure and increased the number of *voyevod*ships (prefectures) from seventeen to forty-nine. This change enhanced the centralization of decision making, the isolation of the administration from its clientele, and the inefficiency of public administration. The interesting aspect is that this highly expensive and consequential overhaul of the administrative and political structure of the state was introduced quickly, without any public discussion, and with great effectiveness. It contributed to the economic crisis and made the Polish state organization a caricature of the French model.[5]

Finally, the preparation, in 1980 and 1981, for the economic reforms of the late 1980s took well over a year, and the implementation did not make much progress during the decade. It took, however, only a few weeks in November 1986 to prepare a complex package of legal proposals that presumed a complete reversal of the reform. This sudden move, calculated to take the country by surprise, failed only because of an immediate public reaction and of the opposition to it on the part of liberal groups that, trusting his desire to implement an economic reform, had supported General Jaruzelski.[6] Thus, Polish "reform," having dragged on for years, is a total failure. Its reversal, had it not been blocked, would undoubtedly have been implemented smoothly and efficiently.

We can draw two conclusions from this evidence. First, it is remarkably easy to implement changes in the system that are in line with its centralist logic, that is, that satisfy the requirements of its internal institutional environment. Only social resistance outside the center may obstruct them. Second, changes consistent with its institutional logic increase the system's maladjustment to its external environment, but those consistent with the requirements of the environment undermine that logic. The irony is that this formulation corresponds to a conflict between the "forces of production" and the "superstructure" that, according to Karl Marx, was characteristic of capitalist and other "antagonistic socioeconomic formations."

Reform and Group Interests

The "logic of an institutional system" is a euphemism that needs to be translated into another theoretical language to make empirical sense. What makes this logic a social fact is that a major constellation of group interests develops on the basis of the institutional system. Under any political regime, it is easy to implement those institutional solutions that fit the dominant interests, unless there is a risk of provoking an active protest by groups outside the political establishment. This is a problem even when political elites consist of many, heterogeneous groups with diverging interests. Considering that the ruling class under an autocratic system is narrow and relatively homogeneous, the tendency toward blocking any measures not advantageous to those interests must be particularly pronounced. Thus, policies that contradict those interests, even if they are accepted as reasonable, are implemented with difficulty and easily reversed when the occasion arises. This may be a more general phenomenon, namely, that it is easy to extend the powers of the state, while it is difficult to curtail them; the extension of state powers is not easily reversible.[7]

Two issues are of interest in this respect. First, can we implement liberal institutional changes without transforming the very identity of the Communist system? Second, where will an opposition to such a reform develop, and how will it articulate itself? The answer to the first question is evident. The central planning and management system was not designed as an auxiliary device for market mechanisms, but as an alternative to markets. It follows that an expansion of market mechanisms within a Communist economy must proceed at the cost of central planning and management. Market reform implies a dramatic change in the property rights system. By handing over some property rights to the level of enterprises, the state also acknowledges the importance of profit and self-interest as legitimate sources of motivation. Successful reform puts effective constraints on governmental powers to interfere with the economy. This implies, in turn, an expansion in the powers of the judiciary, and the availability of autonomous and reliable sources of information as an essential condition for entrepreneurship in the market economy. Even when a reforming Communist economy approaches viable market conditions, it is quickly apparent that the government's powers are too wide and its dependence on other forms of control are too great. An appropriate system is achieved when Montesquieu's principle of using power to check power is extended through the whole system of human affairs. Without effective public control, governmental discretion is too great to prevent gross errors stemming from the arbitrariness of political intervention in the economy. Thus, as public pressure for more participation grows, the issue of the place of parliamentary and electoral processes within the political system is raised. Second, it soon becomes evident that major investment decisions, which are the prerogatives of the government, are not economically rational. Thus, the creation of a capital market as a substitute for direct political interference becomes a public issue. Initially, access to this market may be restricted to state enterprises. Soon this restriction becomes irrelevant, as state enterprises together with private individuals start limited liability companies, and a multitude of various legal forms emerges in the area between "private," "cooperative," and "state" types of ownership. Under a competitive market economy, the distinction itself loses all sense.

A government that has been elected by popular vote and has a genuine desire to bring improvements soon discovers that the distinction between the private sector and the socialized one is an ideological invention without real significance. What is important is to get an economy moving. At that point, special privileges for the state sector must disappear. In a Communist state, the party leadership must stop the process of reform before the changes reach the point at which democratic, free elections become a necessity, and the party-state complex loses its control over the economy.

One may discern two types of opposition to reforms that articulate themselves differently in the political system. The first type, the opposition of interests generated within the party-state complex, was discussed in Chapter 10. If these interests prevail, reform is reduced to an "equilibration of the market" through price increases (the idea being to eradicate shortages by reducing demand but without changing the structure of supply that would have to occur in a true market-oriented reform). The interests are never articulated in public but may sometimes be voiced at closed party meetings. They make themselves effective through the selective implementation and subversion of policies initiated at the center. For the party bureaucracy, decisions of the Central Committee are formally binding, but it can disregard some without running a serious risk and can shirk while implementing others. The veil of secrecy that surrounds the operations of the security services rather effectively protects their interests. The armed forces have had their interests guaranteed not only internally but also through the Warsaw Pact. These groups usually oppose some aspects, or even the idea, of reform itself, but they do not need to do so openly.

The second type, opposition from the working class, manifested itself in strikes and mass protests against price increases. These protests owed their effectiveness not to Marxist-Leninist ideology, whose respect for the working class is debatable, but to the long-term conviction of Communist political elites that "big is beautiful." Communist industrialization has been implemented on a huge scale, resulting in enormous plants employing thousands of often highly qualified, and well-educated workers who want adequate payment. Most of the workers are employed in capital-goods industries. With the whole economic system skewed against the interests of consumer-goods industries, demand generated by the capital-goods sector cannot be met with comparable increases in the production of consumer goods. Thus, increases in wages and salaries in the capital-goods sector contribute to further inflation. Who can oppose a working class army, concentrated in a few huge industrial centers when it gains the ability to act collectively?

When reform starts, the major problem for the reformers at the top, who view the economy in aggregate terms, is to "balance the market." They may do so either by increasing the supply of goods, as Gierek did at the beginning of the 1970s, or by keeping demand under control, which means in practice, reducing demand. Under present conditions in the USSR and Poland, there is no easy way to increase supply, therefore, price increases are the most natural way to reduce demand. Workers in smaller consumer-goods plants are unable to oppose the Communist government. But the thousands, and sometimes tens of thousands, of workers in capital-goods industries, locked in protest in big plants in the centers of big cities, are a different story.

One of the important reasons for the workers' opposition to "price maneuvers" is that they do not believe that reforms initiated by a Communist government will proceed beyond price increases; and they have good grounds for distrust. The challenge that Solidarity presented to the Communist authorities in Poland in

1980 and 1981 to start cooperating with workers in the process of implementing reforms was wasted. Communist authorities are not able to implement effective economic reforms because they do not recognize society as a partner. But, when they are ready to change their attitudes, the problem of sovereignty immediately arises and fatally destabilizes the regime.

An additional factor in the working class opposition to reform is that most of the highly qualified and politically active workers are employed by centrally subsidized plants that are unable to compete in the market, wasteful of material and human resources, and technologically out-of-date. Any market reform implies the necessity of closing most of these plants, creating thereby unemployment among the most politically active and best educated workers, concentrated in a few urban centers. No doubt, this is a very risky political decision even for a legitimate government.

A government in a democratic system can negotiate and try to convince the workers and win their support. A classic Communist government does not recognize any rights inherent in society; society is entitled only to what is benignly conceded by the party leadership. Society is not represented, and thus unable to inform the government of its basic requirements. Under such conditions, it can only revolt. Unable to raise prices, the Communist establishment proclaimed its goodwill while, at the same time, chastising workers for making reforms impossible. We can hope that new non-Communist governments in East-Central Europe will be better equipped to deal with the problem than were their predecessors.

Political democracy and pluralism may help to overcome the two main sources of opposition to reform: first, to provide control mechanisms that would make it impossible for groups within the partisan state to subvert reforms, and second, to win social support for reform, to make Communist leadership credible in the eyes of society. But, reform that puts free elections, political accountability, and so forth into the foreground spells an end to Communist leadership and to the Communist regimes.

Thus, all denials notwithstanding, the political compromise needed for economic reform to succeed is not available under the requirements that enable Communist regimes to survive. More than a quarter of a century ago, Alexander Gerschenkron concluded his discussion of the problem of reformability by saying that ". . . the dictatorship must be as it is or not be at all. Its long-run changeability appears limited indeed" (1962, 604). (Gerschenkron used the term *changeability* in a sense similar to my use of the term *reformability*.) This study generally confirms his position. A Communist system can change through a revolution, possibly instigated and within limits controlled from the top, but it is not reformable in the sense of the term proposed here. Gorbachev has also recognized this:

> If *perestroika* is a revolution—and we agreed that it is—and if it means profound changes in attitudes toward property, the status of the individual, the basics of the political system and the spiritual realm, and if it transforms the people into a real force of change in society, then how can all of this take place quietly and smoothly? ("Gorbachev Urges Purge to Renew Party Leadership," *New York Times*, 22 July 1989)

At this point Marxism converges with "bourgeois" social theory. A change of such proportions is revolutionary indeed.

There is no point in proposing a change of vocabulary. But it is important to remember that when we talk about the reform of a Communist regime we have in mind a revolution. This may be a quiet revolution, a transition. The word *transition* is devoid of the violent implications of the word *revolution.* It is a process of intended, constructive intervention in the constitutional basis of the system. This does not mean that there cannot be a violent revolution in the USSR, but there is still some possibility for a peaceful revolutionary transformation in the governance of Soviet society. If a peaceful transformation occurs in the USSR, the decorative facade of a liberal constitutional order, including the facade of "federalism," will play a decisive role.

SIXTEEN

EAST-CENTRAL EUROPE IN TRANSITION

Let us recapitulate some of the conclusions reached in earlier chapters. The Soviet world system, like its national parts, was built in opposition to the principles of a world-market economy. Its integration, founded mainly in political structures, seriously restricted the national sovereignty of satellite states. Even economic integration had as its purpose a more effective political control. A set of relatively continuous hierarchies related individuals and groups in particular countries to the world order. Each superior level in hierarchy should, ideally, directly control the alternatives open to the subordinate level. A change of direction in the dependency vector would threaten the whole system.

The system was integrated through elaborate networks of formal and informal relations. What assured its existence was the implicit threat of the use of force. There were also positive interests behind it. First, the survival of local Communist political elites in the peripheral countries depended upon Soviet support. They have, therefore, a vested interest in the continuation of dependency. Second, the dysfunctionalities of national economic structures were functional for the system's political integration and, thereby, for the perpetuation of dependence.

When constraints were put upon the use of coercion in governing Communist countries, corruption was a strategy that could, to an extent, substitute for it. Hardly anyone continued to believe the ideology, but compromise and loyalty could be rewarded by privileges and other material rewards. In the short run this worked effectively. In the long run it introduced an informal decentralization into the system that, together with other well-known features of such centralized, bureaucratized regimes, contributed to an escalation of inefficiencies.

The reason that the Communist ruling classes considered economic reform at all was the realization that without reform an economic collapse of the system was imminent, and a political collapse must accompany a failure of the economic system. Two additional considerations can be mentioned in the Soviet case: first, until June 1989, the relative success of the Chinese reform; second, the threat that declining rates of economic growth in the USSR pose for its international political and military position. To continue a high level of military spending while the economy stagnated would be suicidal.

A change in the regulatory mechanism, especially of such vast proportions, can be implemented only at the cost of special privileges of the whole political establishment. Moreover, reform that adapts the economy to the requirements of world markets and makes it more competitive would result in a closer integration of the economies of individual satellites with these markets. This, in turn, must weaken the dependency of any one member country upon the Council for Mutual Economic Assistance and must contribute to the disintegration of the Soviet world system. Thus, an economic reform, however indispensable it is to solving the economic crisis of the Communist bloc, poses a direct threat to its existence and, thereby, to the whole world situation of the USSR. The option of introducing a market-oriented reform in the USSR while forbidding its satellites from doing so was inconceivable.

To imagine the consequences of such a reform for the Communist system, let us return to our picture of this system: It is a hierarchy built upon the principle that each lower level has little autonomy in its dealings with the higher level. Individuals and groups are expected to behave according to the collective interests; private, individual interests are not legitimate. At the level of particular states the party leadership verbalizes the general interest; at the level of the world system, the Soviet Union represents the "internationalist interest of the world proletariat." Steps taken independently by peripheral leaderships are treated by the Soviets as deviations from the correct course, motivated by particularistic, nationalist concerns, a clear indicator of "class betrayal."

The essence of market reform is that it explicitly recognizes and legitimizes private interests. This must always be the case when self-regulating mechanisms are introduced, and individuals and groups enjoy autonomy. But, if reform is carried only to the level of peripheral states, while at the global level traditional integrative mechanisms predominate, serious tensions must follow, for either the Soviet economy is guided by market forces tempered by the influence of state policies or by state policies tempered, to some limited extent, by market forces. Otherwise, we have an organization built upon two contradictory constitutional principles, one in operation at the national level and another at the Soviet world system level. One must take precedence over the other. If the individual states implement market reform, the CMEA loses its ability to impose upon member countries quotas and prescriptions about investment policies, industrial specialization, pricing, and foreign trade policies. An internally consistent global economic organization is possible either when the leadership renounces the reform both on the global and on the local level or when local reforms are accompanied by global measures of reform. If this does not occur, the global Communist system will put effective restraints upon the progress of local reforms or itself be subject to repudiation. Moreover, if the reform is implemented both globally and locally, member countries will have to find it in their interest to continue their membership of the CMEA. If it is not in their interest, the economic organization of the bloc will disintegrate, with obvious repercussions for the political integration.

Thus, we have two possible, logically consistent global systems, but only one is Communist, the unreformed one. Successful reform will result in a variant of the liberal, democratic order that merges into the existing world economy. This we can see happening now, and with all the implications already mentioned. It makes the future of the USSR as a world power, its ability to survive, debatable. Thus, the Soviet leadership faces a Catch-22 situation: both the decision to reform and the decision not to reform carry dramatic threats. The difference is that action carries hope; failure to act carries with it certainty of catastrophe.

CAN THE TRANSITION SUCCEED?

How hopeful can we allow ourselves to be about the success of the present transition? An answer to this question depends on the point of view. We can assume that the transition will be successful, if an institutional transformation takes place without excessive cost in human lives, human welfare, and the world security.

A change that does not affect the workings of basic social institutions and bring about a transformation at the level of the constitutional principles of the system can produce only an internally inconsistent, unstable regime that would either have to resort to some form of a traditional, corrupt system of rule or institute more fundamental changes. A return to the old patterns would mean the long-run resumption of the track leading straight to catastrophe. Moreover, the decision to take this course now after a period of considerable change, when some elements of civil society in different strata of the population have emerged (S. Staar 1988), and it has become quite clear that the USSR has neither the human nor material reserves to make a return to the traditional way a viable alternative, does not seem practical. This does not mean that such a return may not happen. If economic conditions do not improve, a version of a totalitarian regime can reappear as a stage in a continuing decline.

Such a maneuver might succeed in the guise of an understanding with a reunited Germany to which would be offered, for instance, special advantages in economic cooperation and trade if Germany were to abandon NATO and provide massive economic help that would visibly raise the standard of living in the USSR. Then, Gorbachev's successor could criticize mistakes made by liberal reformers and defend the virtues of autocracy. One may doubt, however, if Germany possesses either the resources or the will for that task, especially in view of the political and economic problems it already has with reunification.

Close cooperation between the Russian and the German states has had a long historical tradition. In most instances, this cooperation had a conservative, reactionary influence upon the Russian regime and regressive, disastrous consequences for the countries of East-Central Europe and, at times, for the stability of the world political order. Without West German support, in the form of subsidies and access to modern technology, a retreat to the old system of rule will eventually lead to a resumption of terror on a large scale either in the anarchy of a violent social revolution or after a coup intended to restore order and central control. Nevertheless, the probability of a Soviet-German understanding of the sort described above is very low. Germany is a democratic country, a part of the complex Western economic and political network. In order to enlarge its freedom of action, Germany would have to disengage itself from those networks, which is not simple. The possible advantages of such a step are difficult to imagine.

On these considerations, one could eliminate the possibility of a return to the old Communist patterns. But, when we examine the political structure of the Soviet state, which is more pervasive in its dominance in Russia than it is in East-Central Europe, and the Russian political tradition, we doubt whether the transition can succeed. Both the return to the old Communist regime and a transition to a liberal, democratic regime seem to face major obstacles. The democratic transition would require the simultaneous implementation of two strategies of change: political, with a precedent in Alexander II's reforms of the 1860s; and economic, with a precedent in Stolypin's reforms introduced in the aftermath of the Russian-Japanese war and the revolutionary disturbances in 1905. But this time, the required scale and depth of change are incomparably greater.

There is another problem in carrying through the transformation. The Soviet Union is a failure: it is in the middle of an economic crisis, the life expectancy of its male population has been declining since the mid-1960s, the living standard is low, it is unable to feed its population, and it has a disastrous ecological record. Yet, it has, at least in some areas, been a remarkable success. Territorially, it is the largest state in the world. In military might, it is the only power that can be compared to the United States. Many Soviet citizens, Russians in particular, have been proud of these achievements.

Viewed from this perspective, changes occurring in East-Central Europe, the rise of liberation movements in the countries forcibly incorporated into the USSR, and arms reduction agreements with the United States, are all occurring at the cost of the political and military might of the Soviet Union. That cost is growing, and it is not very clear what its limits are. The defense interests of East-Central European countries only narrowly overlap those of the USSR, so their newly regained independence has made the Warsaw Treaty Organization inoperable. Changes in East Germany raise the issue of the new European political order and nationalistic movements in the USSR are challenging the legality of incorporating some of those countries into the Soviet Union. The empire cracks and disintegrates.

In return for all this, Soviet citizens obtain "openness," more freedoms, and more personal security in legal terms. Had they received more food, better living conditions, and more effective protection against crime, they would probably have offered a stable source of political support for the changes. This is not happening. It is evident that the economic policies of *perestroika* are the least consistent of all, and prospects for a quick economic recovery are not in sight.

It is often said that some of the difficulties in implementing a market-oriented reform lie in the egalitarian attitudes prevailing in Soviet society. We may ask then, How is it possible that a society that has accepted the dramatic inequalities of privilege characteristic of Soviet society at least since the 1930s, has suddenly become revolted by the inequalities generated by the market? The answer can be found in what Tucker (1971, 122) has called the dual conception of Russia. The egalitarian "popular Russia" perceives the privileges of the inegalitarian "official Russia" as external. Defense of egalitarian values permits the "popular Russia" collectively to oppose the "official Russia" in a passive manner. Change that rewards entrepreneurship, individual talent and hard work, and competition pose a threat to this collective solidarity and undermine the "dual image of Russia." This attitude was behind the opposition to Stolypin's reforms and to Gorbachev's cooperatives and small private businesses. By defending "popular Russia," Russians defend at the same time "official Russia," that is, their tradition of autocratic governance.

Also contributing to these inconsistencies may be the lack of a well-developed theory behind the change so that every change appears as a separate policy problem, unrelated to the broader strategy of transition. The economic squeeze coupled with the sense of the declining world power of the Soviet Union might lead to an outburst of Russian xenophobia with dangerous consequences.

The failure of Gorbachev's economic policies is due to the nature of this most dramatic choice in Russian history. As mentioned, one cannot eliminate the possibility of an attempt to rebuild the Soviet state on the grounds of some grand Russian nationalistic ideology and/or the possibility of the disintegration of the Soviet state in a turmoil of civil war that could destablilize not only the region but the world power system at large. Such pessimistic scenarios are easy to devise. It does not follow from this that the outside world can do much to influence the direction of events in the USSR. Those who take the position that substantial, unconditional Western help will make reform less pressing are correct. But the USSR also needs external help to be able to carry on with the changes. Whatever the Western countries do to help Gorbachev must be carefully weighed against the adverse effects that such help may produce.

Global Interdependence

Before we proceed with further considerations, one point should be emphasized: I am not describing here any program of reform explicitly adopted by the Soviet reformers. All I can claim is that, if the present tendencies continue, they are going to lead to certain consequences irrespective of the beliefs and intentions of the actors involved. I do not even believe that there has been or could be a coherent coalition behind Gorbachev's reform efforts. The structure of his support must change from time to time, and the only stable element in it is the political advantage he still draws from his position as first secretary of the party. It seems clear that Gorbachev himself cannot control the forces he helped to release. Perhaps no one could. The result is the ambivalence often criticized by Russian intellectuals between Gorbachev's efforts to liberalize the system and revitalize the society and his attempts to keep the party in hand and maintain the traditional paternalistic posture of both Communist and monarchical leaders.

Let us consider, first, the prospects for a course of events that is less probable and demands a lot more political wisdom and moderation than do the pessimistic scenarios of a return to yet another despotism—a liberal, democratic transition of the USSR, and its impact upon the European order. By a successful transition in the USSR, I mean the emergence of solid institutional grounds for the development of competitive markets, the rule of law, representative government, and of truly federal structures in the organization of the Soviet system, if it survives. This system, if the transition were successful, need not entirely disintegrate as a territorial and political entity.

The success of a liberal, democratic transition will depend on a number of factors. Among the obvious ones the imperative of improving the economic situation has already been mentioned. A requirement of no lesser importance is the need for a fundamental change in Russian political consciousness, not only by breaking with the "dual image of Russia," but also in conceptions that both Soviet leaders and particularly a part of the Russian population have about their special role in the world and their right to subdue and enslave other nations and ethnic groups. Their attitudes toward their neighbors, the international political and legal order, and their global responsibilities all would have to change. Too often the Soviets remind one of the villain deeply and sincerely persuaded that he is the victim. One should add that some Western sovietologists are particularly skillful in supporting the Soviets in this conviction. A successful liberal, democratic transition, besides further stimulating changes in the national consciousness, would have to affect social perceptions in every area of life, strategic and military, economic, and political. It would have to affect the whole social structure of Soviet society, including interethnic and religious relations. Moreover, the social consciousness must recognize that the state cannot solve all problems. People have to acquire self-confidence, learn to trust lateral mechanisms of coordination, and rely on their own initiative and talents instead of relying on the state hierarchy to solve their problems.

The most detrimental effect of the more than seventy years of Communist rule in the USSR has been destruction of elements of the tradition of the civil society that started to emerge in Russia in the late nineteenth century. The civil society is a combination of a universalistic moral basis for community relationships with a technologically competent understanding of the democratic process. The two cannot be separated. The moral community determines the attitude of people toward one other and toward the norms of behavior accepted by a group. The technological competence relates to the ability of individuals and groups to constitute and operate institutions and to function effectively within those institutions. What makes a good judge, for instance, is not only a sound knowledge of the law but also a frame of mind often called a "legal ethic." The great majority of the Soviet population lacks not only the knowledge but also the normative ethos that make for a civilized life. The destruction of civil society is among the most serious impediments to the progress of change in the Soviet Union.

What is the prospect for a peaceful achievement of the revolutionary transition without complete anarchy and the disintegration of the Soviet state? Four interrelated questions seem to be relevant.

1. Can the mobilization potential needed to overcome internal obstacles to revolution from above be generated in Soviet society?

2. Is it possible to introduce a deep change in the principles of the constitutional order in Soviet Russia without creating centrifugal forces that cannot be controlled?

3. Is it possible to implement change in the USSR and its world system without the complete loss of its international position?

4. Would it be possible to create an interest in the countries that are still part of the USSR to remain in it as parts of a federal or confederal structure?

The first question concerns the ability to integrate strategic social groups around a program of liberal, democratic changes; the second, the ability to avoid the total disintegration caused by the side effects of change; the third, the prospects for saving some part of the Soviet/Russian political prominence in the posttransition world; the fourth, the continuation of a special relationship, though based upon very different principles, among the nations that comprised the USSR and perhaps more widely the Soviet bloc.

Assuming that it is possible to mobilize the coalitions necessary to bring about peaceful transition in the Soviet Union, one can point to two bases on which they can arise: some liberal, democratic consensus and a certain brand of Russian nationalism. But here Gorbachev's position is most precarious. Using the central institutions of the party to promote changes, he takes advantage of the Leninist characteristics of the party organization, and succeeds in promoting some changes while neutralizing an open revolt against him in the apparatus. The point is that any continuation of a liberal, democratic transition must weaken the party and, therefore, the political position of Gorbachev as its leader. If he tries to defend his position as party leader, he has to thwart the reforms. His position as the president in a pluralistic political order makes him one among many leading politicians in the country. Their influence depends on the amount of public support they can muster. Moreover, if he surrenders to pressures for further reforms, he will risk dismantling the very organization that keeps him in power and the Soviet Union together. There are signs that the apparatus is already crumbling. He can and does use nationalistic Russian symbols, but he cannot go too far in this direction, for then he risks alienating other Soviet nationalities and legitimizing the extreme right in the Russian nationalist tradition. Moreover, these symbols may be preempted by the increasingly independent leadership of the Russian Republic.

Nonetheless, in time the present strategy of flexible coalitions behind a unified reforming center will have to be abandoned. The only chance for continued reform is the readiness of the Soviet political elites to expose themselves periodically to an electoral process, to accept the prospect of defeat and to accept political pluralism and the implicit emergence of multiple political parties. If the transition is to succeed, the Communist party will have to give way to a number of distinguishable political coalitions with explicit programs for change. These coalitions will have to acquire institutionalized forms. There is little doubt that in this process, at least initially, the intelligentsia in Moscow and Leningrad will play a key role. A successful transition requires a stable network of support reaching deep into the working class and the countryside, cutting across ethnic and national groups. For such a coalition to exist, Russian nationalism would have to acknowledge the rights and legitimate interests of other peoples; the antiintelligentsia obsession among the workers and peasants would have to be tamed. Political elites able to create grounds for working out constructive compromises, to develop new institutional solutions, and to stick to agreements once these are reached, would have to emerge.

That such a process has started is apparent in the growing influence of Boris Yeltsin, the most important challenger to Gorbachev's position. A further development of this process would make possible the co-optation of cultural elites in non-Russian republics in the reform coalition, opening prospects for the emergence of an authenic federal structure. This is the only political option that could alleviate, and even perhaps prevent, ethnic wars, particularly in the Muslim provinces and the areas bordering them. Otherwise, the rise of traditional Russian nationalism will provoke a counterreaction in the escalation of nationalism in other ethnic groups that could threaten not only the existence of the USSR, but also peace in the region.

The Russian nationalist tradition that could play such a positive role has roots in the old party of Constitutional Democrats and seems to find its continuity among some members of the new Supreme

Soviet. This is the only political tradition in contemporary Russian history that is consistent with the concept of the civil society. An open-minded Russian nationalism, respectful of the aspirations of other nationalities and ethnic groups in the USSR, could bring about, in the final stage of change, a truly democratic, federalist political structure. A major factor that will decide, together with the economic situation, the fate of the reform efforts is whether or not there takes place a dramatic change in political culture— one that will permit the Soviet Union, in particular Russia, to create a civil society. We know that such a change is most difficult to attain. One of the main obstacles to liberal, democratic reforms in the Soviet Union is its multinational, multiethnic character. The USSR, like imperial Russia before it, has been correctly called the "prison of nations." None of those nations joined the union of its free will. All of them were coerced into joining. The process of transition from a union based on coercion to one based upon self-interest will be difficult, if possible at all.

A transformation into a true federation depends on the emergence of conditions that would encourage the nations constituting the Union to remain within it rather than to leave. Without satisfying this condition, the USSR must either fall apart or continue as a military police state ruling other nations through oppression— and then no liberal, democratic reform would be possible. Again, the attractiveness of federation would depend on economic and cultural factors. Free access to a very large, dynamically expanding market could still affect the decisions of the Baltic states if they were to be allowed to remain autonomous parts of a confederation. It is also possible that the intelligentsia in the Muslim republics of the USSR would support a loose federation as a defense against the fundamentalist movement in modern Islam.

One should also remember that several legal issues are at stake here. The frontiers of several countries have been arbitrarily changed to the advantage of the Soviet Union. Four sovereign states were forcibly incorporated into the Soviet Union: Georgia in 1921, and the three Baltic states (Lithuania, Latvia, and Estonia) in 1940 on the basis of the Ribbentrop-Molotov Pact. These states, as victims of aggression, should have the right to secession or association on other terms if their populations would so desire. Karelia, Bessarabia, and the Kuril Islands should also be free to change their sovereign associations.

The present ethnic unrest in the USSR is a product of history, of seventy years of disregard for cultural and historical differences, and of contempt and animosity toward all cultural traditions. The Soviet government invaded and forcefully incorporated independent states, moved whole peoples from areas in which they had lived for centuries to regions with which they were not familiar, arbitrarily changed frontiers, undertook deliberate efforts to russify national groups through the educational system, the change of alphabet, and the resettlement of Russian nationals in areas where they had never had large settlements before. Overt ethnic strife has been suppressed, but ethnic animosities have been exacerbated. The Communist system, with its bureaucratic hierarchy and rigid ideology, can create subjection, can even pit one ethnic group or nation against another; it cannot create the integrated communities of interests, spontaneous intercultural contacts, and cooperation that often come with market relationships, comradeship in voluntary associations, and allegiances that are part of the experience of democratic life.

What happens when, after a long period of terror and repression, a policy of liberalization is implemented? Not knowing how to solve their problems by organizing themselves and by cooperation, people begin to terrorize and kill their neighbors of other religions, races, or nations. Having been cut off from whatever universalistic elements they had had in their cultures, they have no moral scruples about giving free expression to their passions. Once nationalist conflicts erupt, it becomes very difficult to stop them. Then, the revival of traditional institutions, instead of taming the passions, provides favorable grounds for their expression. Besides, the state power apparatus, having had no experience with the rule of law, is unable to counter ethnic strife by an appeal to universal principles of fairness and justice. Instead, a command from a superior is presumed to be the law. The task of working out mutually acceptable rules of coexistence and association across ethnic communities is beyond the capabilities of any autocratic regime.

The weakness of the civil society profoundly affects the national and ethnic situations in the USSR. The Soviet ethnic mosaic can survive as a cohesive entity, if only partially, in either of two ways: as a centralized, highly bureaucratized and highly coercive, unified imperial state, or as a complex structure built from the bottom up and kept together by mutual interest and mutual respect. In the second case, the state, and the instruments of coercion, plays a secondary role, while other political, economic, and cultural bonds come to the fore. The first type of order requires only obedience. The second type of organization can survive only in a mature civic culture. The first can exist to the extent that the ethos that defines the civil society is absent. A political system in which coercion plays a minor role and most social activities take place outside the realm of the state, within voluntary associations and private organizations, can exist only when public life is well developed.

The current Soviet transition is an attempt, not always consistent, to move from the first type of order to the second one. The peoples of the Soviet Union, and the Russians in particular, need to reconstruct or build their civil societies and reconstruct the formal institutions of the state. This must be done first in the political domain, because the existing political structures have effectively subverted earlier efforts to change the economy, and because Communist regimes have already succeeded in destroying a sense of public responsibility and the ethos of work.

The only way a moral and spiritual revival of Russian society could occur is as the result of a deep and unflinching reexamination of Stalinism, not as an unfortunate accident or a metaphysical force from nowhere, but as a continuation of Lenin's heritage and of a centuries-long tradition of autocratic rule. Stalin was a product of Russia as Hitler was a product of Germany. Only the moral and intellectual shock produced by serious reflection can bring a modicum of honesty back to social relations; create the readiness to redress crimes committed against its neighbors, the Baltic republics, other nationalities of the USSR, and the Russians themselves; and help to create the conditions necessary to the development of a civil society. Such an effort is already under way, but it is sometimes accompanied by the spread of self-pity that indicates an attempt to reject responsibility. This is particularly striking in the case of the nationalist revival represented by the *Pamyat*. It is impossible to say which of these tendencies will ultimately take over.

East-Central Europe and the Soviet Transition

East-Central Europe is an important element in the success of a liberal, democratic transition of the USSR. Seweryn Bialer has suggested two reasons for this. First, reform is indivisible, that is, to be fully implemented, it has to occur both in the USSR and in its East-Central European dependencies. Second, the danger of political disintegration in the USSR or of the political emancipation of East-Central Europe can create conditions that will cause Gorbachev to be deposed (Bialer 1989, 430–32). As to the second reason, it seems that the East-Central European emancipation has affected the European nationalities of the USSR more than it has the Soviet elites. On the whole, it is evident that what is happening in these countries must affect events in the Soviet "internal empire," and that those events, in turn, must have consequences for East-Central Europe. A serious reversal in the USSR will affect transitional processes taking place in the former satellites.

Historically, what have been the limits of the Soviet political elite's tolerance to changes taking place in East-Central Europe? The limits have evolved over time. Whenever a given Communist country approached these limits, its leadership was castigated at meetings of Communist leaders from the Soviet bloc, and warnings appeared in the Soviet press. When the satellite's leadership continued to be recalcitrant, the country was invaded and the course of events changed. The exception was Hungary, in October 1956; there change took place too fast to make preinvasion warnings possible.

We have a very different situation now. Communists have been removed from power in Poland, Hungary, and Czechoslovakia. The Berlin wall has crumbled, and Germany has been reunited. In the Balkans, Communists, or ex-Communists, are still essentially in power; but the situation has changed even there. These events have been stimulated as much by internal developments, particularly in Hungary and Poland, as by processes of change in the USSR. They have been accompanied by new Soviet peace initiatives that indicate an important change in Soviet foreign policy and conceptions of strategic defense, in the way the Soviet Union perceives its relations with other countries. Soviet tolerance of revolutionary changes occurring in East-Central Europe, where Communism has quietly disintegrated, gives some credibility to the thesis that real change has taken place—at least in the Soviet leadership's perception of its place in the world.

The fact that the West considers the Soviet stance on East-Central Europe a litmus test of its true intentions additionally constrains the Soviets' freedom of maneuver in this area. The USSR seems to have no satisfactory alternative; it must risk continuing the processes of change. Yet, such basic change in the Soviet relationship with the outside world must be a product of mutual concessions. The Soviet Communist leadership will have to demonstrate that what it obtains in return is worth the sacrifice. Thus, some (even if symbolic) relationship with former satellites should be preserved as an insurance for Soviet participation in decisions concerning the future of Europe. This minimum is defined as a temporary survival of something like the Warsaw Treaty Organization and, at least formally, of the Council for Mutual Economic Assistance. If the USSR completely loses its influence in the region, and if important changes that affect Soviet interests keep occurring without any participation by Moscow, the limits of tolerance will probably be reached and the processes of transition disrupted by violence.

The traditional organization of the Soviet bloc, based on direct dependency, created unsurmountable obstacles to liberal, democratic reforms. The key elements of the dependency mechanism were, as I have explained, the imposed Communist elites which, having no considerable internal political support, could only have been maintained in power by the Soviet political and military might. In the name of Moscow, these elites kept the countries they governed in a state of subservience. The dramatic changes occurring in 1989 in East-Central Europe that ended Communist rule in Poland, Hungary, the German Democratic Republic, and Czechoslovakia have been the unavoidable consequences of the Soviet decision to initiate economic and political reforms in the Soviet Union, and of the realization that this could not be done without a change in the Soviet world system that would give the peripheral countries in the Soviet bloc considerable discretion in deciding their own destiny. Yet, it is evident that the Soviet leadership not only accepted the subversion of Communist rule in East-Central Europe, but also that Gorbachev himself did a lot to destabilize some of the Communist leaderships in the region. On several occasions he expressed assurances that the USSR would not interfere with the internal matters of the Soviet-bloc countries. It seems that as was clear in Czechoslovakia, during the critical period between November 20 and 25, 1989, and in East Germany, he even took more direct steps to dislodge conservative Communist leaders. There is an obvious reason for this. Conservative leaderships in the satellite countries could give effective political support to similar elements within the Soviet leadership. Hence, eliminating them was a wise political strategy. Paradoxically, non-Communist elites in East-Central Europe are likely to be much more reliable supporters of the Soviet reformers than were the Communists they replaced.

These events had other important consequences. By accepting changes in the Soviet bloc, Gorbachev demonstrated his goodwill and showed his firm decision to undo the Soviet system of rule both inside and outside the USSR. Thus, his disarmament initiatives and his foreign policy openings gained credibility.

Communist parties have not won power through free elections, and they have difficulty in defending their power positions democratically. The electoral success of ex-Communist parties in Romania and Bulgaria indicates the weakness of the civic culture in these countries. Similarly in Yugoslavia, the Communists are strong in the most backward areas of the country, but in Slovenia and Croatia they were completely defeated at the polls by their opponents.

Communist parties are by their very nature revolutionary. When they abandon their partisan zeal, they turn into reactionary social and political forces, ill-equipped by their ethos and tradition to win significant electoral support. The Soviet leaders realized at the end of the 1980s that, with the growing economic crisis in East-Central

Europe, the Communist leaderships had become a liability. Had they decided to keep those leaders in power at any cost, sooner or later they would have had to face anti-Communist insurrections in at least Poland, Hungary, and Czechoslovakia. The political cost of such events for the USSR would be unbearable and their impact upon the internal situation in its European republics difficult to assess. Thus, the least the Soviet leaders could do was to withdraw their unconditional support and let the world know that there would be no more intervention in the internal affairs of other "socialist nations." This deprived the local Communist elites of their only raison d'être; they were no longer needed. At that moment, the main problem for the East-Central European countries became one of changing the political elites with the least possible disturbance. From every point of view, it was more reasonable to let change take place in an orderly way than to delay and risk a destabilizing revolt.

After World War II, the countries of East-Central Europe had favorable prospects for economic development. The imposition of Communism, changes in the geopolitical situation, and direct Russian domination prevented the realization of those opportunities. They have paid a heavy price. Their industries are out of date. Their economic structures are absurd and reflect the military interests of the Soviet empire instead of those of their own people. Ecologically their countries are in a state of disaster. The standards of living and opportunities in life are far below what their populations could legitimately expect. The labor force is demoralized. In sum, their relative economic and political condition is worse than it was in the aftermath of World War II.

The major problem for the East-Central European countries and for the USSR is, What to do next? Three interrelated strategic issues are of paramount importance: the issues of sources of capital, of the internal political regimes to be adopted, and of their place in the future European and world orders and the shape these global orders will take.

The development of a modern economic infrastructure and a complete restructuring of industry becomes the first requirement for the improvement of economic performance and a rise in the living standards of the population—a necessary condition if the government is to win broad public support and cooperation. Such a restructuring requires tremendous capital investment despite the fact that Soviet-bloc countries, and in particular Poland and Hungary, are already heavily indebted to the West. Among several possible sources of capital are intergovernmental loans, credits from private banks, and loans from international institutions such as the International Monetary Fund (IMF) and the World Bank. Intergovernmental loans can be used in the future as political leverage by the governments from which they originate. Private credits have not been forthcoming yet on a larger scale, because of the uncertainty of the political and economic situation in the region. Loans from the World Bank and from the IMF are accompanied by conditions that, if met, may threaten the political stability of the recipient countries.

There are reasons for hope. Virtually nobody in the world is interested in seeing this region destabilized. When this initial period passes, these countries may already be in the take-off phase of economic development, attracting private capital and enjoying greater political stability. Moreover, credits from the World Bank and the IMF will permit the most needed investments in physical infrastructure and in agriculture.

Better prospects have been opened by the unification of Germany. West German involvement in rebuilding the East German economy will stimulate Western Europe's interest in this region, and Japan and the United States will probably follow suit. The region is strategically located, it has a relatively well-educated labor force, is rich in natural resources, and has a population of over one hundred million people. In addition, it has had long economic, cultural, and political ties both to the West and to the East.

These developments already create major political and economic problems for the Soviet Union, and for its further existence. Already collateral contacts between the Soviets, in particular the inhabitants of the Western republics, and the East-Central Europeans are easier and more frequent. Changes occurring in Poland, Hungary, and Czechoslovakia have had a demonstrable effect on the Balts, the Ukrainians, the Russians, and others, and will further contribute to pressures in the Soviet Union for liberalization. If economic and political changes prove within a short time to be a success, the Soviet Union will be forced to liberalize its economic and political systems further to attract foreign investors. The disintegration of the Soviet unitary state, its transformation into a federation, and the reintegration of its republics into the world economy will continue.

This may be seen as a part of the strategy Gorbachev used for implementing change. He has tried to use his powers as first secretary to control the rigid, irreformable core, while he destabilized and weakened this core by allowing changes to take place in the system's peripheries, that is, in the Soviet bloc. By making the change in East-Central Europe irreversible, he strengthened his own line of reforms in the USSR, but it was in his interests to prevent the change from occurring too rapidly. This was a risky strategy. By destabilizing the core, Gorbachev also weakened his own position in the party. Moreover, he risked creating an effective opposition within the ranks of party bureaucracy. The present changes can be stopped by a dramatic turn of events, such as a military coup in the Soviet Union and the use of the army to win back control over the seceding Baltic republics. The only other way is to try a radical reform, and that in itself is a radical reform. Kremlin leaders do slow down trends toward disintegration whenever they can. Their reactions toward the legislative initiatives taken in the Baltic republics to assure these countries' sovereignty is an instance of such an effort. But these moves can be interpreted in two ways. One is that they stem from a conservative inertia and the inability to act decisively; another is that they are part of an effort to allow the Baltic republics to move ahead with their reforms while keeping the conservative, nationalist opposition in the Russian republic under control. If the latter interpretation is correct, it would appear that the Kremlin has adopted a strategy that can open up the possibility for a quiet, partial dismantling of the USSR and the transformation of the remnants into a democratically ruled federation.

Will East-Central Europe become a part of Europe and, if it will, what effect would that have on the Soviet Union's ability to survive or to undergo a smooth disintegration? Can some special ties between the former USSR, or the independent states that grow out of it, and the former satellites be developed and maintained? What new place will the former Soviet bloc find in the world order? And how will the world order itself evolve? These are fundamental questions, to which I cannot offer satisfying answers. Some general remarks are, however, appropriate.

The new East-Central European governments have only a limited, but not negligible, influence in solving these problems. If they are not offered an opportunity for closer cooperation with Western Europe, they will have to look elsewhere for solutions to their most difficult problems. They might consider some sort of an East-Central European alliance with close but symmetrical ties to the USSR which could, then, have a much better chance for survival, though in a highly modified form. This solution would not create sufficient conditions for a rapid economic recovery, but close cooperation among governments in this strategic area, and wise economic policies could make of it an attractive place for investments.

If East-Central Europe becomes part of a unified European market and develops closer political ties with Western Europe, its relationship with the Soviet Union will become weaker. If the Soviet Union decided to take a similar road, its transition would have to be much more wide ranging. It would have to abandon its unitary structure. The countries of East-Central Europe have a strategic interest in the success and continuation of reforms in the Soviet Union, though not necessarily in its disintegration. Complementary interests of both the West and the East converge toward the reunification of Europe; and, as history shows, the region can function and prosper only under conditions of peace and stability. Preserving and taking advantage of special relations with the Soviet Union, the non-Communist governments of Eastern Europe can exert a favorable influence upon the progress of the Soviet transition. If for the West, the Soviet attitude toward changes in East-Central Europe is the litmus test of Gorbachev's goodwill, for the East-Central Europeans the true test is Moscow's reaction to nationalist tendencies in the Baltic states, the Ukraine, and the Crimea. The successful transformation of the USSR into a democratic federation is clearly in the best interests of the former satellites.

The reunification of Europe and extensive changes in the Soviet Union may give rise to political and economic developments that will result in a new world order. In the face of this possibility we may feel as Tocqueville did when he looked upon the democratic experiment in America.

> Although the revolution which is taking place in the social condition, the laws, the opinions and the feelings of men, is still very far from being terminated, yet its results already admit of no comparison with anything that the world has ever before witnessed. I go back from age to age up to the remotest antiquity: but I find no parallel to what is occurring before my eyes: as the past has ceased to throw its light upon the future, the mind of man wanders in obscurity. (Tocqueville [1840] 1851, 2:352)

Communism is not reformable, but the restructuring of the institutional order of the Soviet system can produce effects of unimaginable proportions. Let us hope that we are capable of meeting the challenge. The failure of Communism does not ensure the success of democracy. Democracy too may be at risk when the Communist threat that has helped to integrate democratic states vanishes. But these are problems of a different kind, and for a new and different world.

NOTES

Chapter 1

1. East-Central Europe is distinguished from Eastern Europe. See Chapter 13 for a geopolitical description of the region.
2. Whether this means a victory of the political right is debatable. The interests of political discourse would not be served adequately if one of the sides loses. The problem of the Left started not in the 1980s, but in 1917, when it, albeit hesitatingly, decided to support the Soviet experiment. Later, on numerous occasions, the Left did condemn the Soviets, but was always ambivalent about the issue of Communism and does not seem to have drawn appropriate lessons from it.
3. Raymond Aron (1966) quite effectively challenged the thesis of environmental determinism in the second part of his book devoted to the geopolitical factors.
4. A similar idea was earlier expressed by Trotsky ([1937] 1972).
5. This has been convincingly demonstrated by Robert C. Tucker (1987, 40–44). The claim that the Mensheviks actively opposed and subverted Bolshevik rule is convincingly refuted by Vera Broido (1987).
6. A fair assessment of the validity of such an argument is provided by Alec Nove:

> We must never for a moment forget that Lenin and his followers, and his opponents too, were operating in an abnormal and indeed desperate situation. Who knows what reforms, policies, remedies they might have proposed in less troubled times? But in less troubled times they would not have been in power. (1969, 45)

7. Darrell P. Hammer, for instance, notes: "In a sense, Lenin's revolution was a culmination of the reforms of Peter the Great. The church was separated from the state; divorce and civil marriage were made legal; and the education of children was made the responsibility of the civil authority" (1986, 21). Hammer is right in pointing out that the modernization strategy the Bolsheviks used has certain similarities to that of Peter the Great. Both strategies resulted in bringing Russia closer to Europe in certain respects while moving it farther away in others.

8. I share Robert C. Tucker's conviction that "the Bolshevik Revolution in October, 1917, followed by the establishment of a one-party dictatorship and the nationalization of the Russian economy, nullified the previous sixty-five years of Russian history, during which, despite many setbacks, a trend of basic liberalization had been making itself felt" (1971, 174).

9. A similar point was made by A. M. Rosenthal in the editorial, "Decades of Historic Falsehood" (*New York Times*, 22 August 1989.)

10. "A constitutional agreement that favours particular interests may be achievable under 'suitable' conditions, but such agreement can be expected to be less robust with regard to potential changes in circumstances than fair arrangements" (Vanberg and Buchanan 1989, 56).

Chapter 2

1. An effort to compare the political cultures of Communist societies was made by Archie Brown and Jack Gray (1977). My impression is, however, that this collection of essays has not successfully defended itself against the troubles that haunt such works, the excessive use of clichés and stereotypes.

2. "The fact that Russia received its Christianity from Byzantium rather than from the West," Richard Pipes noted, "had the most profound consequences for the entire course of Russia's historic development. Next to the geographic considerations . . . it was perhaps the single most critical factor influencing that country's destiny. By accepting the eastern brand of Christianity, Russia separated itself from the main stream of Christian civilization which, as it happened, flowed westward" (1974, 223).

3. For recent lists of elements of the Russian political tradition, see Linden (1983, 2) and White (1977, 34).

4. One should beware, however, of Gerschenkron's warnings against the excessively frivolous use of the terms *historical continuity* and *discontinuity*. "Their meaning appears often blurred, and their users seem unaware of the existing confusion and its manifold sources. Irrelevant intrusion from alien conceptual structures, inferential sloppiness, and

political bias draped in the guise of scientific truth—all these have conspired in tangling the semantic skein" (1968, 11).

5. I shall not spend time discussing Keenan's rejection of the usefulness of studying rituals as mere facades, but it seems that a ritual such as the order in which the Communist leaders appear on official occasions has been telling us an important story about the hierarchy within the top political bodies.

6. The situation became more complicated after Peter's reforms and introduction of the Table of Ranks. This resulted initially in the extension of bureaucratic control over the nobility; but, in the long run, it contributed to the loss of autonomy by the state administration. For a detailed discussion of the Russian administrative tradition, see McKenzie-Pintner and Rowney (1980).

7. According to S. N. Eisenstadt, this is one of the central axes of political process in this type of regime. His book, *The Political Systems of Empires* (1963), is a masterpiece of comparative analysis.

8. See, for instance, Max Weber (1968). He discussed problems of the patrimonial form of traditional authority extensively in both volumes. For the general treatment, see vol. 1, pt. 1, chap. 3.

9. For a detailed examination of Keenan's contribution, see Daniels (1988).

Chapter 3

1. For instance, Darrell P. Hammer thus formulates the main thesis of his book: "Lenin embarked on a visionary program that could not possibly have been carried out; as a realist, he saw the impossibility of the task early in the history of the USSR, and the contradiction between the original vision (in whose name the communist party still holds power) and the reality of Soviet politics still has not been resolved" (1986, ix).

2. See, in particular, Neil Harding (1981). For a different view, see Leszek Kolakowski (1978). (In my original research I used the Polish edition, published in 1977 in Paris by Instytut Literacki, but I cite the English edition here.)

3. It is particularly fashionable to pretend that Lenin developed in this booklet an idea of the socialist state based upon *participatory democracy*. David Lane, for instance, formulates on this basis the opinion that Lenin's "practical political activity in Russia has borne fruit—the Bolsheviks attained power, but his aspirations for a socialist participatory democracy have not been achieved" (1981, 63). Similarly, Jack Gray writes that "in the circumstances which succeeded the seizure of power in 1917, Lenin himself, while continuing to be committed to the democratic

alternative, chose at every critical point the authoritarian alternative" (1977, 260). Two points can be made here. First, British authors seem to cherish the strange conviction that Lenin was a champion of human freedom. Second, when historical facts contradict their claims, they resort to the "accidental events" fallacy that I discussed earlier.

4. I read Polan's book after having written the first draft of this text. Thus, my reading of *State and Revolution*, very close to that of Polan, was not inspired by his important work. I mention this to suggest that perhaps our interpretation is more legitimate than some wish to admit.

5.
> Only in communist society . . . will a truly complete democracy become possible and be realized, a democracy without any exceptions whatever. And only then will democracy begin to *wither away*, owing to the simple fact that, freed from capitalist slavery . . . people will gradually *become accustomed* to observing the elementary rules of social intercourse. . . . They will become accustomed to observing them without force, without coercion, without subordination, *without the special apparatus* for coercion called the state. (Lenin [1917] 1971a, 227–28)

6. See *What Is to Be Done?* ([1902] 1961a), "A Letter to a Comrade" ([1902] 1961b), and "One Step Forward, Two Steps Back (The Crisis in Our Party)" ([1904] 1961e).

7. Alain Besançon noticed that Lenin knew nothing of the intellectual developments of his age, of Weber, Freud, of English logic, and of German critical philosophy (see 1981, 192). Similarly, Kolakowski noted that, unlike Lenin, Marx and Engels fully realized the continuity of human culture and would not have accepted the view that the value of all human actions was reducible to their instrumentality in the service of class interest (1978, 394).

8. According to Leszek Kolakowski (1978, 400), Lenin, with his theory of the party, introduced two novelties to traditional Marxism. The first was the proposition that the spontaneous working class movement could only acquire a bourgeois class consciousness. Second, the fundamental attribute of the proletarian movement is not that it is a working class movement but that it possesses the "correct," that is, Marxist, class consciousness. According to this view, there is no connection between the class composition of the revolutionary party and its class character.

9. Just to illustrate:

> *There could not have been* Social-Democratic consciousness among the workers. It would have to be brought to them from without. The history of all countries shows that the working class,

exclusively by its own effort, is able to develop only trade-union consciousness. . . . [In] Russia, the theoretical doctrine of Social-Democracy arose altogether independently of the spontaneous growth of the working-class movement; it arose as a natural and inevitable outcome of the development of thought among the revolutionary socialist intelligentsia. (Lenin [1902] 1961a, 375–76; see also pp. 399–400, 412, and 422 for similar remarks)

Chapter 4

1. It may be remarked that his pseudonym has become the only identifying term for Ulyanov. It is difficult to find a historical precedent for this. Even his friends from the early days of their revolutionary activities called him Lenin. One may wonder how Nadezhda Krupskaya addressed him during their intimate moments, for in public she also used the party name. Stalin had a first name, Joseph, but few would dare call him anything but Stalin, except for some old friends who called him Koba—but none of them survived the purges of the 1930s. The use of party names seems to have been one of the methods for building charisma, but of a special kind, as if to say, "I have no family, no name, no attachments—my party activities are all I am."

2. That he tried, often unsuccessfully, to maintain iron discipline is obvious. George Denike, one of the most brilliant Bolshevik agitators during the Revolution of 1905, told of his and his friends' treatment by the Bolshevik faction leadership when they dared to present at one of the faction's meetings views on the existing economic situation that differed from those expressed by the leadership. They were sharply rebuffed and forbidden, in the name of "factional discipline," to present their point of view at general party meetings. (Haimson 1987, 332–33)

3. Another example of Lenin's duplicity is revealed in the following story. After his break with Martov, according to Lydia Dan, her husband went to Zurich.

> He wanted to see Lenin and Lenin wanted to see him because he counted very much on his joining the Bolsheviks. The first thing that Lenin said was, "Before talking to you, there is this secret dossier which you should become familiar with." It was a notebook filled with absurd and ridiculous bits of scandal, purely personal, involving Martov and Ekaterina Mihkhailovna Aleksandrova and a number of others. (Ibid., 180)

4. This point was convincingly made by Alexander Rabinovitch in his book *The Bolsheviks Come to Power: The Revolution of 1917 in Petrograd* (1976).

5. "In Russia," Lenin wrote in January–February 1916,

> where the oppressed nations account [for] no less than 57 percent of the population, or over 100 million, where they occupy mostly the border regions, where some of them are more highly cultured than the Great Russians, where the political system is especially barbarous and medieval, where the bourgeois-democratic revolution has not been consummated—there, in Russia, recognition of the right of nations oppressed by tsarism to free secession from Russia is absolutely obligatory for Social-Democrats, for the furtherance of their democratic and socialist aims. (1971b, 166)

6. Also, Leszek Kolakowski (1978, 409–15) points to two constraints put by the Bolsheviks upon the right to self-determination. First, they supported the right to self-determination, but this did not oblige them to give support to all separatists' efforts. Second, the right to self-determination applied to the proletariat and not to the nation as such. One can add a third constraint: as the Bolsheviks arrogated to themselves the decision about what was in the interest of the proletariat and what was not, they also arrogated to themselves the right to decide which movement deserved to be granted self-determination.

7. The Bolsheviks had other ways to control the press. There was a dramatic shortage of paper, and they controlled its supply and so could foreclose access to independent sources of information and alternative viewpoints. At the time, during the very first days of the Revolution, before the civil war and foreign intervention, the Bolsheviks were directing these actions against their ideological and political allies, the Russian Left. Their policies toward the socialist press occasionally were relaxed, but the Bolsheviks were systematically moving toward the destruction of all independent sources of information, all public platforms for the expression of independent opinion. (On the saga of the Menshevik press, see Vera Broido [1987, 53–55].)

8. I made such a comparison in a paper, "James Madison and Vladimir I. Lenin on Factions" (in Polish) (Kaminski 1988). The idea of comparing Madison and Lenin on factionalism occurred earlier, however, to Carl A. Linden (1983, 61–67), though he addressed Lenin's views in general terms without referring to the resolution "On the Unity of the Party."

9. Emblematic of the grim continuity of the purges is that, of a thousand teenagers who at the beginning of the 1920s started

the Menshevik Youth League, only twenty outlived Stalin (Broido 1987, 158).

10. Redemption dues were introduced by the Emancipation Act in 1861. The peasants were to pay those dues during the next fifty years for the land they received. Redemption dues were high, the land on which they were paid was insufficient to sustain them, and they were perceived as one of the main causes of the peasants' misery.

11. As is often remarked, a complete about-face was quite typical for the Soviet regime: they would destroy opponents as "deviationists," and embark upon the very policies the opponents had advocated. When Mensheviks were liquidated, Lenin took their economic program and implemented it as the NEP. When Stalin eliminated Trotsky and his faction, he immediately started to implement their program. Khrushchev, having won his struggle against Malenkov, adopted *his* economic program.

12. On this subject, see Stanislaw Swianiewicz (1965). On the importance of forced labor in the Soviet industrialization, see Steven Rosefielde (1981). On the human sacrifice incurred by the Soviet population at that time, see Rosefielde (1983).

13. According to the estimates by W. F. Scott and H. Fast Scott (1980, 82), between 1930 and 1931 and 1935 and 1937, the production of military aircraft rose 3.5 times, of artillery canons over 2.5 times, of tanks nearly 4.5 times, and of rifles more than 2 times.

14. Whenever a strategic choice was made, it always fell upon a solution that took Russia farther from the democratic path on which it had made some progress during the years preceding World War I.

> At each successive crisis—whether the grain crisis during the Civil War or the industrialization debate at the end of NEP—there was a choice, and in each case the preferred solution was that which more nearly approximated to Tsarist practices, while the feebleness of the opposition in the New Course debate—in which the word "faction" was enough to emasculate the opposition's demands for intra-Party democracy—suggests that the Russian political culture provided no effective barriers to the re-creation of an autocracy prepared to control the thought of citizens, maintain power through a system of secret police and brook no rival power in society. (Gray 1977, 260)

15. See the seminal volume by Karl Wittfogel (1981), first published in 1896.

Chapter 5

1. Take, for instance, the following statement made by the secretary of state for foreign affairs and war in eighteenth-century Portugal:

> I find it absolutely necessary to bring all the commerce of this kingdom and its colonies into companies, then all merchants will be obliged to enter them, or else desist from trading, for they certainly may be assured that I know their interests better than they do themselves and the interest of the whole kingdom. (Valdiz 1980, 108-9)

2. As Samuel Huntington remarked,

> The absence of trust in the culture of the society provides formidable obstacles to the creation of public institutions. Those societies deficient in stable and effective government are also deficient in mutual trust among their citizens, in national and public loyalties, and in organization skills and capacity. Their political cultures are often said to be marked by suspicion, jealousy, and latent or actual hostility toward everyone who is not a member of the family, the village, or, perhaps, the tribe. (1973, 28)

3. The first to propose an interpretation of the socialist state as a class system was Milovan Djilas (1957). Karl Wittfogel (1981, ch. 8) developed a similar analytical perspective.

4. As I understand it, kinship is a natural restraint in the sense that the family is a reproductive unit. A direct interference with its reproductive functions can have a dramatic impact on the biological and cultural reproduction of society. To teach children to inform on their parents to the police by making a hero of Pavka Morozov is an example of the subversion of this constraint.

Chapter 6

1. Weber himself formulated the problem in the following way:

> He who wants to establish absolute justice on earth by force requires a following, a human "machine." He must hold out the necessary internal and external premiums, heavenly or worldly reward, to this "machine" or else the machine will

not function. Under the conditions of the modern class struggle, the internal premiums consist of the satisfying of hatred and the craving for revenge; above all, resentment and the need for pseudo-ethical self-righteousness: the opponents must be slandered and accused of heresy. The external rewards are adventure, victory, booty, power, and spoils. The leader and his success are completely dependent upon the functioning of his machine and hence on his own motives. Therefore he also depends upon whether or not the premiums can be *permanently* granted to the following, that is, to the Red Guard, the informers, the agitators whom he needs. What he actually attains under the conditions of his work is therefore not in his hand, but is prescribed to him by the following's motives, which, if viewed ethically, are predominantly base. The following can be harnessed only so long as an honest belief in his person and his cause inspires at least part of the following, probably never on earth even the majority. This belief, even when subjectively sincere, is in a very great number of cases really no more than an ethical "legitimation" of cravings for revenge, power, booty, and spoils. We shall not be deceived about this by verbiage; the materialist interpretation of history . . . does not stop short of the promoters of revolutions. Emotional revolutionism is followed by the traditionalist routine of everyday life; the crusading leader and the faith itself fade away, or, what is even more effective, the faith becomes part of the conventional phraseology of political Philistines and banausic technicians. (1946, 125)

2. The best review of modern uses of the term can be found in Heidenheimer (1970, ch. 1).

3. For instance, ". . . we will conceive of corruption in terms of a civil servant who regards his public office as a business, the income of which he will, in the extreme case, seek to maximize. The office then becomes a 'maximizing unit'" (van Klaveren 1970, 39).

4.
> This form of "corruption" consists in the vigorous and ruthless pursuit of the interest of one's own administrative (sub)unit. What we have here is not the pursuit of naked self-interest, but of self-interest dressed up as the interest of some collectivity or institution. Direct peer group control is ineffective here, because the members of the group are all involved in the "selfless" pursuit of some transpersonal interest, hoping to receive their personal share of the spoils later on. (van Gunsteren 1986, 277)

5. Eva Etzioni-Halevy, in a recent investigation of political corruption in Great Britain, the United States, and Israel, came to the following conclusion:

> Political corruption through material benefits in return for political support depends not on class characteristics and interests, nor on characteristics and political culture of the rank and file public, but on the elite political culture and on the power structures dominated by the elites. Its presence depends on political and bureaucratic elites and power structures being intermeshed, on politicians and party-politics intruding into the bureaucracy, on the consequent availability of bureaucratic resources for party political purposes and on an elite political culture that treats such deployment of bureaucratic resources as (at least unofficially) acceptable. (1989)

6. One can find elements of this broader thinking about the political system even in Karl Marx's essay, *The Eighteenth Brumaire of Louis Bonaparte* ([1852] 1963), for instance, in the idea of political and literary representatives of social classes.

7. It is not my opinion that all social life should or must be organized in this way in order to have a political system with a dominant bottom-up organization. To introduce democratic principles into an autocratic order is a perversion of this order. The only relevant issue is whether the rules of the game regulating this order may be defended on moral grounds. I think they may.

8. Aaron Wildavsky calls the culture of such groups sectarian egalitarianism (Thompson, Ellis, and Wildavsky 1990).

9. The first, to my knowledge, who introduced the term *partisan state* was Raymond Aron. "Dans un régime de parti unique," he wrote, "l'Etat est partisan, inseparable du parti qui a le monopole de l'activité politique legitime [In a one-party regime, the state itself is partisan, being inseparable from the party, which is the only expression of legitimate party activity—my translation]" (1965, 81). Milovan Djilas (1957) used the term *party state* to express a similar idea.

10. Barrington Moore, Jr., notes that all doctrines proposing an ideal society must question privacy.

> In an ideal society there is by definition no need for a private sphere to which the individual can retreat. If social institutions work perfectly and there is in place an educational system that grinds out new personalities suited to the perfect social order, why should there be any need for privacy? Instead,

privacy begins to look like a cover for the evasion of ethical and social obligations. (1984, 123)

11. This type of indoctrination went so deep that in 1986 a professor at Moscow University, on learning that many Polish workers were giving up their jobs in the state sector to work for private entrepreneurs, exclaimed: "How can it be? This is so unpatriotic?"

12. This subject has been extensively discussed by Vincent Ostrom and Elinor Ostrom (1977).

Chapter 7

1. A very similar view was taken by Robert C. Tucker, although he does not seem to have drawn his inspiration from Weber. See, in particular, Tucker's discussion of the party in chapter 1 of his book, *The Soviet Political Mind* (1971).

2. Zbigniew Brzezinski remarks that "as the regime becomes more stable the old supporters are joined by hordes of opportunists eager to get to the trough. In the absence of external institutions of control such as are found in constitutional societies, totalitarian leadership must proceed in its own way to ensure both loyalty and dynamism" (1956, 18).

3. According to Jerry F. Hough, "the first reason that the new Soviet leaders were moved to change Stalin's system was simply because they were afraid for their lives. . . . The most powerful 50,000 to 100,000 officials in 1937 were eradicated in the Great Purge, and the top officials in 1953 were the ones who most feared a new purge" (1988, 69).

4. In a world of false statistics, those who assess performance take into account either the statistics, showing an optimistic picture, or the real situation. In the first case, they reward; in the second, they punish. The question is not what an individual has done, but whether they want to punish or to reward him.

5. From a different perspective, the relative importance of the education and professional experience of the Communist *apparatchik*s for the functioning of the Soviet political system has been the major preoccupation of Jerry F. Hough (1980).

Chapter 8

1. The concept of the partisan state implies that an organized group seized a monopoly over the state and uses the powers of the state for its own interest. Both the political party and the state are qualitatively different

institutional entities from states and political parties under a liberal, democratic regime. Under Communism, the party is part of the state or, perhaps, vice versa.

2. Darrell P. Hammer aptly appraised the place of the Cheka in the system.

> The early experience of the Cheka established two principles that governed the operations of the political police. First, the Cheka was an instrument of the revolutionary dictatorship unrestricted by law. The initial conflict was between the Cheka and the ministry of justice, as the ministry tried to supervise the Cheka's activities. This conflict was quickly resolved, however, when the Cheka established its power as unrestricted by law. Second, although the Cheka was a part of the state apparatus, it was controlled directly by the party leadership and took its orders from the Politburo. (1986, 165).

3. See, among others, Raymond Aron (1965, ch. 13), Aryeh Unger (1981), and Ghita Ionescu (1967, 59–61).

4. Alexander Yanov (1978) discussed this ideological combination in the Soviet Union. In Central European countries nationalism must be, for obvious reasons, subjected to special cosmetic manipulations and, considering the present campaign by nationalist groups in the Soviet Union, it seems to be weaker there.

5. Effectiveness of these controls varied from sector to sector in the state administration. On the problems with controlling armed forces, see Roman Kolkowicz (1967) and Timothy Colton (1979).

6. The same was (and to some extent still is) true, of course, of the security police (see Berman 1966, 67–72).

7. Eugeniusz Bandosza, the head of the Personnel Policy Department of the Central Committee of the Polish United Workers' Party, stated that, in Poland, ". . . in the 1950s, [the] *nomenklatura* embraced 70 thousand positions but in practice all executive positions were controlled by the party. In the 1970s the *nomenklatura* grew, and at the end of the decade reached 130 thousand such positions, while in the first half of 1980s this figure was doubled" (1989). Now, after recent changes, "political acceptance" is needed only for 30,000 positions.

8. On the historical origins of the *nomenklatura* system in the USSR, see Rigby (1988).

9. For instance, when the draftees who served in the Polish Army during the imposition of martial law on December 13, 1981, were leaving the army for civilian life, General Jaruzelski signed instructions to all state administrative units that the supervisors were to offer positions of

authority to all ex-soldiers from that cohort who might apply for employment. It is impossible to say what the outcome was, but the issue of such an order tells a lot about the way in which political authorities treat the state administration.

10. In a highly interesting account of official corruption in the Soviet Union, Ilya Zemtsov (1985) has described many such cases and quoted the monetary prices paid for posts by their incumbents.

11. The author of this comparison is Stefan Kisielewski, an eminent Polish journalist and writer.

12. I do not quite subscribe to the position taken by Jerry F. Hough (1980, 23-29). Hough correctly notes that marked changes have occurred in the types of people recruited to the party organization. The new recruits usually have a college degree (mostly in engineering) and quite substantial professional experience in industry and ". . . the requirement of the party membership for almost all significant administrative jobs does not mean that the administrative system is staffed by the most opportunistic" (p. 26). I do not think that the data Hough presents support his position. First, we know nothing about social and individual differences between those college graduates who choose to join the party and those who do not. Likewise, we know nothing about such differences between those specialists, party members, who choose to work in the party administration and those who do not. Furthermore, in an environment as highly politicized as a Communist society is, professional criteria must all too often yield to political ones. Political conformism has until recently been, and probably still is, the main virtue of an advancing party activist. If this does not create a conflict between, as Hough says, "'red' and 'expert'," it is because the compromise that resolved this conflict resulted in the disintegration of both the party and the professional ethos with the most detrimental consequences for society.

13. On this subject, see Simis (1982) and Zemtsov (1985). Information no less shocking about the corruption of the Soviet elite has been published since 1987 in the USSR: the cases of Kazakhstan, Uzbekhistan, and the involvement of Leonid Brezhnev's family in those scandals made the Polish revelations of 1980 and 1981 pale in comparison.

Chapter 9

1. Robert W. Campbell describes the level of centralization of the Soviet type of economy in similar terms: "The need for aggregation," he writes, "is directly connected with the attempt to impose on the system a criterion and a set of objectives different from those which would be produced by consensus" (1966, 191). Given a choice, through an open

democratic process, Soviet citizens would probably have chosen another criterion and another order.

2. This distinction does not contradict in any way the basic correctness of the totalitarian paradigm interpreted in terms of an ideal type that reflects important inner patterns within the Communist political order. I mention this because of the debate that took place in the 1970s on the role of interest groups and factions in Soviet politics. I endorse the position represented by William E. Odom (1976) rather than that represented by most of the contributors to the book, *Interest Groups in the Soviet Union* (1971), edited by H. Gordon Skilling and Franklyn Griffiths.

3. A notable exception is the Czechoslovakian armed forces (Rice 1984).

4. For instance, according to some, the politicization of control in the Polish army after the introduction of martial law damaged discipline and morale.

5. Now it is more frequent to rely on nationalism while manipulating the information that officers receive. The purpose of indoctrination is to develop the conviction that the officers' corps is an initiated elite with a better understanding of political problems than that given the rest of society. Under this guise, stories of international conspiracies are presented to them at special meetings or disseminated in supposedly illegal, informally distributed publications.

6. One can doubt, however, the reliability of this source of information. Wladyslaw Bienkowski, a high official in the early years of Gomulka's rule, characterized the value of the source.

> In an inflated police system, the network of confidants does not provide reliable information about processes occurring within the society—one can even say that this is the least important task for this apparatus (that is why it is so often surprised by important social events). This network serves mostly its own interests. (1972, 87)

7. I am relying here on an opinion that is generally held in Poland. All three security agents who, in October 1984, murdered Father Popieluszko had either both or at least one parent employed in the security services.

8. In Poland, it is well known that representatives of the Ministry of Internal Affairs play an important role on the foreign currency black market and they have been (quasi-officially) involved in a number of great smuggling scandals. There is no official and reliable information about the size of the budget of this ministry. What is made public is too small to be true.

9. The press discussion in Poland over the provisions in the penal code that concern mutual relations between the public prosecutor's office and the courts is quite revealing, for the representatives of the Ministry of Internal Affairs behave in full accord with the expectation of minimal formal legal restrictions and savagely defend their "zone of discretion."

10. This element in the cultural ethos of the party apparatus has been particularly emphasized by Maria Hirszowicz (1986, 90–91).

11. The forced-labor mechanism, analyzed from this perspective by Stanislaw Swianiewicz (1965), cannot now be used on a wide scale. See Chapter 4.

12. The trends mentioned here are well known to demographers. I drew my information from Okolski (1983), who presents results of a comparative examination of data from socialist and Western countries.

13. Bihari (1986, 304) made a similar point.

Chapter 10

1. American officials often accuse Japan and other highly dynamic Southeast Asian countries of breaking the rules by pressing their exports while administratively hindering imports. Generally, it is true that the "beggar-thy-neighbor" policies used widely by governments to counter the effects of the depression of the 1930s undermined the market rules of the game, contributing greatly to the seriousness and duration of the crisis.

2. I discussed this problem in a paper, "On the Economic Theory of Planning" (1983).

3. Especially in Poland there has been in recent years an invasion of the families of party and state officials into the private sector; the family members in the private sector exploit the protection offered by relatives in important official positions. Also, more and more party and state officials "serve" on the boards of directors of private companies. The amount of corruption that has taken place where the party administration and the private sector meet must amaze anyone who remembers the ideological and political origins of the Communist party.

4. I assume that, since the formation by Tadeusz Mazowiecki of an interim Polish government, these practices have ceased. But this assumption is not based on any reliable information.

5. Nadezhda Mandelshtam (1970) described in her memoirs an old peasant woman who, during World War II when the USSR was struck with famine, expressed her compassion for Americans. She thought that if things were so bad in the USSR, they must have been much worse in

a country where people were supposed to live, according to official Soviet propaganda, in much worse conditions.

6. My usage has connotations different from those of the internal and the external party in George Orwell's book, *1984*, and different from Robert K. Merton's distinction (1949) between the cosmopolitans and the locals that initially inspired me.

7. When faced with such trends, the inhabitants of the Soviet-bloc countries comment ironically: "The new returns."

8. Mieczkowski assumes that a cut in investments or the redirection of investments can produce in a relatively short time an increase in consumption. This might have been the case earlier in the history of Communist countries. Now, most of the equipment is too specialized for an easy conversion.

9. Bunce expanded these ideas in her book, *Do New Leaders Make a Difference?* (1981).

10. Strzalkowski found that " . . . after 1956 expenditures for administration and national defense clearly declined, after 1970 they remained more or less on the same level, and after 1981 they clearly rose" (1987, 14). This trend, he said, is explained by the declining legitimacy of the Communist regime in Poland.

Chapter 11

1. In Czechoslovakia, more of the change was provoked by conflicts within the leadership. In Hungary and Poland the cause was social dissatisfaction.

2. Warnings about intervention did not occur in Hungary in 1956 and in Czechoslovakia in 1968. The reasons were many: the Hungarian revolution set the precedent for intervention, the Hungarian Communist party quickly disintegrated, and events were happening too fast. In Czechoslovakia, the Dubcek leadership was in control, it trusted the Soviet's goodwill. In Poland, the invasion of Hungary and Czechoslovakia gave to the Communists a powerful argument that they enthusiastically exploited whenever they needed.

3. In Czechoslovakia in 1968, the pressure from below was much less visible; the revolt was initiated and conducted mostly by the party leadership.

4. This situation never occurred in Poland, but seems to have existed in the Soviet Union during the past few years.

5. This view runs counter to the position adopted by Archie Brown, according to whom,

> it is not because a General Secretary's individual power is at its strongest in the earliest years of his tenure of office that much policy change occurs then, but, on the contrary, because his power accumulates so much over time that it becomes increasingly difficult for his colleagues to push through innovatory policies or for institutional interests to effect really significant shifts in priorities. Thus, it is the death or removal of a powerful General Secretary which opens up the way to policy change. (1982, 228)

The difference between my position and Brown's does not stem from the fact that he concentrates upon successions in the USSR, and my focus is on five East-Central European successions. I believe that we start our respective discussions from very different theories of the Communist system. In Brown's view, innovation comes from the top party elite; I see this group as highly conservative.

6. For instance, at the end of the 1970s in Poland, a governmental decree was introduced forbidding state enterprises to use railroad transportation when the distance between the plant and the source of spare parts, raw materials, and so on, or the receiver of the products was closer than a hundred kilometers (that is, about sixty miles). The purpose of the decree was to reduce the railroads' overload by forcing factories to use trucks. The immediate result was that, not having enough trucks, factories adjusted by using sources of raw materials and spare parts in faraway places, a tactic that obviously contributed to increased transportation costs and pressure on the railroads.

7. Some authors speculate that the decisive factor is the memory of the tragic Warsaw Rising, the terrible human toll of which makes both the Soviet leadership and the Polish population slow to provoke a situation in which open conflict would be unavoidable.

Chapter 12

1. Stanislaw Ossowski, a renowned Polish sociologist, is generally known to have used this expression.

2. In specialized policy areas one can find other privileged groups that have direct access to the political center, for instance, the collectivized sector in agriculture, party activists from writers' unions, and so on.

3. Moscow's campaign of mining Afghanistan is a good illustration of this strategy. The number of mines strewn across Afghanistan is

estimated at between ten and thirty million. Many of them resemble toys, balls, and ballpoint pens, which explode when picked up; the victims are mostly children. According to experts quoted by the *New York Times* ("Moscow's Millions of Deadly Seeds," 2 March 1989), these mines have no direct military purpose. In the words of Gay-Leclerc Brennar: "The purpose is really just to maim and terrorize people."

4. In discussing the liquidation of the institutional structure of the old regime in Hungary in the Stalinist period, and the process of the destruction of the existing social structure, Elemer Hankiss wrote:

> The rationale behind this strategy was that the far-reaching goals set by the party could be attained more rapidly and political power more easily consolidated if the society was kept in a diffuse atomized state. As for the economy, a radical program of modernization was announced, which at the time was understood to mean a rapid and extensive industrialization. This led to a certain economic differentiation and to the development of some more advanced forms of the division of labor. However, the process of differentiation was obstructed by the counteraction of central planning and rigorous central control, which penetrated and streamlined the entire economy. Individual economic actors were isolated, their relationships with one another were cut off, the whole economy was pushed into a state of centralized diffuseness and atomization. (1986, 9–10)

5. The term *anomie* was introduced into social science by Emil Durkheim and implies an absence or weakness of moral regulation. It is used here in that sense.

6. I think that Stefan Nowak's diagnosis of Polish society is singularly one-sided. A society characterized, to the extent he postulates, by a so-called sociological vacuum would not have been able to create Solidarity or oppose the Communist regime with any determination. There is no doubt, however, that a sociological vacuum is one of the characteristics of the state of social consciousness that is an important feature of the Polish, and perhaps even more so of other societies ruled by Communists. But again, one has to bear in mind that primary groups oriented toward material acquisition can offer protection to individuals involved in political activities against the system.

7. William E. Griffith noted that

> the Evangelical hierarchy tried to steer a course midway between collaboration and open resistance, thereby combining

some of the Lutheran tradition of loyalty to the state with more of the self-sacrificing opposition of the confessing Church. . . . In practice, this meant walking a tightrope between opposition and collaboration, and thus antagonizing both the SED [Communist Party of East Germany] and the dissidents, especially those who had decided to emigrate but were not allowed to do so. (1989, 329)

8. There were even proposals in the mid-1970s in the Soviet Union and in Poland to make citizens' "rights" dependent upon the fulfillment of their duties to the state.

9. The first situation occurred in Hungary at the beginning of the reform, that is, at the end of the 1960s and beginning of the 1970s; the second, in Czechoslovakia after 1968; the third, in Jaruzelski's Poland. I have discussed these cases in greater detail elsewhere (1989, 85–91) and I tried to explain the structural factors behind the three. Brezhnev's Soviet Union was characterized by a weakening center and strong bureaucracy. Gorbachev's reform efforts can be seen in terms of strengthening the center, imposing more effective forms of control upon the bureaucracy, and encouraging social participation.

Chapter 13

1. Two lines, one joining the extreme northern and southern points, and the other, the extreme western and eastern points of the map of Europe, will cross near the city of Lodz in Poland. Starting from such considerations, Norman Davies entitled his important book on Polish history, *Heart of Europe* (1986).

2. An elaborate statement of this position was initially provided in the work of Sir Halford Mackinder (1919, 1943). The most recent geopolitical analysis, in which this point is demonstrated, is to be found in Zbigniew Brzezinski's book, *Game Plan* (1986).

3. I am interested here mostly in political relations among states. I shall not discuss, therefore, the often highly beneficial German cultural influences in the region.

4. On the cultural and political development of the Commonwealth in this period, see Samuel Fiszman (1988).

5. Adam Ulam takes a different, and not quite consistent, perspective. In his opinion (1968, 133–35), Russia, more than any other large country, needed peace and stability for its economic development and political consolidation. But he also remarks that prosperity and stability in the world would isolate the Soviet Union and diminish chances for

the victory of world Communism. The major question, then, is, If Soviet Russia needed peace and stability, why did its rulers constantly destabilize the country by internal changes of revolutionary proportions? An autarkic economic organization was adopted by the end of 1920, and it does seem that the Russian economy became relatively immune to external factors. Soviet destabilization efforts in Germany, which Ulam described in detail, show that destabilization was high on the Soviet agenda and was renounced only when it created a direct threat to Soviet survival.

6. According to DePorte (1986, 33), General von Seeckt, the commander of the army of the Weimar Republic until 1926, viewed the Treaty of Rapallo that was signed in 1992 as "a means for bringing about the partition of Poland."

7. This interpretation is consistent with Adam Ulam's proposition that the road to the Ribbentrop-Molotov Pact was opened by the declaration made by Chamberlain, the British prime minister, on March 31, 1939, which implied that German aggression against Poland would automatically bring Great Britain and France into a war. For Stalin, according to Ulam, that meant that German aggression against Poland would oblige Germany to turn its armies to the west (1968, 265-70). Interestingly, the same theory was espoused, before World War II, by the then British ambassador in Moscow, Sir William Seeds (see Karski 1985, 343).

8. The area did have some important natural resources and was strategically located, but as it covered only eight hundred square miles, it was in reality a minor problem.

9. See, for instance, A. W. DePorte (1986), who seems to represent the position that a Europe divided across Germany of which one part is supported by the United States of America and the other subdued by the USSR offers much better prospects for stability.

10. As a matter of fact, particularly between 1934 and 1938, Germany pressed the Polish government with proposals to the effect that at ". . . some time in the future the two countries should become partners in a joint enterprise against the USSR, Poland to be rewarded with part of the Ukraine." The Polish government refused consistently on the grounds, among others, of its nonaggression treaty with the Soviet Union (Ulam 1968, 210-11).

11. Whatever other differences between Soviet claims and the original Curzon line, the USSR also incorporated the Lvov and Boryslav region that is to the west of the Curzon line.

12. Recently this argument was mentioned by Condoleezza Rice: "The importance of Eastern Europe as a security buffer is generally acknowledged. This historical memory of invasions through the Polish corridor and the creation of NATO are surely assuaged by Soviet Control of Central Europe" (1986, 244).

Chapter 14

1. This attitude is characteristic, for instance, of some of the contributions to an otherwise highly interesting collection of papers edited by Jan F. Triska (1986).

2. To illustrate the extent to which some Soviets thought that submission to their interests is natural, I can mention a conversation that took place in the fall of 1987 with a Russian scientist, a specialist in the "problems of peace." I asked him about the economic situation in the USSR. He said that the main economic problem was that other members of the Soviet bloc did not want to increase their military expenditures to defend their own frontiers and instead relied on the Soviet Union. I asked then: "Whom do you have in mind when you talk about the threat to our frontiers?" The Russian, without thinking twice, said, "The United States." I responded that I have never heard of an American threat to our frontiers. The professor from Moscow became red with anger and turned his back on me. Yet, this is true: Soviet strategic interests have differed from those of its European satellites, while this was not the case of American and Western European interests in NATO. The exception had been the issue of the western Polish frontier until it was internationally recognized.

3. The historical process of implementing Communist regimes in particular countries, and of changes used to bind countries of East-Central Europe closer to the USSR, are described in detail in a number of important works. See, for instance, Brzezinski (1967) and Hutchings (1983); also, for discussions of particular countries, Staar (1977) and Rakowska-Harmstone and Gyorgy (1979).

4. John Van Oudenaren notes that, "in the event of war, the USSR would administer the non-Soviet forces of the Pact in a manner not fundamentally different from that envisioned by Stalin and his generals—as virtual branches of the Red Army centrally directed from and dependent upon Moscow" (1984, 32). See also Mackintosh (1981, 139) and Rice (1986, 249–50).

5. Thus, at the end of July 1989, during the hearings before the Polish Sejm, General Jaruzelski said that the participation of Polish troops in the invasion of Czechoslovakia in August 1968 had been a sovereign decision of the Polish government and that it was a "good and correct decision." By taking this position he was confirming that he supported the right of the USSR to intervene militarily in the internal affairs of Soviet-bloc countries whenever the political position of those such as Jaruzelski was in trouble.

6. Romania was an exception to this rule, for two reasons. First, Nicolae Ceausescu was in full control of the Romanian political system

and society; hence, it was difficult for the Soviets to mastermind a plot against him. Second, the key to Soviet domination in the Balkans was Bulgaria; any gain from a military intervention in Romania would be negligible, but the costs prohibitive. Only when it became obvious to everyone in the Romanian Communist leadership that only by ousting Ceausescu could they save their own skins, was a successful revolt possible.

7. Polish Communists, for instance, used the argument that support from the USSR was necessary in relation to Poland's western frontier, the areas it acquired from Germany as compensation for the territory lost in the east. After December 1970, this argument became obsolete by the formal recognition of that frontier by the government of the Federal Republic of Germany.

8. Examining Gomulka's succession in Poland in 1956, Zbigniew Brzezinski notes:

> A suspended Soviet threat in the background was . . . a strange source of stability, beneficial not only to Soviet interests but also to Gomulka's survival. Moscow's problem was how to maintain the intricate balance of threat and adjustment without exaggerating the element of threat, which might intensify the tensions, and without diminishing it prematurely, which might encourage those elements elsewhere anxious to imitate Gomulka. (1967, 264-65)

9. The alleged lack of alternatives obviously served particular interests in special cases. The efforts by Mr. Rakowski, the first secretary of the Polish United Workers' party, undertaken in August 1989 to convince the Soviet leadership that a government led by Solidarity would not be a reliable ally show that, whenever an alternative appeared, the peripheral Communist elites were willing to subordinate national interests to their personal interests, for which they were prepared to commit treason.

10.
> Many East European economists would . . . note that the Soviet market's willingness to absorb poor quality goods and obsolete equipment appears to be an advantage to them only in the short run. In the long run, this imposes a large cost because it reduces the pressure and incentive to innovate and produce "for the market," causing their firms to fall more and more behind competitors on the world market. (Marer 1987)

11. The estimates of and methods used by Marrese and Vanous (1983) were criticized by a number of scholars, Marer (1984, 1989), Marer and Poznanski (1986), and Poznanski (1988), among others.

12.
> Issues of crucial significance are tackled in bilateral talks with the Kremlin. The multilateral activities of the bloc countries are devoid of political substance and remain ceremonial performances in a Byzantine style, which is, curiously enough, taken extremely seriously by the actors—probably because this offers them some kind of compensation and satisfaction for lacking freedom of political maneuver. (Schultz 1981, 48)

13. The local residents were well aware of such situations, and Zdenek Mlynar, in his memoirs (1980) of the Prague Spring, gives examples.

14. George Schöpflin goes even so far as to propose that "the East European politburos are an informal part of the central Soviet *nomenklatura* and that the Kremlin actively participates in decisions on promotions and demotions" (1981, 77–78). Reading an interview with an ex-colonel of the Polish People's Army, Ryszard J. Kuklinski, one has no doubt that, at least during crises, Soviet pressure on personnel decisions became direct and decisive (1987, 21). After the Soviet leaders had officially professed noninterference in the internal affairs of East-Central European countries, General Jaruzelski still informed representatives of Solidarity that the USSR, the Czechoslovak Soviet Socialist Republic, and the German Democratic Republic would not accept a Solidarity prime minister (*New York Times,* 27 July 1989). Finally, when the party had no other choice but to accept a Solidarity prime minister, it did so under the condition that key ministries in the government be under Communist control.

15. Other methods of integration were joint investment projects and joint production units, neither of which I shall discuss, except to remark that most of the joint investment projects were located in the USSR.

16. Even its organization structure was modeled on NATO's, but the similarity is rather superficial. They are two very different political and military conceptions of a defense organization (see Mackintosh 1981, 138–39).

17. According to Richard F. Staar, "the true reason for the Warsaw Treaty Organization was probably the USSR's desire to obtain legal justification for stationing its troops in East-Central Europe" (1977, 213).

18. As Robert Hutchings remarks, "One . . . significant aspect of Warsaw Pact exercises is the extent to which they have been used to serve political rather than military or strategic objectives" (1983, 152).

19.
> Clearly there are two institutions involved—the party and the military. The Soviets can influence East European military development through prohibitive control of the domestic Communist party as well. But given Soviet dominance at every

level, it is likely that the Soviet Union for the most part tries to maintain direct ties to the officers corps. . . . The potential for direct Soviet influence with the military professionals is a kind of wedge between the East European parties and their own armed forces. (Rice 1984, 20–21)

20. This paragraph is based on material published by D'Encausse (1983, 292–97).

21. There is general agreement that changes in Hungary and Poland in 1956 were closely interconnected, events in one country affecting what happened in the other. The Soviet invasion of Hungary, and movements of the Soviet units on Polish territory, had a sobering effect upon Poles and on some of the party leaders who supported popular aspirations.

22. The situation in Poland was more complex. Gomulka himself was a staunch Communist and only waited for a favorable moment to reverse the liberal changes that brought him to power. As for Jaruzelski, though he verbally accepted the workers' demands, he had already started preparations for martial law in December 1980. It is probable that this readiness to comply, and the fear that the Poles would resist, prevented Soviet intervention in both cases.

23. As Timothy J. Colton observes:

So intimate is the association [between the USSR and its satellites] springing [out] of occupation by the Red Army and coerced Sovietization after World War II, that forty years later many Soviet politicians still conceive of their policies toward Eastern Europe, and even the internal affairs of the six countries, as an extension of Soviet domestic policy. (1986, 209)

In a similar vein, Seweryn Bialer remarks:

The depth of Soviet elite and popular commitment to the preservation of the empire in Eastern Europe beyond obvious Soviet security needs is great. The issue of how far to go to permit change and accept different forms of socialism in this region is one of the two most sensitive items on Gorbachev's political agenda; the other is the national question in the Soviet Union. (1989, 419)

24. Similarly, according to Zdenek Mlynar (1980), in the spring of 1968 Czech secret agents distributed anti-Russian leaflets in Prague. Their content was immediately conveyed to the Soviet public by the mass media.

25. One of the most revealing examples of this kind of reaction was the debate in the Supreme Soviet over Lithuanian and Estonian demands for autonomy. Many delegates, especially those representing central planning, spoke against autonomy. Then, Svyatoslav N. Fyodorov, a Moscow surgeon, remarked:

> I haven't heard in the deputies' speeches concern that Lithuania and Estonia, in going over to economic independence, would fall apart and become poor. On the contrary, the undertone of the speeches was the envious fear that they would grow richer. This comes from slavery. After all, a slave cannot stand that another slave becomes free. ("More Autonomy for Baltics Stirs Discomfort in Moscow," *New York Times,* 27 July 1989).

Fyodorov, however, is only partly correct. Nearly all the countries dominated by the USSR would have been in every respect better off if they had had autonomy. Professor Fyodorov's thinking would imply that both the Soviet bloc and the USSR should be dismantled.

Chapter 15

1. Some of the reform attempts in agriculture and ecology are discussed in an interesting work by Thane Gustafson, *Reform in Soviet Politics* (1981).

2. Some authors, in contrast to the approach adopted here, consider the problem of identity in terms of social consciousness. See, for instance, Andrzej Rychard (1987, 77–80).

3. The following assessment by Milovan Djilas is even more accurate now than when it was written.

> Everything happened differently in the USSR and other Communist countries from what the leaders . . . anticipated. They expected that the state would rapidly wither away, that democracy would be strengthened. *The reverse happened.* [emphasis added] They expected a rapid improvement in the standard of living—there has been scarcely any change in this respect. . . .
> It was believed that the differences between cities and villages, between intellectual and physical labor, would slowly disappear; instead these differences increased. (1957, 37)

4. One should bear in mind that opposition to liberal, democratic reforms in the Soviet Union, and in particular in its Russian part, is not found solely in the party bureaucracy. Opposition to Western influences has a long history in Russia. *Pamyat,* the contemporary incarnation of this tradition, will gladly join forces with any group among the Communists to stop such changes.

5. Paradoxically, one of the justifications provided for this change was that the adoption of a "well-tried" French model of public administration would be an improvement upon the Polish one. The more probable motive was that Gierek remembered that he waged his successful challenge to Gomulka's leadership from the position of the *voyevod*ship first secretary. Another likely motive was that the prime minister, Jaroszewicz, who was the initiator of the reform, sought to strengthen his position at the cost of the party hierarchy.

6. This puts Jaruzelski's credentials as a reformer into doubt. When he saw the scale of opposition, he disavowed his prime minister, Messner, and pretended that he knew nothing about the proposed changes. This is simply impossible considering the nature of the regime. Moreover, he waited for two years before firing Messner, who had been considered his faithful servant.

7. This is reflected in the efforts, not quite successful up to now, to eliminate state budgetary deficits in most Western countries. It will be interesting to see how the "de-communization" of the Central European societies will affect the place of the state in the socioeconomic structure.

Chapter 16 is not annotated.

BIBLIOGRAPHY

Abalkin, Leonid. 1987. "The Pivot of Economic Life." In *USSR: A Time of Change,* edited by Galina Dzyubenko and Galina Kozlova (translated from Russian). Moscow: Progress Publishers.

Adamski, Jerzy. 1984. *Dno Oka.* Warsaw: Państwowy Instytut Wydawniczy.

Agursky, Mikhail. 1987. *The Third Rome: National Bolshevism in the USSR.* Boulder, Colo.: Westview Press.

Andorka, Rudolf, and L. Bertalan, eds. 1986. *Economy and Society in Hungary.* Budapest: Department of Sociology, University of Economic Science.

Andreski, Stanislav. 1970. "Cleptocracy as a System of Government in Africa." In *Political Corruption,* edited by A. J. Heidenheimer. 2d ed. New Brunswick, N.J.: Transaction.

Aristotle. 1943. *Politics.* Translated by Benjamin Jowett. New York: Modern Library.

Aron, Raymond. 1965. *Démocratie et totalitarisme.* Paris: Editions Gallimard.

———. 1966. *Peace and War: A Theory of International Relations.* New York: Doubleday.

Bandosza, Eugeniusz. 1989. "Nomenklatura—mit i rzeczywistosc" (Nomenklatura—myth and reality). *Trybuna Ludu,* 10 February.

Barghoorn, F. C. 1971. "The Security Police." In *Interest Groups in Soviet Politics,* edited by H. Gordon Skilling and Franklyn Griffiths. Princeton, N.J.: Princeton University Press.

Baron, Samuel. 1962. "Between Marx and Lenin: George Plekhanov." In *Revisionism: Essays on the History of Marxist Ideas,* edited by Leopold Labedz. New York: Praeger.

Beck, Carl, William A. Jarzabek, and Paul H. Ernandez. 1976. "Political Succession in Eastern Europe." *Studies in Comparative Communism* 9 (1/2): 35–61 (spring/summer).

Berman, Harold, ed. 1966. *Soviet Criminal Law and Procedure: The RSFSR Codes.* Cambridge, Mass.: Harvard University Press.
Besançon, Alain. 1978. *The Soviet Syndrome.* New York: Harcourt Brace Jovanovich.
———. 1980. *Présent soviétique et passé russe.* Paris: Hachette.
———. 1981. *The Intellectual Origins of Leninism.* New York: Continuum.
Bialer, Seweryn. 1989. "Central and Eastern Europe, *Perestroika,* and the Future of the Cold War." In *Central and Eastern Europe: The Opening Curtain?* edited by William E. Griffith. Boulder, Colo.: Westview Press.
Bienkowski, Wladyslaw. 1972. *Sociologia Kleski* (The Sociology of Defeat). Paris: Wyd. Kultura.
Bihari, Mihaly. 1986. "The Political System and the Representation of Interests." In *Economy and Society in Hungary,* edited by R. Andorka and L. Bertalan. Budapest: Department of Sociology, Karl Marx University of Economic Sciences.
Bogomolov, Oleg T. 1986. Introduction. In *The World Socialist Economy.* Moscow: USSR Academy of Sciences.
Bova, Russell. 1988. "The Soviet Military and Economic Reform." *Soviet Studies* 40 (3): 385–405 (July).
Broido, Vera. 1987. *Lenin and the Mensheviks: The Persecution of Socialists under Bolshevism.* England: Gower.
Brown, Archie. 1982. "Leadership Succession and Policy Innovation." In *Soviet Policy for the 1980s,* edited by A. Brown and M. Kaser. Bloomington: Indiana University Press.
Brown, Archie, and Jack Gray, eds. 1977. *Political Culture and Political Change in Communist States.* New York: Holmes and Meier.
Brown, J. F. 1989. "Conservatism and Nationalism in the Balkans: Albania, Bulgaria, and Romania." In *Central and Eastern Europe: The Opening Curtain?* edited by William E. Griffith. Boulder, Colo.: Westview Press.
Brzezinski, Zbigniew. 1956. *The Permanent Purge: Politics in Soviet Totalitarianism.* Cambridge, Mass.: Harvard University Press.
———. 1960. "The Patterns of Autocracy." In *The Transformation of Russian Society,* edited by C. E. Black. Cambridge, Mass.: Harvard University Press.
———. 1967. *The Soviet Bloc: Unity and Conflict.* 2d rev. ed. Cambridge, Mass.: Harvard University Press.
———. 1986. *Game Plan: A Geostrategic Framework for the Conduct of the U.S.-Soviet Contest.* New York: Atlantic Monthly Press.
Buchanan, James, and Gordon Tullock. 1965. *The Calculus of Consent: Logical Foundations of a Constitutional Democracy.* Ann Arbor: University of Michigan Press.
Bunce, Valerie. 1980. "The Political Consumption Cycle: A Comparative Analysis." *Soviet Studies* 32 (2): 280–90 (April).

———. 1981. *Do New Leaders Make a Difference? Executive Succession and Public Policy under Capitalism and Socialism.* Princeton, N.J.: Princeton University Press.

Burlatsky, Fyodor. 1987. "Lenin and the Strategy of Radical Change." In *USSR: A Time of Change,* edited by Galina Dzyubenko and Galina Kozlova (translated from Russian). Moscow: Progress Publishers.

Byrnes, Robert F. 1983. "Critical Choices in the 1980s." In *After Brezhnev: Sources of Soviet Conduct in the 1980s,* edited by Robert F. Byrnes. Bloomington: Indiana University Press.

Campbell, Robert W. 1966. "On the Theory of Economic Administration." In *Industrialization in Two Systems: Essays in Honor of Alexander Gerschenkron,* edited by Henry Rosovsky. New York: John Wiley.

———. 1983. "The Economy." In *After Brezhnev: Sources of Soviet Conduct in the 1980s,* edited by Robert F. Byrnes. Bloomington: Indiana University Press.

———. 1988. *The Soviet Telecommunications System.* Indianapolis: Hudson Institute.

Carr, Edward H. 1954. *The Interregnum 1923-1924.* New York: Macmillan.

Churchill, Winston S. 1960. *The Second World War.* Vol. 1, *The Gathering Storm.* London: Cassel.

Colton, Timothy J. 1979. *Commissars, Commanders, and Civilian Authority: The Structure of Soviet Military Politics.* Cambridge, Mass.: Harvard University Press.

———. 1986. *The Dilemma of Reform in the Soviet Union.* 2d rev. ed. New York: Council on Foreign Relations.

Conquest, Robert. 1971. *The Great Terror: Stalin's Purge of the Thirties.* New York: Penguin.

Conrad, Joseph. 1911. *Under Western Eyes.* New York and London: Harper.

Corson, William R., and Robert T. Crowley. 1985. *The KGB: Engine of Soviet Power.* New York: William Morrow.

Coser, Lewis. 1959. *The Functions of Social Conflict.* Glencoe, Ill.: Free Press.

Csaba, Laszlo. 1988. "CMEA and the Challenge of the 1980s." *Soviet Studies* 40 (2): 266-89 (April).

Custine, Marquis de. [1839] 1989. *Empire of the Czar: A Journey Through Eternal Russia.* New York: Doubleday.

Dahrendorf, Ralf. 1959. *Class and Class Conflict in an Industrial Society.* Stanford, Calif.: Stanford University Press.

———. 1974. "Citizenship and Beyond: The Social Dynamics of an Idea." *Social Research* 41 (winter): 673-701.

Dallin, David. 1974. "The Outbreak of the Civil War." In *The Mensheviks: From the Revolution of 1917 to the Second World War,* edited by Leopold H. Haimson. Chicago: University of Chicago Press.

Daniels, Robert V. 1966. "Stalin's Rise to Dictatorship, 1922–29." In *Politics in the Soviet Union,* edited by Alexander Dallin and Alan F. Westin. New York: Harcourt, Brace and World.

———. 1988. *Is Russia Reformable? Change and Resistance from Stalin to Gorbachev.* Boulder, Colo.: Westview Press.

Davies, Norman. 1986. *Heart of Europe: A Short History of Poland.* Oxford and New York: Oxford University Press.

D'Encausse, Hélène Carrère. 1983. *Le grand frère: L'Union soviétique et l'Europe soviétisée.* Paris: Flammarion.

DePorte, A. W. 1986. *Europe Between the Super-Powers: The Enduring Balance.* 2d ed. New Haven, Conn: Yale University Press.

Deutsch, Karl W. 1967. *The Nerves of Government: Models of Political Communication and Control.* London: Free Press of Glencoe.

Djilas, Milovan. 1957. *The New Class: An Analysis of the Communist System.* New York: Praeger.

Dmowski, Roman. 1917. *Problems of Central and Eastern Europe.* London: privately printed.

Dolgorukov, Petr. 1862. *Des réformes en Russie.* Paris: Pagnerre, Libraire-Editeur.

Dostoyevsky, Fyodor. [1873] 1986. *The Possessed.* New York: New American Library.

Eisenstadt, S. N. 1963. *The Political Systems of Empires.* London: Collier-Macmillan.

Engels, Friedrich. [1884] 1942. *The Origin of the Family, Private Property, and the State in the Light of Researches of Lewis H. Morgan.* New York: International Publishers.

Erlich, Alexander. 1960. *The Soviet Industrialization Debate, 1924–1928.* Cambridge, Mass.: Harvard University Press.

Etzioni-Halevy, Eva. 1989. "Tangible Benefits in Return for Political Support: A Comparative Analysis." In *Political Corruption,* edited by A. J. Heidenheimer, Michael Johnston, and Victor LeVine. New Brunswick, N.J.: Transaction Publishers.

Fainsod, Merle. 1953. *How Russia Is Ruled.* Cambridge, Mass.: Harvard University Press.

Fears, J. Rufus, ed. 1985. *Selected Writings of Lord Acton.* Vol. 1, *Essays in the History of Liberty.* Indianapolis: Liberty Classics.

Fiszman, Samuel, ed. 1988. *The Polish Renaissance in Its European Context.* Bloomington: Indiana University Press.

Flerou, F. J. 1971. "Cooptation as a Mechanism of Adaptation: The Soviet Political Leadership System." In *The Behavioral Revolution and Communist Studies,* edited by R. E. Kanet. New York: Free Press.

Friedrich, C. J., and Z. K. Brzezinski. 1956. *Totalitarian Dictatorship and Democracy.* Cambridge, Mass.: Harvard University Press.

Gawda, Witold, Tomasz Kowalczyk, and Andrzej Rychard. 1981. "Social Context of the Organizational Heterogeneity." *Polish Sociological Bulletin* 53 (1).
Gerschenkron, Alexander. 1960. "Problems and Patterns of Russian Economic Development." In *The Transformation of Russian Society*, edited by Cyril E. Black. Cambridge, Mass.: Harvard University Press.
———. 1962. "The Changeability of a Dictatorship." *World Politics* 14 (4): 576–604 (July).
———. 1968. *Continuity in History, and Other Essays*. Cambridge, Mass.: Harvard University Press.
———. 1970. *Europe in the Russian Mirror*. Cambridge: Cambridge University Press.
Gray, Jack. 1977. "Conclusions." In *Political Culture and Political Change in Communist Societies*, edited by A. Brown and Jack Gray. New York: Holmes and Meier.
Griffith, William E. 1989. "The German Democratic Republic." In *Central and Eastern Europe: The Opening Curtain?* edited by William E. Griffith. Boulder, Colo.: Westview Press.
Gustafson, Thane. 1981. *Reform in Soviet Politics: Lessons of Recent Policies on Land and Water*. Cambridge: Cambridge University Press.
Haimson, Leopold H. 1987. *The Making of Three Russian Revolutionaries: Voices from the Menshevik Past*. New York: Cambridge University Press.
Hamilton, Alexander, John Jay, and James Madison. [1787] (n.d.). *The Federalist*, edited by E. M. Earle. New York: Random House, Modern Library.
Hammer, Darrell P. 1986. *The USSR: The Politics of Oligarchy*. 2d ed. Boulder, Colo.: Westview Press.
Hankiss, Elemer. 1986. "The 'Second Economy': Is There a Second Social Paradigm Working in Contemporary Hungary?" Institute of Sociology, Hungarian Academy of Sciences, Budapest. Mimeo.
Hanson, Philip. 1978. "Mieczkowski on Consumption and Politics: A Comment." *Soviet Studies* 30 (4): 553–56 (October).
Harding, Neil. 1981. *Lenin's Political Thought*. London: Macmillan.
Haxthausen, Baron von. 1856. *The Russian Empire*. 2 vols. London: Chapman and Hall.
Hayek, Friedrich von. 1945. "The Use of Knowledge in Society." *The American Economic Review* 35 (4): 519–30.
Heidenheimer, A. J., ed. 1970. *Political Corruption: Readings in Comparative Analysis*. New York: Holt, Rinehart and Winston.
Herspring, Dale R. 1989. "The Soviets, the Warsaw Pact, and the Eastern European Militaries." In *Central and Eastern Europe: The Opening Curtain?* edited by William E. Griffith. Boulder, Colo.: Westview Press.

Hirszowicz, Maria. 1986. *Coercion and Control in Communist Society: The Visible Hand in a Command Economy.* New York: St. Martin's.
Hobbes, Thomas. [1651] 1962. *Leviathan.* Oxford: Clarendon Press.
Holloway, David. 1984. *The Soviet Union and the Arms Race.* 2d ed. New Haven, Conn.: Yale University Press.
Hough, Jerry F. 1980. *Soviet Leadership in Transition.* Washington, D.C.: Brookings Institution.
―――. 1988. *Russia and the West: Gorbachev and the Politics of Reform.* New York: Simon and Schuster.
Huntington, Samuel. 1973. *Political Order in Changing Societies.* New Haven, Conn.: Yale University Press.
Hutchings, Robert. 1983. *Soviet-East European Relations: Consolidation and Conflict, 1960-1980.* Madison: University of Wisconsin Press.
Ionescu, Ghita. 1967. *L'Avenir politique de l'Europe orientale.* Paris: Futuribles.
Jain, R. B. 1987. "Political and Bureaucratic Corruption in India: Some Ethical Dimensions." Paper presented at the conference, "Political Corruption and Political Financing," 18-24 May, at Managgio, Italy.
Jasinska-Kania, Aleksandra. 1987. "Social and Regional Origins, Social Contacts." In *Local Authorities Under Crisis,* edited by J. J. Wiatr (in Polish). Warsaw: Warsaw University Press.
Jowitt, Ken. 1978. *The Leninist Response to National Dependency.* Berkeley: Institute of International Studies, University of California.
―――. 1983. "Soviet Neotraditionalism: The Political Corruption of a Leninist Regime." *Soviet Studies* 35 (3): 275-97 (July).
Kaminski, Antoni Z. 1983. "On the Economic Theory of Planning." *Oeconomica Polona,* no. 2: 163-83.
―――. 1988. James Madison i W. I. Lenin o f(r)akcjach (James Madison and Vladimir I. Lenin on f(r)actions). *Res Publica* (December).
―――. 1989. "Coercion, Corruption, and Reform: State and Society in the Soviet-type Socialist Regime." *Journal of Theoretical Politics* 1 (1): 77-102.
Kaminski, Bartlomiej. 1989. "Council for Mutual Economic Assistance: Division and Conflict on Its 40th Anniversary." In *Yearbook on International Communist Affairs,* edited by Richard F. Staar. Stanford, Calif.: Hoover Institution Press.
Karski, Jan. 1985. *The Great Powers and Poland, 1919-1945.* New York: University Press of America.
Keenan, Edward L. 1986. "Muscovite Political Folkways." *The Russian Review* 45 (2): 115-81.
Keep, John L. H., ed. 1979. *The Debate on Soviet Power. Minutes of the All-Russian Central Executive Committee of Soviets; Second Convocation October 1917-January 1918.* Oxford: Clarendon Press.

Kennan, George F. 1947. "The Sources of Soviet Conduct." *Foreign Affairs* 25 (4): 566–82 (July).
———. 1962. *Russia and the West under Lenin and Stalin*. New York: The American Library.
Kolakowski, Leszek. 1978. *Main Currents of Marxism*. Vol. 2, *The Golden Age*. Oxford: Oxford University Press.
Kolkowicz, Roman. 1967. *The Soviet Military and the Communist Party*. Princeton, N.J.: Princeton University Press.
———. 1969. "The Warsaw Pact: Entangling Alliance." *Survey*, no. 70/71: 86–101 (winter/spring).
———. 1971. "The Military." In *Interest Groups in Soviet Politics*, edited by H. Gordon Skilling and Franklyn Griffiths. Princeton, N.J.: Princeton University Press.
Korbonski, Andrzej. 1976. "Leadership Succession and Political Change in Eastern Europe." *Studies in Comparative Communism* 9 (1/2): 3–26 (spring/summer).
Korbonski, Stefan. 1978. *The Polish Underground State: A Guide to the Underground, 1930–45*. New York: Columbia University Press.
Kornai, Janos. 1980. *Economics of Shortage*. Amsterdam: North Holland.
———. 1986. "The Hungarian Reform Process: Visions, Hopes and Reality." *Journal of Economic Literature* 24 (4): 1687–737 (December).
Kuklinski, Ryszard J. 1987. "Wojna z narodem widziana od środka: rozmowa z byłym płk. dypl. Ryszardem J. Kuklińskim" (War against the nation seen from inside: an interview with ex-colonel R. J. Kulinski). *Kultura* (Paris), no. 4: 3–57.
Lane, David. 1969. *The Roots of Russian Communism: A Social and Historical Study of Russian Social-Democracy 1898–1907*. Assen, Netherlands: Van Gorcum.
———. 1981. *Leninism: A Sociological Interpretation*. New York: Cambridge University Press.
Lawrence, Paul R., and Jay W. Lorsch. 1967. *Organization and Environment*. Boston, Mass.: Graduate School of Business Administration, Harvard University.
Lednicki, Waclaw. 1967. *Wspomnienia* (Memoirs), vol. 2. London: Swiderski.
Lenin, V. I. 1949. *Selected Works* (in Polish). Warsaw: KIW.
———. [1902] 1961a. "What Is to Be Done?" In *Collected Works*, vol. 5. Moscow.
———. [1902] 1961b. "A Letter to a Comrade on Our Organisational Tasks." In *Collected Works*, vol. 6. Moscow.
———. [1903] 1961c. "Report on the Party Rules." In *Collected Works*, vol. 6. Moscow.
———. [1903] 1961d. "Letter to Iskra." In *Collected Works*, vol. 7. Moscow.

———. [1904] 1961e. "One Step Forward, Two Steps Back (The Crisis in Our Party)." In *Collected Works,* vol. 7. Moscow.

———. [1917] 1971a. "State and Revolution." In *Lenin: Essential Aspects of Lenin's Contributions to Revolutionary Marxism.* New York: International Publishers.

———. 1971b. "The Socialist Revolution and the Right of Nations to Self-Determination." In *Lenin: Essential Aspects of Lenin's Contributions to Revolutionary Marxism.* New York: International Publishers.

Linden, Carl A. 1983. *The Soviet Party State: The Politics of Ideocratic Despotism.* New York: Praeger.

MacGregor, Douglas A. 1986. "Uncertain Allies? East European Forces in the Warsaw Pact." *Soviet Studies* 38 (2): 227–47 (April).

Maciejewski, Wojciech. 1989. "Adjustment Processes in Planned Economies." In *Poland: The Economy in the 1980s,* edited by R. A. Clarke. London: Longman.

Maciejewski, Wojciech, and Mario Nutti. 1985. "Economic Integration Between CMEA Countries and Prospects for East-West Trade." DOC 127/85. Florence: European University Institute.

McKenzie-Pintner, W., and D. K. Rowney. 1980. *Russian Officialdom: The Bureaucratization of Russian Society from the Seventeenth to the Twentieth Century.* Chapel Hill: University of North Carolina Press.

Mackinder, Sir Halford. 1919. *Democratic Ideals and Reality: A Study in the Politics of Reconstruction.* New York: Holt.

———. 1943. "The Round World and the Winning of the Peace." *Foreign Affairs* 21 (4): 595–605.

Mackintosh, Malcolm. 1981. "Military Considerations in Soviet–East European Relations." In *Soviet–East European Dilemmas: Coercion, Competition, and Consent,* edited by K. Davisha and P. Hanson. London: Heinemann.

Mandelshtam, Nadezhda. 1970. *Hope Against Hope: A Memoir.* New York: Atheneum.

Marcuse, Herbert. 1957. *Soviet Marxism: A Critical Analysis.* New York: Columbia University Press.

Marer, Paul. 1984. "The Political Economy of Soviet Relations with Eastern Europe." In *Soviet Policy in Eastern Europe,* edited by Sarah M. Terry. New Haven, Conn.: Yale University Press.

———. 1987. "Soviet–East European Economic Relations: A Historical Perspective." *Advances in International Comparative Management,* suppl. 2: 45–53.

———. 1989. "The Economies and Trade of Eastern Europe." In *Central and Eastern Europe: The Opening Curtain?* edited by William E. Griffith. Boulder, Colo.: Westview Press.

Marer, Paul, and K. Poznanski. 1986. "Costs of Domination, Benefits of Subordination." In *Dominant Powers and Subordinate States: The United States in Latin America and the Soviet Union in Eastern Europe,* edited by Jan F. Triska. Durham, N.C.: Duke University Press.

Marrese, Michael, and Jan Vanous. 1983. *The Soviet Subsidization of Trade with Eastern Europe.* Berkeley: Institute of International Studies, University of California.

Marx, Karl. [1852] 1963. *The Eighteenth Brumaire of Louis Bonaparte.* New York: International Publishers.

Marx, Karl. [1843] 1970. *Critique of Hegel's "Philosophy of Right."* Cambridge: Cambridge University Press.

Mastny, Vojtech. 1989. "Eastern Europe and the West in the Perspective of Time." In *Central and Eastern Europe: The Opening Curtain?* edited by William E. Griffith. Boulder, Colo.: Westview Press.

Merton, Edwina. 1981. "Foreign Policy Perspectives in Eastern Europe." In *Soviet-East European Dilemmas: Coercion, Competition, and Consent,* edited by K. Davisha and P. Hanson. London: Heinemann.

Merton, Robert K. 1949. *Social Theory and Social Structure.* Glencoe, Ill.: Free Press.

Mieczkowski, Bogdan. 1978. "The Relationship Between Changes in Consumption and Politics in Poland." *Soviet Studies* 30 (2): 262–69 (April).

Mlynar, Zdenek. 1980. *Nightfrost in Prague: The End of Human Socialism.* New York: Karz-Kohl.

Montesquieu, Charles-Louis de Secondat, Baron de La Brède et de. [1750] 1886. *The Spirit of Laws,* translated by Thomas Nugent, vol. 1. Cincinnati, Ohio: Robert Clarke.

Moore, Barrington, Jr. 1974. *Social Origins of Dictatorship and Democracy: Lord and Peasant in the Making of the Modern World.* Harmondsworth, Middlesex, England: Penguin.

———. 1984. *Privacy: Studies in Social and Cultural History.* Armonk, N.Y.: Sharpe.

Morawski, Witold. 1980. "Society and the Strategy of Imposed Industrialization: The Polish Case." *Polish Sociological Bulletin* 52 (4).

Mosca, Gaetano. 1939. *The Ruling Class.* New York: McGraw-Hill.

North, Douglass. 1981. *Structure and Change in Economic History.* New York: Norton.

———. 1986. "Institutions, Economic Growth and Freedom: An Historical Introduction." Paper prepared for the symposium, "Economic, Political and Civil Freedom," sponsored by the Liberty Fund, 5–8 October, in the Napa valley, California.

Nove, Alec. 1969. *An Economic History of the U.S.S.R.* New York: Penguin.

Nowak, Jan. 1982. *The Courier to London.* Detroit: Wayne State University Press.

Nowak, Stefan. 1980. "Values and Attitudes of the Polish People." *Polish Sociological Bulletin* 2.
Odom, William E. 1976. "A Dissenting View on the Group Approach to Soviet Politics." *World Politics* 28 (4): 542–67 (July).
Okolski, Marek. 1983. "Transformacja demograficzna w Polsce" (Demographic transition in Poland). *Ekonomista*, no. 1: 9–57.
Ostrom, Vincent. 1974. *The Intellectual Crisis in American Public Administration.* Tuscaloosa: University of Alabama Press.
———. 1987. *The Political Theory of a Compound Republic: Designing the American Experiment.* Lincoln: University of Nebraska Press.
———. 1991. *The Meaning of American Federalism: Constituting a Self-Governing Society.* San Francisco: ICS Press.
Ostrom, Vincent and Elinor Ostrom. 1977. "Public Goods and Public Choices." In *Alternatives for Delivering Public Services: Toward Improved Performance,* edited by E. S. Savas. Boulder, Colo.: Westview Press.
Pipes, Richard. 1954. *The Formation of the Soviet Union: Communism and Nationalism 1917–1923.* Cambridge, Mass.: Harvard University Press.
———. 1974. *Russia under the Old Regime.* New York: Charles Scribner's Sons.
———. 1980. "Militarism and the Soviet State." *Daedalus* 109 (4): 1–12 (fall).
———. 1984. "Can the Soviet Union Reform?" *Foreign Affairs* 63 (1):47–61.
———. 1988. "The Bolsheviks Dissolve the Constituent Assembly." *Survey* 30 (3): 148–75 (October).
Polan, A. J. 1984. *Lenin and the End of Politics.* London: Methuen.
Poznanski, Kazimierz Z. 1988. "Opportunity Cost in Soviet Trade with Eastern Europe: Discussion of Methodology and New Evidence." *Soviet Studies* 40 (2): 290–307.
Rabinovitch, Alexander. 1976. *The Bolsheviks Come to Power: The Revolution of 1917 in Petrograd.* New York: Norton.
Rakowska-Harmstone, Teresa. 1976. " 'Socialist Internationalism' and Eastern Europe—a New Stage." *Survey* 22 (1): 38–54 (winter).
———. 1979. "Nationalism and Integration in Eastern Europe: The Dynamics of Change." In *Communism in Eastern Europe,* edited by T. Rakowska-Harmstone and A. Gyorgy. Bloomington: Indiana University Press.
Rakowska-Harmstone, Teresa, and Andrew Gyorgy, eds. 1979. *Communism in Eastern Europe.* Bloomington: Indiana University Press.
Rice, Condoleezza. 1984. *The Soviet Union and the Czechoslovak Army, 1948–1983: Uncertain Allegiance.* Princeton, N.J.: Princeton University Press.
———. 1986. "The Military as an Instrument of Influence and Control." In *Dominant Powers and Subordinate States: The United States in Latin*

America and the Soviet Union in Eastern Europe, edited by Jan F. Triska. Durham, N.C.: Duke University Press.

Rigby, T. H. 1981. "Early Provincial Cliques and the Rise of Stalin." *Soviet Studies* 33 (1): 3–28 (January).

———. 1988. "Staffing USSR Incorporated: The Origins of the Nomenklatura System." *Soviet Studies* 40 (4): 523–37 (October).

Rosefielde, Steven. 1981. "An Assessment of the Sources and Uses of Gulag Forced Labour 1929–1956." *Soviet Studies* 33 (1): 51–87 (January).

———. 1983. "Excess Mortality in the Soviet Union: A Reconsideration of the Demographic Consequences of Forced Industrialization 1929–1949." *Soviet Studies* 35 (3): 385–409 (July).

Rousseau, Jean-Jacques. [1762] 1948. *The Social Contract: Or, Principles of Political Right*. London: Allen and Unwin.

Rush, Myron. 1974. *How Communist States Change Their Rulers*. Ithaca, N.Y.: Cornell University Press.

———. 1980. "The Problem of Succession." In *The Soviet Union: Looking to the 1980s*, edited by Robert Wesson. Stanford, Calif.: Hoover Institution Press.

Russian Communist party, Tenth Congress. 1970. *Minutes* (in Polish). Warsaw: Ksiozka i Wiedza.

Rychard Andrej. 1987. Wladza i Interesy w gospodarce (Power and Interests in the Economy). Warsaw: Warsaw University Press.

Schapiro, Leonard. 1956. *The Origin of the Communist Autocracy: Political Opposition in the Soviet State, First Phase, 1917–1922*. Cambridge, Mass.: Harvard University Press.

———, ed. 1972. Introduction. In *Political Opposition in One-Party States*. London: Macmillan.

———. 1984. *The Russian Revolutions of 1917: The Origins of Modern Communism*. New York: Basic Books.

Schöpflin, George. 1981. "The Political Structure of Eastern Europe as a Factor in Intra-bloc Relations." In *Soviet–East European Dilemmas: Coercion, Competition, and Consent*, edited by K. Dawisha and P. Hanson. London: Heinemann.

Schultz, Eberhard. 1981. "New Developments in Intra-bloc Relations in Historical Perspective." In *Soviet–East European Dilemmas: Coercion, Competition, and Consent*, edited by K. Dawisha and P. Hanson. London: Heinemann.

Schumpeter, Joseph. [1918] 1954. *The Crisis of the Tax State*, translated by W. F. Stolper and R. A. Musgrave. International Economic Papers, no. 4. New York: Macmillan.

Scott, W. F., and H. Fast Scott. 1980. "Military Stance and Outlook." In *The Soviet Union: Looking to the 1980s*, edited by R. Wesson. Millwood, N.Y.: Kraus International Publications.

Sharlet, Robert. 1989. "Human Rights and Civil Society in Eastern Europe." In *Central and Eastern Europe: The Opening Curtain?* edited by William E. Griffith. Boulder, Colo.: Westview Press.

Shepard, Herbert A. 1963. "Innovation-Resisting and Innovation-Producing Organizations." In *The Planning of Change,* edited by W. G. Bennis, K. D. Benne, and R. Chin. New York: Holt, Rinehart and Winston.

Simis, Konstantin. 1982. *USSR: Secrets of a Corrupt Society.* London: Dent.

Simon, Herbert. 1973. "The Organization of Complex Systems." In *Hierarchy Theory: The Challenge of Complex Systems,* edited by Howard H. Pattee. New York: Braziller.

Skilling, H. Gordon, and Franklyn Griffiths, eds. 1971. *Interest Groups in Soviet Politics.* Princeton, N.J.: Princeton University Press.

Skocpol, Theda. 1979. *States and Social Revolutions.* Cambridge: Cambridge University Press.

Slomczynski, K., and W. Wesolowski. 1975. "Zmniejszanie Nierownosci Spolecznych A Rozbieznosc Czynnikow Statusu" (Reduction in social inequalities and the divergence among status factors). *Studia Socjologiczne* 56 (1): 36-46.

Smith, Hedrick. 1976. *The Russians.* New York: Ballantine.

Staar, Richard F. 1977. *Communist Regimes in Eastern Europe.* 3d ed. Stanford, Calif.: Hoover Institution Press.

Staar, S. Frederic. 1988. "Soviet Union: A Civil Society." *Foreign Policy,* no. 70: 26-41 (spring).

Strzalkowski, Piotr. 1987. "Polityka Budzetowa w Polsce, 1946-1985" (Budget politics in Poland, 1946-1985). Institute of Sociology, Warsaw University. Manuscript.

Sulek, Antoni. 1985. "Life Values of Two Generations." *Polish Sociological Bulletin,* nos. 1-4.

Swianiewicz, Stanislaw. 1965. *Forced Labour and Economic Development: An Enquiry into the Experience of Soviet Industrialization.* London: Oxford University Press.

Szamuely, Tibor. 1974. *The Russian Tradition,* edited by Robert Conquest. New York: McGraw-Hill.

Tarkowski, Jacek. 1983. "Patronage in a Centralized, Socialist System: The Case of Poland." *International Political Science Review* 4 (4): 495-518.

Tocqueville, Alexis de. [1835, 1840] 1851. *Democracy in America.* New York: A. S. Barnes.

———. [1856] 1955. *The Old Regime and the French Revolution.* Garden City, N.Y.: Doubleday.

Thompson, Michael, Richard Ellis, and Aaron Wildavsky. 1990. *Cultural Theory.* Boulder, Colo.: Westview Press.

Toranska, Teresa. 1987. *"Them": Stalin's Polish Puppets.* New York: Harper and Row.
Trimberger, Ellen. 1978. *Revolutions From Above: Military Bureaucrats and Development in Japan, Turkey, Egypt, and Peru.* New Brunswick, N.J.: Transaction.
Triska, Jan F., ed. 1986. *Dominant Powers and Subordinate States: The United States in Latin America and the Soviet Union in Eastern Europe.* Durham, N.C.: Duke University Press.
Trotsky, Leon (Lev). [1937] 1972. *The Revolution Betrayed: What Is the Soviet Union and Where Is It Going?* translated by Max Eastman. 5th ed. New York: Pathfinder Press.
Tucker, Robert C. 1971. *The Soviet Political Mind: Studies in Stalinism and Post-Stalin Change.* Rev. ed. New York: Norton.
———. 1987. *Political Culture and Leadership in Soviet Russia.* New York: Norton.
Ulam, Adam. 1968. *Expansion and Coexistence: The History of Soviet Foreign Policy, 1917–1967.* New York: Praeger.
———. 1976. *A History of Soviet Russia.* New York: Praeger.
Unger, Aryeh. 1981. *Constitutional Development in the USSR: A Guide to the Soviet Constitutions.* London: Methuen.
Urban, George. 1985. "The People are Coming!" *Encounter* September/October: 16–20.
Valdiz, Claudio. 1980. *The Centralist Tradition of Latin America.* Princeton, N.J.: Princeton University Press.
Valenta, Jiri. 1986. "Military Interventions: Doctrines, Motivations, Goals, and Outcomes." In *Dominant Powers and Subordinate States: The United States in Latin America and the Soviet Union in Eastern Europe,* edited by J. F. Triska. Durham, N.C.: Duke University Press.
Vanberg, Viktor, and James M. Buchanan. 1989. "Interests and Theories in Constitutional Choice." *Journal of Theoretical Politics* 1 (1): 49–62 (January).
van Gunsteren, Herman R. 1986. "The Ethical Context of Bureaucracy and Performance Analysis." In *Guidance, Control, and Evaluation in the Public Sector,* edited by F. X. Kaufmann, G. Majone, and V. Ostrom. Berlin and New York: Walter de Gruyter.
Vankatappiach, B. 1970. "Misuse of Office." In *International Encyclopedia of the Social Sciences,* edited by David L. Sills. New York: Macmillan.
van Klaveren, Jacob. 1970. "The Concept of Corruption." In *Political Corruption: Readings in Comparative Analysis,* edited by A. J. Heidenheimer. New York: Holt, Rinehart and Winston.
Van Oudenaren, John. 1984. *The Soviet Union and Eastern Europe: Options for the 1980s and Beyond.* Santa Monica, Calif.: Rand Corporation.

———. 1989. "The Soviet Bloc and Eastern Europe: New Prospects and Old Dilemmas." In *Central and Eastern Europe: The Opening Curtain?* edited by William E. Griffith. Boulder, Colo.: Westview Press.

Walenta, Jiri. 1986. "Military Interventions: Doctrines, Motives, Goals and Outcomes." In *Dominant Powers and Subordinate States,* edited by Jan F. Triska. Durham, N.C.: Duke University Press.

Wallerstein, Immanuel. 1974. *The Modern World-System.* New York: Academic Press.

Wasilewski, Jacek. 1981. Kariery Spoleczno-Zawodowe dyrektorōw (The socio-professional careers of top managers). Warsaw: Panstwowe Wydawnictwo Naukowe.

Wat, Aleksander. 1985. *Swiat na haku i pod kluczem* (The world locked and suspended). London: Polonia.

———. 1988. *My Century: The Odyssey of a Polish Intellectual.* Berkeley: University of California Press.

Weber, Max. 1960. "Politics as a Vocation and Politics as a Profession." In *From Max Weber: Essays in Sociology,* edited by H. H. Gerth and C. W. Mills. New York: Oxford University Press.

———. 1968. *Economy and Society.* New York: Bedminster Press.

Wedel, Janine. 1986. *The Private Poland.* New York: Facts on File.

Weissberg-Cybulski, Aleksander. 1951. *The Accused.* New York: Simon and Schuster.

Weit, Erwin. 1973. *At the Red Summit: Interpreter Behind the Iron Curtain,* translated by Mary Schofield. New York: Macmillan.

White, Stephen. 1977. "The USSR: Patterns of Autocracy and Industrialism." In *Political Culture and Political Change in Communist Societies,* edited by A. Brown and Jack Gray. New York: Holmes and Meier.

Wildavsky, Aaron. 1979. *Speaking Truth to Power: The Art and Craft of Policy Analysis.* Boston: Little, Brown.

Wiles, Peter. 1962. *The Political Economy of Communism.* Cambridge, Mass.: Harvard University Press.

Wisniewski, Marian. 1985. "Ekonomiczne determinanty drugiego obiegu w Polsce" (Economic determinants of the 'second economy' in Poland). In *Problemy patologii i przestepczosci,* edited by P. Wojcik. Warsaw: Academy of Social Sciences, Central Committee, Polish United Workers' Party.

Wittfogel, Karl. [1896] 1981. *Oriental Despotism.* New Haven, Conn.: Yale University Press.

Yanov, Alexander. 1978. *The Russian New Right: Right Wing Ideologies in the Contemporary USSR.* Berkeley: University of California Press.

Zand, Helena. 1977. *Leninowska koncepcja partii* (The Leninist conception of the party). Warsaw: Ksiazka i Wiedza.

Zemtsov, Ilya. 1985. *The Private Life of the Soviet Elite.* New York: Crane Russak.
Zimmerman, William. 1986. "What Do Scholars Know about Soviet Foreign Policy?" In *Soviet Foreign Policy in a Changing World,* edited by Robbin F. Laird and Erik P. Hoffmann. New York: Aldine.

Name Index

Abalkin, Leonid, 323–24
Adamski, Jerzy, 160
Alexander I, 38
Alexander II, 313, 337
Andorka, Rudolf, 184
Andreski, Stanislav, 124
Aristotle, 20–21, 24, 37, 116, 122–23, 127, 137
Aron, Raymond, 277, 279, 355n3, 364n9, 366n3
Avanesov, V. A., 78–79
Axelrod, Pavel, 69

Bandosza, Eugeniusz, 366n7
Barghoorn, F. C., 192
Baron, Samuel, 59
Beck, Carl, 227
Benes, Edward, 276
Bentham, Jeremy, 127
Beria, Lavrenti, 151
Berman, Harold, 162–63, 366n6
Bertalan, L., 184
Besançon, Alain, 41, 102, 254, 258, 358n7
Bialer, Seweryn, 289, 310, 347, 378n23
Bienkowski, Wladyslaw, 368n6
Bihari, Mihaly, 179, 184, 369n13
Bogomolov, Olga, 288

Bova, Russell, 211
Brennar, Gay-Leclerc, 371–72n3
Brezhnev, Leonid, 152, 154, 238, 300
Broido, Vera, 80, 355n5, 360–61n9
Brown, Archie, 227, 308, 356n1, 370–71n5
Brzezinski, Zbigniew K., 115, 144, 148–49, 276, 283, 303, 365n2, 373n2, 375n3, 376n8
Buchanan, James, 14, 21, 356n10
Bukharin, N. I., 91, 93, 152
Bunce, Valerie, 223–24, 241, 370n9
Burlatsky, Fyodor, 314, 315

Campbell, Robert W., 298, 367–68n1
Ceausescu, Nicolae, 295, 309, 375–76n6
Chicherin (Bolshevik), 75
Churchill, Winston S., 278, 279
Clausewitz, Karl von, 279
Colton, Timothy J., 190, 366n5, 378n23
Conquest, Robert, 151
Conrad, Joseph, 69

Corson, William R., 149, 191
Coser, Lewis, 134
Crowley, Robert T., 149, 191
Csaba, Laszlo, 300
Custine, Astolphe de, 29, 101, 321, 322

Dahrendorf, Ralf, 109
Dallin, David, 81
Dan, Lydia, 69
Daniels, Robert V., 91–92, 357n9, 314
Davies, Norman, 373n1
D'Encausse, Hélène C., 273, 287, 306, 307–8, 378n20
Denike, George, 70–71, 359n2
Denikin, Anton, 75
DePorte, A. W., 374nn6, 9
Deutsch, Karl, 316
Djilas, Milovan, 248, 362n3, 364n9, 379n3
Dmowski, Roman, 272
Dolgorukov, Petr, 313, 315
Dostoyevsky, Fyodor, 148
Dubcek, Alexander, 183, 212, 228, 238, 293, 296, 309
Durkheim, Emil, 372n5
Dzerzhinsky, Felix, 80, 92

Eisenstadt, S. N., 39, 357n7
Ellis, Richard, 364n8
Engels, Friedrich, 46, 47, 51, 111, 112, 196, 358n7
Erlich, Alexander, 88, 93
Ernandez, Paul H., 227
Etzioni-Halevy, Eva, 364n5

Fainsod, Merle, 79
Fears, J. Rufus, 271
Fiszman, Samuel, 373n4
Flerou, F. J., 227

Friedrich, C. J., 144
Fyodorov, Svyatoslav N., 379n25

Gawda, Witold, 218
Gerschenkron, Alexander, 42–43, 332, 356–57n4
Gierek, Edward, 222, 228, 303, 326, 330, 380n5
Gomulka, Wladyslaw, 222, 228, 238, 295, 309, 376n8, 378n22, 380n5
Gorbachev, Mikhail, 24, 155, 332
Gray, Jack, 356n1, 357n3, 361n14
Griffith, William, 372–72n7
Griffiths, Franklyn, 368n2
Gustafson, Thane, 379n1
Gyorgy, Andrew, 375n3

Haimson, Leopold H., 70, 359nn2, 3
Hamilton, Alexander, 108, 113
Hammer, Darrell P., 356n7, 357n1, 366n2
Hankiss, Elemer, 258, 372n4
Hanson, Philip, 223
Harding, Neil, 357n2
Haxthausen, A. F. L. M. von, 29
Hayek, Friedrich von, 133, 321
Hegedus, Andras, 146–47
Heidenheimer, A. J., 363n2
Herspring, Dale R., 306
Hirszowicz, Maria, 174, 252, 369n10
Hitler, Adolf, 273, 274, 277, 278, 279, 280
Hobbes, Thomas, 17
Holloway, David, 209, 210
Hough, Jerry F., 365nn3, 5, 367n12
Hume, David, 108
Huntington, Samuel, 362n2
Hutchings, Robert, 289, 304, 375n3, 377n18

Name Index

Ignatov, Y. N., 82–83
Ionescu, Ghita, 366n3
Ivan IV, 38, 43

Jain, R. B., 125
Jaroszewicz, Piotr, 187
Jaruzelski, Woijcek, 160, 195, 228, 239, 327, 366–67n9, 375n5, 380n6
Jasinska-Kania, Aleksandra, 218
Jay, John, 113
Jowitt, Ken, 142–45

Kadar, Janos, 227
Kamenev, Lev, 74, 78, 91, 93
Kaminski, B., 286, 304, 360n8
Kania, Stanislaw, 228, 239
Karamzin, Nikolai, 38
Karelin (Left Social Revolutionary), 79
Karski, Jan, 274, 374n7
Kautsky, Karl, 54
Keenan, Edward, 30–35, 38–39, 41–42, 104, 131, 357n5
Keep, John L. H., 78, 79
Kennan, George, 10, 12
Khrushchev, Nikita, 152, 154, 209, 228, 238, 361n11
Kisielewski, Stefan, 367n11
Kolakowski, Leszek, 357n2, 358nn7, 8, 360n6
Kolkowicz, Roman, 190, 191, 209, 306, 366n5
Korbonski, A., 227
Kornai, Janos, 170, 248–49, 259
Kosygin, A. N., 152, 238
Kowalczyk, Tomasz, 218
Krylenko, N. V., 149
Kuklinski, Ryszard, 289

Lane, David, 71, 357n3
Lednicki, Waclaw, 76
Lenin, V. I., 6, 11–13, 17, 45–65, 67–90, 93, 95–99, 111–13, 131–32, 142–43, 148–49, 196, 216, 322, 357–58n3, 358nn5, 7, 358–59n9, 359nn1, 3, 360nn5, 8
Lerner, Max, 137
Ligachev, Yegor, 184
Linden, Carl A., 356n3, 360n8
Locke, John, 108, 109
Luxemburg, Rosa, 54

MacGregor, Douglas A., 192, 306–7
Maciejewski, Wojciech, 286, 300
McKenzie-Pintner, W., 357n6
Mackinder, Halford, 373n2
Mackintosh, Malcolm, 375n4, 377n16
Madison, James, 82, 108, 109, 112–13, 360n8
Malenkov, G. M., 209
Mandelshtam, Nadezhda, 369–70n5
Mao Zedong, 4, 309
Marcuse, Herbert, 158
Marer, Paul, 286, 376nn10, 11
Marrese, Michael, 301, 376n11
Martov, Yuli, 69, 359n3
Marx, Karl, 8, 46, 47, 50, 51, 54, 112–13, 131–32, 237, 317, 322, 327, 358n7, 364n6
Mastny, Vojtech, 272, 281
Mazowiecki, Tadeusz, 369n4
Merton, Edwina, 306
Merton, Robert K., 370n6
Mieczkowski, Bogdan, 223, 370n8
Mises, Ludwig von, 321
Mlynar, Zdenek, 377n13, 378n24
Moczar, Mieczyslaw, 188

Montesquieu, Charles-Louis de, 24, 37, 105, 108, 109, 122–23, 126–28, 134, 328
Moore, Barrington, Jr., 15, 364–65n10
Mosca, Gaetano, 105, 121–24, 156, 200

Nagy, Imre, 228, 238, 293, 296, 309
Napoleon, 280
Nicholas II, 72, 84
Nogin, Viktor P., 77–78
North, Douglass C., 203–4
Nove, Alec, 86, 89, 355n6
Nowak, Stefan, 252, 372n6
Nutti, Mario, 286

Odom, William E., 368n2
Ogatai, 10
Okolski, Marek, 369n12
Orwell, George, 370nn6
Ossowski, Stanislaw, 371n1
Ostrom, Elinor, 365n12
Ostrom, Vincent, 109, 117–18, 128, 204, 260, 317, 322, 365n12

Pareto, Vilfredo, 297
Peter the Great, 40–43, 85, 89, 107
Pilatowicz, Stanislaw, 303
Pipes, Richard, 30–31, 35–38, 39, 40–43, 75, 79, 81, 84, 314, 356n2
Plekhanov, George, 59, 68, 69
Pokol, Bela, 184
Polan, A. J., 46–47, 50, 53, 358n4
Poznanski, K., 376n11
Preobrazhensky, E. A., 91

Rabinovitch, Alexander, 360n4
Rakowska-Harmstone, Teresa, 288, 295, 375n3

Rakowski (first secretary of Polish United Workers' party), 376n9
Rice, Condoleezza, 211, 368n3, 374n12, 375n4, 377–78n19
Rigby, T. H., 145, 165, 366n8
Roosevelt, Franklin D., 278, 279
Rosefielde, Steven, 151, 361n12
Rosenthal, A. M., 356n9
Rowney, D. K., 357n6
Rush, Myron, 227
Rychard, Andrzej, 218, 379n2
Rykov, Alexei, 91, 93

Schapiro, Leonard, 77, 78, 83, 184
Schöpflin, George, 377
Schultz, Eberhard, 377n12
Schumpeter, Joseph, 198, 317, 318–19
Scott, H. Fast, 361n13
Scott, W. F., 361n13
Sharlet, Robert, 253
Shepard, Herbert A., 61
Sikorski, Wladyslaw, 278
Simis, Konstantin, 163, 367n13
Simon, Herbert, 128
Skilling, H. Gordon, 368n2
Skocpol, Theda, 16
Smith, Adam, 108, 109
Smith, Hedrick, 207–8
Socrates, 116
Staar, Richard F., 336, 375n3, 377n17
Stalin, Joseph, 21, 60, 74, 91–92, 95, 145, 152, 302, 359n1, 361n11
Stolypin, Peter A., 16, 86, 337
Strzalkowski, Piotr, 224, 370n10
Sulek, Antoni, 252
Suslov, Mikhail, 238
Swianiewicz, Stanislaw, 151, 361n12, 369n11

Name Index

Szalajda, Zbigniew, 213
Szamuely, Tibor, 30

Talleyrand-Périgord, Charles M. de, 276
Tarkowski, Jacek, 171, 182
Thompson, Michael, 364n8
Tito, Josip Broz, 4
Tocqueville, Alexis de, 24, 29, 37, 98, 101, 105, 137–38, 292, 354
Tomsky, Mikhail, 91, 93
Trimberger, Ellen, 319
Triska, Jan F., 293, 375n1
Trotsky, Leon (Lev), 80, 81, 91, 93, 355n4, 361n11
Tucker, Robert C., 106, 151, 338, 355n5, 356n8, 365n1
Tullock, Gordon, 14, 21

Ulam, Adam, 83, 92, 373n5, 374nn7, 10
Ulbricht, Walter, 293–94
Ulyanov, Vladimir Ilyich. *See* Lenin, V. I.
Unger, Aryeh, 131, 154, 366n3
Urban, George, 147

Valdiz, Claudio, 362n5.1
Vanberg, Victor, 356n10
van Gunsteren, Herman, 363n4
Vankatappiach, B., 167
van Klaveren, Jacob, 363n3

Van Oudenaren, John, 293, 375n4
Vanous, Jan, 301, 376n11

Walenta, Jiri, 280
Wallerstein, Immanuel, 9, 284
Wasilewski, Jacek, 217
Wat, Aleksander, 245
Weber, Max, 37, 112, 121–24, 142, 144, 156, 321, 357n8, 362–63n1
Wedel, Janine, 251
Weissberg, Alexander, 145
Weit, Erwin, 294
White, Stephen, 41, 356n3
Wildavsky, Aaron, 364n8
Wiles, Peter, 89–90
Wisniewski, Marian, 257
Witte, Sergey, 85, 89
Wittfogel, Karl, 39, 362n3, 361n15
Wrangel, Peter, 75

Yanov, Alexander, 366n4
Yeltsin, Boris, 183, 343
Yudenich, Nicolas, 75

Zand, Helena, 11–12
Zarzabeck, William A., 227
Zasulich, Vera I., 69
Zemtsov, Ilya, 367nn10, 13
Zimmerman, William, 306
Zinovyev, Grigory, 78, 91, 93, 97

Subject Index

Agrarian reform, postwar, 291
Agricultural sector
  Bolshevik policy for, 86–87
  collectivization of, under Communist regime, 85, 94–95, 209, 298
  revolutionary abolition of property rights in, 102
  See also Agrarian reform
Albania, 308–9
Anti-Comintern Pact (1939), 272
Apparatchik, 168
Aristocracy, 123
Armed forces
  economic interests of, 209–12
  rationale for powerful, 178, 330
Army
  mission of, 178
  political control by party in, 190–92
Austro-Hungarian Empire, 270–72

Balkan countries
  shift in Communist power in, 347–48
  strategic significance of, 308
Banking system, USSR, 92
Bessarabia, 345

Black market, 88
Bolshevik Council of People's Commissars, 77
Bolshevik revolution
  effect of, 97, 107
  origins of, 7
  unitary nature of, 99
Bolsheviks
  Communist regime of, 21
  defeat of opponents by, 77, 81–84, 98
  ethnic and class composition of, 71–72
  under Lenin, 70–90
  neopatrimonial state of, 103–4
  repression by, 80–81
  role of, in formation of Communist International, 96
Brest-Litovsk Treaty (March 1918), 75, 80
Bretton Woods agreements, 205, 317
Bulgaria, 307, 308
Bund (Jewish socialist party), 69
Bureaucracy
  as component of partisan state, 261
  nomenklatura in, 165–66

402

Capitalism
  Marx's and Lenin's views of, 54, 64, 112
  survival qualities of, 17
Capitalist exploitation, 103
Catholic church, 253
Center of partisan state
  function of, 205, 229–30
  party leadership as, 261
  as source of power, 178–79
  source of strength for, 261–62
Centralization
  of economic decision making, 298–99
  with forced succession, 241
  Lenin's interest in idea of, 49–50, 58–60, 90
  of political decision making, 74–98
  Tocqueville's remarks on, 105
  See also Decentralization
Charisma, 142–46
Cheka. See Secret police (Cheka)
China, People's Republic of
  Communist regime in, 4
  Cultural Revolution in, 116
  ideological differences of, 308–9
Class consciousness, 55
Class struggle, 13, 159
CMEA. See Council for Mutual Economic Assistance (CMEA)
Cold War, 281
Comintern. See Communist International (Comintern)
Communism, 18
  changes in, 155
  final stage of, 157–58
  gains of, after World War II, 279–80
  Marx's and Lenin's views of, 54
  as modernization strategy, 14–16

See also Marxist-Leninist ideology
Communist bloc nations
  creation of, 273–81
  effect of market reform by, 335
  factors contributing to integration of, 299–300
  as foundation for Soviet world system, 24–25
  methods of control in, 283–310
  organization of, 287
  Soviet theory of relations among, 288
  See also Balkan countries
Communist International (Comintern)
  Lenin's and Stalin's roles in, 96–97
  purpose and function of, 96–97
Communist party
  changes in, 155–56
  control over organizational hierarchies of, 162, 166–67
  defense of monopoly position by, 206
  effect of control by, 184–86
  extralegal status of, 163
  four main positions in Russian, 81–82
  functioning components in, 229–39
  fusion of, with state, 158
  increased autonomy of, 95–96
  informal networks in, 151–56, 166–67, 174, 237
  international focus of, 97
  legitimation of, 159–62
  Lenin's conception of, 11–12, 54–60, 113–15, 142, 146
  in postwar Communist-dominated countries, 290

Communist party
(*continued*)
  recruitment mechanism in, 215–17, 292–94, 367n12
  as replacement for traditional structure, 130
  role of apparatus in, 188–90
  role of bilateral and multilateral conferences of, 302–3
  role of members of, 134
  in Soviet political system, 141–42
  use of purges by, 147–48
  See also Party activists; Party apparatus; Party cells
Communist system
  conditions for reform of, 314–32
  despotic nature of, 121–22
  effect of peaceful revolution in, 5–6
  effect on Soviet society of, 341
  hierarchical control in, 334–35
  inadequacies of, 4
  institutional design of, 21
  Marxist-Leninist doctrine sanctified in, 18
  promoting nationalism under, 294–96
  shortages in economic and political arenas of, 248–55
  social order of, 16–20
  terms used to describe, 18–20
  See also Marxist-Leninist ideology; Soviet world system; State; State, partisan
Constituent Assembly, Russia, 79
Constitution, USSR (1977), 154
Constitutional Democrats (Kadety), 83, 84
Constitutions, Soviet bloc countries, 307

Corruption
  causes of, 130, 138
  collective, 258–61
  definitions of, 124, 143–46
  effect of ruling through, 260–61, 334
  modern approach to, 127
  Montesquieu's idea of government, 122–23, 126–28
  occurrence of, 124–27
  term as used by Jowitt, 144–46
Council for Mutual Economic Assistance (CMEA), 288, 299–300
  economic policies of, 301, 304
  effect of individual countries' market reform on, 335
  role of Khrushchev in, 302, 303
  weaknesses of, 304–5
Cultural Revolution, China, 116
Currency
  loss of value of, 89
  stabilization of, under Stalin, 92
  transfer rubles as, 304
Curzon line, 278
Czechoslovakia
  fall of Communists in, 347–48
  formation of, 273
  ideological differences of, 307–8
  invasion of, 4
  relations of, with Hungary and Romania, 276
  relations of, with Poland, 275–76
  Soviet efforts to destabilize, 349
  during World War II, 278
  See also Iron triangle

Decentralization
  corruption as factor in, 334
  Lenin's perception of, 58–60
  in partisan state, 200
  Red Army opposition to
    economic, 209
Deception, 219, 244–45, 250,
  254, 323–25, 365n4
Defense policy, USSR, 192,
  209–11
Democracy
  Lenin's idea of, 48–50,
    60–61, 64
  moral character of government
    in, 123
  Social Democrats' ideas of, 68
  See also Democratic centralism;
    Social democracy movement;
    Social-Democratic party
Democratic centralism, 60–63
Democratic Centralists (Detsysts),
  81
Democratic institutions, 117
Democratic tradition, 159–61
  See also Rational-legal order
Democratic transition
  interdependence of USSR and
    satellites for, 347–48
  obstacles to, 344, 348
  prospect for peaceful, 341
  requirements for Soviet, 337,
    340–41
  role of East-Central Europe in,
    347–48
Dependency theory. See Soviet
  world system
Depersonalization, 134–35, 137,
  150, 254
Despotism, 121–22, 123, 128
  Montesquieu's interpretation
    of, 122–23, 128
  Weber's interpretation of,
    123–24

See also Corruption
Dictatorship of the proletariat
  dream of, 157
  Lenin's version of democracy
    under, 48–49, 64–65
  Lenin's view of, 50, 63–65,
    113, 131, 132
  state as tool serving, 116,
    164–65

East-Central European nations
  destabilization of, by
    Gorbachev, 349
  effect of Communist regime
    on, 350
  effect of independence of, 338
  effect of Western Europe on,
    353
  external debt of, 300
  lack of natural resources in,
    299
  loans from World Bank and
    IMF for, 351
  postwar Communist domination in, 3, 291–98
  revival of strong society in, 24
  Soviet economic system in,
    298
  strategic location of, 269–70
  See also Bulgaria;
    Czechoslovakia; Hungary;
    Poland; Romania
Economic activity
  attention focused on, 185
  role of political influences in,
    186–87
Economic performance
  requirements to improve,
    350–51
  of Soviet economy, 8
Economic policy
  of Communist governments,
    298

Economic policy
   (*continued*)
   with forced succession,
      239–42
   politicized nature of, 185–87,
      204–5
   role of consumer goods and
      services in, 212
   of Russia, 85, 89
   See also Market economy; War
      communism
Economic policy, USSR
   effect of defense-based,
      210–11
   failure of Gorbachev's,
      339–40
   Five-Year Plans, 85, 95, 249
   for industrialization, 86,
      88–89
   opposition of security
      organizations to, 208
   under Stalin's regime, 90,
      92–95
   See also Defense policy; Gosplan
      (State Planning Commission);
      Industrial sector; Military
      sector; War communism
      policy
Economic reform. *See* Reform,
   economic
Economic system
   of Communist party, 204–5
   effect of, on state priorities,
      196–97
Education, 155–56, 365n5
Elections, Communist system,
   183
Elite, ruling
   conditions for survival of,
      333–34
   cost to maintain, 4
   entrenchment of, 325–26, 328
   of imperial Russia, 35–38
   internal and external groups
      of, 214–20
   in political and administrative
      hierarchy, 173
   in post–World War II Poland,
      292–93
   recruitment of members for,
      215–17, 292–94, 367n12
   role of, in formation of Com-
      munist bloc, 294–98
Entrepreneurship, 328
Environment, 318
Estonia, 344
Europe, Western
   effect on Russia of market
      system in, 9
   influence of, on Russia, 40–41
   Social Democrats in, 68

Factions, political
   under different degrees of
      power, 194–95
   formation and role of,
      182–84, 187–88
   perceived importance of, 185
   relationship of, to interest
      groups, 186–88
   supression of, under Lenin
      and Stalin, 81–84, 95
Federalism, 69, 332
Freedom of the press
   Bolshevik position on, 78–79,
      360n7
   purge as substitute for, 150

Gdansk, 278
Geopolitical importance, Com-
   munist bloc nations, 308
Georgia, 344
German Democratic Republic
   ideological differences of, 307
   Soviet destabilization efforts
      in, 349

German Democratic Republic
  (*continued*)
  See also Iron triangle
German-Soviet Treaty of
  Nonagression (1939), 275,
  277, 344
Germany
  influence of, in East-Central
    Europe, 270
  military agreement between
    USSR and (1922), 92
  reunification of, 347, 351
  See also Prussia
Gosplan (State Planning Commission), 88
Great Britain, 277
Great Purge (1936-1938), 92

Habsburg Empire. *See* Austro-Hungarian Empire
Hungary
  democratic coalition in, 22
  fall of Communists in, 347-48
  ideological differences of,
    307-8
  invasion of, 4

Imperialism
  rationale for Russian and
    Soviet, 103
  of USSR as superpower, 154
Impersonality, 134-35
Income equalization policy
  (*uravnilovka*), 47
Individual in partisan state,
  133-39
Industrial sector
  defense industries in, 210-11
  effect of support for, 330
  heavy industry favored in
    Communist, 298-99
  priority for heavy industry in,
    178
  Red Army support for heavy
    industry in, 209-10
Inflation, 197
Information
  deliberate withholding of,
    104-5
  effect of market reform on,
    328
  hindrances to exchange of,
    207
  shortages of, 250
Institutional order
  existence of, dependent on
    society, 24, 39
  reaction to and shaping of environment by, 6-7
Interdependence, country, 285-86
Interest groups
  of Communist state, 188-95
  condition for exploitation by,
    257-61
  under different degrees of
    power, 194-95
  economic concerns of, 206-12
  emergence of influential, 202
  factors for effective functioning of, 184
  in liberal, democratic state, 184
  manipulation of, by Stalin, 92
  of non-party and state affiliation, 177, 199, 201
  of party-state affiliation, 177,
    184-86, 199
  relationship of, to factions,
    186-87
  secrecy and power of, 186
Interests, regional, 213
International Monetary Fund
  (IMF), 351
Iron triangle, 308

Kadets. *See* Constitutional
  Democrats (Kadety)

Karelia, 345
KGB, 290
Kronstadt rising, 63, 85
Kuril Islands, 345

Labor force, 299, 330
Land ownership, Russian reforms in (1908-1911), 86, 87
Latvia, 344
League of Nations, 278
Left Social Revolutionaries, 77, 78, 78-79
Legal system
    contradictory nature of rules in, 163-64
    effect of reform on, 328-29
    party control of, in partisan state, 162-63
Legislation, partisan state, 162-64
Leninist ideology, 294
Liberalism, European, 107-10
Lithuania, 344

Market economy
    difficulties of implementing, 260-61
    effect of rejecting, 117
    effect of, on centrally planned economy, 213
    government services provided under, 198
    Lenin's prediction for, 51-52
    liberal perception of, 108-10
    military sector in, 210
    under NEP, 87-88
    separation of economy and government in, 325
    social mechanism of, 8
    as threat to Communist party bureaucracy, 206
    See also Black market
Marshall Plan, 303

Marxism
    modification of, by Lenin, 45-55
    origins of, 7
    social and economic doctrine of, 3, 8
Marxist-Leninist ideology
    change in role of, 155, 159, 294
    defense of, by party apparatus, 189-90
    distinction between public and private domains by, 131-32
    as doctrine to rationalize partisan state, 116-18, 159, 161, 196
    immorality of public good in, 134
    influence of accidental and environmental determinants on, 9-13
    lack of concern for one's country in, 309
    language of, 219, 244-45, 250, 254, 323-25
    perception of Communist system in, 8
    perception of society in, 132, 331
    in postcolonial developing countries, 4
    process of establishing communism using, 157-58
    rigidity of, 322-23
    role of, in Communist regimes, 130-31
    social division of labor under, 111-12, 126-27
    as state religion, 15
    theory of the state under, 111-12
    use of patriotic symbolism to support, 246

Marxist-Leninist ideology
(*continued*)
See also Leninist ideology;
Revolutionary ideology;
Socialist movement
Marxist social doctrine,
Russia, 3
Mensheviks
elimination of, 361n11
ethnic and class composition
of, 71
within Social-Democratic
party, 70–71
Military cooperation, Soviet–
German (1922), 92
Military doctrine,
Czechoslovakia, 211–12
Military power
of Soviet Union, 338
under Stalin's regime, 95, 99
Military sector
political role of, 209
spending for, 209–12
Millenarianism, Russian, 97–98
Modernization strategy
Communism as, 14–16
of Communist regimes, 9–10,
115–16
of prerevolutionary Russia,
15–16
Monarchy, 123

Nationalism, Russian
as basis for democratic transition, 342–44
in party politics, 71–72
rejection of, in Marxist-
Leninist ideology, 96, 310
Nationalization, USSR, 89
NEP. *See* New Economic Policy
(NEP)
Networks, informal, 151–56,
166–67, 174

New Economic Policy (NEP)
of Communist party, 85, 314
effect of, 86–90
support for and opposition to,
91–94, 209
See also Agricultural sector
NKVD. *See* People's Commissariat
of Internal Affairs (NKVD)
Nomenklatura system, 8, 162,
165–66, 189, 206, 366n7
North Atlantic Treaty Organization (NATO), 305

October Revolution (1917), 3, 107
Oil price shocks, 300
Orthodox church, 103, 253
Ottoman Empire, 270

Party activists, 168–70, 189,
229–31
Party apparatus, 188–90, 229–31,
234–35
Party cells, 229, 234
Patronage, 170–72, 182
People's Commissariat of Internal
Affairs (NKVD), 294
Perestroika
Communist institutional
design as target of, 22
economic policies of, 338–39
Personnel system
party apparatus control of,
189, 206
party control over assignments
of, 162, 165–66
political influences in, 186–87
security organizations as policy
makers of, 207
See also *Nomenklatura* system
Poland
compensation after World
War II, 279
elite of ruling class in, 217–20

Poland
  (*continued*)
  fall of Communists in, 347–48
  ideological differences in, 307–8
  issue of boundaries of, 273, 278, 283
  relations of, with Czechoslovakia, 275
  response to economic reform in, 213–14
  role of, in decline of Communist bloc, 25
  during World War II, 278
  See also Iron triangle
Polish-Lithuanian Commonwealth, 271
Political culture, Russia, 105–7
Political order
  bottom-up organization of, 128–30
  features of Soviet-type, 320–27
  top-down organization of Soviet-type, 177–78, 302–310, 319–20, 321
Political system
  compromise required of, 331–32
  consistency of, with economic system under Stalin, 94–95
  control of, by Communist party, 158–59, 188–95
  effect of social control by, 167–75
  elements of opposition to reform in, 329
  formalization of influence of, 179–80
  integration of, in Soviet bloc countries, 307
  interest groups dominant in, 205
  in market economy, 8–9
  NEP incompatibility with, 86–87
  role of Communist party in Soviet, 141–42
  in Soviet world system, 333
  Stalin's shaping of, 90–96
Population
  growth under Stalin of urban, 94
  surplus rural, 94–95
Postal service, Germany, 50–51
Potsdam Conference, 279
Prague Spring (1968), 211, 310
Price mechanism
  in CMEA, 301
  control of, under Communist regime, 205
Privacy, 132–33
Private domain
  effect of purges on, 146–50
  interdependence of, with public domain, 129–30
  Marxist-Leninist ideology delegitimizes, 132–33, 139
  recognition of, in market system, 335
Privatization
  conditions for, in partisan state, 253–54
  in Marxist-Leninist state, 135–36, 149, 195
Proletarian internationalism, 288
Property rights
  effect of abolition of, 133, 321
  effect of economic reform on, 328
  effect of transfer to private sector of, 136
  liberal idea of, 109
  in market economy, 8
  revolutionary abolition of, 102

Property rights, Russia
  reform involving, 86
  under tzar, 102
Provisional Government (1917), 84
Prussia, 271
Public domain, 127–29
  interdependence of, with private domain, 130
  negation of, in Marxist-Leninist ideology, 132–33, 139
  See also Private domain
Public good, 134
Public interest
  effect of privatization on, 135–36
  in political order, 128
Public life, 128–29
Purges
  abolition of, 294
  functions of, 147–51
  use of, in Stalin's regime, 43, 84, 92, 196, 360–61n9

Rational-legal order, 159–61
Rationing
  as Communist economic policy, 298
  effect of, 205, 210, 221
  under war communism policy, 89
Red Army
  organized by Trotsky, 80
  position of, on economic activity, 209
  role in imposing Soviet regime, 290
Reform, economic
  ability to initiate and sustain, 314–17
  difficulties in initiating, 317–26
  effect of, on property rights, 328
  with forced succession, 240–41
  necessity to consider, 334
  political compromise as requirement for, 331–32
  political opposition to, 329
  response in Poland to, 213–14
  role of military in Gorbachev's, 211
  ruling through policies of, 259–61
  working class opposition to, 330–31
Reform, political
  instances of success for, 326–27
  and Lenin, 89–90
Reform conditions, 314–32
Religious life, 253
Revolutionary ideology, 159, 161
Ribbentrop-Molotov Pact. See German-Soviet Treaty of Nonagression (1939)
Romania
  ideological differences of, 307–9
  strategic significance of, 308
Rubles, transfer, 304
Rule of law, 20–21, 38, 150, 325
Russia
  dual conception of, 338–39
  effect of World War I on economy of, 72–73
  expansion of, into East-Central Europe, 270
  political culture and system of, 31–44
  political revival in (late 1800s), 67–68
  prerevolutionary modernization strategy in, 15–16
  Provisional Government in, 72–76

Russia
  (*continued*)
  as imperial power, 271
  similarities to Communist system of old regime in, 29–30
  Social Democrats in, 68–69
Russian Orthodoxy, 15

Secrecy, 104, 177, 210–11, 231, 245, 322, 329–30
Secret police (Cheka), 80–81, 92, 158, 366n2
Security organizations
  opposition of, to democratic tendencies, 208
  role of, in Communist party, 192–94, 206–7
Serfdom, 86
Social democracy movement, Russia, 67–68
Social-Democratic party, 68
  division of, into Bolsheviks and Mensheviks, 70
  Lenin's concept of hierarchy in, 56–58
  Lenin's perception of centralization in, 60, 69
  Lenin's role in, 69–72
  See also Bolsheviks; Mensheviks
Socialism, 19, 68
Socialist movement
  effect of, 110
  identification of Soviet interests in, 97
  ideology of, 110–11
  international focus of, 96
Social Revolutionary party, 68, 76, 78–79, 81, 83
  See also Left Social Revolutionaries
Social services, 198–200, 315
Social system
  of Communist regimes, 130
  regulation of private lives in, 134
  character of environment shaped by, 13
Society
  asymmetrical relations of, with partisan state, 244
  in Communist state, 261–62
  control of state by, 128–29, 167–75
  under different levels of coercion, 261–65
  diversity of East-Central European, 255
  effect in East-Central Europe of Communist domination of, 291
  effect of Communist system on Soviet, 341
  effect of peaceful revolution on, 5–6
  effect of purges on, 146–50
  factors influencing maintenance of public domain by, 129–30
  informal networks in, 250–51
  lack of autonomy for, 248
  Marxist-Leninist ideology delegitimizes, 132, 331
  pattern of subjugation of Russian, 102
  repressed and terrorized, 246–47
  revival of strong, 24
  role of Communist party in changing, 114–15
  top-down organization of, 102–7, 248, 321
  See also Depersonalization; Terror
Society, USSR
  elimination of social groups in, 107
  political organization of, 102

Solidarity movement, 22, 319, 330–31
Soviet, 18
Soviet bloc. *See* Communist bloc nations
Soviet-German military agreement (1922), 92
Soviet Union
  change in foreign policy of, 348
  dominance of, after World War II, 283–84
  effect of loss of influence by, 348
  effect of economic and political ties between Western Europe and, 353
  legal issues of democratic transition in, 344–45
  military power of, 3–4
  multinational, multiethnic character of, 344–46
  role of Communist bloc for interests of, 287
  strategic interest of, in iron triangle, 308
  successes and failures of, 337–38
  territorial gains of, from World War II, 279–80
  See also Soviet world system
Soviet world system
  centralization, integration, and control in, 21, 289–90, 333
  core of, 5
  dependency and interdependency relationships of, 284–86
  effect of political and economic reform on, 348–49
  establishing balance under, 296–98
  formal, informal, and secret aspects of, 302–10, 333
  ideological differences within, 307–8
  performance of East-Central European nations in, 298–302
  role of Brezhnev in, 305–6
  threat to use force in, 333, 347
  See also Communist bloc nations; East-Central Europe
Stalinism, 346–47
State
  Aristotle's view of role of, 127
  condition of privatization of, 135
  control of, by Communist party, 158, 162–67
  different types of restraint for, 115
  difficulties in reversing powers of, 327–28
  as instrument of oppression, 138
  Lenin's concept of withering away of, 49, 52–53, 65
  Lenin's interpretation of role of, 114–15, 138–39
  liberal conception of, 108–9, 114
  organized force of, 102–7
  party and administrative hierarchy in, 166–67
  party control over, 184, 188–95
  role of, in public domain, 127–28
  role of, in Soviet society, 102
  as tool for move to socialism, 158
  withering away of Communist, 22

State, partisan
  asymmetric relations of, with society, 244–48
  components of, 261
  concept of, 365–66n1
  doctrines used to rationalize, 159–62
  domination of, by party, 158–59, 162–67
  effect of different levels of coercion by, 261–65
  effect of, on society, 116–17
  neglect of social services under, 198–200, 315
  political struggle within, 180–88
  political system formed by, 173–74
  post-Stalin autonomy of, 159
  privacy in, 133–39
  private interests in, 256–61
  purges in, 146–51, 196
  rationalization of, 159–61
  revolutionary ideology as rationale for, 159, 161
  See also Center of partisan state
State intervention, 265
Successions, forced
  economic policy with, 239–42
  effect of, 228, 239
  process of, in Poland, 232–42
System of ideas, 17–18

Teheran Conference, 279, 283
Terror
  by Bolsheviks, 80–81
  effect of discarding tactics of, 254, 256
  purges as form of, 149–50
  role of, in Communist regimes, 138
  used in Communist-dominated countries, 246–47, 291

Totalitarian regime, 246, 336
Trade unions, 55–56
Treaty of Riga (1920), 273

Uravnilovka. See Income equalization policy

Vanguard
  dictatorship and function of, 132, 321
  in transition period of communism, 158
  See also Dictatorship of the proletariat
Versailles Conference, 272, 276, 277

War communism policy, 89–90
Warsaw Treaty Organization (WTO), 288–89
  contradiction of, 211–12
  factors causing disintegration of, 338
  role of Khrushchev in, 302
  threat of, in Soviet world system, 233, 242, 305–7, 330
Workers' Opposition, 81–82
Working class
  movement of, 56–57
  opposition to reform by, 330–31
World Bank, 351
WTO. *See* Warsaw Treaty Organization (WTO)

Yalta Conference, 279, 283
Yugoslavia
  cultural differences in, 272–73
  ideological differences of, 308–9
  joins Communist bloc, 4

About the Author

Antoni Z. Kaminski is deputy director in charge of the West and North European Divisions, Department of Europe, in the Foreign Affairs Ministry of the Republic of Poland and is director of the Polish Institute for International Affairs. Trained as a sociologist, Dr. Kaminski has coordinated a program in institutional design and policy analysis at the National School of Public Administration in Warsaw and has taught at the University of Warsaw. He has held visiting appointments at the University of East Anglia, the University of British Columbia, Oxford University, and Indiana University. Dr. Kaminski has published widely in both Polish and English.

Related Books from ICS Press

The Moral Collapse of Communism
Poland as a Cautionary Tale
by John Clark and Aaron Wildavsky

Why did the myriad and powerful communist institutions of repression fail to hold the communist system together and maintain government control? Using Poland as their model, Clark and Wildavsky describe how the struggle to survive under state socialism damaged the very fabric of society. They show that the Marxist theory of capitalism as corrupt and doomed more accurately applies to communism. Polish citizens were forced to lie, bribe, and steal to secure even the basic essentials of life. This book illuminates the realities of life in a repressive state and explains why the collapse of communism is ultimately a moral collapse.

1990, 431 pp., $24.95 (cloth)

The Meaning of American Federalism
Constituting a Self-Governing Society
by Vincent Ostrom

Any system founded on the illusion that "the government" governs and can function as an all-competent problem solver is destined for failure. So argues Vincent Ostrom, who demonstrates that the principles of American federalism, as it was conceived and meant to function, offer the conceptual basis for achieving a free society of self-governing citizens. There is a profound message in this book for people everywhere—from American neighborhoods to the reemerging nations of Eastern Europe, the changing Soviet Union, and the countries of the third world.

1991, 301 pp., $24.95 (cloth)

The Emergence of Autocracy in Liberia
Tragedy and Challenge
by Amos Sawyer

Liberia is a nation whose history is intricately tied to America's past and Africa's future. Liberian president Amos Sawyer traces the country's history from its colonization in the nineteenth century by free blacks from the United States and explains how autocratic government emerged from a tradition of patrimonial authority, culminating in a military dictatorship. The country recently endured a brutal civil war to restore its freedom. Important reading for everyone concerned about the fate of freedom in Africa—and the world.

1992, 395 pp., $29.95 (cloth), $15.95 (paper)

To order call: 1-800-326-0263 (contiguous United States only, 8:30–5 PST)
ICS PRESS/Institute for Contemporary Studies
Dept. BBI, 243 Kearny Street, San Francisco, CA 94108